Study Guide

for

Nairne's

Psychology

HALF PRICE BOOKS®

Half Price Books
1835 Forms Drive
Carrollton, TX 75006
OFS OrderID 39482208

Thank you for your order, ABE TP Orders!

Thank you for shopping with Half Price Books! Please contact Support@hpb.com. if you have any questions, comments or concerns about your order (738044911)

Visit our stores to sell your books, music, movies games for cash.

SKU	ISBN/UPC	Title & Author/Artist	Shelf ID	Qty	OrderSKU
S478493150	9780495031550	Nairne's Psychology Nairne, James S.	DB 15.16.6	1	

SHIPPED STANDARD TO:
ABE TP Orders
800 Avondale Ave
Columbus OH 43212
help@textbookrush.com

ORDER# **738044911**
Abebooks

Study Guide

for

Nairne's

Psychology

Fourth Edition

Janet Proctor
Purdue University

THOMSON
WADSWORTH

Australia • Brazil • Canada • Mexico • Singapore • Spain • United Kingdom • United States

Printed in the United States of America

1 2 3 4 5 6 7 09 08 07 06 05

Printer: Thomson West

ISBN 0-495-03155-0

Thomson Higher Education
10 Davis Drive
Belmont, CA 94002-3098
USA

For more information about our products, contact us at:
Thomson Learning Academic Resource Center
1-800-423-0563

For permission to use material from this text or product, submit a request online at
http://www.thomsonrights.com.
Any additional questions about permissions can be submitted by email to **thomsonrights@thomson.com.**

TABLE OF CONTENTS

INTRODUCTION

Throughout your text you will find an emphasis on the *adaptive mind*, the fact that we use our brains in a purposive and strategic fashion to meet the challenges of a changing environment. Each chapter will address certain problems or issues most organisms must resolve.

As a student in this introductory psychology class, you face certain demands, also. Stated most broadly, you must learn the material presented in class and in the text, and you must demonstrate your knowledge on tests and other assignments. The purpose of this study guide is to help you successfully meet these demands.

USING THE STUDY GUIDE

Part of the challenge of introductory psychology is the amount of material to be learned. The study guide's organization breaks down the material into manageable units. Studying an entire chapter at one time is overwhelming to many students and can lead to very poor learning. Taking too big a bite of food can lead to choking; trying to tackle too much new material at one time can have a similar effect. Therefore, each chapter in this study guide is divided into smaller units that follow the major sections of the text.

Exercises designed to help you learn the vocabulary, practice recalling specific facts, and evaluate your basic comprehension of the material are provided for each section of the chapter. You will not need to study the entire chapter before doing these early exercises in the study guide. You can study one topic, work with the material, and evaluate your comprehension before moving on to another topic. Then, at the end of each chapter there are additional exercises that revisit the entire chapter and give you additional opportunity to practice working with the material and to evaluate your readiness for an exam. I hope this will encourage you to study for mastery on a daily basis, rather than trying to learn an entire chapter (or chapters, worse yet) in a single marathon study session a day or two before your exam.

Establishing Learning Goals

Each study guide chapter begins with a set of learning goals. These will provide a quick summary of what the text chapter covers, and what you should be trying to accomplish. Review them before you read the text, and use them to test your comprehension of each section. If your instructor gives essay exams, use these objectives as possible essay questions, and practice formulating a response to them. If your exams will include only multiple choice questions, use the objectives to evaluate your knowledge. If you can recite the relevant information for each objective, you probably have a good understanding of the material.

Mastering the Material

Mastering the Vocabulary. Each section of the chapter has a list of important terms. In most cases these terms are defined and printed in bold in your text. You might develop a set of note cards instead of writing the definitions in the study guide. Many students keep their note cards handy to pull out and review during short breaks. You will be surprised at your progress if you use those occasional spare minutes.

Mastering the Concepts. These fill-in-the-blanks exercises will give you practice recalling the vocabulary and basic conceptual material from a section of the text. When completed, you will have a reasonably detailed review to use when doing your final work before an exam. If you have great difficulty with this section, you need to go back and work with the text again. An answer key is provided, but try to complete the exercise on your own first, working with the text if necessary.

Evaluating Your Progress. Each section includes multiple choice questions to help you evaluate whether you have achieved at least a basic level of mastery of the facts and vocabulary. For the most part, these questions will require lower levels of comprehension than the questions in the pretests found at the end of each chapter. Many will emphasize definitions or will address general issues. Errors here indicate you have missed some basic information or don't know the important terms. Go back and fill in those gaps before you begin new material. Note that the answer key includes explanations about why the wrong answers are wrong. Use this feature to understand your mistakes and learn even more.

Making Final Preparations

You should work on this section after you feel you have achieved a basic mastery of the entire chapter. In fact, it is a good idea to wait a day or two before beginning this section. As you will learn in Chapter 8, the most significant forgetting occurs soon after the original learning period. You will overestimate your mastery if you complete these exercises right after studying the chapter.

Short Essay Questions. Each chapter includes several practice essay questions. Answering essay questions requires that you recall the information, rather than just recognize it, so essay questions provide a more difficult test of your knowledge. Answering essay questions is excellent practice regardless of the format of your exams, but it is essential if your exams will include essay questions. Sample answers are provided, but write your own answers first.

Matching. This exercise provides practice with a matching format and requires that you link terms with their definitions or their importance to the chapter. This is also the exercise that tests your recognition of the names of notable people. Some instructors require their students to know the names of major researchers or theorists; others don't. Find out your instructor's policy before your first exam.

Multiple Choice Pretests. Two pretests are provided to give you practice answering multiple-choice questions and to help you evaluate your mastery of the text material prior to your exams. Pretest 1 tends to focus more on specific factual information than Pretest 2. Pretest 2 emphasizes application and prediction. Can you recognize a concept in action? Can you take a theory and make predictions about what will happen in a new situation? Can you see the relationships between concepts? These questions require more complete conceptual understanding.

If you have no trouble with Pretest 1, but make many errors on Pretest 2, you probably know facts but don't really understand them or their significance. You might try discussing the material with a study partner or friend, or go to your instructor and ask for some help in reaching this level of comprehension. Also, be sure to look at the explanations for the incorrect alternatives given in the answer key. Knowing *why* something is wrong is often as informative as knowing that something is right.

Language Development Guide

This material, originally prepared by Mary Beth Foster, will help you understand some of the more difficult vocabulary. This section explains non-technical terms and idioms that might be unfamiliar (especially to non-native English readers).

Core Terms. These words may or may not appear in the chapter, but you are very likely to hear them in lecture. They are words that instructors sometimes use *without ever explaining them.* Understanding them should help you get more out of the lectures and the text. You might want to read this part before the lectures on a given chapter begin.

Idioms. A list of difficult words and "idioms" -- phrases that have a special meaning (e.g., "has its roots," or "coined a term") and their explanations are provided. Because of the large number of idioms in each chapter, these lists include only those most likely to be difficult to interpret without context.

Pronunciation. New to this edition of the study guide is a section to help you learn how to pronounce some of the more challenging words in the chapter. The words included are those that are important terms or names and are most likely to give non-native English speakers trouble because of unusual letter to sound relationships.

Answers and Explanations

Use this feature to evaluate why you made a mistake and to help you understand difficult material. Each question is page-referenced to direct you to the relevant material in the text. Even if you answer correctly, review the explanations of incorrect answers and see if your reasoning was similar.

STRATEGIES FOR MASTERING THE MATERIAL

Being a successful student requires more than a text and study guide. The best materials are worthless if the student approaches the course inappropriately or uses poor study strategies. This section discusses some basic behaviors that are important for success in any class, not just introductory psychology.

Go to Class Regularly. This seems pretty obvious, right? Still, many students miss class frequently, especially in large lecture classes in which their absence is unlikely to be noticed. Going to class has many benefits. First, the lectures might be the only source of some of the information you are expected to learn. Second, the focus of the lectures may be a good guide to the topics your instructor feels are important, and exams are likely to reflect this emphasis. Third, your instructor will present the material in a different "voice" or perhaps from a different orientation than your text. Material in the text that you have difficulty understanding might be easier to understand when presented in class. Also, the different style or form of presentation may help create more retrieval cues. The more ways and times information is presented, the more likely you are to remember it. Also, demonstrations, videos, and exercises that are included in class can provide wonderful memory cues for the related material and keep things interesting.

Simply showing up for class is insufficient, however. To get the most benefit from your attendance you need to come prepared and you need to be an active participant. Try to survey the material to be discussed. Look through the chapter, paying attention to section headings, figures, and tables. Familiarize yourself with the topic and some of the vocabulary. If you go to class with a foundation, the lecture will be easier to understand, and you will be able to take notes more effectively.

Pay attention in class. If you are socializing rather than paying attention, you not only miss the information you supposedly came to class to learn, but you also interfere with your neighbors' ability to pay attention.

Try to sit in the front of the class, especially in large lecture halls. You will be better able to see and hear, and there will be fewer distracting things between you and the instructor.

Get involved in the lecture. Think about what is being said; don't just listen passively. Active involvement in learning produces better memory for the material. Taking notes is one way to actively process the information, but don't try to write down every word. Be selective, and use your own words except in cases in which exact recall will be necessary. Have an organization to your notes. Indicate major topic headings and the supporting information, and include enough information to make your notes meaningful. Find a time soon after class to review your notes. If something is unclear then, it certainly will be unclear later when you begin studying. Clarify those points as soon as possible.

Use Your Textbook. Failing to read your textbook is similar to cutting class: you are wasting an important source of information, not to mention the money you spent. Why buy a book and then not use it?

Your textbook not only presents the information you will be expected to know, but also includes many features that will help make your studying easier and more effective. The important terms are highlighted and defined right in the chapter. Summary tables for concepts and theories are provided and make great study aids. Use them to quickly review the concepts and compare the different theories. Figures and other illustrations provide a clear visual representation of information. Learning goals and self-tests help you organize your studying and evaluate your progress. Chapter summaries offer a chance to preview the material before you begin your reading and to review the material when you are preparing for an exam.

Ask Questions. Asking questions serves several purposes. Most obviously, if you don't understand something, asking questions can get you the needed information. If you are unable to ask questions during class, talk with your instructor or TA before or after class or during their office hours. Don't be shy about asking for help understanding something. This is also true during exams. If you don't understand a question or a specific word, ask for help interpreting it. If you are generally struggling in class, ask your instructor or TA for help or go to your school's learning center for suggestions.

Asking questions is also a wonderful way to get involved in the material and to process it to a deeper level of understanding. As you study and as you listen in class, ask yourself what the information really means or what the point of the discussion is. The more deeply you process material, the more you will remember.

Make a Plan. Once you have a syllabus for each of your classes, evaluate what each class will require and mark important assignments on your calendar. For most courses you should plan to study about two hours per week for every hour spent in class. Carve out a regular study time for each class and consider those work periods comparable to a job. You don't put off going to work; don't put off studying. Don't waste free time between classes. Use it to study, or make it part of your planned recreational time.

Each time you sit down to study, set objectives about how long you will study and what material you will cover. Be realistic about your objectives. Consider both the study time needed and your attention span. If you have trouble concentrating for more than 30 minutes, don't plan to study 3 hours. Plan shorter but more frequent study sessions, or plan brief breaks within a study session.

Study As You Go. This requires discipline, but it is essential for most students. For classes that cover a large amount of material, waiting until a few days before an exam to begin serious study is deadly and is a mistake that many students make.

As you will learn in Chapter 8, massed practice (cramming) produces poorer memory than distributed (day by day) practice. Study for mastery on a daily (or at least weekly) basis, focusing on a small amount of material as if you will have a test the next day. By the time the actual exam approaches, you will have learned most of what you need to know, and you can spend the final study periods filling in details and expanding your comprehension to deeper levels. You will be less likely to end up with everything in a jumble in your mind than if you try to learn it all at the last minute.

Study Effectively When You Study. A popular study technique is the SQ3R method: *S*urvey, *Q*uestion, *R*ead, *R*ecite, *R*eview. My recommendations don't conform to this plan exactly, but the emphasis is similar: To study effectively requires action and thought on the part of the student.

1. Know where you are headed when you begin to study. Have learning goals. To formulate goals, briefly survey the material and identify the general issues. Compare your goals to those listed in this study guide.

2. Organize your studying and reading. Focus on a topic to be mastered. Integrate your class notes with the text material. The topic context will help you learn and remember the information. Develop outlines or create tables that summarize and relate material. Make use of the Concept Summary tables in your text. Expand these tables with information from lectures.

3. Be an *active* reader and learner. Reading passively and hoping that the material will find its way into your memory automatically is not an adaptive strategy. You might understand everything you read, but understanding and remembering are two different things. You need to understand something to maximize the chance you will remember it, but remembering requires more. Simple repetition is better than nothing, but thinking deeply is the best way to ensure you will remember. Look for relationships or critical differences

between terms or concepts. Apply the concepts to your own life. Generate your own examples. Tell somebody what you have learned. Get involved.

4. Develop materials for later review. As mentioned before, some students find note cards with a term on one side, and a definition and other important material on the other side to be very useful. You might also develop outlines, or create summary tables similar to your text's Concept Summary tables mentioned above. Your active involvement will help you remember the information, and you will be creating study materials for use during final preparations for exams.

5. Periodically evaluate your progress. Use the learning goals as cues for recall. Recite the basic ideas and the important details. Answer the questions in the study guide to quiz yourself. Don't move to new material until you understand and can recall the current material.

Be A Teacher. Teaching a concept to someone else is an excellent way to ensure you will remember that information for a long time. It also is one of the quickest ways to find out that you don't really understand something and that you need to do more work. Teaching a parent or friend will work, but taking turns with a study partner is best. Encourage your "student" to ask questions to test your comprehension. The act of recalling, organizing, and presenting information develops additional retrieval cues and reviews the material at the same time.

Practice, Practice, Practice. Review material right after you finish reading and frequently during the following week. Don't consider it learned and then never think about it again. Make part of each study session a quick review of past material. Each time you review material you are strengthening the retrieval cues for that information.

Practice answering questions similar to those you will encounter on the exam. The study guide has questions in different formats. Ask your instructor if any old exams are available. Sometimes dorms or campus organizations maintain test files. Don't assume that your exam will focus on the same material or be exactly the same difficulty. Use old tests simply to practice using your knowledge, not to figure out what will be on your exam. You might also find a different study guide and use the questions in it for additional practice. Most introductory psychology texts overlap considerably in what they cover, so many of the exercises will be appropriate.

Adapt Your Strategies. Evaluate your study strategies periodically. If you don't perform well on the first exam, try to figure out why. Look over your exam, and ask your instructor or TA for suggestions. Modify your strategies to fit your particular learning style and the demands of your particular course.

STRATEGIES FOR TAKING TESTS

Although how well you comprehend the material is certainly the most critical determinant of test performance, taking tests is somewhat an acquired skill. Poor test-taking behaviors can undo much of the hard work done to prepare for the test. Here are some general suggestions concerning taking tests:

Come Prepared. As stated above, the critical requirement for doing well on an exam is to know the material. Being well prepared has another benefit, though. Feeling confident about your knowledge reduces the anxiety you will experience during the exam. Being a little nervous is a good thing, but in large doses it interferes with the ability to concentrate and think. No matter how well prepared you are, there likely will be a question or two that will require you to stop and think for a minute.

Come Alert and Well-Rested. Being tired increases the chance you will make careless mistakes and degrades your ability to reason through difficult questions. As you will discover in Chapter 6, sleeping several hours after studying can improve memory for the material, too.

Survey the Test Before You Begin. Review the format of the questions, and evaluate how to budget your time. If you are unsure what you are supposed to do on some parts of the exam, ask for assistance.

Budget Your Time. Figure out approximately how long you can work on each question. For essay or other non-objective questions, the point value provides information about how complete an answer should be and how much time you might need for a question. Don't spend 30 minutes on one 5-point question and 5 minutes on a 25-point question. If you encounter a question you cannot answer in your budgeted time, make your best guess (if multiple choice), mark it for reconsideration, and move on. After finishing the rest of the questions, go back and spend any extra time on the ones that need more thought.

Be an Intelligent Test-Taker. Read the entire question before formulating an answer. Don't focus on one or two key terms and then assume you know what the question is asking. Be careful to notice critical words such as "not" or "except." On multiple choice questions, try to figure out the answer before you look at the alternatives. If your answer is listed (make sure it really says what you think it says), it probably is the right choice. However, read all the alternatives to be sure your choice is the best.

If you don't immediately know the answer to a question, don't panic. First, reread the question to make sure you know what it is asking. For multiple choice questions, reread the alternatives. Sometimes the alternatives will alert you to important details to consider. Then ask yourself what you *do* know about the topic. Use this information to reconsider the possibilities and to eliminate any answers that are clearly inappropriate. Finally, if all else fails, guess. For a multiple choice question, you probably will be able to eliminate one or two of the alternatives, increasing your odds of picking the correct answer. Essay questions are a greater challenge, but if you know anything, you have a chance for partial credit.

Don't be afraid to change an answer. Your first impression is not always right. Information you find later in the exam or a miraculous release from your blocked memory might show you an earlier answer needs to be reconsidered. If you can clearly explain why your first choice is wrong, change it.

Adapt Your Strategies to the Type of Test. Obviously, an essay exam requires a different strategy than a multiple-choice exam. First, make sure you know what the question is asking. A great answer to the wrong question is worthless. Second, take a minute to plan your answer. Jot down the important points, and think about how to organize those points. A poorly organized answer suggests you don't really understand the material and often will receive a lower grade. Also, information is more likely to be overlooked if your answer is a jumble of unorganized facts. Third, be concise. Include adequate details, but don't add irrelevant information. Get to the point, and stay there. Fourth, make sure your answer says what you intend. You know what you mean to say, but sometimes that is not what actually ends up on paper. Finally, write legibly and use reasonable grammar. What cannot be read or understood will earn no points.

A FINAL WORD

I hope this study guide helps you reach your goals in introductory psychology. I welcome any comments that you care to share with me. Let me know what worked well for you, what didn't, and what you think would be valuable to include in future editions.

Janet Proctor, Ph.D.

100 N. University Street, Room 1114

Purdue University

West Lafayette, Indiana 47907-1364

jproctor@purdue.edu

CHAPTER 1

AN INTRODUCTION TO PSYCHOLOGY

ESTABLISHING LEARNING GOALS

Use these learning goals as a preview of the chapter, a guide for active reading, and to evaluate your mastery of the material. Review the relevant goals as you begin and end your reading of each major section of the chapter.

I. Define and describe psychology.
   A. Understand the modern definition of psychology.
      1. Explain what is meant by mind.
      2. Explain what is meant by behavior.
   B. Distinguish among clinical, applied, and research psychologists.
      1. Describe the activities and typical workplace of clinical, applied, and research psychologist.
      2. Compare clinical and counseling psychologists.
      3. Distinguish between psychologists and psychiatrists.

II. Trace the history of scientific psychology.
   A. Understand what is meant by the mind-body problem.
      1. Describe Descartes' position on the mind-body problem.
      2. Describe the modern approach to the mind-body problem.
   B. Contrast the different viewpoints on the origins of knowledge.
      1. Describe the empiricist view of the origin of knowledge.
      2. Describe the nativist view of the origin of knowledge.
      3. Define natural selection and explain how it relates to the debate about the origin of knowledge and behavior.
      4. Discuss the current view of the influence of "nature" and "nurture" on the mind and behavior.
   C. Trace the development of the first scientific schools of psychology.
      1. Identify the event that marked the birth of psychology as a science.
      2. Describe the guiding focus and methods of structuralism, functionalism, and behaviorism.
      3. Identify the major figures associated with each school of psychology.
      4. Explain why these different approaches to the study of psychology developed.
   D. Note the early clinical contributions of Freud and the humanists.

1. Compare the central concepts and techniques of psychoanalysis and humanistic psychology.
2. Identify the major figures associated with each approach.

E. Highlight the contributions of women to the development of psychology as a field.

III. Understand and describe the focus of modern psychology.

A. Understand what it means to adopt an eclectic approach.

B. Understand the factors that started the cognitive revolution.

C. Trace recent developments in biology and evolutionary psychology and discussing how they influence modern psychology.

D. Explain why psychologists think cultural factors are important determinants of behavior and mind.

MASTERING THE MATERIAL

PREVIEW & DEFINING AND DESCRIBING PSYCHOLOGY (PP. 1-7)

MASTERING THE VOCABULARY

Define or explain each of the following terms.

1. psychology
2. mind
3. behavior
4. clinical psychologists
5. psychiatrists
6. applied psychologists
7. research psychologists

MASTERING THE CONCEPTS

Fill in the blanks to create a summary of the section.

Psychology is defined as the [1] ____________ study of [2] ____________ and mind. The [3] ____________ is the content and processes of subjective experience. Behavior includes any activity that can be systematically [4] ____________ and measured, including internal activity.

[5] ____________ psychologists treat psychological problems or counsel people about parenting or relationships. [6] ____________ are not psychologists; they are medical doctors trained in psychology who treat mental disorders. [7] ____________ psychologists, such as human factors or industrial/organizational psychologists, extend principles of psychology to industry. [8] ____________ psychologists explore basic principles of psychology by conducting experiments, often in laboratories at universities.

EVALUATING YOUR PROGRESS

Select the best response. If you make any errors, reread the relevant material before proceeding.

1. Behavior
   a. is the content and processes of subjective experience.
   b. is conscious and intentional activity.
   c. is activity that can be observed and measured in a systematic way.
   d. is studied only by indirect techniques and inferences.

2. Psychology and philosophy may deal with similar issues, but psychology
   a. emphasizes the use of the scientific method.
   b. developed before philosophy.
   c. studies only behavior, not the mind.
   d. studies abnormal behavior rather than normal behavior.

3. More than half of all psychologists work in
   a. business settings.
   b. mental health treatment centers.
   c. research facilities.
   d. elementary schools or high schools.

4. Which of the following people is most likely to be considered an applied psychologist?
   a. Tom, who helps people cope with divorce
   b. Chris, who studies the cognitive development of children
   c. Maria, who treats patients with serious mental disorders such as schizophrenia
   d. Ellen, who uses principles of psychology to improve teamwork and productivity in a large corporation

5. Psychiatrists must earn
   a. a Doctor of Philosophy degree (Ph.D.).
   b. a Doctor of Psychology degree (Psy.D.).
   c. a Doctor of Medicine degree (M.D.).
   d. a Doctor of Pharmacy degree (Pharm.D.).

THE SCIENCE OF PSYCHOLOGY: A BRIEF HISTORY (PP. 7-16)

MASTERING THE VOCABULARY

Define or explain each of the following terms.

1. empiricism
2. nativism
3. Gestalt psychology
4. structuralism
5. systematic introspection
6. functionalism
7. behaviorism
8. psychoanalysis
9. humanistic psychology

MASTERING THE CONCEPTS.

Fill in the blanks to create a summary of the section.

The roots of psychology are in [1] ____________ and [2] ____________ and date back to ancient Greece. Psychology merges these, studying both the mind and the biological processes of mental activity. How the mind relates to the body is known as the [3] ____________ question. The philosopher Descartes said that the mind and body are [4] ____________ , but the mind controls the body through the [5] ____________ gland. Psychologists now view the mind as brain activity and inseparable from the body.

Another question that interests psychologists concerns the origins of knowledge. Aristotle's [6] ____________ view states knowledge is obtained through experience, whereas Kant's [7] ____________ view states some knowledge is innate. The [8] ____________ psychologists suggested perceptual organization is one of these innate abilities. [9] ____________ concept of natural selection predicts adaptive traits are likely to be passed on in the genes, making inherited behavioral tendencies possible. Most modern psychologists agree both [10] ____________ (innate factors) and [11] ____________ (experience) are important.

Wilhelm Wundt founded psychology in [12] ____________ when he established the first psychology [13] ____________ , and psychology became a distinct scientific discipline. [14] ____________ , such as Wundt and Titchener, sought to study the mind by breaking experiences into basic components using systematic [15] ____________ . Later, [16] ____________ emerged in America and emphasized the function and purpose of mental operations. In the 20th century, the [17] ____________ , including Watson, argued that scientific psychology should study observable [18] ____________ rather than conscious experience. This approach remains influential today.

Clinical psychology changed in the early 20th century with the development of Freud's theory of mind and therapy called [19] ____________ . Here, the emphasis was on [20] ____________ determinants of behavior, which could only be discovered through the symbolic analysis of such things as dreams. Disliking Freud's negative view, the [21] ____________ , such as Rogers and Maslow, proposed that humans possess the potential for positive growth and self-awareness. Mary Calkins, Margaret Washburn, and Helen Thompson Wooley are some of the women who contributed to early psychology, in spite of intense discrimination. Women continue to play an important role in psychology today.

EVALUATING YOUR PROGRESS

Select the best response. If you miss any questions, reread the relevant material before proceeding.

1. The philosophical position that suggests experience is the origin of knowledge is called
   a. nativism.
   b. humanism.
   c. structuralism.
   d. empiricism.

2. "Nurture" in the nature-nurture issue refers to
   a. innate factors that influence behavior.
   b. the influence of experience.
   c. the unconscious mind.
   d. Gestalt influences on behavior.

3. Which movement in psychology suggested humans are born with unchangeable rules for organizing sensory input?
   a. behaviorism
   b. Gestalt psychology
   c. humanistic psychology
   d. psychoanalysis

4. Who is considered the founder of modern scientific psychology?
   a. William James
   b. Charles Darwin
   c. Wilhelm Wundt
   d. Sigmund Freud

5. Systematic introspection was a research technique used mostly by
   a. the structuralists.
   b. the behaviorists.
   c. the humanists.
   d. the functionalists.

6. Darwin's theory of evolution and natural selection most influenced the development of
   a. structuralism.
   b. functionalism.
   c. behaviorism.
   d. psychoanalysis.

7. The view that psychology should study only observable behavior and attempt to relate changes in the environment to changes in behavior is most characteristic of
   a. the humanistic perspective.
   b. nativism.
   c. structuralism.
   d. behaviorism.

8. Freud's psychoanalytic approach to psychology gave great importance to
   a. the therapist being a friend and supporter of the client.
   b. the role of natural selection in determining behavior.
   c. discovering hidden conflicts and desires in the unconscious mind.
   d. immediate conscious experience.

THE FOCUS OF MODERN PSYCHOLOGY (PP. 16-21)

MASTERING THE VOCABULARY

Define or explain each of the following terms.

1. eclectic approach

2. cognitive revolution

3. evolutionary psychology

4. culture

MASTERING THE CONCEPTS

Fill in the blanks to create a summary of the section.

Modern psychology is best described as [1] ____________ , not tied to one point of view, but an emphasis of cognitive, evolutionary, and biological factors is common. The cognitive [2] ____________ was stimulated by the invention of the [3] ____________ . This renewed interest in mental processes represented a [4] ____________ in the influence of behaviorism, and it emphasized an appreciation of how thoughts and perception influence behavior. New technology also advanced the study of biological aspects of behavior. Although renewed interest in natural selection's impact characterizes the controversial approach called [5] ____________ psychology, modern psychologists also carefully consider the role that shared values, customs, and beliefs, or [6] ____________ , has in behavior.

EVALUATING YOUR PROGRESS

Select the best response. If you miss any questions, reread the relevant material before proceeding.

1. Most modern psychologists use a variety of perspectives when studying behavior. In other words modern psychology uses
   a. a structuralist approach.
   b. a functionalist approach.
   c. a behaviorist approach.
   d. an eclectic approach.
2. With the cognitive revolution, behaviorism
   a. began to describe behavior in terms of computer models.
   b. turned from emphasizing the environment to emphasizing biological factors.
   c. lost some of its influence among psychologists.
   d. began to focus on the role of conflicts in the unconscious mind.
3. Improvements in technology have led to advances in the cognitive approach and
   a. the psychoanalytic approach.
   b. the biological approach.
   c. the cultural approach.
   d. the behaviorist approach.
4. A renewed interest in the adaptive value of behavior has contributed to the recent movement in psychology known as
   a. evolutionary psychology.
   b. psychobiology.
   c. cultural psychology.
   d. cognitive psychology.

5. The idea that humans have innate mental mechanisms that have been acquired through natural selection, represents
   a. cognitive psychology.
   b. behaviorism.
   c. evolutionary psychology.
   d. human factors psychology.

6. Modern psychologists recognize that the values and shared beliefs of the community are important influences on behavior. In other words, they recognize the importance of
   a. innate factors.
   b. cultural factors.
   c. humanistic factors.
   d. natural selection factors.

MAKING FINAL PREPARATIONS

Complete these sections without consulting your book or notes. For a more accurate estimate of how well you know this material, wait at least a day or two after studying the chapter before working on the questions. Some of the material you "know" immediately after working with the chapter will be quickly forgotten. Exercises done too soon after studying will overestimate what you know well.

SHORT ESSAY QUESTIONS

Write a brief answer to each question.

1. Compare the education and activities of counseling psychologists, clinical psychologists, and psychiatrists.

   ____

   ____

2. Compare the structuralist and behaviorist views about the proper focus and techniques of psychology.

   ____

   ____

3. Compare Freud's psychoanalytic approach with the humanistic approach of Rogers.

   ____

   ____

4. Explain how technology has affected modern psychology.

____

____

MATCHING

Select the correct definition or description for each item.

1. _______ systematic introspection
2. _______ tabula rasa
3. _______ Wundt
4. _______ nature-nurture issue
5. _______ Watson
6. _______ Calkins
7. _______ empiricism
8. _______ Descartes
9. _______ nativism
10. _______ Freud
11. _______ evolutionary psychology
12. _______ developmental psychology
13. _______ Rogers
14. _______ Wooley
15. _______ Titchener
16. _______ James

a. was especially interested in the mind-body problem
b. founded behaviorism
c. a prominent humanistic psychologist
d. view that certain knowledge is innate
e. idea that knowledge comes from experience
f. the idea that at birth the mind is a "blank slate"
g. issue of the role of innate & environmental factors
h. major figure in functionalism
i. favorite technique of structuralists
j. brought structuralism to America
k. original structuralist
l. studies how behavior changes through the lifespan
m. studies innate behavioral tendencies
n. early researcher in the field of sex differences
o. founder of the psychoanalytic approach
p. one of the first female psychologists

MULTIPLE CHOICE PRETEST 1

Select the one best response.

1. According to your text, psychology is currently defined as
   a. the scientific study of behavior and mind.
   b. the systematic study of mental processes.
   c. the systematic study of brain activity.
   d. the scientific study of mental illness.

2. Prior to the 1800s, the mind was studied mostly by
   a. sociologists and historians.
   b. psychiatrists and surgeons.
   c. poets and medical doctors.
   d. philosophers and physiologists.

3. The nativist view suggests that personality is determined by
   a. cultural factors.
   b. inborn biological or genetic characteristics.
   c. very early childhood experiences.
   d. unconscious conflicts.

4. Who is credited with establishing psychology as a science?
   a. William James
   b. Sigmund Freud
   c. John Watson
   d. Wilhelm Wundt

5. Psychologists who work in schools and industry are classified as
   a. clinical psychologists.
   b. research psychologists.
   c. applied psychologists.
   d. evolutionary psychologists.

6. "Yes, there are four basic tastes, but I'm interested in how this has helped us adapt and survive." What kind of psychologist is most likely to make such a statement?
   a. a psychoanalyst
   b. a structuralist
   c. a behaviorist
   d. a functionalist

7. The intensity of the lights in Jim's car increase when he pushes a control lever up, and decrease when he pushes control lever down. Using natural mappings like these in design is a principle favored by
   a. functionalists.
   b. psychoanalytic psychologists.
   c. human factors psychologists.
   d. social psychologists.

8. Which of the following are correctly paired?
   a. Descartes; natural selection
   b. structuralism; systematic introspection
   c. behaviorism; unconscious motivation
   d. empiricism; the mind-body problem

9. Who proposed that there are innate rules for perceptual organization?
   a. the empiricists
   b. the Gestalt psychologists
   c. John Watson
   d. Helen Wooley

10. Which school believed that psychology should study the mind by identifying the basic elements of immediate conscious experience and how they are combined?
    a. structuralism
    b. behaviorism
    c. humanism
    d. functionalism

11. Which statement most likely would be heard in a therapy session with a Freudian psychoanalytic psychologist?
    a. "There is a great person in there if you'll just let her out."
    b. "I don't want to hear about your dream. I'd rather talk about what you think is making you anxious."
    c. "I want you to tell me as completely as possible what you experience as you feel this satin cloth."
    d. "Your fear of dogs is just a symptom of some conflict deep in your unconscious mind."

12. Calkins and Washburn are notable for
    a. establishing the first psychology laboratory.
    b. developing humanistic psychology.
    c. first studying cross-cultural differences in behavior.
    d. being among the first female psychologists.

13. Behaviorism dismissed structuralism as unscientific because structuralists
    a. studied subjective events.
    b. emphasized negative urges rather than positive potential.
    c. studied animal behavior instead of human behavior.
    d. emphasized highly variable cultural influences on behavior.

14. The cognitive revolution refers to
    a. the development of computers modeled after human cognitive processes.
    b. the renewed interest in studying the mind after years of studying only directly observable behavior.
    c. the rapid shift in thinking that accompanied each transition from one view of psychology to another.
    d. the controversy created by Freud's theory of sexual urges during childhood.

15. Evolutionary psychology explores the influence of natural selection and
    a. shared values and customs.
    b. changes in brain chemistry.
    c. innate mental mechanisms.
    d. immediate conscious experience.

16. Utilizing a variety of theoretical approaches rather than a single approach is referred to as the
    a. humanistic approach.
    b. nativist approach.
    c. eclectic approach.
    d. behaviorist approach.

17. Research on the effects of racial diversity in complex thinking found that diversity in a discussion group
    a. increased flexibility and complexity of thought during the discussion and in later exercises.
    b. increased flexibility and complexity of thought during the discussion, but not in later exercises.
    c. had no effect during the discussion, but increased flexibility and complexity of though in later exercises.
    d. increased flexibility and complexity of thought only when topics related to racism were employed.

MULTIPLE CHOICE PRETEST 2

Select the one best response.

1. Pat hopes to complete medical school and then work as a therapist treating people with serious mental disorders. If Pat is successful, she will be
   a. a clinical psychologist.
   b. a psychiatrist.
   c. an applied psychologist.
   d. a cognitive psychologist.
2. School psychologists help identify children with learning disabilities or other problems that impact education, and they develop plans for helping these children perform well in school. School psychologists are one type of
   a. clinical psychologist.
   b. research psychologist.
   c. applied psychologist.
   d. counseling psychologist.
3. Descartes' answer to the mind-body problem proposes
   a. the mind is the same thing as the body.
   b. the mind is what the brain does.
   c. the mind and body are separate, but they can influence each other.
   d. the mind and body are separate and do not interact at all.
4. The Psychology Department is located in a building named after the founder of scientific psychology. The name of the building must be
   a. Wundt Hall
   b. Titchener Hall.
   c. James Hall
   d. Freud Hall.
5. Frieda knows how the environment produces physical reactions in the nervous system that then produce brain activity. What she has trouble understanding is how cellular activity becomes consciousness, emotion, or knowledge. Frieda is considering the
   a. cognitive revolution.
   b. structuralist-functionalist debate.
   c. nature-nurture problem.
   d. mind-body problem.

6. Which person-item pair is incorrectly linked?
   a. Carl Rogers---unconscious mind
   b. John Watson---observable behavior
   c. Wilhelm Wundt---systematic introspection
   d. William James---adaptive function

7. A psychologist observes rats that are in either crowded or uncrowded cages and counts the number of times rats bite or make other aggressive responses. To what "school" does this psychologist probably belong?
   a. structuralist
   b. behaviorist
   c. functionalist
   d. cognitive

8. You believe that psychology should strive to discover the elements of immediate experience and how they combine to produce meaningful wholes. Your view is most similar to
   a. functionalism.
   b. behaviorism.
   c. structuralism.
   d. psychoanalysis.

9. A major difference between Watson's behaviorism and Freud's psychoanalysis is that
   a. behaviorism stresses the function of the mind, but psychoanalysis stresses potential for growth.
   b. behaviorism stresses potential for growth, but psychoanalysis stresses unconscious urges.
   c. behaviorism stresses biological activity, but psychoanalysis stresses observable behavior.
   d. behaviorism stresses observable behavior, but psychoanalysis stresses unconscious urges.

10. If you believe "nature" in the nature-nurture controversy is most important, you are most likely to agree that
    a. Aristotle and the empiricists were correct to say the mind is a "tabula rasa" at birth.
    b. personality is determined more by one's genes than by one's early childhood experiences.
    c. people who are violent probably became that way because of violence in their environment.
    d. sex differences in behavior are mostly due to cultural beliefs about how males and females should act.

11. A capacity for self-awareness and personal growth is most associated with
    a. psychoanalysis.
    b. empiricism.
    c. humanistic psychology.
    d. cognitive psychology.

12. Dr. Hart is interested in the differences in dating behavior found in communities with different religious, ethnic, and socioeconomic characteristics. Dr. Hart's research emphasizes
    a. a humanistic view.
    b. a psychoanalytic view.
    c. a cognitive view.
    d. a cultural view.

13. Dr. Flores believes successful treatment of depression requires changing brain chemistry, attitudes and perceptions, and environmental conditions that are associated with stress or conflict. Dr. Flores' approach is best described as?
    a. behaviorist
    b. cognitive
    c. psychoanalytic
    d. eclectic

14. Important historical figures like Wundt, James, Freud, and Skinner were all men. What role have women played in psychology?
    a. Women have held prominent positions in psychology since the very early 1900's.
    b. Because of severe discrimination, no woman received a Ph.D. in psychology until 1930.
    c. The first female psychologists appeared in the 1940s when the need for therapists increased greatly.
    d. Early clinical psychology included many women, but women were excluded from research until the 1950s.

15. Marta believes that innate mechanisms help us learn language, find a mate, and engage in certain types of social behavior. She believes these innate mechanisms have developed because of natural selection. Marta's beliefs suggest she is
    a. an evolutionary psychologist.
    b. a behaviorist.
    c. a humanist.
    d. a human factors psychologist.

LANGUAGE DEVELOPMENT GUIDE

CORE TERMS

You might hear the word ***discipline*** or ***school*** in a discussion of psychology. Psychology, sociology, anthropology, history, etc., are all disciplines -- branches of knowledge -- that study behavior, but each has its own unique focus and methods of study. Even within a discipline there may be different ***schools*** of thought -- different ideas about the best way to study or explain something.

Psychology is considered a ***social science***, which means that it uses the principles of scientific investigation to study individual people and groups. As in sciences like chemistry and biology, psychology has ***theories***

-- detailed explanations -- that are tested through experiments. ***Empirical research***, including experiments, involves the systematic observation of an event or behavior. Similarly, the philosophical view of ***empiricism*** that is discussed in your text suggests that knowledge comes from a person's own observations (experience).

IDIOMS

p. 1	ultimately	final or highest
p. 7	in a sense	in some ways
p. 11	inherited predisposition	tendency to behave in a specific way that is passed in the genes to an organism's offspring
p. 11	act in concert	act together
p. 14	slip of the tongue	an error in word choice
p. 14	determinants of	things which cause
p. 15	drawing special attention to	emphasizing
p. 17	getting its…feet wet	in an early stage; taking a small step in
p. 17	to infer	to guess or predict based upon what you already know
p. 17	conceive of	think of in a new way, develop a way of thinking about
p. 20	an integral part	an important, necessary part; essential
p. 21	think critically	to ask questions and actively think about a topic

PRONUNCIATION

psychology (sy-col′-o-gee) *p. 1*
psychiatrists (sy-ky′-a-trist) *p. 4*
empiricism (im-peer′-i-siz-um) *p. 7*
nativism (nay′-ti-viz-um) *p. 8*
Gestalt (ge-stalt') *p. 9*
eclectic (ee-klek′-tik) *p. 17*

SOLUTIONS

PREVIEW & DEFINING AND DESCRIBING PSYCHOLOGY (PP. 1-7)

MASTERING THE CONCEPTS

1. scientific (p. 1)
2. behavior (p. 1)
3. mind (p. 4)
4. observed (p. 4)
5. Clinical (p. 4)
6. Psychiatrists (p. 4)
7. Applied (p. 5)
8. Research (p. 6)

EVALUATING YOUR PROGRESS

1. C, Correct (p. 4)
   A. Wrong. The content and processes of subjective experience defines mind.
   B. Wrong. Cellular activity is behavior, and it is not conscious.
   D. Wrong. Behavior may be studied directly. Mind must be studied indirectly.
2. A, Correct (p. 3)
   B. Wrong. Psychology began in the 1800s. Philosophy is much, much older.
   C. Wrong. Psychology is the scientific study of behavior and mind.
   D. Wrong. Psychology focuses on normal behavior, too.
3. B, Correct (p. 4)
   A, B, C. Wrong. Most psychologists work in mental health treatment.
4. D, Correct (p. 5)
   A. Wrong. Tom is a counseling psychologist.
   B. Wrong. Chris is a research psychologist.
   C. Wrong. Maria is a clinical psychologist or psychiatrist.
5. C, Correct (p. 4)
   A. Wrong. Psychologists earn a Ph.D. or a Psy.D.; psychiatrists are medical doctors (M.D.).
   B. Wrong. Psychiatrists are medical doctors (M.D.). Some clinical psychologists earn a Psy.D. degree.
   D. Wrong. Although psychiatrists prescribe medication, they do not earn a Doctor of Pharmacy degree.

THE SCIENCE OF PSYCHOLOGY: A BRIEF HISTORY (PP. 7-16)

MASTERING THE CONCEPTS.

1. philosophy (p. 7)
2. physiology (p. 7)
3. mind-body (p. 8)
4. separate (p. 8)
5. pineal (p. 8)
6. empiricist (p. 8)
7. nativist (p.8)
8. Gestalt (p. 9)
9. Darwin's (p. 10)
10. nature (p. 10)
11. nurture (p. 11)
12. 1879 (p. 11)
13. laboratory (p. 11)
14. Structuralists (p. 11)
15. introspection (p. 11)
16. functionalism (p. 12)
17. behaviorists (p. 13)
18. behavior (p. 13)
19. psychoanalysis (p. 14)
20. unconscious (p. 14)
21. humanists (p. 15)

EVALUATING YOUR PROGRESS

1. D, Correct (p. 7)
   A. Wrong. Nativism emphasizes that knowledge is present at birth.
   B. Wrong. Humanism stresses humans' positive potential. It doesn't relate to the origin of knowledge.
   C. Wrong. Structuralism proposed experience can be broken down into smaller elements.
2. B, Correct (p. 11)
   A. Wrong. "Nature" is associated with innate factors. "Nurture" relates to experience.
   C. Wrong. The unconscious mind is not involved in the nature-nurture issue.
   D. Wrong. Gestalt psychologists emphasized "nature," not "nurture."
3. B, Correct (p. 9)
   A. Wrong. Behaviorism stressed the role of experience, not innate factors.
   C. Wrong. Humanistic psychology stressed the potential for growth, not perceptual organization.
   D. Wrong. Psychoanalysis stressed the unconscious mind's importance, not rules of perception.
4. C, Correct (p. 11)
   A. Wrong. James was an important functionalist. Wundt was the founder of scientific psychology.
   B. Wrong. Darwin proposed the theory of evolution. He was not a psychologist.
   D. Wrong. Freud founded psychoanalysis significantly after Wundt founded scientific psychology.
5. A, Correct (p. 11)
   B. Wrong. Behaviorists felt systematic introspection was too subjective. Structuralists used systematic introspection.
   C. Wrong. Systematic introspection was used by structuralists to study the mind.
   D. Wrong. Functionalists emphasized function, so systematic introspection was not popular. Structuralists used systematic introspection.
6. B, Correct (p. 12)
   A. Wrong. Darwin's theory emphasizes adaptation and function, major ideas in functionalism.
   C. Wrong. Darwin's theory emphasizes adaptation and function, major ideas in functionalism. Behaviorism emphasizes the current environmental influences, not evolutionary ones.
   D. Wrong. Darwin's theory emphasizes adaptation and function, major idea in functionalism. Freud emphasized the role of the unconscious mind, not evolutionary pressures.
7. D, Correct (p. 13)
   A. Wrong. Humanistic psychologists do not believe only observable behavior is important.
   B. Wrong. Nativism proposed inborn characteristics, not the influence of the environment.
   C. Wrong. Structuralism emphasized subjective experience, not just observable behavior.
8. C, Correct (p. 14)
   A. Wrong. This is characteristic of client-centered therapy, a humanistic approach, not psychoanalysis.
   B. Wrong. Natural selection is relevant to functionalism, not Freud's psychoanalytic approach.
   D. Wrong. This is characteristic of structuralism. Freud emphasized unconscious influences.

THE FOCUS OF MODERN PSYCHOLOGY (PP. 16-21)

MASTERING THE CONCEPTS

1. eclectic (p. 17)
2. revolution (p. 17)
3. computer (p. 17)
4. decrease (p. 17)
5. evolutionary (p. 19)
6. culture (p. 19)

EVALUATING YOUR PROGRESS

1. D, Correct (p. 17)
   A, B, C. Wrong. Modern psychology is described as eclectic, or not tied to one approach.
2. C, Correct (p. 17)
   A. Wrong. Cognitive psychology often used computer analogies, not behaviorism.
   B. Wrong. Behaviorism still emphasizes environmental influences, not a biological approach.
   D. Wrong. Psychoanalysis stresses the unconscious mind. Behaviorism still emphasizes the environment.
3. B, Correct (p. 18)
   A. Wrong. Psychoanalysis doesn't depend on technology. The biological approach does.
   C. Wrong. The cultural approach wasn't influenced greatly by technology. The biological approach was.
   D. Wrong. Behaviorism isn't greatly influenced by technology. The biological approach is, however.
4. A, Correct (p. 19)
   B. Wrong. Adaptation value is central to evolutionary psychology, not psychobiology.
   C. Wrong. Although cultural factors are seen as important in modern psychology, they are not usually associated with the concept of adaptive value.
   D. Wrong. Cognitive psychology doesn't usually emphasize adaptive value. Adaptive value is critical in evolutionary psychology.
5. C, Correct (p. 19)
   A. Wrong. Cognitive psychology stresses the role of thoughts and perception, not natural selection.
   B. Wrong. Behaviorism stresses experience, not natural selection and innate tendencies.
   D. Wrong. Human factors stresses behavioral tendencies of the human user, not natural selection.
6. B, Correct (p. 19)
   A. Wrong Innate factors are present at birth and are not due to environmental influences.
   C. Wrong The environment has a role in humanism, but this question refers to cultural factors.
   D. Wrong. Natural selection is a process by which traits either persist or die out through evolution.

MAKING FINAL PREPARATIONS

SHORT ESSAY QUESTIONS

1. Counseling and clinical psychologists differ in the types of problems they most commonly treat, but not in the type of education they complete. Counseling psychologists tend to focus on adjustment problems such as marital problems or grief, whereas clinical psychologists tend to treat psychological disorders such as depression or serious anxiety. Both earn a graduate degree, often a doctorate (Ph.D.). Psychiatrists also treat psychological disorders such as depression, but they attend medical school and earn a medical degree (M.D.). They also have the ability to prescribe drugs as part of treatment, unlike psychologists. (p. 4)
2. The structuralists focused on immediate conscious experience and attempted to determine the basic elements of the mind and how they combine into meaningful wholes. They sought to understand the structure of the mind. To do so, they employed the research technique of systematic introspection, in which trained observers gave detailed accounts of their subjective experiences. Behaviorists, on the other hand, argued that to be a science, psychology should not attempt to study the mind or consciousness because its subjective nature made direct observation impossible and placed it outside of science. Instead, they proposed studying only overt behavior and how changes in environmental events affect behavior. (pp. 11-12)
3. Freud's psychoanalytic approach emphasized the role of unconscious influences. He felt that people had little insight into these unconscious, animalistic urges, conflicts, and memories. Mental problems would be solved only by insight through an analysis of the symbolic content of dreams, slips of the tongue, etc. His view was a very pessimistic, deterministic view of people. Humanists such as Rogers had a more optimistic view. They proposed that people had great abilities to achieve growth, self-awareness, and self-determination. The therapist's role is to nurture these strengths to allow the person to develop to their potential. (pp. 13-15)
4. The invention of the computer stimulated the use of computer-related concepts to describe and study cognitive behavior. Mental processes were likened to the stages of information processing performed by computers. Also, technology has provided new ways to study the brain. Brain activity can be more precisely measured, and highly detailed images of the brain are possible. New technology has also advanced the study of the biochemistry of the brain, and this has led to a greater emphasis on the biological determinants of mental disorders. (pp. 17-18)

MATCHING

1. i (p. 11)
2. f (p. 7)
3. k (p. 11)
4. g (p. 10)
5. b (p. 13)
6. p (p. 15)

7. e (p. 7)
8. a (p. 8)
9. d (p. 8)
10. o (p. 14)
11. m (p. 19)
12. l (p. 7)
13. c (p. 15)
14. n (p. 15)
15. j (p. 11)
16. h (p. 12)

MULTIPLE CHOICE PRETEST 1

1. A, Correct (p. 1)

   B. Wrong. Psychology is a science and it studies more than mental processes.

   C. Wrong. Psychology is a science and studies more than just brain activity.

   D. Wrong. Psychology studies more than just mental illness.

2. D, Correct (p. 3)

   A. Wrong. The origins of psychology are in philosophy and physiology.

   B. Wrong. Physiologists, but not these medical doctors, studied the mind.

   C. Wrong. Philosophers and physiologists, not poets and doctors, originally studied the mind.

3. B, Correct (p. 8)

   A. Wrong. Nativists stress innate factors, not environmental ones.

   C. Wrong. Nativists stress innate factors, not experiences after birth.

   D. Wrong. Conflicts arise from experience. Nativists stress innate factors.

4. D, Correct (p. 11)

   A. Wrong. James founded functionalism after psychology had become a science.

   B. Wrong. Freud is important in the development of clinical, but not scientific, psychology.

   C. Wrong. John Watson founded behaviorism after psychology had become a science.

5. C, Correct (p. 5)

   A. Wrong. Clinical psychologists work in mental health clinics.

   B. Wrong. Research psychologists work in universities and research institutes.

   D. Wrong. Evolutionary psychologists are research psychologists and work mostly in universities.

6. D, Correct (p. 12)

   A. Wrong. A psychoanalyst is interested in unconscious determinants of behavior, not adaptation.

   B. Wrong. A structuralist is interested in the structure of mind, rather than its adaptive value.

   C. Wrong. A behaviorist is interested in environmental determinants of behavior, not function.

7. C, Correct (p. 5)

   A. Wrong. Functionalists study the function of specific behaviors. They don't design functional products.

   B. Wrong. Psychoanalysts treat psychological disorders. They don't strive for natural mappings in design.

   D. Wrong. Social psychologists study interpersonal relationships, not natural mappings in design.

8. B, Correct (p. 11)

   A. Wrong. Descartes discussed the mind-body problem; Darwin discussed natural selection.

   C. Wrong. Psychoanalysis addresses the unconscious. Behaviorism focuses on observable behavior.

   D. Wrong. Empiricism stressed experience, not the relationship between body and mind.

9. B, Correct (p. 9)

   A. Wrong. Empiricists focus on the role of experience, not innate factors.

   C. Wrong. John Watson was a behaviorist who emphasized the role of experience in behavior.

   D. Wrong. Helen Wooley's research was on sex differences in behavior, not perceptual organization.

10. A, Correct (p. 11)

    B. Wrong. Behaviorists didn't study the mind. They studied only directly observable behaviors.

    C. Wrong. Humanism is an viewpoint related to personality or clinical psychology. It does not seek to identify the basic elements of the mind.

    D. Wrong. Functionalists emphasized function, not the structure or basic elements of the mind.

11. D, Correct (p. 14)
    A. Wrong. Psychoanalysis is more negative. This is probably from a humanistic therapist.
    B. Wrong. A psychoanalyst would analyze dreams. This is probably from a humanistic therapist.
    C. Wrong. This describes systematic introspection, not a therapy.
12. D, Correct (p. 15)
    A. Wrong. Wilhelm Wundt established the first psychology lab.
    B. Wrong. Carl Rogers developed humanistic psychology.
    C. Wrong. Washburn studied consciousness, and Calkins studied learning, not cultural differences.
13. A, Correct (p. 13)
    B. Wrong. This is the point of disagreement between psychoanalysis and humanism.
    C. Wrong. This is not true, and behaviorists used animals in much of their research.
    D. Wrong. This is not true of structuralism.
14. B, Correct (p. 17)
    A. Wrong. Theories of mind were influenced by the computer, not the reverse.
    C. Wrong. Cognitive revolution only refers to the shift from behaviorism to a cognitive view.
    D. Wrong. Freud's theory was controversial, but it did not lead to the cognitive revolution.
15. C, Correct (p. 19)
    A. Wrong. Evolutionary psychology studies innate mechanisms, not cultural influences.
    B. Wrong. Evolutionary psychology studies innate mechanisms, not biochemical changes.
    D. Wrong. Evolutionary psychology deals with evolutionary pressures, not immediate experience.
16. C, Correct (p. 17)
    A. Wrong. The humanistic approach utilizes a single philosophy, centered on personal growth.
    B. Wrong. The nativist approach emphasizes the influence of innate tendencies.
    D. Wrong. The behaviorist approach utilizes a single philosophy, centered on experience.
17. A, Correct (p. 6)
    B. Wrong. Diversity impacted both the discussion and performance in later exercises .
    C. Wrong. Diversity impacted both the discussion and performance in later exercises.
    D. Wrong. The diversity effect did vary by topic, but it was not limited to topics related to race.

MULTIPLE CHOICE PRETEST 2

1. B, Correct (p. 4)
   A. Wrong. Clinical psychologists don't get a medical degree. Psychiatrists have medical degrees.
   C. Wrong. Applied psychologists work with practical environmental problems, not mental problems.
   D. Wrong. Cognitive psychologists study primarily normal thought processes, not mental problems.
2. C, Correct (p. 5)
   A. Wrong. School psychologists are not a type of clinical psychologist. They are applied psychologists.
   B. Wrong. Research psychologists might study the cause of learning disabilities, rather than find a way for a student to overcome them.
   D. Wrong. Counseling psychologists treat mental health problems. They do not develop educational plans.
3. C, Correct (p. 8)
   A. Wrong. Descartes believed the mind and body should be considered separate.
   B. Wrong. This is the modern view, not the view of Descartes.
   D. Wrong. Descartes did not believe in complete separation. He believed the mind could affect the body.

4. A, Correct (p. 11)

   B. Wrong. Titchener was not the founder of scientific psychology; Wundt is considered the founder.

   C. Wrong. James was an early functionalist. He did not found scientific psychology.

   D. Wrong. Freud might be credited with founding clinical psychology, but not scientific psychology.

5. D, Correct (p. 8)

   A. Wrong. The cognitive revolution was a change in the focus of psychology, not how mind and body relate.

   B. Wrong. Structuralists and functionalists debated the proper focus of psychology, not mind-body issues.

   C. Wrong. The nature-nurture problem involves the origin of knowledge, not mind-body issues.

6. A, Correct (p. 15)

   B. Wrong. Watson, a behaviorist, stressed studying observable behavior.

   C. Wrong. Wundt, a structuralist, used systematic introspection.

   D. Wrong. James, a functionalist, was interested in the adaptive function of the mind and behavior.

7. B, Correct (p. 13)

   A. Wrong. Structuralism was more concerned with the mind than stimulus-response relations.

   C. Wrong. Functionalism was more concerned with the adaptive function of behavior.

   D. Wrong. Cognitive psychologists are more concerned with the mental processes behind behavior.

8. C, Correct (p. 11)

   A. Wrong. Functionalism stresses discovering the function of an experience, not the contents.

   B. Wrong. Behaviorism stresses studying only observable behaviors, not consciousness.

   D. Wrong. Psychoanalysis stresses the discovery of hidden conflicts that affect behavior.

9. D, Correct (pp. 13-14)

   A. Wrong. These represent functionalism and humanism.

   B. Wrong. These represent humanism and psychoanalysis.

   C. Wrong. These represent the biological approach and behaviorism.

10. B, Correct (p. 9)

    A. Wrong. Tabula rasa emphasizes the importance of experience, and is more consistent with "nurture."

    C. Wrong. This view is more consistent with the "nurture" (experience or environment) position.

    D. Wrong. This view is more consistent with the "nurture" (learned) position.

11. C, Correct (p. 15)

    A. Wrong. Psychoanalysis stresses the unconscious and determinism.

    B. Wrong. Empiricism is the idea that knowledge results from experience.

    D. Wrong. Cognitive psychology stresses information processing.

12. D, Correct (p. 19)

    A. Wrong. Humanism stresses the potential for personal growth, not cultural variables.

    B. Wrong. Psychoanalysis emphasizes unconscious influences, not cultural differences.

    C. Wrong. Cognitive research involved memory and thinking, not differences in dating behavior.

13. D, Correct (p. 17)

    A. Wrong. Behaviorist aspects are present, but the variety of factors describes an eclectic approach.

    B. Wrong. Cognitive aspects are present, but the variety of factors describes an eclectic approach.

    C. Wrong. Nothing was said about unconscious components or other aspects of psychoanalytic theory.

14. A, Correct (p. 15)

    B. Wrong. Severe discrimination did occur, but Margaret Washburn received her Ph.D. in 1894.

    C. Wrong. In spite of discrimination, women have worked as psychologists since the late 1800's.

    D. Wrong. Some of the earliest (late 1800s, early 1900s) important research was conducted by women.

15. A, Correct (p. 19)

    B. Wrong. Belief in innate mechanisms is not very characteristic of behaviorists.

    C. Wrong. Humanists emphasize the potential for self-growth, not innate mechanisms of behavior.

    D. Wrong. Human factors psychologists believe humans have certain behavioral tendencies, but not necessarily that these are innate or due to natural selection.

CHAPTER 2

THE TOOLS OF PSYCHOLOGICAL RESEARCH

ESTABLISHING LEARNING GOALS

Use these learning goals as a preview of the chapter, a guide for active reading, and to evaluate your mastery of the material. Review the relevant goals as you begin and end your reading of each major section of the chapter.

I. Describe the role of the scientific method in psychology.

  A. Describe the scientific method.

  B. Identify the roles of observation and operational definitions.

II. Understand how best to observe and describe behavior.

  A. Describe the techniques and goals of descriptive research.
    1. Define reactivity and external validity.
    2. Explain how reactivity affects external validity.

  B. Explain how psychologists conduct naturalistic research.
    1. Explain how reactivity may be avoided.
    2. Describe the role of naturalistic observation in research.

  C. Discuss the gains and costs of case studies and surveys.
    1. Discuss the problems of external validity and verification in relation to surveys and case studies.
    2. Explain how and why representative samples are obtained.

  D. Describe the major purpose of psychological tests.

  E. Explain how statistics can summarize and help interpret data.
    1. Define central tendency and variability, and discuss why both types of measures are needed.
    2. Compare descriptive and inferential statistics.

III. Describe techniques for predicting behavior.

  A. Define correlation and discuss how correlations can be used to predict behavior.
    1. Compare positive and negative correlations, and give examples of each.
    2. Characterize the relationship between two variables based on the correlation coefficient.

  B. Explain why correlations cannot normally be used to determine the cause of behavior.

IV. Describe techniques for explaining why a behavior occurs.

A. Explain how and why experiments are conducted.

B. Discuss the differences between independent and dependent variables.

C. Explain what is meant by experimental control and how it allows for the determination of causality.
   1. Discuss the problem of confounding variables and how they can be avoided.
   2. Describe random assignment, and explain why it is used.

D. Describe the problems created by expectancies and biases and how these problems are solved.

E. Discuss the problems associated with generalizing experimental conclusions.

V. Describe the ethics of research involving humans and animals.

A. Explain the principle of informed consent.

B. Discuss the roles of debriefing and confidentiality in research.

C. Discuss the ethical issues involved in animal research.

MASTERING THE MATERIAL

PREVIEW & OBSERVING BEHAVIOR: DESCRIPTIVE RESEARCH (PP. 27-39)

MASTERING THE VOCABULARY

Define or explain each of the following terms.

1. scientific method
2. operational definition
3. descriptive research
4. reactivity
5. external validity
6. naturalistic observation
7. case study
8. survey
9. random sampling
10. achievement test
11. aptitude test
12. mean

13. mode
14. median
15. variability
16. range
17. standard deviation
18. descriptive statistics
19. inferential statistics

MASTERING THE CONCEPTS

Fill in the blanks to create a summary of the section.

Psychology uses the [1] ____________ method to examine the mind and behavior. This approach involves four steps: [2] ____________ of a behavior, detection of [3] ____________ in the data, the generation of a [4] ____________ , and additional observations to check the [5] ____________ of the hypothesis. To ensure that psychological terms or concepts can be observed, [6] ____________ definitions are used.

This chapter examines four goals of research: observing and [7] ____________ behavior; predicting behavior; [8] ____________ behavior; and treating research participants [9] ____________ .

[10] ____________ research involves observing and describing behavior. One possible problem is that the observer's presence can cause [11] ____________ , a change in behavior caused by being observed. As a result, observations may not [12] ____________ to other situations and will lack external [13] ____________ . This problem can be reduced by using unobtrusive techniques such as [14] ____________ observation, in which behavior is observed in its natural environment without interference by the experimenter. In a related method, [15] ____________ observation, the experimenter becomes a participant in the activities of interest. [16] ____________ observation, examining the aftereffects of a behavior, is also useful for avoiding reactivity.

A [17] ____________ involves detailed observations of a single person. The detailed information helps develop [18] ____________ , but because only one person is observed, external validity may be poor, and verifying the [19] ____________ of the information is difficult. [20] ____________ relationships cannot be determined.

Another approach, using [21] ____________ , gathers less detailed information from many individuals. To get representative data and to avoid bias, [22] ____________ sampling must be used. Every member of a population must have an equal chance of participation. Limitations of surveys include a lack of in-depth information and the [23] ____________ of the information may be poor.

Psychological tests can be used to measure [24] ____________ differences. [25] ____________ tests measure current level of knowledge, while aptitude tests measure potential ability.

[26] ____________ are used to summarize and interpret the results of observations. Measures of [27] ____________ tendency describe the point at which scores tend to cluster and include the mean (average), the [28] ____________ (most frequent), and the [29] ____________ (middle score). Measures of [30] ____________ describe how far apart scores are spread and include the range and the [31] ____________ deviation.

[32] ____________ statistics are used to decide whether the data are representative and to evaluate the probability that observed differences are due to chance. If the probability of being due to chance is 5% or less, the difference is statistically [33] ____________ .

Without a statistical education, people often draw inappropriate conclusions. The law of [34] ____________ , which states larger samples are more likely than smaller samples to accurately represent the entire population, may be ignored and result in errors.

EVALUATING YOUR PROGRESS

Select the one best response. If you make any errors, reread the relevant material before proceeding.

1. The first and last step in the scientific method is
   a. observation.
   b. data analysis.
   c. operationally defining variables.
   d. detecting regularities in behavior.

2. An operational definition defines a concept in terms of
   a. the most current hypothesis concerning the concept.
   b. its most common characteristics.
   c. how the concept can be measured.
   d. the most general and abstract characteristics of the concept.

3. What technique is used when a researcher studies one person in great detail?
   a. inferential statistics
   b. a case study
   c. naturalistic observation
   d. a survey

4. People's behavior sometimes changes simply because they are being observed. This effect is known as
   a. reactivity.
   b. external validity.
   c. standard deviation.
   d. experimental control.

5. One reason researchers use naturalistic observation is
   a. to increase reactivity in their results.
   b. to improve the external validity of their findings.
   c. to establish cause and effect.
   d. to increase the standard deviation of their observations.

6. Random sampling of a population is most likely to
   a. produce a representative sample.
   b. reduce external validity
   c. reduce reactivity.
   d. allow validation of the data.

7. The mean, median, and mode are measures of
   a. external validity.
   b. variability.
   c. central tendency.
   d. statistical significance.

8. Inferential statistics are used to help
   a. increase external validity.
   b. measure the central tendency of the data.
   c. reduce the variability in the data.
   d. interpret the results of research.

9. What is the law of large numbers?
    a. The larger the sample size, the more likely observations will accurately represent the population.
    b. The larger the number of possible outcomes, the more likely the conclusion will be wrong.
    c. The more people surveyed, the less agreement there will be in the responses.
    d. The larger the number of observations, the more chance there will be careless errors.

PREDICTING BEHAVIOR: CORRELATIONAL RESEARCH (PP. 40-43)

MASTERING THE VOCABULARY

Define or explain each of the following terms.

1. correlation
2. positive correlation
3. negative correlation
4. zero correlation

MASTERING THE CONCEPTS.

Fill in the blanks to create a summary of the section.

Another purpose of research is to predict behavior. Correlational research looks for [1] ____________ between behaviors. A correlation (or correlation coefficient) reflects the way and degree to which two measures of behavior vary systematically together. [2] ____________ correlations indicate that the measures vary in the same direction; [3] ____________ correlations indicate that the measures vary in opposite directions. The [4] ____________ of the correlation is indicated by how close the coefficient is to 1.0 (or -1.0). Zero correlations indicate no predictable relationship exists. Correlations describe relationships, but they do not prove [5] ____________ and effect, mainly because of the problem of possible [6] ____________ variables.

EVALUATING YOUR PROGRESS

Select the one best response. If you make any errors, reread the relevant material before proceeding.

1. Significant correlations permit researchers to
   a. determine cause-effect relationships.
   b. use one behavior to predict another.
   c. identify third variable relationships.
   d. assume that the relationship has good external validity.

2. As Behavior A decreases, Behavior B decreases equally. This pattern reflects a
   a. negative correlation.
   b. zero correlation.
   c. positive correlation.
   d. a third variable correlation.

3. Behavior A will most reliably predict Behavior B if their correlation coefficient equals.
   a. +0.60
   b. +0.40
   c. -0.10
   d. -0.80

EXPLAINING BEHAVIOR: EXPERIMENTAL RESEARCH (PP. 44-50)

MASTERING THE VOCABULARY

Define or explain each of the following terms.

1. experimental research
2. independent variable
3. dependent variable
4. confounding variable
5. internal validity
6. random assignment
7. placebo
8. single-blind study
9. double-blind study

MASTERING THE CONCEPTS.

Fill in the blanks to create a summary of the section.

Experiments can evaluate the cause of behavior because [1] ____________ is possible. Experiments differ from correlational studies because the experimenter directly [2] ____________ some environmental condition thought to influence the behavior being studied. The condition that is varied is the [3] ____________ variable. The experimenter observes behavior to see whether it changes when conditions change. The behavior observed and measured is called the [4] ____________ variable.

To make cause-effect statements, the only systematic changes in the experimental conditions that can occur are those of the independent variable. For this reason, two groups are used: an [5] ____________ group, which receives the independent variable manipulation, and a [6] ____________ group, which does not. If a [7] ____________ variable, an uncontrolled variable that varies systematically with the independent variable, is present, differences between groups might be due to this variable rather than the independent variable, and the experiment will have poor [8] ____________ validity. Experimenters control as many variables as possible and use [9] ____________ assignment to reduce initial differences between groups.

The expectations of the subjects and the experimenter can influence their behavior and the research outcome. [10] ____________ studies keep the experimental condition secret from the subject to avoid subject expectancy effects. [11] ____________ studies keep group membership secret from subjects and experimenter to avoid both subject and experimenter expectancy effects.

Laboratory research often has good [12] ____________ validity and generalizes to natural environments, but the control needed to prove cause-effect may lead to behavior that would not occur in natural environments.

EVALUATING YOUR PROGRESS

Select the one best response. If you make any errors, reread the relevant material before proceeding.

1. In an experiment, the researcher
   a. makes observations of naturally occurring behavior and does not interfere in any way.
   b. changes some aspect of the environment and observes the effect of that change.
   c. takes measurements of two variables for every person in the group being observed.
   d. examines one person in great detail.

2. The behavior that is measured by the experimenter is
   a. the independent variable.
   b. the dependent variable.
   c. the confounding variable.
   d. the internal variable.

3. An uncontrolled factor that varies systematically with the independent variable is
   a. an internal variable.
   b. a placebo variable.
   c. a random variable.
   d. a confounding variable.

4. A control group in an experiment
   a. does not receive the experimental treatment or change.
   b. is used to prevent subject and experimenter biases.
   c. usually improves the external validity of the data.
   d. is not necessary if random assignment or a "blind" procedure is used.

5. If random assignment is used, researchers assume differences in group performance are not due to
   a. experimenter expectancies about the experiment.
   b. subject expectancies about the experiment.
   c. differences in the personal characteristics of subjects in each group.
   d. the environmental conditions that are intentionally manipulated in the experiment.

6. A placebo is used in drug studies to
   a. equate subject expectancies.
   b. avoid the need for a control group.
   c. fulfill the requirements for ethical research.
   d. increase the likelihood of confounding variables.

7. To avoid experimenter expectancy effects, researchers use
   a. a control group.
   b. at least two dependent variables.
   c. a single-blind procedure.
   d. a double-blind procedure.

THE ETHICS OF RESEARCH: HUMAN AND ANIMAL GUIDELINES (PP. 51-54)

MASTERING THE VOCABULARY

Define or explain each of the following terms.

1. informed consent
2. debriefing
3. confidentiality

MASTERING THE CONCEPTS

Fill in the blanks to create a summary of the section.

Researchers follow ethical guidelines to protect the rights of research participants. One requirement is [1] ____________ consent, consent given after information about the risks and procedures of the research have been provided. Deception is allowed if it does not involve potential harm and would not affect the person's willingness to participate. Researchers also [2] ____________ participants by explaining the research, and must protect their privacy by maintaining the [3] ____________ of personal information.

Ethical requirements have been established that require animals be treated humanely and be given proper care. Animal research is important because of the greater ability to [4] ____________ the environment, to complete studies rapidly, and to deal with simpler systems. In spite of criticisms that conclusions from animal research are invalid for humans, many findings do generalize.

EVALUATING YOUR PROGRESS

Select the one best response. If you make any errors, reread the relevant material before proceeding.

1. The use of deception in research is controversial because it conflicts with the ethical requirement of
   a. confidentiality.
   b. compensation.
   c. debriefing.
   d. informed consent.

2. Keeping personal information about research participants private is part of the ethical requirement of
   a. compensation.
   b. confidentiality.
   c. debriefing.
   d. informed consent.

3. Which of the following is not an advantage of using animals in research?
   a. There are no ethical requirements to be followed with animals.
   b. The environment and experiences of the animals can be tightly controlled.
   c. Some animals have simpler systems than humans, which makes research simpler.
   d. Animals often have short lifespans, so developmental research may be conducted more quickly.

MAKING FINAL PREPARATIONS

Complete these sections without consulting your book or notes. For a more accurate estimate of how well you know this material, wait at least a day or two after studying the chapter before working on the questions. Some of the material you "know" immediately after working with the chapter will be quickly forgotten. Exercises done too soon after studying will overestimate what you know well.

SHORT ESSAY QUESTIONS

Write a brief answer to each question.

1. Briefly outline the four steps of the scientific method.

   ____

   ____

2. What do measures of central tendency and measures of variability tell us, and why are both needed?

   ____

   ____

3. Explain what a correlation describes, and give examples of positive and negative correlations.

   ____

   ____

4. Compare reactivity and expectancy effects, and explain how they can be reduced in research.

   ____

   ____

5. Why can experiments establish cause-effect relationships but correlational research cannot?

____

____

6. What is random assignment, and why is it used in experiments?

____

____

7. Identify and briefly explain the three major ethical requirements for research with humans.

____

____

MATCHING

Select the correct definition or description for each item.

1. _______ positive correlation
2. _______ standard deviation
3. _______ case study
4. _______ external validity
5. _______ reactivity
6. _______ inferential statistics
7. _______ dependent variable
8. _______ median
9. _______ negative correlation
10. _______ participant observation
11. _______ internal validity
12. _______ independent variable
13. _______ descriptive statistics
14. _______ single-blind study

a. ability of data to generalize to other situations
b. a change in behavior because of being observed
c. mathematical techniques used to describe data
d. detailed description of a single person
e. subjects do not know their group assignment
f. observing while taking part in the observed activity
g. measure of how much a score differs from the mean
h. mathematical techniques for evaluating data and estimating whether differences are due to chance
i. behavior that is measured in an experiment
j. two variables related such that a change in one is accompanied by an opposite change in the other
k. condition manipulated by the experimenter
l. the middle point or score in a set of scores
m. two variables related such that a change in one is accompanied by similar changes in the other
n. amount of control over confounding variables

MULTIPLE CHOICE PRETEST 1

Select the one best response.

1. According to your text, forming a hypothesis is the ______ step in the scientific method.
   a. first
   b. second
   c. third
   d. last

2. Naturalistic observation, case studies, and surveys are all examples of
   a. descriptive research.
   b. experimental research.
   c. double-blind research designs.
   d. single-blind research designs.

3. What technique helps ensure that survey data represent the opinions of the population as a whole?
   a. informed consent
   b. participant observation
   c. random sampling
   d. double-blind design

4. You obtained the following data (1, 1, 2, 4, 7). The mean, median, and mode of these data are
   a. 2, 1, 4.
   b. 3, 2, 1.
   c. 2, 3, 1.
   d. 1, 4, 2.

5. To study age differences in personal space, researchers sat in a mall and watched people walking and sitting together. What research approach did they use?
   a. a case study
   b. an experiment
   c. a survey
   d. naturalistic observation

6. Correlations
   a. identify cause-effect relationships.
   b. are measures of central tendency.
   c. predict behavior.
   d. require the manipulation of some aspect of the environment.

7. Inferential statistics
   a. describe the value around which scores tend to cluster.
   b. help interpret research results.
   c. show how far from the mean a score is located.
   d. control for confounding variables.

8. Which represents a negative correlation?
   a. People with a high activity level tend to have a high metabolic rate.
   b. Young adults recall more words in a memory test than do older adults.
   c. Children who wear large shoes tend to have better reading skills than children who wear small shoes.
   d. People with lower education tend to have lower salaries than people with higher education.
9. You read that there is a statistically significant difference in the rate of depression among men and women. This means that the difference is not likely to be due to
   a. chance.
   b. reactivity.
   c. a confounded variable.
   d. an expectancy effect.
10. When results from laboratory research fail to predict behavior in the real world, the research lacks
    a. external validity.
    b. internal validity.
    c. an independent variable.
    d. a dependent variable.
11. Researchers manipulated the temperature of the room in which 4 groups of students were asked to solve 10 math problems. Students in the 60 and 70 degree rooms had more correct answers than students in the 80 and 90 degree rooms. The dependent variable in this experiment is
    a. the temperature of the room.
    b. the number of groups of students.
    c. the number of math problems correctly solved.
    d. the time students spent in the room.
12. What potential problem of correlational research limits the types of conclusions possible?
    a. negative correlations
    b. participant observation
    c. standard deviation
    d. third variables
13. When the subjects do not know to which group they have been assigned, but the experimenter recording their behavior does, the experiment
    a. has a confounding variable.
    b. has no control group.
    c. used a single-blind design.
    d. used a double-blind design.

14. When the experiment session ended, Raj told the subjects the purpose of the experiment, what he hoped to learn, and who to contact for further information about the results. This was part of the ethical requirement of
    a. confidentiality.
    b. humane treatment.
    c. informed consent.
    d. debriefing.

15. To help ensure that uncontrolled individual differences in participants are equated across the groups in an experiment, researchers are most likely to use
    a. random assignment.
    b. a placebo.
    c. a single-blind design.
    d. a double-blind design.

MULTIPLE CHOICE PRETEST 2

Select the one best response.

1. Sometimes the observations from case studies fail to generalize to other individuals or situations. This represents a problem with
    a. reactivity.
    b. a third or confounding variable.
    c. internal validity.
    d. external validity.

2. Many cable news programs ask viewers to participate in online surveys, but when reporting the outcome, they usually include a warning that the survey was unscientific and the results might not represent the beliefs of the population in general. Why is this warning very appropriate?
    a. These surveys rarely use a double-blind procedure.
    b. Inferential statistics are not commonly used.
    c. Participants are not selected randomly.
    d. These surveys are likely to include a third variable.

3. Production at the factory was poor, so management had a team of observers film the workers on the job. The films showed everyone working at top speed, and production was the highest in a year. A likely explanation for the change in the workers' behavior is
    a. external validity.
    b. reactivity.
    c. a placebo effect.
    d. random assignment.

4. Channel 6 News heard reports that security regulations were being ignored at the local airport. They had a reporter get a job at the airport so he could find out how security was maintained. This technique is
   a. a case study.
   b. introspection.
   c. participant observation.
   d. naturalistic observation.

5. To determine a person's potential for success in a particular occupation, rather than the person's current level of knowledge, researchers would use
   a. an aptitude test.
   b. an achievement test.
   c. measures of central tendency.
   d. correlation coefficients.

6. Range and standard deviation represent
   a. variability.
   b. correlations.
   c. the average score.
   d. central tendency.

7. The primary advantage of experimental research over correlational research is that experiments
   a. are easier to conduct than correlational studies.
   b. use descriptive statistics rather than inferential statistics.
   c. involve more natural behavior than correlational studies.
   d. can determine cause-effect relationships.

8. Sam, an autistic boy, took part in Dr. Omar's new therapy program. Dr. Omar reported Sam's behavior in great detail to argue his new program works. The research technique used here was
   a. an experiment.
   b. naturalistic observation.
   c. a case study.
   d. a single-blind procedure.

9. After reading that children's shoe size and reading ability are positively correlated, Tom said, "Getting older probably explains both increased shoe size and reading skill. Which problem associated with interpreting correlations did Tom point out?
   a. an expectancy effect
   b. a reactivity effect
   c. an unrepresentative sample effect
   d. a third variable effect

10. Assume there is a moderate correlation between the IQ of identical twins, such that if one twin has a low IQ, the other twin is also likely to have a low IQ. Which of the following most likely represents that correlation?
    a. +1.00
    b. +0.45
    c. -0.45
    d. -0.75

11. To discover whether highlighting terms in texts help students learn, researchers had one group of students read a biology chapter with highlighted terms and had another group read the same chapter with the terms in normal type. Both groups then took the same 10-item test, and their test scores were recorded. The independent variable in this experiment was
    a. the format of the chapter (highlighted terms or no highlighting).
    b. the students' test performance (the test score).
    c. the content of the chapter (the factual material).
    d. the personal backgrounds of the students who participated (intelligence, age).

12. Fred's advisor noticed that he had not included the same words in each list used to test whether the color of ink affects memory. The lists differed in both content and ink color. Fred can't easily interpret his results because
    a. reactivity occurred.
    b. his data have poor external validity.
    c. his experiment included a confounding variable.
    d. he did not use a control group.

13. Before beginning each experiment session, Kit reads aloud a description of what participants will be asked to do. Kit is fulfilling the ethical requirement of
    a. humane treatment.
    b. informed consent.
    c. debriefing.
    d. confidentiality.

14. Teachers in a small town are protesting because their pay raises are based on teaching evaluations of one class period each year. They claim that such limited sampling of their teaching is likely to produce inaccurate evaluations, and they want at least five observations. What concept supports their argument?
    a. operational definition
    b. random assignment
    c. placebo effect
    d. law of large numbers

15. The research participants were not told which of three types of pills they were prescribed (a new drug, an old drug, or a sugar pill). Lakisha, the researcher who observes and rates each person's behavior, doesn't know which type of pill they received, either. This is an example of
    a. a double-blind design.
    b. a single-blind design.
    c. the use of deception.
    d. participant observation.

LANGUAGE DEVELOPMENT GUIDE

CORE TERMS

When you signed up for this course, you probably thought that a certain amount of what you would study would be "common sense." But it's the job of psychologists to question common sense, and to want to test it. Instead of "common sense," psychologists would use the term ***intuitive*** -- that is, coming from your intuition. You can't build a science on intuition or common sense; a science requires that before a fact is accepted as a fact it must be tested empirically. That means that psychologists have to set up some experiments to check whether things really work the way they seem to work.

Your instructor might use the term ***classic*** study or ***seminal*** study when describing an experiment. This is research that is very important because it proved some major fact to be true or because it changed the way people viewed a topic. *Seminal experiments* usually lead to a new theory and inspire many new experiments. When discussing a classic study, your professor might say something like, "This study clearly establishes ***causality*** between a lack of dopamine and Parkinson's disease." That means that the experiment is important because it showed that one thing (the amount of dopamine) causes another thing (Parkinson's disease). Remember, though, that some "classic" studies are discussed because of their impact in the past, not their current value. For example, because of problems with confirming it's accuracy, Freud's theory of personality is not the most popular theory, but it is discussed because of its past and current influence on psychology.

You might also hear other unfamiliar terms. The first is ***methodology***, the specific procedures used in research. Your instructor might describe a study as having ***rigorous*** methodology, which means that the procedures used were very good and very carefully planned. In many cases, this will mean proper ***controls*** were used. The term control has several uses. The experimenter *controls* (has the power to determine or influence) the conditions in an experiment, such as controlling whether a room is cool or hot. The experimenter *controls for* (takes steps to avoid) differences in conditions that are not intended. A ***control group*** is an "untreated" group in an experiment, a neutral condition. Also, when your professor says an experiment must be ***replicated***, the experiment must be repeated to show that the same results can be obtained again.

IDIOMS

p. 29	meet this criterion	to have the necessary characteristics; to meet one necessary requirement. (A criterion is one requirement; criteria are several.)
p. 29	potential pitfall	possible problem
p. 32	had themselves committed	asked to be admitted to a mental hospital
p. 32	a poor vehicle for determining causality	not a good way to tell whether one thing causes another
p. 32	establish the generality of	to show that something is common; to show that it is usually what happens
p. 33	place all their (theoretical) eggs in one basket	to unwisely depend upon just one thing to support you; for example, to build a whole theory on one example
p. 35	to characterize a person's tendencies to act in consistent ways	to describe the ways that a person usually acts
p. 38	attributed to chance	"blamed on" random factors; caused by chance
p. 42	a social outcry for the monitoring of televised violence	lots of people saying that they want violence on TV to be monitored by the government
p. 48	clouding interpretation of the results	making sense of the results will be difficult
p. 50	"cooked"	dishonestly changed or created
p. 50	a devastating critique	criticism that will make something useless
p. 53	justify the invasive procedures	have good reasons for using methods that invade (and might permanently hurt)
p. 53	advocated	spoke out for
p. 54	can result in censure	can mean you are formally criticized

PRONUNCIATION

placebo (pla-see'-bo) *p.49*

debriefing (dee-breef'-ing) *p.52*

SOLUTIONS

PREVIEW & OBSERVING BEHAVIOR: DESCRIPTIVE RESEARCH (PP. 27-39)

MASTERING THE CONCEPTS

1. scientific (p. 28)
2. observation (p. 28)
3. regularities (p. 28)
4. hypothesis (p. 28)
5. accuracy (p. 28)
6. operational (p. 29)
7. describing (p. 29)
8. explaining (p. 29)
9. ethically (p. 30)
10. Descriptive (p. 30)
11. reactivity (p. 31)
12. generalize (p. 31)
13. validity (p. 31)
14. naturalistic (p. 31)
15. participant (p. 31)
16. Indirect (p. 32)
17. case study (p. 33)
18. hypotheses (p. 33)
19. accuracy (p. 33)
20. Cause-effect (p. 33)
21. surveys (p. 33)
22. random (p. 34)
23. accuracy (p. 35)
24. individual (p. 35)
25. Achievement (p. 35)
26. Statistics (p. 36)
27. central (p. 36)
28. mode (p. 40)
29. median (p. 36)
30. variability (p. 37)
31. standard (p. 37)
32. Inferential (p. 38)
33. significant (p. 38)
34. large numbers (p. 39)

EVALUATING YOUR PROGRESS

1. A, Correct (p. 28)

   B. Wrong. Data analysis is done late in the process, but not at the beginning.

   C. Wrong. Operational definitions are established early in the process, not at the end.

   D. Wrong. Detecting regularities in the data is done after observation.

2. C, Correct (p. 29)

   A. Wrong. Measurement, not hypotheses, are the basis of operational definitions.

   B. Wrong. Measurement, not common characteristics, is the basis of operational definitions.

   D. Wrong. Operational definitions are based on specific, objective measurements of the concept.

3. B, Correct (p. 33)

   A. Wrong. Inferential statistics are not standard with single participant research.

   C. Wrong. Although naturalistic observation may involve a single person, this term would not be used to describe single participant studies in general.

   D. Wrong. Surveys involve many people, not just one.

4. A, Correct (p. 31)

   B. Wrong. External validity is the generalizability of observations or conclusions to other situations.

   C. Wrong. Standard deviation is a descriptive statistic reflecting the variability of the data.

   D. Wrong. Experimental control involves controlling or equating variables in an experiment.

5. B, Correct (p. 31)

   A. Wrong. Reactivity should be avoided. Good naturalistic observation procedures reduce reactivity.

   C. Wrong. Naturalistic observation cannot establish cause and effect.

   D. Wrong. Changing variability is not a goal of naturalistic observation, especially not increasing it.

6. A, Correct (p. 34)

   B. Wrong. Random sampling produces representative samples, which would tend to increase external validity.

   C. Wrong. Reactivity occurs due to observation itself. Sampling techniques have no impact.

   D. Wrong. Sampling influences the representativeness of data, but not how easily it can be verified.

7. C, Correct (p. 36)
   A. Wrong. External validity refers to the extent to which data will generalize to other situations.
   B. Wrong. Range and standard deviation are measures of variability.
   D. Wrong. Statistical significance relates to the probability that differences are due to chance.

8. D, Correct (p. 38)
   A. Wrong. The ability to generalize the results is not influenced by the statistic used.
   B. Wrong. Measures of central tendency and variability are descriptive, not inferential statistics.
   C. Wrong. Statistics do not influence variability; they sometimes measure it.

9. A, Correct (p. 39)
   B, C, D. Wrong. The law of large numbers involves the benefits of numerous observations.

PREDICTING BEHAVIOR: CORRELATIONAL RESEARCH (PP. 40-43)

MASTERING THE CONCEPTS.

1. relationships (p. 40)
2. Positive (p. 41)
3. negative (p. 41)
4. strength (p. 41)
5. cause (p. 42)
6. third (p. 42)

EVALUATING YOUR PROGRESS

1. B, Correct (p. 40)
   A. Wrong. Correlations lack experimental control, so they can't determine cause-effect.
   C. Wrong. Correlations involve two variables. Third variables are one reason why correlations can't be used to determine cause-effect.
   D. Wrong. External validity is the ability to generalize to other situations. A significant correlation can still have poor external validity.

2. C, Correct (p. 41)
   A. Wrong. Negative correlations involve changes in opposite directions.
   B. Wrong. Zero correlations occur when one behavior cannot predict another, unlike the situation described.
   D. Wrong. There is no such thing as a third variable correlation. Third variable problems are one reason correlations don't determine cause-effect.

3. D, Correct (p. 41)
   A. Wrong. The absolute value of the correlation indicates reliability. The sign denotes the nature of the relationship.
   B. Wrong The absolute value of the correlation indicates reliability, and .40 is less than .60 and .80.
   C. Wrong. The absolute value of the correlation indicates reliability, and .10 is the smallest choice.

EXPLAINING BEHAVIOR: EXPERIMENTAL RESEARCH (PP. 44-50)

MASTERING THE CONCEPTS.

1. control (p. 44)
2. manipulates (p. 44)
3. independent (p. 44)
4. dependent (p. 45)
5. experimental (p. 46)
6. control (p. 46)
7. confounding (p. 46)
8. internal (p. 47)
9. random (p. 47)
10. Single-blind (p. 49)
11. Double-blind (p. 50)
12. external (p. 50)

EVALUATING YOUR PROGRESS

1. B, Correct (p. 44)

   A. Wrong. This describes naturalistic observation, not an experiment.

   C. Wrong. This describes the correlational research method, not an experiment.

   D. Wrong. This describes the case study method, not an experiment.

2. B, Correct (p. 45)

   A. Wrong. The independent variable is the variable that the experimenter manipulates, not measures.

   C. Wrong. Confounding variables are uncontrolled variables.

   D. Wrong. There is no such thing as an internal variable.

3. D, Correct (p. 46)

   A. Wrong. There is no such thing as an internal variable. An uncontrolled, systematic variable is a confounding variable.

   B. Wrong. A placebo is a control for expectancy.

   C. Wrong. Random and systematic are not compatible. An uncontrolled, systematic variable is a confounding variable.

4. A, Correct (p. 46)

   B. Wrong. "Blind" procedures are used to prevent bias. Control groups provide information about what happens when participants are not exposed to the experimental treatment, an important comparison.

   C. Wrong. Control groups don't influence whether results generalize to other situations (external validity).

   D. Wrong. Random assignment helps avoid initial differences between groups, and blind procedures reduce expectancy effects. Control groups provide a no-treatment comparison.

5. C, Correct (p. 47)

   A. Wrong. Experimenter expectancy effects are not eliminated by random assignment.

   B. Wrong. Subject expectancy effects are not eliminated by random assignment.

   D. Wrong. Differences are more likely to be due to the experimental manipulation.

6. A, Correct (p. 49)

   B. Wrong. Placebos are usually given to the control group.

   C. Wrong. Placebos are not required by ethical rules.

   D. Wrong. Confounding variables (expectancy differences) are less likely with placebos.

7. D, Correct (p. 50)

   A. Wrong. A control group does not reduce experimenter expectancy effects.

   B. Wrong. Expectancy is not related to the number of dependent variables.

   C. Wrong. Single-blind procedures reduce subject expectancy effects.

THE ETHICS OF RESEARCH: HUMAN AND ANIMAL GUIDELINES (PP. 51-54)

MASTERING THE CONCEPTS

1. informed (p. 52)
2. debrief (p. 52)
3. confidentiality (p. 52)
4. control (p. 53)

EVALUATING YOUR PROGRESS

1. D, Correct (p. 52)
   A. Wrong. Confidentiality involves keeping personal information private.
   B. Wrong. There is no requirement that participants be compensated, but some are.
   C. Wrong. Debriefing is disclosing the purpose of the research at its conclusion.
2. B, Correct (p. 52)
   A. Wrong. There is no requirement that participants be compensated, but some are.
   C. Wrong. Debriefing is discussing the purpose of the research after someone participates.
   D. Wrong. Informed consent involves getting the person's consent to participate after providing information about the risks and nature of the research.
3. A, Correct (p. 53)
   B, C, D. Wrong. These are major advantages of using animals, but there are ethical requirements for animal research.

MAKING FINAL PREPARATIONS

SHORT ESSAY QUESTIONS

1. The four steps of the scientific method are: (1) Observations of a behavior are made. (2) The data are examined for systematic regularities. (3) A hypothesis is formulated. (4) More observations are made to evaluate the accuracy of the hypothesis. (p. 28)
2. Measures of central tendency describe the point around which most data cluster. They describe a typical score. Measures of variability describe how the distribution of scores is spread out. Both measures are needed to have the full description of the score distribution. (pp. 37-37)
3. A correlation describes a relationship between two variables. In a positive correlation, both variables change in the same direction (e.g., height and shoe size: Taller people tend to have bigger feet than shorter people). In a negative correlation the variables change in opposite directions (e.g., class absences and grades: Students with many absences tend to have lower grades than those with few absences). (pp. 40-42)
4. Reactivity and expectancy effects are biases that can occur. Reactivity, a change in a subject's behavior caused by being observed, can lead to inaccurate conclusions. Expectancy effects, changes in a subject's (or experimenter's) behavior caused by their expectations about the research, also lead to errors. A solution is to restrict the subject's knowledge about the research. Naturalistic observation or other unobtrusive observation techniques can reduce reactivity. "Blind" designs, in which group assignments are not known, reduce expectancy effects. Deception also can be used. (pp. 31; 32, 49)

5. Correlational research lacks the experimental control that is possible in experiments. This lack of control makes is possible that unobserved variables are responsible for the behaviors. By controlling for the influence of other variables, behavior changes can be attributed to the variables under study. (pp. 42-44)

6. In random assignment, participants have an equal chance to be assigned to any group in the experiment. This reduces group differences in uncontrolled variables and equates the characteristics of the groups. When groups may be assumed to be relatively equal initially, subsequent differences may be attributed to the influence of the manipulated variables (pp. 47-48)

7. (1) Informed consent: Participants must be informed of the nature of the research and any possible effects of their participation and must give their consent prior to participating. (2) Debriefing: Participant must be informed about the purpose of the experiment and any deception after their participation. (3) Confidentiality: Personal information about participants must not be disclosed to other people. (pp. 51-53)

MATCHING

1. m (p. 41)
2. g (p. 37)
3. d (p. 33)
4. a (p. 31)
5. b (p. 31)
6. h (p. 38)
7. i (p. 45)
8. l (p. 36)
9. j (p. 41)
10. f (p. 31)
11. n (p. 47)
12. k (p. 44)
13. c (p. 38)
14. e (p. 49)

MULTIPLE CHOICE PRETEST 1

1. C, Correct (p. 28)

   A. Wrong. Observation comes first and is the basis of later hypothesis formation.

   B. Wrong. The second step is looking for regularities in the data.

   D. Wrong. The last step is more observation to verify the relationships.

2. A, Correct (pp. 31-33)

   B. Wrong. Experiments involve manipulation of conditions; case studies, etc., don't.

   C, D. Wrong. "Blind" designs restrict information about group assignment in experiments.

3. C, Correct (p. 34)

   A. Wrong. Informed consent is an ethical requirement. It does not impact the validity of surveys.

   B. Wrong. Participant observation is a technique for naturalistic observation, not surveys.

   D. Wrong. Double-blind designs can't be used in surveys; subjects aren't assigned to groups.

4. B, Correct (p. 36)

   A, C, D. Wrong. The mean (average) = (sum of scores / number of scores) = 15/5 = 3. The median is the middle score (2). The mode is the most common score (1).

5. D, Correct (p. 31)

   A. Wrong. A case study is a detailed study of one person; here, many people were observed.

   B. Wrong. They didn't manipulate any condition, so it wasn't an experiment.

   C. Wrong. Surveys are interviews or paper-and-pencil questionnaires.

6. C, Correct (p. 40)

   A. Wrong. Correlations can't establish cause-effect relationships due to a lack of control.

   B. Wrong. Measures of central tendency include mean, median, and mode, not correlations.

   D. Wrong. Experiments involve manipulations; correlations involve only observations.

7. B, Correct (p. 38)
   A. Wrong. This answer describes measures of central tendency, which are descriptive statistics.
   C. Wrong. This answer describes standard deviation, which is a descriptive statistic.
   D. Wrong. Confounding variables are an experimental design problem. Statistics don't deal with that.
8. B, Correct (p. 41)
   A, C, D. Wrong. Relationships in which variable change in the same direction equal positive correlations.
9. A, Correct (p. 38)
   B, C, D. Wrong. Statistical significance only indicates a result is unlikely to be due to chance. It does not address whether or not the data are accurate or unbiased.
10. A, Correct (p. 31)
    B. Wrong. Internal validity relates to having the proper controls, not generalizing to other settings.
    C. Wrong. Poor generalization can occur in experiments with independent variables.
    D. Wrong. If there are results from an experiment, there is a dependent variable.
11. C, Correct (p. 45)
    A. Wrong. The temperature of the room is the independent variable.
    B, D. Wrong. The dependent variable is the behavior that is measured.
12. D, Correct (p. 42)
    A. Wrong. Negative correlations are a specific type of relationship, not a problem that limits conclusions.
    B. Wrong. Participant observation is an observation technique, not a problem that limits conclusions.
    C. Wrong. Standard deviation is a measure of variability, not a problem that limits conclusions.
13. C, Correct (p. 49)
    A. Wrong. Confounding variables are uncontrolled variables that vary systematically with the independent variable.
    B. Wrong. A control group doesn't receive the experimental manipulation. Knowledge about group assignment does not define control groups.
    D. Wrong. A double-blind design keeps group membership secret from both the subject and experimenter.
14. D, Correct (p. 52)
    A. Wrong. Confidentiality is the right to have personal information kept private.
    B. Wrong. Humane treatment is proper care (usually referring to animals).
    C. Wrong. Informed consent is obtained before a person participates.
15. A, Correct (p. 47)
    B. Wrong. A placebo controls for expectancy. It doesn't balance individual differences across groups.
    C. Wrong. A single-blind design controls subject expectancy effects, not differences across groups.
    D. Wrong. A double-blind design addresses subject and experimenter expectancy effects, not differences across groups.

MULTIPLE CHOICE PRETEST 2

1. D, Correct (p. 31)

   A. Wrong. Reactivity is a change in behavior due to being observed, not a failure of results to generalize.

   B. Wrong. A third or confounding variable causes poor *internal* validity. Poor generalization is poor external validity.

   C. Wrong. Internal validity is a problem when confounding variables occur, not when generalization is poor.

2. C, Correct (p. 34)

   A. Wrong. Double-blind procedures cannot be used in surveys. People are not in different groups.

   B. Wrong. The type of statistics used does not address the issue of being representative of the entire population's beliefs.

   D. Wrong. Whether results are representative of the entire population depends on the sampling procedure used. Third variables are not an issue.

3. B, Correct (p. 31)

   A. Wrong. External validity refers to the extent to which data will generalize to other situations.

   C. Wrong. No placebo was used. Being observed was the key factor and caused a change in behavior.

   D. Wrong. Workers were not assigned to groups, so random assignment is not relevant.

4. C, Correct (p. 31)

   A. Wrong. A case study is a detailed description of a person's behavior. The reporter was not observed.

   B. Wrong. The observations would focus on external events, not internal, subjective experiences.

   D. Wrong. In naturalistic observation the observer doesn't participate in the activities being studied.

5. A, Correct (p. 35)

   B. Wrong. Achievement tests evaluate a person's current state of knowledge or competence.

   C. Wrong. Measures of central tendency are statistics that describe data, not tests potential success.

   D. Wrong. Correlation coefficients are the mathematical representation of a correlation, not tests of potential success.

6. A, Correct (p. 37)

   B. Wrong. Range and standard deviation represent variability, not a relationship between two variables.

   C. Wrong. An average represents central tendency; range and standard deviation represent variability.

   D. Wrong. Mean, median, and mode represent central tendency.

7. D, Correct (p. 44)

   A. Wrong. Experiments often are more complicated than correlational studies.

   B. Wrong. The data from experiments are analyzed using inferential statistics.

   C. Wrong. Experiments are sometimes criticized for their artificial behaviors and settings.

8. C, Correct (p. 33)

   A. Wrong. An experiment requires more than one person and systematic manipulation of a variable.

   B. Wrong. Dr. Johnson did not merely observe Sam in his natural environment.

   D. Wrong. Single-blind procedures require an experiment; this is not an experiment.

9. D, Correct (pp. 42-43)

   A. Wrong. The third variable (age or getting older) is important here. Expectancy wasn't involved.

   B. Wrong. The third variable (age or getting older) is important here. Nobody was being observed.

   C. Wrong. The third variable (age or getting older) is important here, not how participants were selected.

10. B, Correct (p. 41)

    A. Wrong. +1.0 is the strongest possible positive correlation, not a moderate positive correlation.

    C. Wrong. -0.45 is a moderate negative correlation, not a moderate positive correlation.

    D. Wrong. -0.75 is a strong negative correlation, not a moderate positive correlation.

11. A, Correct (p. 44)

    B. Wrong. Test performance is the dependent variable.

    C. Wrong. Content was held constant; independent variables are manipulated by the experimenter.

    D. Wrong. Personal background was not manipulated, so it isn't the independent variable.

12. C, Correct (p. 46)

    A. Wrong. There is no indication that responses were influenced by being observed.

    B. Wrong. Confounding variables yield poor internal validity. No information about generalizability (external validity) is provided in this question.

    D. Wrong. This experiment didn't require a true control group. It did have the required comparison group.

13. B, Correct (p. 52)

    A. Wrong. Humane treatment involves the experimental manipulation or living conditions, not knowing what the experiment is about.

    C. Wrong. Debriefing is telling the person about the purpose of the experiment after it is over.

    D. Wrong. Confidentiality involves keeping information about participants private.

14. D, Correct (p. 39)

    A. Wrong. There's no argument over defining good teaching, just the accuracy of single samples.

    B. Wrong. Randomly assigning subject to groups is not involved here.

    C. Wrong. A placebo effect, subject expectancies influencing behavior, is not an issue here.

15. A, Correct (p. 53)

    B. Wrong. Single-blind designs keep group identity secret from subjects only.

    C. Wrong. Information was withheld, but no deception occurred.

    D. Wrong. The researcher didn't make observations while participating in the observed behavior.

CHAPTER 3

BIOLOGICAL PROCESSES

ESTABLISHING LEARNING GOALS

Use these learning goals as a preview of the chapter, a guide for active reading, and to evaluate your mastery of the material. Review the relevant goals as you begin and end your reading of each major section of the chapter.

I. Discuss how the nervous system communicates internally, linking world and brain.

   A. Describe the structure, type, and function of neurons.
      1. Identify three types of neurons, and explain their functions.
      2. Describe how a reflex operates, and explain why reflexes are important.
      3. Identify the component parts of a neuron, and explain their functions.

   B. Explain how neurons transmit information.
      1. Define resting potential, and explain its role in neural transmission.
      2. Explain how action potentials are generated and travel down the axon.
      3. Explain the role of neurotransmitters and identify three common neurotransmitters.
      4. Explain how drugs effect the nervous system to alter behavior.

   C. Explain how neurons work together to communicate.

II. Discuss how the nervous system initiates and coordinates behavior efficiently.

   A. Describe the basic organization of the nervous system.

   B. Describe the techniques researchers use to study the brain.

   C. Describe the major structures of the brain and their functions.
      1. Identify the structures of the hindbrain, midbrain, and forebrain and their major functions.
      2. Describe the organizational structure of the cortex, and identify the higher mental functions associated with each area.

   D. Discuss how the two hemispheres coordinate brain functions.
      1. Describe what happens when the two hemispheres are surgically "split."
      2. Summarize the current view concerning lateralization of hemispheric functions.

III. Discuss how growth and internal functions are regulated.

   A. Explain how the endocrine system controls long-term and widespread communication needs.

   B. Discuss the role that hormones play in establishing sexual identity and gender-specific behaviors.

IV. Discuss how the genetic code is stored and transmitted.

A. Review natural selection and adaptation.

B. Describe the basic principles of genetic transmission.

C. Explain how psychologists study genetic influences on behavior.

MASTERING THE MATERIAL

PREVIEW & COMMUNICATING INTERNALLY: CONNECTING WORLD AND BRAIN (PP. 61-71)

MASTERING THE VOCABULARY

Define or explain each of the following terms.

1. neuroscience
2. central nervous system
3. peripheral nervous system
4. neuron
5. sensory neuron
6. interneuron
7. motor neuron
8. glial cell
9. myelin sheath
10. reflexes
11. dendrites
12. soma
13. axon
14. terminal buttons
15. synapse
16. resting potential
17. action potential
18. depolarization

19. hyperpolarization
20. neurotransmitters
21. acetylcholine
22. dopamine
23. serotonin
24. GABA
25. endorphins
26. refractory period

MASTERING THE CONCEPTS

Fill in the blanks to create a summary of the section.

The field of [1] ____________ studies brain-behavior relationships. Brain cells interact to form a communication network and to control behavior. The brain and [2] ____________ make up the [3] ____________ nervous system. The [4] ____________ nervous system, the remaining nerves, links the central nervous system and the body.

This chapter addresses four major issues: How does internal communication occur? How does the brain initiate and [5] ____________ behavior? How are [6] ____________ and internal functions regulated? How is the [7] ____________ code stored and transmitted?

Neurons are cells of the nervous system and come in three major types. [8] ____________ neurons contact the environment and carry messages to the spinal cord and brain. [9] ____________ serve as links between neurons. [10] ____________ neurons carry information from the brain and spinal cord to muscles and glands. The nervous system also contains [11] ____________ cells that perform "housekeeping" functions and form the [12] ____________ sheath, a kind of insulation on some neurons. Not all behavior is controlled by the brain. The spinal [13] ____________, in which responses originate in the spinal cord, allows a speedier response than one initiated in the brain.

Neurons are composed of four major parts. [14] ____________ are branches that receive and transfer input to the [15] ____________, the main body of the cell. The [16] ____________ transmits input (in the form of an action potential) to another cell. In the end of the axon's branches are [17] ____________ that contain chemicals that communicate with the next cell. Neurons are separated by a space, the [18] ____________ .

If inactive, neurons have a [19] ____________ , or imbalance of ions inside and outside the cell. Stimulation causes ion movement and either [20] ____________ or [21] ____________ , depending on whether the stimulation is excitatory or inhibitory. If excitatory stimulation is strong enough, depolarization occurs, and an [22] ____________ is generated. Action potentials are [23] ____________ ; they either occur or not. They have a constant speed and intensity, but axon size affects the speed. The [24] ____________ are gaps in the myelin that increase transmission speed.

Neurotransmitters flow into the synapse and contact the next cell, stimulating or inhibiting initiation of another action potential. Neurotransmitters include acetylcholine, serotonin, GABA and [25] ____________ . Imbalances cause physical and mental disorders. Some drugs act as [26] ____________ and mimic neurotransmitters, or as [27] ____________ and block neurotransmitter action. [28] ____________ , natural painkillers in the body, are neuromodulators that influence neurotransmitter levels.

Information is represented by the [29] ____________ of activation across many neurons and by changes in the neuron's [30] ____________ . The neuron's firing rate is limited by the [31] ____________ period, a period following an action potential in which the neuron cannot fire again.

EVALUATING YOUR PROGRESS

Select the best response. If you make any errors, reread the relevant material before proceeding.

1. The type of neuron that carries messages from the brain to muscles and glands is a
   a. motor neuron.
   b. sensory neuron.
   c. glial neuron.
   d. interneuron.

2. Neurotransmitters are released by the
   a. cell body.
   b. axon.
   c. terminal buttons.
   d. dendrites.

3. A reflex requires all of the following EXCEPT:
   a. a sensory neuron.
   b. a motor neuron.
   c. the brain.
   d. neurotransmitters.

4. The resting potential is caused by
   a. an uneven distribution of charged ions inside and outside the neuron.
   b. neurotransmitters being released by the terminal buttons of the neuron.
   c. a change in the axon cell membrane that allows depolarization of the neuron.
   d. strong input from another neuron stimulating the dendrites of the cell.

5. Action potentials
   a. are larger if the stimulus is intense rather than weak.
   b. travel faster if the stimulus is intense rather than weak.
   c. are generated along the axon.
   d. all of the above

6. The synapse is
   a. the part of the neuron that contains the cell nucleus.
   b. the fluid-filled space between neurons.
   c. the place in the neuron where the action potential begins.
   d. a gap in the axon's myelin sheath.

7. The neural impulse is transferred to the next neuron via
   a. interneurons.
   b. glial cells in the terminal buttons.
   c. the sodium-potassium pump.
   d. neurotransmitters.

8. A major theory suggests that schizophrenia is caused by an imbalance of
   a. endorphins.
   b. dopamine.
   c. serotonin.
   d. acetylcholine.

9. The maximum firing rate of a neuron is limited by
   a. the type of neurotransmitter involved.
   b. whether it is in the central or peripheral nervous system.
   c. the refractory period.
   d. the number of neurons with which it synapses.

INITIATING BEHAVIOR: A DIVISION OF LABOR (PP. 71-86)

MASTERING THE VOCABULARY

Define or explain each of the following terms.

1. nerves
2. somatic system
3. autonomic system
4. electroencephalograph (EEG)
5. computerized tomography scan (CT scan)
6. positron emission tomography (PET)
7. magnetic resonance imaging (MRI)
8. hindbrain
9. medulla
10. pons
11. reticular formation
12. cerebellum
13. midbrain
14. forebrain
15. cerebral cortex
16. thalamus
17. hypothalamus
18. limbic system
19. amygdala
20. hippocampus
21. frontal lobe
22. parietal lobe
23. temporal lobe
24. occipital lobe
25. corpus callosum

MASTERING THE CONCEPTS.

Fill in the blanks to create a summary of the section.

The two divisions of the nervous system are the [1] ____________ and the [2] ____________ nervous systems. Messages are sent to the brain via [3] ____________ (sensory) pathways and out from the brain via [4] ____________ (motor) pathways. The peripheral nervous system contains the [5] ____________ nervous system, which serves the sensory and motor systems, and the [6] ____________ nervous system, which controls basic bodily functions and adjusts the body to meet emergency situations.

Brain function is studied by recording brain activity, stimulating the brain, and examining the effects of [7] ____________ . Changes in behavior associated with stimulation or destruction help link a function to an area of the brain. EEG, PET, and functional MRI record brain activity; MRI and CT reveal structures.

The brain is organized into three major regions: the hindbrain, [8] ____________ , and [9] ____________ . The hindbrain contains the [10] ____________ and pons, which control life-support systems, the reticular formation, which controls arousal, and the [11] ____________ , which is important for coordinated movements. The midbrain contains the tectum, which includes areas used to relay sensory input, and the substantia nigra, which produces dopamine. Damage to the substantia nigra reduces dopamine and causes [12] ____________ disease. The forebrain includes the [13] ____________ and subcortical structures, including the thalamus, hypothalamus, and limbic system. The thalamus processes and relays [14] ____________ input. The [15] ____________ is involved in eating, drinking, body temperature, sexual behavior and the control of the pituitary. The [16] ____________ includes the amygdala, which is involved in emotion and motivation, and the hippocampus, which is important for [17] ____________ , and several other structures.

The cerebral hemisphere has four lobes. The [18] ____________ lobes contain the motor cortex, and areas important for planning and thought. The [19] ____________ lobes contain the somatosensory area for touch. The motor and somatosensory cortex are arranged topographically (areas close on the body are handled by areas close in the brain) and the size of a body part's brain area is related to the sensitivity or level of control of the body part. Auditory and language comprehenshion centers are in the [20] ____________ lobe, with language usually processed by the [21] ____________ hemisphere. The occipital lobe processes visual input.

Processing also is lateralized, with each hemisphere handling certain tasks. The right hemisphere receives input from and controls the [22] ____________ side of the body and the left visual field; the left hemisphere receives input from and controls the right. The right hemisphere is important for [23] ____________ tasks; the left hemisphere is important for verbal tasks. Input is available to both hemispheres due to eye movements and because a bridge of tissue, the [24] ____________, allows information from one side to transfer to the other. Split-brain patients with no corpus callosum behave normally except in situations that restrict both how information is received and how responses are made. Although processing is lateralized, the hemispheres usually work together.

EVALUATING YOUR PROGRESS

Select the best response. If you miss any questions, reread the relevant material before proceeding.

1. The autonomic nervous system is part of the
   a. central nervous system.
   b. afferent nervous system.
   c. somatic nervous system.
   d. peripheral nervous system.

2. The nerves that transmit information to the muscles are part of the
   a. autonomic nervous system.
   b. somatic nervous system.
   c. parasympathetic nervous system.
   d. sympathetic nervous system.

3. PET, EEG, and functional MRI
   a. are lesioning techniques used to study brain function.
   b. are primarily used with animals.
   c. provide information about brain activity.
   d. stimulate the brain so that changes in behavior can be observed.

4. The hindbrain is very important for
   a. controlling life-support systems (e.g., heart rate, respiration).
   b. complex thought and planning.
   c. processing sensory information.
   d. controlling basic motivational processes (e.g., eating, sexual behavior, etc.).

5. Which is not part of the forebrain?
   a. thalamus
   b. cerebellum
   c. hippocampus
   d. hypothalamus

6. Parkinson's disease patients lack an adequate amount of dopamine due to malfunction of the
   a. substantia nigra.
   b. medulla and pons.
   c. hypothalamus.
   d. cerebral cortex.
7. Damage to the limbic system is likely to affect
   a. visual perception.
   b. consciousness and arousal.
   c. language production or comprehension.
   d. emotional behaviors.
8. Based on the case of Phineas Gage and other cases of brain damage, we might reasonably conclude that the sense of self or personality is associated with activity in the
   a. parietal lobe.
   b. temporal lobe.
   c. frontal lobe.
   d. occipital lobe.
9. Which statement is false concerning the motor cortex?
   a. Adjacent areas of the body are represented in adjacent areas of the motor cortex.
   b. The motor cortex is located in the parietal lobes.
   c. Areas of the body with fine motor control are associated with large areas in the motor cortex.
   d. Certain neurons in the motor cortex respond when we observe someone performing certain actions.
10. If a brain injury causes a loss of language comprehension, the location of the injury probably includes
    a. the occipital lobe.
    b. the frontal lobe.
    c. the parietal lobe.
    d. the temporal lobe.
11. Most psychologists would agree that
    a. the idea of localization or lateralization of brain function has little scientific support.
    b. localization occurs for functions handled by subcortical structures, but not for cortical functions.
    c. almost all functions are highly localized or lateralized; each area works almost independently.
    d. even highly localized or lateralized tasks involve much cooperation between different brain areas.

REGULATING GROWTH AND INTERNAL FUNCTIONS: EXTENDED COMMUNICATION (PP. 86-89)

MASTERING THE VOCABULARY

Define or explain each of the following terms.

1. endocrine system

2. hormones
3. pituitary gland

MASTERING THE CONCEPTS

Fill in the blanks to create a summary of the section.

The [1] ____________ system uses hormones to regulate growth and biological systems. Its activity is more widespread and of [2] ____________ duration than neural activity. The brain, mostly the hypothalamus, controls the "master" endocrine gland, the [3] ____________ , which controls other endocrine glands, including those important for sexual and "fight or flee" behavior. Prenatal [4] ____________ hormones may affect the brain and later gender behavior. Adult hormone levels may produce gender differences in mental tasks.

EVALUATING YOUR PROGRESS

Select the best response. If you miss any questions, reread the relevant material before proceeding.

1. The "master gland" of the body is the
   a. adrenal gland.
   b. ovary or testes.
   c. pineal gland.
   d. pituitary gland.

2. The brain structure that controls the endocrine system is
   a. the cerebellum.
   b. the hippocampus.
   c. the hypothalamus.
   d. the medulla.

3. The communication system provided by the endocrine system complements that of the nervous system because the actions of the endocrine system are
   a. more localized and more short-term.
   b. more localized and more long-term.
   c. more widespread and more short-term.
   d. more widespread and more long-term.

4. Research on gender differences in behavior has found that high spatial ability is correlated with
   a. testosterone levels at the time of testing.
   b. estrogen levels at the time of testing.
   c. epinephrine levels during the prenatal period of development.
   d. norepinephrine levels during the prenatal period of development.

5. In the "flight-or-flee" activation, which adapts the body in threatening situations, epinephrine is released by
   a. the pituitary gland.
   b. the hypothalamus.
   c. the adrenal glands.
   d. ovaries or testes.

ADAPTING AND TRANSMITTING THE GENETIC CODE (PP. 89-93)

MASTERING THE VOCABULARY

Define or explain each of the following terms.

1. adaptation
2. genes
3. genotype
4. phenotype
5. mutation
6. family studies
7. twin studies

MASTERING THE CONCEPTS

Fill in the blanks to create a summary of the section.

The genetic code has two adaptive functions: providing a flexible blueprint for development, and providing for specific traits to be transmitted to future generations. Humans have 23 pairs of chromosomes which contain the [1] ____________ that determine personal traits. [2] ____________ genes cause the expression of a trait even if the two genes for the trait differ. A matching pair of genes is needed for the expression of a [3] ____________ trait. Most physical traits and behaviors are influenced by a complex interaction of many genes and environmental conditions. [4] ____________ studies look for similarities in behavior among blood relatives. Comparisons of traits in identical and fraternal twins raised in same or different environments provide even better data about the genetic component of a trait.

EVALUATING YOUR PROGRESS

Select the best response. If you miss any questions, reread the relevant material before proceeding.

1. A chromosome segment that contains instructions for the development of a hereditary trait is called
   a. a phenotype.
   b. an efferent.
   c. an afferent.
   d. a gene.

2. When a trait has been selected by nature because it increases the odds of survival the trait is said to be
   a. a mutation.
   b. an adaptation.
   c. a recessive trait.
   d. a dominant trait.

3. A person's phenotype concerning a genetic trait describes
   a. how many gene pairs determine the trait.
   b. whether the trait is dominant or recessive.
   c. the person's observable characteristics regarding a trait.
   d. the person's specific genetic pattern (AA, Aa, aa) regarding a trait.

4. If identical twins do not share some trait, that trait probably is
   a. a recessive trait.
   b. a mutation originating in a parent.
   c. genetically determined.
   d. environmentally determined.

5. To be an adaptation, a trait must be adaptive, economical, and
   a. dominant.
   b. recessive.
   c. physical.
   d. universal.

MAKING FINAL PREPARATIONS

Complete these sections without consulting your book or notes. For a more accurate estimate of how well you know this material, wait at least a day or two after studying the chapter before working on the questions. Some of the material you "know" immediately after working with the chapter will be quickly forgotten. Exercises done too soon after studying will overestimate what you know well.

SHORT ESSAY QUESTIONS

Write a brief answer to each question.

1. Explain how drugs work in the nervous system to cause changes in behavior.

2. Movement can be initiated either by the usual neural pathway or by a spinal reflex. Compare these pathways for removing your hand from a sharp object. Explain a spinal reflex's adaptive value.

3. Describe three techniques to determine structure-function relationships for the brain.

4. Imagine your left hemisphere has been removed. Describe and explain at least two effects.

5. Explain how twin studies are used to differentiate genetic and environmentally determined traits.

MATCHING

Select the correct definition or description for each item.

1. _______ cerebellum
2. _______ amygdala
3. _______ hippocampus
4. _______ glial cell
5. _______ medulla
6. _______ axon
7. _______ substantia nigra
8. _______ terminal button
9. _______ reticular formation
10. _______ soma
11. _______ corpus callosum
12. _______ hypothalamus
13. _______ thalamus
14. _______ dendrite
15. _______ somatosensory cortex
16. _______ pituitary

a. allows transfer of information between hemispheres
b. releases neurotransmitters
c. processes touch and temperature input
d. aids formation of memories
e. regulates basic functions (heart rate, respiration)
f. coordinates smooth movements
g. relays sensory information to the cortex
h. controls cellular metabolism of neuron
i. controls other endocrine glands
j. receives neural input from a sense organ or neuron
k. controls eating, drinking and sexual behaviors
l. generates and transmits the action potential
m. produces dopamine
n. insulates and assists in function of neuron
o. controls aggression and motivational behaviors
p. controls general arousal and consciousness

MULTIPLE CHOICE PRETEST 1

Select the one best response.

1. Messages to the muscles that initiate movement are sent from the brain via
   a. motor neurons.
   b. sensory neurons.
   c. glial cells.
   d. hormones.

2. The correct sequence describing the pathway neural information travels is
   a. axon, soma, dendrite, terminal button.
   b. terminal button, axon, soma, dendrite.
   c. dendrite, soma, axon, terminal button.
   d. soma, dendrite, axon, terminal button.

3. Researchers are recording the gross electrical activity of a man's brain. This procedure probably is
   a. a PET scan.
   b. brain lesioning.
   c. an EEG.
   d. a CT scan.

4. The adaptive value of the spinal reflex is due to its
   a. speed of response.
   b. use of no neurotransmitters.
   c. long-lasting communication capabilities.
   d. use of hormones to communicate.

5. Depolarization is associated with
   a. inhibition.
   b. refractory period.
   c. resting potential.
   d. action potential.

6. Terminal buttons
   a. insulate the neuron to assist transmission.
   b. physically attach one neuron to another.
   c. receive incoming stimulation from another neuron.
   d. store and release neurotransmitters.

7. If a neuron is hyperpolarized
   a. an action potential will soon occur.
   b. the incoming message was inhibitory.
   c. all the neurotransmitters have been released.
   d. the previous message was very intense.

8. Where do neurotransmitters and receptor molecules chemically interact?
   a. the axon
   b. the synapse
   c. the myelin sheath
   d. the postsynaptic membrane

9. The substantia nigra in the midbrain of Parkinson's disease patients no longer produces appropriate levels of
   a. acetlycholine.
   b. serotonin.
   c. dopamine.
   d. an endorphin.

10. Sharika's hindbrain was damaged when she hit her head. She is likely to experience
   a. problems understanding language.
   b. sensory deficits such as loss of touch sensations.
   c. personality changes and poorly controlled emotions.
   d. problems regulating heart rate, respiration, and blood pressure.

11. The lobes of the brain that are most important for vision are
    a. the parietal lobes.
    b. the occipital lobes.
    c. the temporal lobes.
    d. the frontal lobes.

12. Drugs that mimic the action of neurotransmitters are called
    a. agonists.
    b. endorphins.
    c. antagonists.
    d. efferents.

13. Grandpa's stroke affected Broca's area in the brain. Grandpa probably has difficulty
    a. making and carrying out plans.
    b. producing language (speaking).
    c. storing or recalling new memories.
    d. recognizing faces or objects.

14. Damage to the hypothalamus, a limbic system structure, is least likely to affect
    a. sexual behavior.
    b. changes in learning and memory.
    c. eating behavior.
    d. hormonal changes.

15. A split-brain patient is briefly shown a cup on the far left and a hat on the far right. If asked to indicate what object appeared, when will cup be selected?
    a. only when the left hand is used to select the object
    b. only when the right hand is used to select the object
    c. only when a spoken response is allowed
    d. when either the right hand is used or a vocal response is allowed

16. Behaviors, thought, and feelings are represented in the nervous system by
    a. the length of the refractory period.
    b. the pattern of activation of groups of neurons.
    c. the particular neurotransmitter that has been released.
    d. the particular node of Ranvier stimulated.

17. The somatosensory cortex is important for
    a. regulating heart rate.
    b. language production.
    c. processing touch sensations.
    d. controlling eating and drinking.

18. When your roommate slammed the door and started screaming, you felt your heart race and your muscles tense. These physical changes were due to
    a. GABA.
    b. endorphins.
    c. serotonin.
    d. epinephrine.

19. The trait of nearsightedness is recessive. If you are nearsighted, you can conclude that you must have
    a. no nearsightedness genes.
    b. only one nearsightedness gene.
    c. at least one (maybe two, but not necessarily) nearsightedness genes.
    d. two nearsightedness genes.

MULTIPLE CHOICE PRETEST 2

Select the one best response.

1. Compared to neurons without myelin, neurons with myelin
    a. are more likely to release excitatory neurotransmitters.
    b. are more likely to release inhibitory neurotransmitters.
    c. usually have more dendrites.
    d. usually have faster transmission rates.

2. When sodium ions flow into the neuron
    a. hyperpolarization occurs.
    b. depolarization occurs.
    c. a resting potential is established.
    d. the refractory period ends.

3. The adaptive value of the resting potential is that it
    a. allows quick response to stimulation.
    b. protects the cell from over-stimulation.
    c. slows neurotransmitter loss.
    d. inhibits nearby neurons.

4. The morphine-like neuromodulators produced by the brain are
    a. endorphins.
    b. efferents.
    c. L-dopa compounds.
    d. GABA compounds.

5. Which of the following are very important for transmitting sensory information to the cerebral cortex?
    a. the thalamus and the hypothalamus
    b. the amygdala and the hippocampus
    c. the midbrain and the thalamus
    d. the hippocampus and the hypothalamus

6. Which neurotransmitter is important in the regulation of sleep and is thought to be involved in depression and several other psychological disorders?
   a. acetylcholine
   b. epinephrine
   c. serotonin
   d. dopamine

7. Alzheimer's disease involves serious memory disorders. This suggests Alzheimer's disease affects
   a. the medulla and pons.
   b. the tectum.
   c. the cerebellum.
   d. the hippocampus.

8. Tia's smooth, coordinated gymnastic movements are primarily the result of her well-functioning
   a. reticular formation.
   b. cerebellum.
   c. limbic system.
   d. tectum.

9. Aunt Bess no longer can plan activities or make decisions sensibly. She has also become very uninhibited, undressing in public. Her doctor probably suspects Aunt Bess has damage to
   a. the pons.
   b. the substantia nigra.
   c. the frontal lobe.
   d. the occipital lob.

10. To reduce the aggressive behavior of a wolverine, which limbic system structure should be lesioned?
    a. the hippocampus
    b. the superior colliculus
    c. the tectum
    d. the amygdala

11. What happens if a stimulus arrives during a neuron's refractory period?
    a. The neuron will release an inhibitory neurotransmitter.
    b. The action potential will be faster than usual.
    c. Saltatory conduction will occur.
    d. No action potential will occur.

12. Grandma's stroke left her unable to move her left hand and arm. Her stroke probably was located in
    a. the left frontal lobe.
    b. the right frontal lobe.
    c. the left parietal lobe.
    d. the right parietal lobe.

13. Dr. Sperry stimulated the patient's brain and the patient's mouth moved. Based on the topographic organization of the brain, if the patient's brain is stimulated slightly to one side of the first spot, we should expect the patient to
    a. say something.
    b. report seeing a spot of light.
    c. twitch her cheek.
    d. report tasting something.

14. Which of the following does not provide information about brain activity or function?
    a. CT scan
    b. functional MRI
    c. EEG
    d. PET

15. When the parasympathetic nervous system is activated
    a. sensory neurons increase their firing rate.
    b. heart rate and blood pressure are reduced.
    c. most activity occurs in the form of spinal reflexes.
    d. the body is readying itself for action.

16. Some data links "tomboy" behavior (rough and tumble play) in girls to
    a. prenatal exposure to testosterone.
    b. prenatal exposure to estrogen.
    c. early childhood (age 6) exposure to epinephrine.
    d. early childhood (age 6) exposure to pituitary growth hormone.

17. The pituitary gland is often described as the "master gland," but it is really the brain that controls the pituitary gland. Which brain area controls the pituitary gland?
    a. the amygdala
    b. the hypothalamus
    c. the corpus callosum
    d. the reticular formation

18. A trait's phenotype refers to
    a. its observable characteristics.
    b. its genetic components (e.g., two of the same genes or one of each gene type).
    c. whether it is dominant of recessive.
    d. whether it is adaptive or a mutation.

19. If an adaptive trait is economical,
    a. it is found in all members of the species.
    b. it is not costly to the survival of the organism.
    c. it solves specific adaptive problems the organism faces.
    d. the genes involved have undergone a spontaneous, sudden change.

LANGUAGE DEVELOPMENT GUIDE

CORE TERMS

In the lectures on this chapter, there are a few terms you are almost certain to hear. The first is ***physiology***, the study of how a part of the body works. There are two ways to study body parts: you can look at their ***structure*** (their cells or how they are put together) or their ***function*** (what the parts do). Your instructor will probably cover both structure and function for each of the ***anatomical features*** (brain parts) discussed. The discussion will range all the way from the ***grossest*** structures (meaning the largest) to the ***finest*** (smallest), from whole sections of the brain to the inner workings of individual brain cells.

The nervous system is a ***hierarchy***, a strictly organized system with definite divisions and subdivisions, but organizing its functions is not simple. The discussion of the functions of each ***hemisphere*** (half) of the brain will probably include the terms ***lateralized*** (found in only one of the halves) and ***localized*** (found in one specific area). Some functions seem to be controlled by a specific brain region. At the same time, other functions may be described as ***diffuse*** (spread among several locations). You also need to keep in mind the ***malleability*** and ***plasticity*** of the brain. Both of these terms mean that the brain is somewhat flexible in how it works, and can change some aspects of its functioning if necessary.

IDIOMS

p. 68	a mimicking of	behaving just like; seeming just like
p. 69	modulating	controlling the effects of; keeping an effect from being too extreme
p. 70	tapped briefly into	gotten a quick look into
p. 72	via	by way of
p. 74	capitalizing on	making use of
p. 75	gross electrical activity	a general picture of the electrical activity of the brain
p. 75	global	overall, throughout the whole thing
p. 76	pictorial blueprint	a picture that maps out the parts in great detail
p. 77	base camp	starting point; place from which an expedition begins
p. 79	kick starts	initiates or stimulates; pushes into action
p. 82	fine motor control	ability to move very small muscles in precise ways
p. 84	firebreak	a region with nothing that will catch fire, and as a result, stops a fire's movement; a device that prevents spreading to other locations
p. 85	personal anecdotes	stories of personal experiences told by individuals
p. 94	try to disentangle the relative contributions of	try to figure out which of two or more elements have contributed more

PRONUNCIATION

neuroscience (nur′-o-sy-ince) *p. 62*
glial (glee′-ul) *p. 63*
synapse (sin′-aps) *p. 65*
acetylcholine (a-see′-tull-koh-leen) *p. 68*
dopamine (doh′-pa-meen) *p. 68*
serotonin (se-re-toh′-nin) *p. 68*
tomography (toh-mog′-ra-fee) *p. 75*
myelin (my′-e-lin) *p. 63*
soma (so′-muh) *p. 64*
substantia nigra (sub-stan′-shia ny′-gra) *p. 78*
amygdala (a-mig′-duh-luh) *p. 79*
parietal (puh-ry′-i-tull) *p. 82*
endocrine (in′-doh-krin) *p. 86*
pituitary (pi-too′-i-tair-ee) *p. 87*

SOLUTIONS

PREVIEW & COMMUNICATING INTERNALLY: CONNECTING WORLD AND BRAIN (PP. 61-71)

MASTERING THE CONCEPTS

1. neuroscience (p. 62)
2. spinal cord (p. 62)
3. central (p. 62)
4. peripheral (p. 62)
5. coordinate (p. 62)
6. growth (p. 62)
7. genetic (p. 62)
8. Sensory (p. 63)
9. Interneurons (p. 63)
10. Motor (p. 63)
11. glial cells (p. 63)
12. myelin (p. 63)
13. reflex (p. 63)
14. Dendrites (p. 64)
15. soma (p. 64)
16. axon (p. 64)
17. terminal buttons (p. 64)
18. synapse (p. 65)
19. resting potential (p. 65)
20. depolarization (p. 66)
21. hyperpolarization (p. 66)
22. action potential (p. 66)
23. all or none (p. 66)
24. nodes of Ranvier (p. 67)
25. dopamine (p. 68)
26. agonists (p. 69)
27. antagonists (p. 69)
28. Endorphins (p. 69)
29. pattern (p. 71)
30. firing rate (p. 71)
31. refractory (p. 71)

EVALUATING YOUR PROGRESS

1. A, Correct (p. 63)
   B. Wrong. Sensory neurons link sensory receptors with the brain.
   C. Wrong. Glial cells (aren't neurons!) fill space and perform "housekeeping" duties for neurons.
   D. Wrong. Interneurons link other neurons only and have no contact with the world.
2. C, Correct (pp. 64, 67)
   A. Wrong. The cell body receives input from the dendrites and contains the cell's nucleus.
   B. Wrong. Axons transmit the impulse from the cell body to the next neuron or body organ.
   D. Wrong. Dendrites receive input from a sensory organ or another neuron.
3. C, Correct (p. 63)
   A. Wrong. A sensory neuron is the first neuron in a spinal reflex.
   B. Wrong. A motor neuron is the last neuron in a spinal reflex.
   D. Wrong. Neurotransmitters are needed in all neural transmission.
4. A, Correct (p. 65)
   B. Wrong. Neurotransmitters are released when the cell is active, not resting.
   C. Wrong. Depolarization creates the action potential, not the resting potential.
   D. Wrong. The resting potential is present when the neuron is inactive and not being stimulated.
5. C, Correct (p. 66)
   A. Wrong. For a given neuron, the action potential is the same magnitude for all stimuli.
   B. Wrong. For a given neuron, the action potential has the same speed for all stimuli.
   D. Wrong. Only one is correct.
6. B, Correct (p. 65)
   A. Wrong. The nucleus is in the soma. The synapse is a space between neurons.
   C. Wrong. The axon hillock is the location where the action potential begins.
   D. Wrong. Nodes of Ranvier are gaps in the myelin sheath. The synapse is a gap between neurons.
7. D, Correct (p. 67)
   A. Wrong. Interneurons are a type of neuron. The impulse crosses the synapse via neurotransmitters.
   B. Wrong. Glial cells are supportive cells and make up the myelin sheath. They are not in terminal buttons.
   C. Wrong. The sodium-potassium pump maintains the ion distribution in the neuron.

8. B, Correct (p. 68)

   A. Wrong. Endorphins are substances produced by the brain that mimic the action of morphine.

   C. Wrong. Serotonin is associated with sleep, depression, and other mental disorders.

   D. Wrong. A shortage of acetylcholine is associated with memory loss in Alzheimer's disease.

9. C, Correct (p. 69)

   A. Wrong. Neurotransmitters don't limit the firing rate; the refractory period does.

   B. Wrong. The system in which the neuron is located isn't important; the refractory period is the limitation.

   D. Wrong. The number of synapses might influence whether a neuron fires, but not its maximum firing rate.

INITIATING BEHAVIOR: A DIVISION OF LABOR (PP. 71-86)

MASTERING THE CONCEPTS.

1. central (p. 72)
2. peripheral (p. 72)
3. afferent (p. 73)
4. efferent (p. 73)
5. somatic (p. 73)
6. autonomic (p. 73)
7. brain damage (p. 73)
8. midbrain (p. 78)
9. forebrain (p. 78)
10. medulla (p. 77)
11. cerebellum (p. 77)
12. Parkinson's (p. 78)
13. cerebral cortex (p. 78)
14. sensory (p. 79)
15. hypothalamus (p. 79)
16. limbic system (p. 79)
17. memories (p. 80)
18. frontal (p. 81)
19. parietal (p. 82)
20. temporal (p. 83)
21. left (p. 83)
22. left (p. 84)
23. spatial (p. 86)
24. corpus callosum (p. 84)

EVALUATING YOUR PROGRESS

1. D, Correct (p. 73)

   A. Wrong. The autonomic nervous system goes beyond the brain and spinal cord (central nervous system).

   B. Wrong. The afferent pathway contains sensory neurons. The autonomic system goes to internal organs.

   C. Wrong. The somatic and autonomic nervous systems together make up the peripheral nervous system.

2. B, Correct (p. 73)

   A. Wrong. The autonomic nervous system controls basic bodily functions, not movements.

   C. Wrong. The parasympathetic nervous system returns the body to normal after emergencies.

   D. Wrong. The sympathetic nervous system activates the body to deal with emergencies.

3. C, Correct (pp. 75-76)

   A. Wrong. To lesion is to destroy an area of cells. These techniques merely record brain activity.

   B. Wrong. Because they are generally non-invasive, these techniques are commonly used with humans.

   D. Wrong. These techniques record brain activity. They do not stimulate the brain.

4. A, Correct (p. 77)
   B. Wrong. The forebrain controls complex thought and planning.
   C. Wrong. The midbrain contains neural relay stations, particularly for sensory information.
   D. Wrong. The forebrain (especially the hypothalamus) controls basic motivational processes.
5. B, Correct (pp. 77-79)
   A, C, & D. Wrong. These are all in the forebrain. The cerebellum is in the hindbrain.
6. A, Correct (p. 78)
   B. Wrong. The medulla and pons control breathing, respiration, and other life support systems.
   C. Wrong. The hypothalamus is involved in eating, drinking, temperature, and sexual behavior.
   D. Wrong. The cerebral cortex in involved in higher mental processes.
7. D, Correct (p. 79)
   A. Wrong. Damage in the occipital lobe causes visual perception problems.
   B. Wrong. Damage in the reticular formation affects arousal and consciousness.
   C. Wrong. Damage to the frontal or temporal lobes affects language.
8. C, Correct (pp. 80-81)
   A. Wrong. The parietal lobe is responsible for the skin senses and some higher visual processes.
   B. Wrong. The temporal lobe is responsible for auditory processing and aspects of language.
   D. Wrong. The occipital lobe is responsible for visual processing.
9. B, Correct (p. 81)
   A, C, & D. Wrong. These are all true, but the motor cortex is in the frontal, not parietal lobes.
10. D, Correct (p. 82)
    A. Wrong. The occipital lobe processes vision. Language comprehension is a function of the temporal lobe.
    B. Wrong. Language comprehension is a function of Wernicke's area (temporal lobe). The frontal lobe is important for language production.
    C. Wrong. Language comprehension is a function of Wernicke's area (temporal lobe).
11. D, Correct (p. 84-86)
    A. Wrong. Data support some amount of localization or lateralization of function.
    B. Wrong. Cortical functions are at least as lateralized or localized as sub-cortical functions.
    C. Wrong. Data support cooperative processes in addition to some localization of function.

REGULATING GROWTH AND INTERNAL FUNCTIONS: EXTENDED COMMUNICATION (PP. 86-89)

MASTERING THE CONCEPTS

1. endocrine (p. 86)
2. longer (p. 86)
3. pituitary (p. 87)
4. sex (p. 88)

EVALUATING YOUR PROGRESS

1. D, Correct (p. 87)
   A. Wrong. Adrenal hormones energize the body for action, but don't control other glands.
   B. Wrong. The ovaries and testes produce sex hormones, but don't control other glands.
   C. Wrong. The pineal gland is involved with biological cycles, but doesn't control other glands.
2. C, Correct (p. 87)
   A. Wrong. The cerebellum is involved in coordination of movement, not endocrine control.
   B. Wrong. The hippocampus is responsible for memory functions, not endocrine control.
   D. Wrong. The medulla controls life-support functions like heart rate, not the endocrine system.
3. D, Correct (p. 86)
   A. Wrong. Endocrine system effects are more widespread and longer-term.
   B. Wrong. Endocrine system effects are more widespread, not localized.
   C. Wrong. Endocrine system effects are longer-term.

4. A, Correct (p. 88)
   B. Wrong. Estrogen (female hormone) has been linked to verbal skill, in which women excel.
   C. Wrong. Sex hormones, not prenatal epinephrine, may be linked to behavioral gender effects.
   D. Wrong. Sex hormones, not prenatal norepinephrine, may be linked to behavioral gender effects.
5. C, Correct (p. 87)
   A. Wrong. The pituitary doesn't secrete epinephrine; it stimulates the adrenal glands to do so.
   B. Wrong. The hypothalamus doesn't secrete the epinephrine; it stimulates the pituitary, which stimulates the adrenal glands to do so.
   D. Wrong. The ovaries and testes secrete sex hormones (estrogen and testosterone), not epinephrine.

ADAPTING AND TRANSMITTING THE GENETIC CODE (PP. 89-93)

MASTERING THE CONCEPTS

1. genes (p. 91)
2. Dominant (p. 91)
3. recessive (p. 91)
4. Family (p. 92)

EVALUATING YOUR PROGRESS

1. D, Correct (p. 91)
   A. Wrong. A phenotype is a person's observable characteristic, such as eye color.
   B. Wrong. Efferent refers to a neural pathway carrying information away from the brain.
   C. Wrong. Afferent refers to a neural pathway carrying information to the brain.
2. B, Correct (p. 90)
   A. Wrong. A mutation is a change in the genetic code that often occurs by chance.
   C. Wrong. A recessive trait requires two recessive genes to be present. It isn't necessarily related to survival likelihood.
   D. Wrong. A dominant trait can be maladaptive. Dominance involves how the trait is controlled.
3. C, Correct (p. 91)
   A. Wrong. Phenotypes describe the observable characteristics of a trait, not the number of genes.
   B. Wrong. Phenotypes describe the observable characteristics of a trait, not dominant/recessive.
   D. Wrong. The specific genetic pattern is described by the genotype.
4. D, Correct (p. 93)
   A. Wrong. Identical twins are essentially genetically identical, so both would show a recessive trait.
   B. Wrong. Identical twins receive the same genes, so a parental mutation would appear in both twins.
   C. Wrong. If genetically determined, both twins will show the trait. Identical twins share the same genes.
5. D, Correct (p. 90)
   A. Wrong. Adaptations can involve recessive traits, too.
   B. Wrong. Adaptations can involve dominant traits, too.
   C. Wrong. Behavioral traits, not just physical ones, can be adaptations.

MAKING FINAL PREPARATIONS

SHORT ESSAY QUESTIONS

1. Drugs act like natural neurotransmitters (agonists), by increasing the effectiveness of natural neurotransmitters (neuromodulators), or by blocking neurotransmitter activity (antagonists). The behavioral effects will depend on the specific combinations of inhibition and excitation of the nervous system. (p. 69)
2. In the usual pathway, sensory input about the object is carried via sensory neurons to the spinal cord and then to the brain. The brain initiates commands to move which are carried via motor neurons to the spinal cord and the muscles. In a spinal reflex the sensory input is carried by sensory neurons to the spinal cord. Commands to move are initiated in the spinal cord (without involving the brain) and carried to the muscles by motor neurons. The spinal reflex allows more rapid responses because input does not have to travel all the way to and from the brain. This is advantageous in dangerous situations. (p. 63)
3. Brain functions are studied by damaging, recording, or stimulating the brain. The function of a brain area is inferred based on changes in behavior after brain damage, or based on changes in that area's level of activity during a particular behavior, or when a change in behavior occurs when that area is stimulated. (pp. 73-76)
4. Because the left hemisphere controls language in most people, I would lose the ability to use and comprehend speech. Sensory input from the right side of the body and right visual field is handled in the left hemisphere, so I would lose sight, touch, temperature, and pain information from the right. The left hemisphere controls movement on the right side of the body, so I'd be paralyzed in my right arm and leg. (pp. 83-86)
5. Identical twins share essentially identical genes, so traits that are not shared by both twins are likely to be environmentally induced. When both twins share a trait, the origin of the trait is not clear because identical twins also usually share very similar environments. However, by examining identical twins raised in different environments from infancy, the impact of the genes and the environment may be untangled. When the incidence of a trait in separated identical twin pairs is compared to that in fraternal twins raised together, further information about the influence of the genes is possible. (p. 92-93)

MATCHING

1. f (p. 77)
2. o (p. 79)
3. d (p. 79)
4. n (p. 63)
5. e (p. 77)
6. l (p. 64)
7. m (p. 78)
8. b (p. 64)
9. p (p. 77)
10. h (p. 64)
11. a (p. 84)
12. k (p. 79)
13. g (p. 79)
14. j (p. 64)
15. c (p. 82)
16. i (p. 87)

MULTIPLE CHOICE PRETEST 1

1. A, Correct (p. 63)
   B. Wrong. Sensory neurons carry input from the sensory organs to the brain.
   C. Wrong. Glial cells do not transmit impulses. They provide support services to neurons.
   D. Wrong. Hormones do not transmit movement commands to the muscles.
2. C, Correct (p. 64)
   A. Wrong. The axon is not the first structure. Dendrite--soma--axon--terminal button.
   B. Wrong. The terminal button is the last structure. Dendrite--soma--axon--terminal button.
   D. Wrong. The soma is not the first structure. Dendrite--soma--axon--terminal button.
3. C, Correct (p. 75)
   A. Wrong. PET involves imaging metabolic activity in specific locations, not gross electrical activity.
   B. Wrong. Lesioning involves destroying brain tissue, not recording its electrical activity.
   D. Wrong. CT scans provide an image of brain structure.
4. A, Correct (p. 63)
   B. Wrong. Neurotransmitters are used in all neural transmission.
   C. Wrong. Hormones, not the spinal reflex, provide long-lasting communication.
   D. Wrong. The spinal reflex is neural, not hormonal, activity.
5. D, Correct (p. 66)
   A. Wrong. Inhibition would be related to hyperpolarization.
   B. Wrong. The refractory period is the time after a neural impulse when the cell can't fire again.
   C. Wrong. The resting potential is the charge present in the neuron when at rest, not when depolarized.
6. D, Correct (p. 64)
   A. Wrong. The myelin insulates some neurons.
   B. Wrong. Neurons are not attached. They are separated by a fluid filled space, the synapse.
   C. Wrong. The dendrites receive incoming stimulation, not the terminal buttons.
7. B, Correct (p. 66)
   A. Wrong. Hyperpolarization is associated with a reduced chance of an action potential (inhibition).
   C. Wrong. Hyperpolarization is associated with inhibitory input, so neurotransmitters were not released.
   D. Wrong. Hyperpolarization prevents neural firing. The intensity of the previous message isn't important.
8. D, Correct (p. 68)
   A. Wrong. Neurotransmitters generally contact the dendrites, not the axon.
   B. Wrong. Neurotransmitters flow across the synapse and make contact with the postsynaptic membrane.
   C. Wrong. The myelin sheath insulates the axon and is not influenced by neurotransmitters.
9. C, Correct (p. 78)
   A. Wrong. Acetylcholine is associated with Alzheimer's disease, not Parkinson's disease.
   B. Wrong. Serotonin is important in sleep and some psychological disorders, but not Alzheimer's.
   D. Wrong. Endorphins are morphine-like substances, not a factor in Alzheimer's.
10. D, Correct (p. 77)
    A. Wrong. This problem would be associated with temporal lobe damage (Wernicke's area).
    B. Wrong. This problem would be associated with parietal lobe damage (somatosensory cortex).
    C. Wrong. This problem would be associated with frontal lobe damage or limbic system damage.
11. B, Correct (p. 83)
    A. Wrong. The parietal lobes are important for the sense of touch, not the visual sense.
    C. Wrong. The temporal lobes are important for hearing, not vision.
    D. Wrong. The occipital lobes are critical for vision. The frontal lobes are not major sensory areas.
12. A, Correct (p. 69)
    B. Wrong. Endorphins are neuromodulators (not agonists) that are involved in the pleasure system.
    C. Wrong. Antagonists block the action of neurotransmitters, not mimic them.
    D. Wrong. Efferents are motor pathways, not drugs.

13. B, Correct (p. 81)
    A. Wrong. Broca's area is important for speech production. Planning is a frontal lobe behavior.
    C. Wrong. The hippocampus is important in memory.
    D. Wrong. Object and facial recognition is associated with the parietal lobe, not with Broca's area.
14. B, Correct (p. 79)
    A., C., & D. Wrong. The hypothalamus is important for eating, sexual behavior, and controlling the endocrine system, but not for memory.
15. A, Correct (p. 84)
    B. Wrong. Cup will go to the right hemisphere, which controls the left hand.
    C. Wrong. Cup will go to the right hemisphere, but speech is generally controlled by the left hemisphere.
    D. Wrong. Input will go to the right hemisphere, which doesn't control the right hand or speech.
16. B, Correct (p. 71)
    A. Wrong. The refractory period is a characteristic of a neuron, not a neural code.
    C. Wrong. Neural activity, not specific neurotransmitters represent the information.
    D. Wrong. Nodes of Ranvier are gaps in the myelin and do not represent information.
17. C, Correct (p. 82)
    A. Wrong. The medulla and other hindbrain areas control heart rate.
    B. Wrong. Broca's area in the frontal lobe is important for controlling language production.
    D. Wrong. The hypothalamus is important for controlling eating and drinking.
18. D, Correct (p. 87)
    A. Wrong. GABA is a brain neurotransmitter, not a fight-or-flee adrenal hormone.
    B. Wrong. Endorphins are morphine-like substances in the brain, not a fight-or-flee adrenal hormone.
    C. Wrong. Serotonin is associated with sleep and mood, not a fight-or-flee response.
19. D, Correct (p. 91)
    A. Wrong. Two dominant (normal) genes produce the dominant trait (normal vision).
    B. Wrong. Recessive traits appear only if both genes are the recessive (nearsightedness) type.
    C. Wrong. One recessive (nearsightedness) gene will not produce the recessive trait. It takes two.

MULTIPLE CHOICE PRETEST 2

1. D, Correct (p. 63)
    A, B, C. Wrong. Myelin is an insulating substance on the axon that helps speed neural transmission.
2. B, Correct (p. 66)
    A. Wrong. Hyperpolarization occurs if more sodium is pushed out or chloride comes in.
    C. Wrong. The resting potential occurs when the neuron is inactive and sodium is not flowing in.
    D. Wrong. The refractory period ends when the resting potential is reestablished.
3. A, Correct (p. 65)
    B. Wrong. The resting potential is the charge of the neuron at rest, and unrelated to protection.
    C. Wrong. The resting potential is the charge of the neuron at rest, not a neurotransmitter issue.
    D. Wrong. Activity inhibits other neurons, not the charge of the neuron at rest (resting potential).

4. A, Correct (p. 69)
   B. Wrong. Efferents are motor pathways, not brain chemicals.
   C. Wrong. L-dopa is a drug used to treat Parkinson's disease. It is not morphine-like.
   D. Wrong. GABA is a brain neurotransmitter, but it is not similar to morphine.
5. C, Correct (p. 79)
   A. Wrong. The thalamus is a sensory relay structure, but the hypothalamus is not involved in sensory input.
   B. Wrong. These structures are in the limbic system, which is not involved in transmitting sensory input.
   D. Wrong. The hippocampus is important for memory, and the hypothalamus is important fro sexual behavior and eating behavior. Neither plays a significant role in transmitting sensory information.
6. C, Correct (p. 68)
   A. Wrong. Acetylcholine is influential in Alzheimer's disease, but not sleep or depression.
   B. Wrong. Epinephrine is not important in sleep. It is generally a stimulant.
   D. Wrong. Dopamine is not important in sleep. It is thought to be involved in schizophrenia, not depression.
7. D, Correct (p. 68)
   A. Wrong. The medulla and pons control basic functions like breathing and blood pressure.
   B. Wrong. The tectum of the midbrain has important sensory pathways.
   C. Wrong. The cerebellum controls coordination of movements.
8. B, Correct (p. 77)
   A. Wrong. The reticular formation is important for arousal and consciousness. Coordination is cerebellar.
   C. Wrong. The limbic system is involved with motivation and emotion, not coordination.
   D. Wrong. The tectum contains sensory centers important for responding to sensory events.
9. C, Correct (p. 81)
   A. Wrong. The pons regulates basic bodily functions, not higher cognitive processes.
   B. Wrong. The substantia nigra produces dopamine and is involved in Parkinson's disease.
   D. Wrong. The occipital lobe is important for vision, not thinking.
10. D, Correct (p. 79)
    A. Wrong. The hippocampus is involved with memory, not aggression.
    B. Wrong. The superior colliculus is a sensory area in the midbrain.
    C. Wrong. The tectum is the midbrain area with sensory functions.
11. D, Correct (p. 71)
    A. Wrong. Neurons do not respond at all during the refractory period.
    B. Wrong. The action potential doesn't vary in speed.
    C. Wrong. Saltatory conduction occurs when the action potential moves from one Node of Ranvier to another. Neurons do not generate action potentials during the refractory period.
12. B, Correct (pp. 80-81)
    A. Wrong. The left side of the body is controlled by the right hemisphere, not the left.
    C. Wrong. The left side of the body is controlled by the right hemisphere, and the motor cortex is in the frontal lobe.
    D. Wrong. The motor cortex is in the frontal lobe, not the parietal lobe.
13. C, Correct (p. 81)
    A. Wrong. Speech and movement aren't as closely linked in the brain as movements of nearby areas.
    B. Wrong. Visual functions are not near motor functions in the brain.
    D. Wrong. Body part and related functions are not necessarily nearby in the brain.
14. A, Correct (p. 75)
    B. Wrong. The functional MRI measures brain activity. CT scans only show structure.
    C. Wrong. The EEG measures brain activity. CT scans only show structure.
    D. Wrong. PET measures brain activity in different brain areas. CT scans only show structure.
15. B, Correct (p. 73)
    A. Wrong. Sensory neurons are not part of, nor affected by, the parasympathetic system.
    C. Wrong. Spinal reflexes are "hardwired" and are unaffected by the autonomic nervous system.
    D. Wrong. Activation of the sympathetic nervous system produces the "fight or flee" reaction.

16. A, Correct (p. 88)
    B. Wrong. Estrogen is a female hormone and would facilitate normal "female" development.
    C. Wrong. Epinephrine is an adrenal hormone with general activation, not sexual, effects.
    D. Wrong. Pituitary growth hormone controls bone growth and is normally present in childhood.

17. B, Correct (p. 87)
    A. Wrong. The amygdala is involved in aggressive behavior.
    C. Wrong. The corpus callosum is the structure that allows the two hemispheres to communicate.
    D. Wrong. The reticular formation is important for controlling general arousal and consciousness.

18. A, Correct (p. 91)
    B. Wrong. The genetic pattern represents the trait's genotype, not phenotype.
    C. Wrong. The type of inheritance pattern (e.g., dominant) is not relevant. The manifestation of the trait is.
    D. Wrong. The phenotype is what is observed. The value or origin of the trait is irrelevant.

19. B, Correct (p. 90)
    A. Wrong. Being common to all members makes the trait universal.
    C. Wrong. Solving problems makes the trait adaptive.
    D. Wrong. A spontaneous change in genes describes mutation.

CHAPTER **4**

HUMAN DEVELOPMENT

ESTABLISHING LEARNING GOALS

Use these learning goals as a preview of the chapter, a guide for active reading, and to evaluate your mastery of the material. Review the relevant goals as you begin and end your reading of each major section of the chapter.

I. Discuss how the individual develops physically through the life span.
   - A. Describe the physical changes that occur prenatally.
     1. Describe the three periods of prenatal development and the major events of each.
     2. Discuss the factors that influence or disrupt prenatal development.
   - B. Discuss how we grow from infancy through adolescence.
     1. Discuss the influence of "nature" and "nurture" on the development of motor skills.
     2. Describe physical growth from infancy through adolescence.
   - C. Discuss adulthood and the aging body and brain.
     1. Describe the physical and mental changes associated with menopause.
     2. Describe the neural changes in the brain and how they relate to behavioral changes.

II. Discuss how individuals develop the intellectual skills needed to deal effectively with the constantly changing circumstances encountered throughout life.
   - A. Explain the research tools used to study infant perception and memory.
   - B. Describe an infant's perceptual capabilities.
   - C. Characterize memory loss in the elderly.
   - D. Discuss and evaluate Piaget's theory of cognitive development.
     1. Discuss the characteristics of the stages of cognitive development and how changes occur.
     2. Discuss the criticism of Piaget's theory of cognitive development.
   - E. Discuss and evaluate Kohlberg's theory of moral development.
     1. Describe moral reasoning in the preconventional, conventional, and postconventional stages.
     2. Evaluate Kohlberg's theory in terms of its general approach and its applicability to all cultures.

III. Discuss how individuals form social relationships and a personal identity.
   - A. Discuss the short- and long-term consequences of early attachments.
     1. Describe the artificial mother research and how it relates to humans.

2. Identify four types of attachment.
3. Discuss the role of friendships in development.
4. Discuss the impact of child care on social and intellectual development.

B. Explain Erik Erikson's stage theory of personal identity development.
1. Describe the personal crises characteristic of each stage, and explain their importance.
2. Evaluate Erikson's theory.

C. Discuss the issues that affect gender role development.

D. Discuss the psychological issues associated with death and dying.
1. Discuss ageism.
2. Describe Kubler-Ross' stages of confronting death.

MASTERING THE MATERIAL

PREVIEW & DEVELOPING PHYSICALLY (PP. 99-108)

MASTERING THE VOCABULARY

Define or explain each of the following terms.

1. development
2. zygote
3. germinal period
4. embryonic period
5. fetal period
6. teratogens
7. puberty
8. menopause
9. dementia

MASTERING THE CONCEPTS

Fill in the blanks to create a summary of the section.

[1] ___________ is the age-related change in behavior and physical features that occurs over time. Developmental psychologists consider development to be due to the [2] ___________ of biological

and environmental factors. This chapter involves three issues: How does the individual develop [3] ____________ , [4] ____________ , and socially or personally?

Physical development begins with the formation of the single-celled [5] ____________ at conception. Not all survive the two-week [6] ____________ period and implant in the uterus. During the six-week [7] ____________ period the cells develop into a more recognizable structure and sexual differentiation occurs. From the ninth week until birth, the [8] ____________ period, development continues. Development can be disrupted if the mother exposes the developing child to [9] ____________ , environmental agents that harm development. Alcohol use can lead to [10] ____________ syndrome. Structures have critical periods of susceptibility to teratogens, but exposure at any time can be dangerous.

Although the brain is only 25% of its adult weight at birth, its growth involves development of branches and interconnections, not significantly increased numbers of neurons. Plasticity allows the brain to respond to [11] ____________ influences. Development of the nervous system occurs in a [12] ____________ and out fashion and produces a predictable sequence of motor development, although the timing may be modified by the environment. Growth slows during early childhood, and increases again at [13] ____________ when the release of estrogen or androgen initiates a growth spurt accompanied by [14] ____________ development. Age at puberty varies with sex and environment.

After age 20, a gradual [15] ____________ in physical condition begins. Women reach [16] ____________ at about age 50. The brain loses cells, and by age 80 Alzheimer's disease or other types of [17] ____________ may appear. However, cell loss might be offset by adaptation of other cells to compensate and maintain function.

EVALUATING YOUR PROGRESS

Select the best response. If you make any errors, reread the relevant material before proceeding.

1. The fertilized egg is called the
   a. embryo.
   b. fetus.
   c. zygote.
   d. teratogen.

2. Sexual differentiation, the development of the sexual reproductive system, occurs during the
   a. early germinal period.
   b. middle of the germinal period.
   c. late embryonic period.
   d. late fetal period.

3. The structures that are most likely to be affected by a teratogen are those that
   a. develop first (nervous system and heart).
   b. are undergoing initial development when the teratogen is present.
   c. have just completed their initial development when the teratogen is present.
   d. would be affected by the teratogen in adulthood (alcohol--liver).

4. The brain grows dramatically in size from birth to age 2 due to
   a. a rapid increase in the number of neurons present.
   b. a rapid growth of blood vessels within the brain.
   c. the development of the ventricles, fluid filled spaces found in the normal adult brain.
   d. the increase in the number of glial cells and the complexity of the neurons.

5. Prenatal development sets down basic neural circuitry, but environmental factors influence final circuitry. This describes the principle of
   a. schemata.
   b. habituation.
   c. plasticity.
   d. conservation.

6. Neural development and motor development follow a predictable sequence that is best described as
   a. up and out.
   b. down and out.
   c. up and in.
   d. down and in.

7. The developmental period during which individuals mature sexually is called
   a. puberty.
   b. menarche.
   c. the climacteric.
   d. menopause.

8. The age of the onset of puberty has decreased 3-4 years in the last century, probably due to
   a. changes in the genetic makeup of people today.
   b. poor diets that are high in junk foods.
   c. the emphasis on strenuous daily exercise and sports.
   d. improved medical care and living conditions.

9. Which of the following is FALSE?
   a. Most physical functions decline during adulthood.
   b. Most women do not experience depression or other serious mood problems during menopause.
   c. Neurons in the elderly may have larger and more complex dendrites than in the middle-aged.
   d. Most people in their 80's develop Alzheimer's disease or other serious mental deterioration.
10. The physically based loss in mental functioning is called
    a. dementia.
    b. the climacteric.
    c. teratogenesis.
    d. menarche.

DEVELOPING INTELLECTUALLY (PP. 109-123)

MASTERING THE VOCABULARY

Define or explain each of the following terms.

1. longitudinal design
2. cross sectional design
3. preference technique
4. habituation
5. schemata
6. assimilation
7. accommodation
8. sensorimotor period
9. object permanence
10. preoperational period
11. principle of conservation
12. egocentrism
13. concrete operational period
14. formal operational period
15. morality
16. preconventional level
17. conventional level
18. postconventional level

MASTERING THE CONCEPTS.

Fill in the blanks to create a summary of the section.

Developmental research often uses either a cross-sectional research design or a [1] ____________ design. Infants' limited ability to respond makes infant perception research difficult, but three characteristics of infants are useful: they show [2] ____________ ; they notice [3] ____________ ; and they can learn to make a response. In the [4] ____________ technique, looking at one stimulus longer than another suggests that the infant can tell the two stimuli are different. Another method for testing an infant's ability to remember or discriminate stimuli is to use the [5] ____________ technique, repeating a stimulus until the infant quits responding, then changing to a new stimulus and noting any response. Also, rewarding a simple action such as sucking or kicking produces responses that can be used to study infant abilities.

The infant's perceptual system is immature, but it functions well. All senses are operational. Adaptive capabilities, such as recognizing the mother by [6] ____________ , are particularly sophisticated. Their acuity is poor, but "visual cliff" experiments show infants perceive [7] ____________ . In general, their perceptual systems need to be fine-tuned by maturation and experience.

Memory skills improve during childhood, mostly due to improved [8] ____________ . Loss of memory skill is common in older adults, but the way memory is tested is very important. [9] ____________ is most likely to be affected by aging.

Piaget proposed that people develop [10] ____________ , mental models of the world that influence their interpretation of their experiences. Piaget suggested development proceeds in [11] ____________ characterized by different schemata. The [12] ____________ of development is variable, but the [13] ____________ is the same for all children. Cognitive development involves both assimilation and accommodation. [14] ____________ occurs when the child fits new experiences into existing schemata. In [15] ____________ , schemata are modified to fit the new experiences.

Behavior in Piaget's first stage, the [16] ____________ period, includes survival reflexes such as the [17] ____________ and the sucking reflex. Children move from reflexive to deliberate interaction with the world. They develop object [18] ____________ , the ability to symbolically represent objects not in view.

From about age 2 to 7, children are in the [19] ____________ period, and they lack an understanding of [20] ____________ . Due to [21] ____________ , or focusing on one dimension, and difficulty with reversibility, children think that changing shape causes a change in amount. Preoperational children also have difficulty seeing the world from others' perspectives, a trait called [22] ____________ . Children between 7 and 11 are in the [23] ____________ operations period, and the ability to think abstractly is greatly limited. [24] ____________ thought and systematic problem solving is characteristic of the formal operations period.

Piaget's theory has been criticized for underestimating what children know, for proposing sudden shifts from stage to stage, and for failing to explain the processes of change and the role of [25] ____________ context. In contrast, Vygotsky, emphasized the importance of social and cultural influence.

Kohlberg proposed morality develops in 3 stages: the [26] ____________ , conventional, and [27] ____________ stages. He assessed moral development by examining the [28] ____________ given for deciding right or wrong. [29] ____________ reasoning is based on the external results of an action (e.g., punishment). Conventional reasoning is based on how an action affects the [30] ____________ . [31] ____________ reasoning is based on abstract principles that may conflict with accepted norms.

Research supports the sequence of development and the link to cognitive skills. Criticisms of Kohlberg's theory include that it does not generalize across sexes or [32] ____________ , and that analyzing reasoning is not adequate.

EVALUATING YOUR PROGRESS

Select the best response. If you miss any questions, reread the relevant material before proceeding.

1. A stimulus is presented repeatedly until response rate declines, and then a new stimulus is presented and any change in response rate is noted. This describes
   a. the habituation method.
   b. the reward method.
   c. the preference method.
   d. the cross-sectional method.

2. Research has shown that infants just a few days old can do all of the following EXCEPT
   a. recognize their mother's voice.
   b. recognize their mother's smell.
   c. see clearly.
   d. taste sour, sweet, and salty substances.

3. Comparing the behavior of a group of today's 7-year-olds to a group of today's12-year-olds is an example of a
   a. cross-sectional design.
   b. longitudinal design.
   c. time-linked design.
   d. continuous design.

4. The process of altering schemata to fit new information is called
   a. generalization.
   b. centration.
   c. accommodation.
   d. assimilation.

5. Piaget's stages, in order from first to last, are
   a. preoperational, sensorimotor, concrete operational, formal operational.
   b. concrete operational, formal operational, sensorimotor, preoperational.
   c. preoperational, formal operational, concrete operational, sensorimotor.
   d. sensorimotor, preoperational, concrete operational, formal operational.

6. At the beginning of the sensorimotor period
   a. object permanence is present.
   b. behavior is mostly reflexive.
   c. children begin to acquire conservation.
   d. reversibility is understood.

7. Object permanence is the knowledge that
   a. the basic properties of an object don't change if superficial changes are made.
   b. if one operation causes a change, another operation can reverse that change.
   c. an object can still exist even if it is not currently in view or other sensory contact.
   d. changes in one dimension can be offset by changes in another dimension.

8. The rooting reflex is the tendency to
   a. consider only one dimension of an object or situation.
   b. consider an action in relation to others.
   c. suck on anything that comes in contact with the mouth.
   d. turn the head toward the side of the cheek that was touched.

9. The conservation concept develops by the end of Piaget's
   a. preoperational period.
   b. formal operational period.
   c. sensorimotor period.
   d. concrete operational period.

10. The formal operational period is characterized by
    a. centration.
    b. abstract thought.
    c. egocentrism.
    d. only limited object permanence.

11. A 9-year-old is likely to be in the
    a. preoperational period.
    b. formal operational period.
    c. sensorimotor period.
    d. concrete operational period.

12. All of the following are criticisms of Piaget's theory of cognitive development EXCEPT:
    a. Research shows that children's schemata are not the same as adults'.
    b. Children know more, and sooner, than Piaget proposed.
    c. Piaget doesn't address the role social context plays in cognitive development.
    d. Children do not make sudden transitions from one stage to another as Piaget proposes.

13. Kohlberg's theory of moral reasoning proposes that
    a. moral reasoning develops differently in different countries.
    b. children's moral reasoning is developed fully by the time they are 6.
    c. development proceeds through a series of orderly stages.
    d. the "yes" or "no" decision about a moral dilemma determines the level of moral reasoning.

14. Postconventional moral reasoning is based on
    a. whether the action disrupts or maintains the social order.
    b. the personal consequences of the action.
    c. abstract moral principles.
    d. the standards of morality defined by an authority figure.

15. Research on Kohlberg's theory of moral development has found that
    a. the moral reasoning of men and women differs greatly in most circumstances.
    b. moral reasoning in India is quite different from moral reasoning in Western cultures.
    c. the orderly progression of moral reasoning is found only in Western cultures, not elsewhere.
    d. the analysis of reasoning judgments accurately predicts moral values.

DEVELOPING SOCIALLY AND PERSONALLY (PP. 124-137)

MASTERING THE VOCABULARY

Define or explain each of the following terms.

1. attachments
2. temperament
3. strange-situation test
4. personal identity
5. gender roles
6. ageism

MASTERING THE CONCEPTS

Fill in the blanks to create a summary of the section.

Attachment, the [1] ____________ ties to another individual, may be controlled by biological predispositions in both parent and child. Harlow's research with monkeys suggests contact [2] ____________ , pleasant physical contact, is more important for attachment than being a food source. Parental responsiveness is also important and is influenced by the child's [3] ____________ , which can be easy or difficult, uninhibited or inhibited. Attachment is evaluated using the [4] ____________ situation test. Most children have [5] ____________ attachment, 20% have avoidant attachment, and a smaller percentage have resistant or disorganized/disoriented attachment. Secure attachment is associated with social and intellectual benefits. Assessments are not always stable, attachment can vary across parents, the data is correlational, and later experiences are important. Friendships are also beneficial. Research on the effects of day care indicates it has little effect on attachment and may benefit social and [6] ____________ development, depending on the quality of care and other factors.

Erikson states that personal [7] ____________ is shaped by a series of psychosocial crises confronted in life. They extend from the trust vs. mistrust crisis of infancy to the integrity vs. despair crisis of [8] ____________ . The ideas of life-long development and the importance of [9] ____________ and cultural interactions are valid contributions. Criticisms of the theory include the problem of distinct stages, the lack of an explanation as to how progress occurs, and its testability.

Basic gender identity seems to be present by age [10] ____________ . By school age, gender identity is seen as permanent, and behavior reflects gender [11] ____________ , behavior fitting society's concept of male or female behavior. In [12] ____________ theory, gender roles develop because certain behaviors are rewarded. Gender roles lead to gender schemas, beliefs about men and women that guide behavior.

Many beliefs about the elderly are myths, but the elderly do face physical concerns, difficult end-of-life decisions, and [13] ____________ , prejudice against the elderly. Kubler-Ross proposed a theory of dying: denial, anger, bargaining, depression, and [14] ____________ . Her theory has been criticized for its stage format. Dying trajectories provide an alternative without implying a "right" way to die. End-of-life decisions are influence by personal beliefs and values, but most people facing difficult situations choose to try to continue, rather than choose to end life.

EVALUATING YOUR PROGRESS

Select the best response. If you miss any questions, reread the relevant material before proceeding.

1. The strong emotional bond between individuals is known as
   a. personal identity.
   b. contact comfort.
   c. dependency.
   d. attachment.

2. Harlow's research found that most monkeys raised with artificial mothers formed attachments if
   a. the "mother" provided the infant monkey's food.
   b. the "mother" had a warm, fuzzy cover.
   c. the "mother" was made out of wire mesh with no cover.
   d. all of the above conditions led to attachment in most monkeys.

3. The technique researchers use to evaluate attachment is called the
   a. contact comfort test.
   b. strange situation test.
   c. stress reaction test.
   d. social stressor test.

4. Which of the following is not a classification of attachment?
   a. resistant attachment
   b. avoidant attachment
   c. antagonistic attachment
   d. secure attachment

5. Tina is described as an "easy" child who is fairly uninhibited. This is a description of
   a. temperament.
   b. moral development.
   c. attachment.
   d. cognitive development.

6. Recent studies of day care suggest that
   a. essentially all day care harms the development of attachment.
   b. even quality day care is associated with poor social development.
   c. quality day care is associated with improved cognitive skills for almost all children.
   d. general conclusions are difficult because of the many factors that interact.

7. Erikson's stage theory of personal identity development proposes
   a. contact comfort is more important than supplying food.
   b. development begins at puberty.
   c. identity is determined by several psychosocial crises.
   d. friends are the primary determinants of personal identity.

8. At what point in life do people try to resolve the crisis of integrity vs. despair?
   a. adolescence
   b. early adulthood
   c. middle adulthood
   d. late adulthood

9. The social learning theory of gender role development states that gender roles develop because
   a. children are rewarded for certain "masculine" or "feminine" behavior.
   b. children have few models for gender-appropriate behavior.
   c. children quickly determine that their genitals are different from others'.
   d. children are innately programmed to behave in stereotypically "masculine" or "feminine" ways.

10. Kubler-Ross' stages of death and dying are, in order,
   a. denial, anger, bargaining, depression, acceptance.
   b. denial, depression, anger, bargaining, acceptance.
   c. denial, bargaining, depression, anger, acceptance.
   d. denial, bargaining, anger, depression, acceptance.

MAKING FINAL PREPARATIONS

Complete these sections without consulting your book or notes. For a more accurate estimate of how well you know this material, wait at least a day or two after studying the chapter before working on the questions. Some of the material you "know" immediately after working with the chapter will be quickly forgotten. Exercises done too soon after studying will overestimate what you know well.

SHORT ESSAY QUESTIONS

Write a brief answer to each question.

1. Discuss why exposure to a teratogen during the first three months produces different effects than exposure during the last three months of pregnancy.

2. Describe a newborn infant's perceptual capabilities and how and why they change with time.

3. Describe the preference technique and explain what it tells us about an infant's perceptual capabilities.

4. Give an example of preconventional, conventional, and postconventional moral reasoning for the druggist moral dilemma and explain why each exemplifies the relevant level.

5. Identify three types of attachment and describe how each is reflected in the strange situation test.

6. Evaluate Erikson's theory of personal identity.

7. Compare the gender identities of a 3-year-old and a 7-year-old.

MATCHING

Select the correct definition or description for each item.

1. _______ schemata
2. _______ Harlow
3. _______ fetal period
4. _______ habituation
5. _______ Erikson
6. _______ concrete operational period
7. _______ sensorimotor period
8. _______ gender schema
9. _______ Piaget
10. _______ embryonic period
11. _______ menopause
12. _______ preconventional level
13. _______ germinal period
14. _______ conventional level
15. _______ dementia
16. _______ Kohlberg
17. _______ centration
18. _______ attachment

a. first two weeks of prenatal period
b. set of beliefs about men and women
c. loss of mental function due to physical causes
d. morality based on external consequences of action
e. time of final development of physical systems
f. proposed theory of personal identity development
g. time of initial development of physical systems
h. proposed theory of moral development
i. found importance of contact comfort in attachment
j. mental models of the world
k. considering only one aspect of a stimulus
l. proposed theory of cognitive development
m. morality based on maintaining social order
n. period when woman's menstrual cycles cease
o. reflexive behavior and no object permanence
p. can't deal with abstract or hypothetical situations
q. emotional ties formed to other people
r. decline in responsiveness to a repeated stimulus

MULTIPLE CHOICE PRETEST 1

Select the one best response.

1. During the third through eighth weeks of development, the organism is called a(n)
   a. fetus.
   b. embryo.
   c. zygote.
   d. menarche.

2. The disease rubella produces heart defects if contracted during the first 6 weeks of pregnancy, but it is unlikely to produce heart defects if contracted later. Why does this pattern occur?
   a. The heart doesn't develop until well after the sixth week.
   b. The heart has mostly completed its development after the sixth week, so damage is less likely.
   c. The fetus' immune system doesn't develop until later in pregnancy and can't protect the heart until then.
   d. The fetus' immune system is overly aggressive during the first six weeks.

3. The sequential development of motor skills is most dependent on
   a. the sequential development of muscle strength.
   b. the sequential development of bone strength.
   c. the sequential development of neural connections.
   d. the sequence of behaviors to which parents pay most attention.

4. Which is true?
   a. Most women do not experience significant depression or very disruptive physical problems during menopause.
   b. A majority of 80 year olds show signs of Alzheimer's disease.
   c. In elderly brains there are fewer neurons and the cells are less complex than in middle-aged brains.
   d. The physical decline is usually limited to muscle strength, rather than affecting many areas.

5. To study moral development, researchers tested a group of fifty 3-year-olds at yearly intervals over the next 20 years. This procedure is an example of
   a. a cross-sectional design.
   b. a trajectory technique.
   c. longitudinal design.
   d. the centration technique.

6. Which is false?
   a. Infants perceive depth at least by the time they are 6 months old.
   b. Infants have at least basic color vision at birth.
   c. Infants prefer pictures of normal faces more than "scrambled" faces.
   d. A newborn's visual acuity is about 20/20.

7. A decline from peak physical functioning typically begins between the ages of
   a. 20-30.
   b. 40-50.
   c. 50-60.
   d. 60-70.

8. The process of fitting new information into existing schemata is called
   a. accommodation.
   b. conservation.
   c. assimilation.
   d. relativistic thinking.

9. In the standard conservation of liquid task, preoperational children pay attention to the "height" of the liquid and ignore the "width" of the liquid. This tendency to consider only one dimension is called
   a. centration.
   b. accommodation.
   c. egocentrism.
   d. ageism.

10. Kiri acts as if her toy doesn't exist when it rolls under the sofa. Kiri is probably in Piaget's
    a. formal operational period.
    b. concrete operational period.
    c. preoperational period.
    d. sensorimotor period.

11. Dee understands conservation, but she can't handle questions that deal with the abstract. She is in
    a. the sensorimotor period.
    b. the formal operational period.
    c. the preoperational period.
    d. the concrete operational period.

12. Object permanence research suggests that
    a. even 1-4 month-olds show surprise when an object does not reappear when a screen is removed.
    b. Piaget's estimate of good object permanence by about age 1 is reasonably accurate.
    c. children do not develop object permanence until they are close to age 3, rather than by age 1.
    d. children have object permanence for living things at birth, but not for nonliving things.

13. Memory research indicates that older adults
    a. show no deficits if their verbal ability is equal to the comparison group's.
    b. show deficits primarily on indirect tests of memory, rather than on conscious memory tests.
    c. perform poorly on recall tests, but not on recognition tests.
    d. perform worse than younger adults on memory tasks of all types and formats.

14. Fred said that stealing a drug would be wrong because if caught, the man would go to jail. This is an example of Kohlberg's
    a. preconventional reasoning.
    b. postconventional reasoning.
    c. conventional reasoning.
    d. concrete operational reasoning.

15. Attachment is strongly influenced by all of the following EXCEPT
    a. a biological predisposition for attachment behavior in the infant.
    b. a biological predisposition for attachment behavior in the parent.
    c. contact comfort.
    d. providing a source of food.

16. Tom rarely acts nervous in strange situations and pays little attention to his mother's presence or absence. Tom would most likely be classified as having
    a. secure attachment.
    b. avoidant attachment.
    c. resistant attachment.
    d. disorganized/disoriented attachment.

17. Billy believes boys are stronger, noisier, better at math, and make better doctors, engineers, and police officers than girls. These beliefs about males and females represent
    a. gender schemas.
    b. gender roles.
    c. gender identities.
    d. gender trajectories.

18. If Mike is struggling to achieve generativity rather than stagnation, Mike is probably
    a. an adolescent.
    b. a young adult.
    c. middle-aged.
    d. elderly.

19. Ed is no longer angry he is dying of lung cancer. If Kubler-Ross is correct, Ed will now experience
    a. acceptance.
    b. denial.
    c. depression.
    d. bargaining.

20. Which best represents the conclusions of research on the effects of day care on most children?
    a. Day care seriously damages normal social development.
    b. Day care seriously damages normal cognitive development.
    c. Day care seriously damages both social and cognitive development.
    d. Day care has no serious long-term effects on social or cognitive development.

MULTIPLE CHOICE PRETEST 2

Select the one best response.

1. The critical factor that causes a female reproductive system to develop is
    a. testosterone release in the 7th-8th week of development.
    b. estrogen release in the 7th-8th week of development.
    c. having no testosterone released in the 7th-8th week of development.
    d. having a Y sex chromosome.

2. Although avoiding drugs, alcohol, smoking, and other toxins throughout pregnancy is best, generally the most important time to avoid them in order to prevent abnormalities is
    a. the first 2 weeks of the prenatal period.
    b. the first three months of the prenatal period.
    c. the middle three months of the prenatal period.
    d. the last three months of the prenatal period.

3. The adaptive value of the plasticity of the brain is
   a. the stability provided by having neural circuits firmly established and operating in a set way.
   b. the capability of adjusting to a particular environment and compensating for cell loss.
   c. the ability to prevent teratogens from entering the brain.
   d. the advantage of being able to grow new neurons to replace those lost through damage or aging.

4. Eduardo's body was encased in a cast during the first 9 months of his life. He probably will
   a. show life-long problems in motor development, especially walking.
   b. begin to walk at least 1 year later than children given free movement.
   c. begin to walk at least 6 months later than children given free movement.
   d. begin to walk at about the same time as children given free movement.

5. The same red light was presented repeatedly until the infant quit responding, then a new, slightly different colored light was presented, and the infant responded again. This is an example of the
   a. longitudinal technique.
   b. habituation technique.
   c. preference technique.
   d. use of reward.

6. In general, the role of experience in perceptual development is
   a. to establish all the basic neural circuits used in perception.
   b. to establish the basic neural circuits used for taste and touch, but not for the other senses.
   c. to make adjustments to the basic neural circuits already established at birth.
   d. very minimal; the neural circuits present at birth allow perception like that in adulthood.

7. To study changes in processing speed with age, Ted is currently testing a group of 20-year-olds, a group of 30-year-olds and a group of 40-year-olds and comparing their speeds. This is an example of
   a. a horizontal design.
   b. a vertical design.
   c. a cross-sectional design.
   d. a longitudinal design.

8. Meg knows cats are small furry animals. When she saw a mink at the zoo, she kept calling it a cat, even after being told it was a mink. Meg's behavior represents
   a. conservation.
   b. object permanence.
   c. accommodation.
   d. assimilation.

9. To stop Rudy's fussing for an attractive (but dangerous) object, Rudy's mother put it in her pocket. "Out of sight, out of mind," she said, and it worked. Rudy's mother made use of his lack of
   a. conservation.
   b. object permanence.
   c. rooting reflex.
   d. assimilation.

10. Although she saw both pieces taken out of their cans, Amy now thinks that she has less clay than her brother because his has been squashed flat. Amy does not understand
    a. object permanence.
    b. proximal development.
    c. conservation.
    d. seriation.

11. James can view events only from his own unique perspective; he can't consider the viewpoints of others. This represents
    a. accommodation.
    b. reversibility.
    c. habituation.
    d. egocentrism.

12. Kim decided that stealing a drug would be wrong because it is against the law, and because laws are needed to maintain social order. Kim is reasoning at Kohlberg's
    a. postconventional level.
    b. conventional level.
    c. preconventional level.
    d. preoperational level.

13. Mal is struggling to develop a sense of initiative. Mal is probably
    a. between 3 and 6 years old.
    b. between 6 and 12 years old.
    c. a young adult.
    d. middle aged.

14. Which of the following accurately represents the results of temperament research?
    a. Inhibited toddlers tend to become inhibited adults.
    b. Genetics appear to have little impact on temperament.
    c. Temperaments are not identifiable until age 2.
    d. All of the above

15. Perhaps the most valid criticism of Kohlberg's theory of moral development is that
    a. men and women reason very differently about morality.
    b. people do not seem to go through orderly stages of moral reasoning.
    c. moral development has no relationship to cognitive development.
    d. cross-cultural differences in moral reasoning are not handled well by his theory.

16. Based on Harlow's artificial mother research, hospitals might best promote parent-child attachment if
    a. parents are encouraged to cuddle their newborn often.
    b. parents are encouraged to give their baby its bottle right from the start.
    c. parents are encouraged to wait a few minutes before seeing to the baby's needs.
    d. parents are encouraged to change the baby's diaper right from the start.

17. Evaluations of attachment indicate that about 70% of children have
    a. resistant attachment.
    b. disorganized/disoriented attachment.
    c. secure attachment.
    d. avoidant attachment.

18. Frank, age 70, can't find a part-time job because many employers mistakenly believe all the elderly are sickly, unable to think clearly, and cranky. Frank is experiencing the effects of
    a. ageism.
    b. stagnation.
    c. assimilation.
    d. dementia.

19. A strength of Erikson's psychosocial theory of the development of personal identity is
    a. its proposal that personal identity development is a lifelong process.
    b. its clear and precise description of the psychological mechanisms that resolve the crises.
    c. its scientific rigor (ability to be tested scientifically).
    d. its emphasis on genetic determinants.

20. Because not all people follow Kubler-Ross' proposed stages, many psychologists prefer to discuss death in terms of
    a. death watches.
    b. death trajectories.
    c. death schemata.
    d. death cascades.

LANGUAGE DEVELOPMENT GUIDE

CORE TERMS

In this chapter, you can expect the terms ***quantitative*** and ***qualitative*** to be used. Your instructor may say something like, "the differences between children's cognitive development are not merely quantitative, but qualitative." What they are saying is that children don't think *less* than adults do, but *differently* than adults do. The form, or quality, of their thinking is different.

Another pair of terms you might hear are ***abstract*** and ***concrete***. Something that is concrete can be touched, seen, and so on. Something that is abstract cannot. For example, a math problem using real beads or coins is concrete; a math problem using just numbers is abstract.

Some other terms have to do with the models of development. Most of these models present development as a ***continuum*** or ***spectrum***, straight lines with different points along the way. You might imagine a number-line or time-line as a continuum, and the colors of a rainbow as a spectrum. Your instructor may talk about someone moving ***sequentially*** -- that is, step by step in one direction -- through the stages of development. But another pattern of movement is ***recursive*** -- that is, moving forward a bit, and then stepping back, and then moving forward.

IDIOMS

p. 100	milestones	important points along a path
p. 103	Russian roulette	a game of chance in which, if you lose, you die
p. 107	teen, teenage	ages 13-18
p. 109	devise a way to infer perceptual capabilities	figure out a way to determine what someone can perceive with their senses
p. 110	immobile, largely uncommunicative infants	babies who can't move around or say much
p. 110	switching their relative positions from trial to trial	switching them around each time before showing them to the subject
p. 111	biological equipment	senses, brains and bodies
p. 111	sophisticated perceptual processing	complex ways of understanding what is seen, heard, etc.
p. 113	attend selectively to pertinent information	pay attention only to things that are important right now
p. 113	help us interpret ambiguous stimuli	help us perceive things that aren't straightforward or clear
p. 116	attaining adequate nourishment	getting enough food
p. 116	initial stirrings	first signs of; first movements
p. 119	hypothetical outcomes	thinking through an imaginary situation to see what would happen next in it
p. 122	the resident authority figures	the people in charge
p. 122	society's dictum	society's rule
p. 128	well-adjusted	mentally happy and healthy
p. 129	multifaceted concept	an idea with many different possible perspectives
p. 133	rudimentary foundations	basic building-blocks
p. 135	at an economic disadvantage	to be poor
p. 136	sensitized legions of surgeons	made a great many surgeons aware of
p. 136	dismissed out of hand	ignored or put aside without careful consideration

PRONUNCIATION

embryonic (im-bree-on′-ick) *p. 102*
fetal (fee′-tul) *p. 102*
puberty (pew′-ber-tee) *p. 106*
schemata (skee-ma′-ta) *p. 115*

egocentrism (ee-go-sin′-tris-um) *p. 118*

gender (jin′-der) *p. 133*

SOLUTIONS

PREVIEW & DEVELOPING PHYSICALLY (PP. 99-108)

MASTERING THE CONCEPTS

1. Development (p. 99)
2. interaction (p. 99)
3. physically (p. 100)
4. intellectually (p. 100)
5. zygote (p. 101)
6. germinal (p. 102)
7. embryonic (p. 102)
8. fetal (p. 102)
9. teratogens (p. 103)
10. fetal alcohol (p. 103)
11. environmental (p. 104)
12. down (p. 104)
13. puberty (p. 106)
14. sexual (p. 106)
15. decline (p. 107)
16. menopause (p. 107)
17. dementia (p. 108)

EVALUATING YOUR PROGRESS

1. C, Correct (p. 101)
   A. Wrong. The fertilized egg develops into an embryo after two weeks.
   B. Wrong. The developing child isn't called a fetus after the eighth week of development.
   D. Wrong. A teratogen is an environmental agent that causes prenatal damage.
2. C, Correct (p. 102)
   A. Wrong. Differentiation occurs at 7-8 weeks. The germinal period is the first 2 weeks.
   B. Wrong. Differentiation occurs at 7-8 weeks, not at 1-2 weeks.
   D. Wrong. Differentiation occurs at 7-8 weeks, not during the 8th or 9th month.
3. B, Correct (p. 103)
   A. Wrong. Order is not important; whatever is in early stages of development is affected most.
   C. Wrong. Once initial development is over, the threat is greatly reduced.
   D. Wrong. The adult effect is not relevant; the structure in its early development is at most risk.
4. D, Correct (p. 104)
   A. Wrong. Neurons do not significantly increase in number after birth.
   B. Wrong. Blood vessel growth is minimal compared to that of neural branches and glial cells.
   C. Wrong. Ventricle enlargement is minimal compared to that of neuron size and complexity.
5. C, Correct (p. 104)
   A. Wrong. Schemata are mental models of the world, not the adaptability of neural circuitry.
   B. Wrong. Habituation is the reduction in responsiveness to repeated stimuli.
   D. Wrong. Conservation involves understanding that changes in form do not necessarily affect mass or other stimulus dimensions. It does not directly relate to environmental influences on neural circuitry.
6. B, Correct (p. 104)
   A, C, D. Wrong. Development generally goes from the head down, and the center to the outside.
7. A, Correct (p. 106)
   A. Wrong. Menarche is the onset of menstruation, not a developmental period.
   C. Wrong. The climacteric is the loss of reproductive ability in older men.
   D. Wrong. Menopause is the cessation of menstruation in older women.
8. D, Correct (p. 107)
   A. Wrong. Age of puberty seems linked to environmental factors, not genetics.
   B. Wrong. Unhealthy lifestyles are associated with later, not earlier, puberty onset.
   C. Wrong. Too much strenuous exercise tends to delay, not speed up, puberty.
9. D, Correct (pp. 107-108)
   A. Wrong. The physical decline tends to be across the board, not limited to one physical dimension.
   B. Wrong. The idea that menopause is traumatic for most women is a myth.
   C. Wrong. These are all common changes after age 50.

10. A, Correct (p. 108)
    B. Wrong. The climacteric is the loss of male reproductive capacity.
    C. Wrong. Teratogens disrupt prenatal development. Teratogenesis is a fabricated term.
    D. Wrong. Menarche is the first menstrual flow.

DEVELOPING INTELLECTUALLY (PP. 109-123)

MASTERING THE CONCEPTS.

1. longitudinal (p. 109)
2. preferences (p. 110)
3. novelty (p. 110)
4. preference (p. 110)
5. habituation (p. 110)
6. smell (p. 113)
7. depth (p. 113)
8. strategies (p. 113)
9. Recall (p. 113)
10. schemata (p. 115)
11. stages (p. 116)
12. timing (p. 116)
13. order (p. 116)
14. Assimilation (p. 115)
15. accommodation (p. 115)
16. sensorimotor (p. 116)
17. rooting (p. 116)
18. permanence (p. 116)
19. preoperational (p. 117)
20. conservation (p. 117)
21. centration (p. 117)
22. egocentrism (p. 118)
23. concrete (p. 118)
24. Abstract (p. 119)
25. social (p. 120)
26. preconventional (p. 122)
27. postconventional (p. 122)
28. reasons (p. 122)
29. Preconventional (p. 122)
30. social order (p. 122)
31. Postconventional (p. 122)
32. cultures (p. 123)

EVALUATING YOUR PROGRESS

1. A, Correct (p. 110)
   B. Wrong. The reward method teaches the infant to make a simple response in order to get a reward.
   C. Wrong. The preference method presents two stimuli together and measures which is attended to most.
   D. Wrong. The cross-sectional method looks at groups of different ages to study changes in behavior.
2. C, Correct (p. 110)
   A, B, D. Wrong. These are all possible, but the infant has poor visual acuity.
3. A, Correct (p. 110)
   B. Wrong. A cross-sectional design would test groups of people of different ages all at once.
   C. Wrong. There is no such thing as a time-linked design.
   D. Wrong. There is no such thing as a continuous design.
4. C, Correct (p. 115)
   A. Wrong. Generalization is the application of a concept or response to new, similar situations.
   B. Wrong. Centration is the tendency to take into account only one dimension.
   D. Wrong. Assimilation involves fitting new information into existing schemata.
5. D, Correct (p. 116)
   A, B, C. Wrong. These are all out of order. The sensorimotor period is first.
6. B, Correct (p. 116)
   A. Wrong. Object permanence develops later in the sensorimotor period.
   C. Wrong. Conservation skills develop during the preoperational period.
   D. Wrong. Reversibility is not understood until late in the preoperational period.

7. C, Correct (p. 116)
   A. Wrong. This describes conservation.
   B. Wrong. This describes reversibility.
   D. Wrong. This describes the ability to avoid centration.
8. D, Correct (p. 116)
   A. Wrong. This describes centration.
   B. Wrong. This describes relativistic thinking.
   C. Wrong. This describes the sucking reflex.
9. A, Correct (pp. 117-118)
   B, C, D. Wrong. Conservation develops during the preoperational period.
10. B, Correct (p. 119)
    A. Wrong. Centration is characteristic of the early preoperational period.
    C. Wrong. Egocentrism is characteristic of the preoperational period.
    D. Wrong. Object permanence is quite developed by the end of the sensorimotor period.
11. D, Correct (p. 118)
    A. Wrong. The preoperational period usually includes ages 2 through 7.
    B. Wrong. The formal operational period begins at about age 12.
    C. Wrong. The sensorimotor period runs from about birth to age 2.
12. A, Correct (pp. 119-120)
    B. Wrong. Research shows earlier object permanence, for example, than Piaget proposed.
    C. Wrong. Vygotsky suggests that social context is a critical factor in cognitive development.
    D. Wrong. Different conservation skills are acquired at different times, producing a gradual transition.
13. C, Correct (p. 122)
    A. Wrong. His theory is supposedly applicable world-wide (but critics say it isn't).
    B. Wrong. He proposes development continues into adulthood.
    D. Wrong. He examines the justification for the "yes" or "no," not the "yes" or "no" itself.
14. C, Correct (p. 122)
    A. Wrong. This is conventional reasoning.
    B. Wrong. This is preconventional reasoning.
    D. Wrong. This is conventional reasoning.
15. B, Correct (p. 123)
    A. Wrong. Research finds minimal sex differences in moral reasoning.
    C. Wrong. Cross-cultural research confirms an orderly progression of reasoning.
    D. Wrong. Research suggests Kohlberg's technique is not adequate.

DEVELOPING SOCIALLY AND PERSONALLY (PP. 124-137)

MASTERING THE CONCEPTS

1. emotional (p. 124)
2. comfort (p. 125)
3. temperament (p. 126)
4. strange (p. 127)
5. secure (p. 127)
6. cognitive (p. 129)
7. identity (p. 130)
8. old age (p. 132)
9. social (p. 132)
10. two or three (p. 133)
11. roles (p. 133)
12. social learning (p. 134)
13. ageism (p. 135)
14. acceptance (p. 136)

EVALUATING YOUR PROGRESS

1. D, Correct (p. 124)
   A. Wrong. Personal identity is one's sense of self.
   B. Wrong. Contact comfort is important for forming attachments, but is not attachment.
   C. Wrong. Dependency is a reliance on, or need for, another person or thing.
2. B, Correct (pp. 125-126)
   A. Wrong. Attachment was not based on being provided food.
   C. Wrong. Monkeys did not become attached to wire mothers.
   D. Wrong. A & C did not produce attachment.
3. B, Correct (p. 127)
   A, C, D. Wrong. The strange situation test is used to evaluate attachment.
4. C, Correct (p. 127)
   A, B, D. Wrong. These are all types of attachment.
5. A, Correct (p. 126)
   B, C, D. Wrong. Easy vs. difficult, and uninhibited vs. inhibited are dimensions of temperament.
6. D, Correct (p. 129)
   A. Wrong. Early studies showed this, but recent ones show little, if any, negative effect.
   B. Wrong. Quality care is associated with improved social development.
   C. Wrong. Cognitive benefits are found only if the child's home environment is deficient.
7. C, Correct (p. 130)
   A. Wrong. Contact comfort is Harlow's idea and relates to attachment, not identity.
   B. Wrong. Erikson proposed personal identity development begins during early infancy.
   D. Wrong. Friendship is not a major component in Erikson's theory.
8. D, Correct (p. 132)
   A. Wrong. The crisis of adolescence is identity vs. role confusion.
   B. Wrong. The crisis of early adulthood is intimacy vs. isolation.
   C. Wrong. The crisis of middle adulthood is generativity vs. stagnation.
9. A, Correct (p. 134)
   B. Wrong. Many models are available through other people, television, etc.
   C. Wrong. Genitals influence gender identity but don't relate to social learning theory.
   D. Wrong. The learning in social learning refers to the impact of experience, not innate factors.
10. A, Correct (p. 136)
    B. Wrong. Depression is out of place.
    C. Wrong. Anger is out of place.
    D. Wrong. Bargaining is out of place.

MAKING FINAL PREPARATIONS

SHORT ESSAY QUESTIONS

1. Teratogens usually affect whatever is undergoing initial development. Most organs undergo most of their development in the first three months of pregnancy, so teratogens during that period are likely to cause damage. The specific damage depends on the exact timing of the teratogen. Teratogens during the last three months are less likely to have an effect, because most development is complete except for the central nervous system. Thus, the nervous system is the likely site of damage from late teratogens. (p. 103)
2. All of the newborn's senses are operational, but they do not have the capabilities of an older child. In general, the senses lack the precision and perhaps the sensitivity of more mature systems. Changes occur due to maturation of the nervous system, and to some extent, experience. (pp. 111-113)
3. In the preference technique, two stimuli are presented and the amount of time spent looking at each is recorded. If the infant looks at one more than the other (controlling for position, etc.) the infant must be able to discriminate one from the other. Thus, this technique can evaluate color vision, pattern perception, pattern recognition variables, etc. (p. 110)
4. Preconventional (focus on external consequences): He shouldn't steal the drug because he will get caught and sent to jail. Conventional (focus on maintaining social order): He shouldn't steal the drug because stealing is against the law. If everyone stole what they needed, it would be chaos. Postconventional (focus on abstract principles): He shouldn't steal the drug because it is not right to take someone else's property. (p. 122)
5. Secure attachment: The child is upset by the mother's absence or a stranger but is calmed by the mother's return. Resistant attachment: The child is upset by the mother's absence or stranger but is not calmed by the mother's return. Avoidant attachment: The child is not upset by the mother's absence or a stranger. The mother's return receives little attention. (p. 127)
6. Erickson's theory is important because it recognizes the personal development continues through the lifespan, and because it emphasizes the importance of the influence of social and cultural interactions. However, this theory is criticized for being a stage theory, especially given the mechanism for progression is not identified. Also, the theory is difficult to test and lacks scientific rigor. (p. 132)
7. A basic gender identity (I'm a girl) is present at age 3, but it is not stable. The 3-year-old will likely say that a boy can change into a girl if he grows his hair long or wears a dress. By age 7, the gender identity is stable (dresses don't make a boy a girl), and the child will be operating within well-developed gender roles (behavior consistent with society's view of appropriate male or female behavior). (pp. 133-134)

MATCHING

1. j (p. 115)
2. i (p. 125)
3. e (p. 102)
4. r (p. 110)
5. f (p. 130)
6. p (p. 118)
7. o (p. 116)
8. b (p. 134)
9. l (p. 115)

10. g (p. 102)
11. n (p. 107)
12. d (p. 122)
13. a (p. 102)
14. m (p. 122)
15. c (p. 108)
16. h (p. 122)
17. k (p. 117)
18. q (p. 124)

MULTIPLE CHOICE PRETEST 1

1. B, Correct (p. 102)
   A. Wrong. The term fetus is used after the 8th week.
   C. Wrong. The term zygote is used in the 1st-2nd week.
   D. Wrong. The term menarche refers to the onset of menstruation in females.
2. B, Correct (p. 103)
   A. Wrong. The heart develops much earlier than the sixth week. Development is mostly over by then.
   C. Wrong. The immune system isn't the issue. The key is when the initial development of the heart occurs.
   D. Wrong. The immune system isn't the issue, and it is not aggressive at that early time.
3. C, Correct (p. 104)
   A. Wrong. Without neural development, muscle strength is a minor factor.
   B. Wrong. Without neural development, bone strength is a minor factor.
   D. Wrong. The expectations of parents are not important in determining the sequence.
4. A, Correct (pp. 107-108)
   B. Wrong. No more than about 20% of 80-year-olds have Alzheimer's disease.
   C. Wrong. The brain cells are less numerous, but more complex.
   D. Wrong. Physical decline is usually described as "across the board."
5. C, Correct (p. 109)
   A. Wrong. A cross-sectional design would test people of different ages at one point in time.
   B. Wrong. Trajectory is not a research technique.
   D. Wrong. Centration is not a research technique. It is a limitation of early thought.
6. D, Correct (p. 113)
   A, B, C. Wrong. Infants do all these things, but their acuity is about 20/600.
7. A, Correct (p. 107)
   B, C, D. Wrong. The decline begins earlier.
8. C, Correct (p. 115)
   A. Wrong. Accomodation involves changing schemata in response to new information.
   B. Wrong. Conservation is the idea that superficial changes don't change the basic properties.
   D. Wrong. Relativistic thinking involves considering the relative nature of things.
9. A, Correct (p. 117)
   B. Wrong. Accommodation involves changing schemata to fit new information.
   C. Wrong. Egocentrism is an inability to consider other people's views or perspectives.
   D. Wrong. Ageism is prejudice based on age.
10. D, Correct (p. 116)
    A. Wrong. A lack of object permanence is not typical of the formal operational period.
    B. Wrong. A lack of object permanence is not typical of the concrete operational period.
    C. Wrong. A lack of object permanence is not typical of the preoperational period.
11. D, Correct (p. 118)
    A. Wrong. Neither conservation nor the abstract are understood during the sensorimotor period.
    B. Wrong. Both conservation and the abstract are understood during the formal operational period.
    C. Wrong. Neither conservation nor the abstract are understood during the preoperational period.
12. A, Correct (p. 120)
    B, C. Wrong. Research shows object permanence develops earlier than Piaget's estimate.
    D. Wrong. A living-nonliving distinction has not been made, especially as an innate ability.
13. C, Correct (p. 113-114)
    A. Wrong. Deficits are found even if verbal ability and education are equated across groups.
    B. Wrong. Deficits are more common in conscious memory tests than in indirect tests.
    D. Wrong. Performance is basically equal on recognition tests.

14. A, Correct (p. 122)
    B. Wrong. Postconventional reasoning is based on abstract principles, not personal consequences.
    C. Wrong. Conventional reasoning is based on maintaining social order, not personal consequences
    D. Wrong. This is not one of Kohlberg's levels of moral reasoning.
15. D, Correct (pp. 124-125)
    A, B. Wrong. Both infant and child seem to be predisposed to attachments.
    C. Wrong. Contact comfort is an important influence, probably for both monkeys and humans.
16. B, Correct (p. 127)
    A. Wrong. A securely attached child explores a situation and the mother's whereabouts is important.
    C. Wrong. Resistant attachment involves strong fear of strange situations, but little affection shown to the mother upon her return.
    D. Wrong. Disorganized/ disoriented attachment involves behavior that is inconsistent, sometimes appearing secure and very disordered at other times.
17. A, Correct (p. 134)
    B. Wrong. Gender roles are patterns of behavior consistent with society's ideas of males and female behavior.
    C. Wrong. Gender identities are the genders people assign themselves.
    D. Wrong. Gender theories is a fabricated term.
18. C, Correct (p. 132)
    A. Wrong. Adolescents struggle with identity vs. role confusion.
    B. Wrong. Young adults struggle with intimacy vs. isolation.
    D. Wrong. The elderly struggle with integrity vs. despair.
19. D, Correct (p. 136)
    A. Wrong. Acceptance is the fifth stage. Ed is just entering the third.
    B. Wrong. Denial is the first stage. Ed is just entering the third.
    C. Wrong. Depression is the fourth stage. Ed is just entering the third.
20. D, Correct (p. 129)
    A, B, C. Wrong. Day care does not produce serious problems in social or cognitive development.

MULTIPLE CHOICE PRETEST 2

1. C, Correct (p. 102)
   A. Wrong. Testosterone produces a male system; the lack of testosterone produces a female system.
   B. Wrong. The lack of testosterone, not the presence of estrogen, produces a female system.
   D. Wrong. A Y would cause testosterone release, which would cause male genitals to develop.
2. B, Correct (p. 103)
   A. Wrong. Little differentiation occurs during the first two weeks, so susceptibility is limited.
   C, D. Wrong. Susceptibility is greatest when systems are undergoing initial development. Initial development occurs between the 3rd and 12th weeks (first 3 months).
3. B, Correct (p. 104)
   A. Wrong. Plasticity involves changeable circuits, not set ones.
   C. Wrong. Plasticity involves changeable circuits, not set ones. It is not a barrier to teratogens.
   D. Wrong. Plasticity is not this great; lost neurons cannot be replaced with new ones.
4. D, Correct (p. 106)
   A, B, C. Wrong. Children learn to walk at about the same time as long as some opportunity to move around is available prior to the normal age of walking (12 months).
5. B, Correct (p. 110)
   A. Wrong. The longitudinal technique tests people at different times to examine development.
   C. Wrong. The preference technique compares the length of time an infant looks at each of two stimuli.
   D. Wrong. Reward is used to teach an infant a response.

6. C, Correct (p. 113)
   A. Wrong. Infants have relatively good perception at birth; the basic neural circuits are in place.
   B. Wrong. The basic circuits for taste and touch are present at birth, along with those for other senses.
   D. Wrong. Experience influences perceptual development significantly.
7. C, Correct (p. 109)
   A., B. Wrong. These are not actual designs.
   D. Wrong. A longitudinal design repeatedly tests groups of same-age people over time.
8. D, Correct (p. 115)
   A. Wrong. Conservation is the idea that superficial changes don't change the amount of a substance.
   B. Wrong. Object permanence is the ability to know an object still exists even if it is out of sight.
   C. Wrong. Accommodation is changing schemata to fit new experiences. Here, no change occurred.
9. B, Correct (p. 116)
   A. Wrong. Conservation is knowledge that objects' basic properties don't change with surface changes.
   C. Wrong. The rooting reflex is turning the head to the side toward the cheek that was touched.
   D. Wrong. Assimilation is the fitting of new experiences into existing schemata.
10. C, Correct (p. 117)
    A. Wrong. Object permanence is the understanding that an object still exists when out of sight.
    B. Wrong. Proximal development is a concept concerning the impact of social interactions.
    D. Wrong. Seriation is the ability to put things in ordered sequences.
11. D, Correct (p. 118)
    A. Wrong. Reversibility is the ability to understand that actions can be reversed.
    B. Wrong. Accommodation occurs when schemata are changed to fit new information.
    C. Wrong. Habituation is the reduction of a response to repeated stimulation.
12. B, Correct (p. 122)
    A. Wrong. Postconventional reasoning uses abstract principles, not protecting the social order.
    C. Wrong. Preconventional reasoning is based on the personal consequences of an action.
    D. Wrong. The preoperational level is one of Piaget's levels, not Kohlberg's.
13. A, Correct (p. 131)
    B. Wrong. At ages 6-12, the crisis is industry vs. inferiority.
    C. Wrong. In early adulthood, the crisis is intimacy vs. isolation.
    D. Wrong. The crisis of middle age is generativity vs. stagnation.
14. A, Correct (p. 126)
    B. Wrong. Identical twins show more similar temperaments than fraternal twins raised together.
    C. Wrong. Temperament is identifiable in very early infancy.
    D. Wrong. Answers B and C are both wrong.
15. D, Correct (p. 122-123)
    A. Wrong. Research indicates that sex differences are minimal.
    B. Wrong. Research supports an orderly progression in moral reasoning.
    C. Wrong. The link between cognitive development and moral reasoning is well accepted.
16. A, Correct (p. 126)
    B. Wrong. Being the food supplier, especially in a bottle, is not a major factor in attachment.
    C. Wrong. Attachment is more likely if parents react promptly to the infant's needs.
    D. Wrong. Providing basic physical needs is not the most important factor in attachment.
17. C, Correct (p. 127)
    A. Wrong. About 10% have resistant attachment.
    B. Wrong. Less than 10% have disorganized/disoriented attachment.
    D. Wrong. About 20% have avoidant attachment.
18. A, Correct (p. 135)
    B. Wrong. Stagnation is a feeling of meaninglessness in middle age.
    C. Wrong. Assimilation is a concept in cognitive development, not prejudice against the elderly.
    D. Wrong. Dementia is a cognitive problem, not prejudice against the elderly.
19. A, Correct (p. 132)
    B. Wrong. It does not clearly describe the psychological mechanisms of crisis resolution.
    C. Wrong. It is not scientifically rigorous; it's concepts are vague and difficult to test.
    D. Wrong. Erikson emphasizes personal, social challenges, not genetics.

20. B, Correct (p. 136)

    A. Wrong. A death watch involves waiting with a person who is near death.

    C. Wrong. Death schemata are personal versions of a concept of death.

    D. Wrong. This is not a valid term.

CHAPTER 5

SENSATION AND PERCEPTION

ESTABLISHING LEARNING GOALS

Use these learning goals as a preview of the chapter, a guide for active reading, and to evaluate your mastery of the material. Review the relevant goals as you begin and end your reading of each major section of the chapter.

I. Describe how an internal representation of the external world is created.

   A. Distinguish between sensation and perception.

   B. Describe three fundamental problems common to all sensory systems.

II. Describe how an effective perception of visual information is created.

   A. Explain how light gets translated into the electrochemical language of the brain.
      1. Describe the path light travels through the eye, and explain the function of each eye structure.
      2. Describe the process of dark adaptation.

   B. Describe how basic features of the visual message, such as color, are identified by the brain.
      1. Trace the neural pathway from eye to brain, and describe the processing done at each level.
      2. Explain how color information is extracted and different colors perceived.

   C. Explain how a stable interpretation of visual information is created, and why the interpretation process sometimes produces visual illusions.
      1. Compare bottom-up and top-down processing.
      2. Discuss how information is organized into groups or forms and then recognized.
      3. List and describe types of information used to create a perception of depth.
      4. Discuss perceptual constancy, and explain its relationship to depth perception and illusions.

III. Describe how an effective perception of auditory information is created.

   A. Explain how sound, the physical message, is translated into the electrochemical language of the brain.
      1. Describe the physical stimulus for sound.
      2. Describe the path sound travels through the ear, and explain the function of each structure.

   B. Discuss how pitch information is pulled out of the auditory message.
      1. Describe the place theory of pitch, and indicate its strengths and limitations.
      2. Describe the frequency theory of pitch, and indicate its strengths and limitations.

   C. Explain how the auditory message is interpreted and how sound is localized.

IV. Describe how an effective perception of information from the skin and body is created.

   A. Explain how sensory messages delivered to the skin (touch and temperature) are translated and interpreted by the brain.

   B. Describe how we perceive and interpret pain.

   C. Discuss the operation and function of the body senses of movement and balance.

V. Describe how an effective perception of information from the chemical senses is created.

   A. Describe how chemical stimuli lead to neural activities that are interpreted as different odors and tastes.

VI. Describe how the relationship of the physical and psychological event is quantified.

   A. Explain stimulus detection, including techniques designed to measure it.

   B. Define difference threshold, and explain Weber's Law.

   C. Discuss stimulus adaptation and its adaptive value.

MASTERING THE MATERIAL

PREVIEW & VISION: THE WORLD OF COLOR AND FORM (PP. 143-165)

MASTERING THE VOCABULARY

Define or explain each of the following terms.

1. sensations
2. perception
3. light
4. hue
5. brightness
6. transduction
7. cornea
8. lens
9. pupil
10. iris

11. accommodation
12. retina
13. rods
14. cones
15. fovea
16. visual acuity
17. receptive field
18. blind spot
19. dark adaptation
20. feature detectors
21. trichromatic theory
22. opponent-process theory
23. bottom-up processing
24. top-down processing
25. Gestalt principles of organization
26. recognition by components
27. monocular depth cues
28. binocular depth cues
29. retinal disparity
30. convergence
31. phi phenomenon
32. perceptual constancy
33. perceptual illusions

MASTERING THE CONCEPTS

Fill in the blanks to create a summary of the section.

This chapter explores how environmental stimuli are translated into neural activity, how the message components are analyzed, and how stable interpretations are produced. The basic components of experience, [1] ____________, are processed to produce an interpretation or [2] ____________ of the stimulus. Light coming directly from a source or reflected by an object enters the eye, is transduced into [3] ____________ energy, and is processed in the brain to create a perception of form and color. The [4] ____________ and lens of the eye focus light on the retina, where it stimulates rods and [5] ____________ , the visual receptors. Rods work in low light, whereas cones work in normal light and provide color vision and good [6] ____________ , the ability to see detail. [7] ____________ adaptation is needed for top efficiency.

Receptor activity causes a neural response in the bipolar and ganglion cells. Most signals are carried by the optic nerve to the [8] ____________ and then to the primary visual cortex. [9] ____________ detectors, single cells that respond to specific stimuli (e.g., 45° lines), are found in the visual cortex in a very organized arrangement. Other cortical areas are involved in more complex, visual processing.

Color vision is made possible by three types of cones, each selectively responsive to short, medium, or long [10] ____________ of light. [11] ____________ theory states color is perceived based on the relative activity in three cone types. Color [12] ____________ occurs when one photopigment is missing. [13] ____________ process theory proposes colors are paired, and each member produces opposite neural responses. Data suggest trichromatic processes apply in the retina, and opponent processes apply at higher levels.

Form perception involves both bottom-up (sensory) analysis and top-down analysis using context or [14] ____________ . The Gestalt psychologists proposed principles of [15] ____________ , including proximity, similarity, closure, good continuation, and common fate. Recognition by components theory states complex forms are recognized from [16] ____________ , their simpler components.

Cues for depth, such as linear perspective, shading, convergence and [17] ____________ disparity, allow a 3-dimensional perception. Motion perception provides information about object shape, location, and figure-ground relationships. Retinal image movement is an inadequate cue for motion, and the [18] ____________ phenomenon proves that no real movement is required to perceive motion. Although sensory input is variable, we are able to maintain an unchanging perception, or perceptual [19] ____________ . Depth cues serve as cues for constancy, but if misapplied, [20] ____________ occur.

EVALUATING YOUR PROGRESS

Select the best response. If you make any errors, reread the relevant material before proceeding.

1. Varying the wavelength of a light generally changes the light's
   a. hue.
   b. acuity.
   c. brightness.
   d. accommodation.

2. Ellen sees the world as blurry shapes unless she wears her glasses. She probably has a defective
   a. retina.
   b. pupil.
   c. lens.
   d. iris.

3. Which is a characteristic of the cones?
   a. provide accommodation
   b. work well in low light conditions
   c. provide color vision
   d. have poorer acuity than rods

4. Sensitivity to light increases during dark adaptation because
   a. photopigments are replenished.
   b. the receptive fields get larger.
   c. the brain "fills in" missing information.
   d. the cornea becomes larger.

5. Single cells in the cortex that respond best to lines at a specific angle are called
   a. akinetopsias.
   b. photoreceptors.
   c. bipolar cells.
   d. feature detectors.

6. The firing rate of some visual pathway cells increases when red light is present and decreases when green light is present. This best supports
   a. opponent process theory.
   b. recognition by components theory.
   c. Gestalt theory.
   d. trichromatic theory.

7. The laws of proximity, closure, and similarity govern
   a. depth perception.
   b. perceptual organization.
   c. motion perception.
   d. center-surround receptive fields.

8. The parallel lines of a railroad track appear to converge as they get farther away. This depth cue is
   a. convergence.
   b. retinal disparity.
   c. linear perspective.
   d. common fate.

9. The role knowledge and context have in perception relates to
   a. bottom-up processing.
   b. top-down processing.
   c. opponent processing.
   d. feature processing.

10. The phi phenomenon is an illusion of
   a. color.
   b. depth.
   c. size.
   d. motion.

11. The retinal image of a ball changes in size as it rolls away, but its size is not perceived to change. This is an example of
   a. the Mueller-Lyer illusion.
   b. recognition by components.
   c. retinal disparity.
   d. perceptual constancy.

HEARING: IDENTIFYING AND LOCALIZING SOUNDS (PP. 166-170)

MASTERING THE VOCABULARY

Define or explain each of the following terms.

1. sound
2. pitch
3. pinna
4. tympanic membrane
5. middle ear
6. cochlea
7. basilar membrane
8. place theory
9. frequency theory

MASTERING THE CONCEPTS.

Fill in the blanks to create a summary of the section.

Sound is mechanical energy from the movement of molecules within a physical medium such as air. The rate of these vibrations, measured in hertz (Hz), produces the [1] ____________ of the sound, and their amplitude (energy) produces the [2] ____________ , which is measured in units called decibels (dB).

Sound is captured by the [3] ____________ , and travels down the auditory canal to the tympanic membrane, which vibrates. Three tiny [4] ____________ in the middle ear transfer the vibration to the oval window of the [5] ____________ in the inner ear. This vibration moves the cochlear fluid, causing the [6] ____________ membrane to move. The movement bends [7] ____________ cells, the auditory receptors, and generates a neural impulse that travels via the auditory nerve to the brain. Input from each ear is processed primarily by the [8] ____________ hemisphere. Neurons respond most to specific frequencies and less to others. Auditory cortex cells respond selectively to particular sequences of tones.

Different sound frequencies produce different patterns of movement of basilar membrane, and thus, stimulate different hair cells. Low frequencies cause movement near the [9] ____________ end of the coiled basilar membrane; high frequencies peak near the [10] ____________ . This location information is used to discriminate pitch, according to the [11] ____________ theory. The brain interprets activity in neurons from a specific location as reflecting a particular pitch (frequency). This is compatible with patterns of deafness, but it is limited by a lack of independence in hair cell activity. The [12] ____________ theory of pitch suggests the rate (frequency) of neural firing signals pitch. That is, high frequency impulses reflect a high frequency (high pitch). The firing rate across groups of neurons, or [13] ____________ , extends frequency information. Simple and complex auditory feature detectors are found in the [14] ____________ lobes of the brain.

Ambiguity in auditory input limits identification based only on physical characteristics. Auditory figure-ground is organized on the basis of [15] ____________ , timing, and top-down factors such as knowledge and [16] ____________ . Location is determined by input intensity and timing differences at the two ears.

EVALUATING YOUR PROGRESS

Select the best response. If you miss any questions, reread the relevant material before proceeding.

1. The frequency of a sound stimulus corresponds most closely to its
   a. intensity.
   b. pitch.
   c. location.
   d. purity.

2. The structure that contains the auditory receptor cells is the
   a. semicircular canal.
   b. tympanic membrane.
   c. cochlea.
   d. incus.

3. The auditory neural response is generated when
   a. the neurons on the tympanic membrane are vibrated.
   b. the malleus, incus, and stapes push against the eardrum.
   c. hair cells are bent due to movement of the basilar membrane.
   d. a chemical change occurs in the fluid of the cochlea.

4. The malleus, incus and stapes are
   a. bones in the middle ear.
   b. membranes in the cochlea.
   c. types of hair cells.
   d. specific characteristics of the auditory waveform.

5. The place theory states that pitch is perceived based on
   a. the frequency of the neural impulses generated in the cochlea.
   b. the strength of the neural impulses generated in the cochlea.
   c. the number of neurons activated by the sound.
   d. which specific neurons are firing the most during a sound.

6. Which is false?
   a. The auditory cortex is located mostly in the temporal lobes.
   b. Auditory messages from the right ear go mostly to the right hemisphere.
   c. Top-down processing is not important in auditory perception.
   d. Many auditory cortex cells are frequency-sensitive.

7. The primary factor that allows good auditory localization is
   a. having two ears.
   b. having good pitch discrimination.
   c. knowing the content of the message.
   d. having good frequency detectors in the auditory cortex.

THE SKIN AND BODY SENSES: FROM TOUCH TO MOVEMENT (PP. 170-174)

MASTERING THE VOCABULARY

Define or explain each of the following terms.

1. cold fibers
2. warm fibers
3. pain
4. gate control theory
5. kinesthesia
6. semicircular canals
7. vestibular sacs

MASTERING THE CONCEPTS

Fill in the blanks to create a summary of the section.

The skin senses are touch, [1] ____________ , and pain. Different types of pressure-sensitive receptor cells respond to different aspects of touch stimuli. Touch input goes to the [2] ____________ cortex. Cold fibers and warm fibers react to [3] ____________ in skin temperature.

The response to injury-causing stimuli, [4] ____________ , involves stimulus factors and psychological factors. The gate control theory states physical or [5] ____________ factors can block pain signals by closing a "gate" in the [6] ____________ . Pain also can be reduced by release of [7] ____________ in the brain.

[8] ____________ is the ability to sense the movement and position of body parts. Receptors in the skin, tendons, muscles, and [9] ____________ send input to the somatosensory cortex. The [10] ____________ sense responds to movement, acceleration, and posture changes. Receptors in the [11] ____________ canals and vestibular sacs also send input to the somatosensory cortex. Disturbances of the vestibular system cause dizziness or nausea.

EVALUATING YOUR PROGRESS

Select the best response. If you miss any questions, reread the relevant material before proceeding.

1. Neural responses for touch are generated when touch receptors in the skin are stimulated by
   a. mechanical energy.
   b. electromagnetic energy.
   c. endorphins.
   d. chemical energy.
2. The gate control theory suggests cognitive factors influence pain by opening or closing a "gate" in
   a. the free nerve endings.
   b. the tympanic membrane.
   c. the spinal cord.
   d. the somatosensory cortex.
3. Receptors for the kinesthetic sense are located in the
   a. cortex.
   b. muscles, joints, tendons, and skin.
   c. semicircular canals.
   d. cochlea.
4. A lot of activity coming from your semicircular canals indicates you probably
   a. are moving.
   b. are touching something.
   c. are experiencing a change in temperature.
   d. are feeling pain.
5. The semicircular canals are in the
   a. spine.
   b. muscles of the eyes, neck, and head.
   c. skin.
   d. inner ear.

THE CHEMICAL SENSES: SMELL AND TASTE (PP. 174-177)

MASTERING THE VOCABULARY

Define or explain each of the following terms.

1. chemoreceptors
2. olfaction
3. gustation
4. flavor

5. taste buds

MASTERING THE CONCEPTS

Fill in the blanks to create a summary of the section.

The receptors for smell and taste are called [1] ____________ . Olfactory receptors found in the roof of the nasal cavity bind with odorant molecules, and a neural impulse is generated and transmitted to the [2] ____________ and the limbic system. Some odors, pheromones, are related to [3] ____________ behavior or other specific behavior patterns.

Taste, or gustation, relies on receptors found in [4] ____________ in the papillae of the tongue. Input is sent to the somatosensory cortex. Although there are [5] ____________ basic tastes, receptors do not respond to only one. The pattern across many receptors is critical. Some tastes are dependent on information about smell.

EVALUATING YOUR PROGRESS

Select the best response. If you miss any questions, reread the relevant material before proceeding.

1. The receptors for smell and taste are called
   a. vestibular sacs.
   b. free nerve endings.
   c. chemoreceptors.
   d. mechanoreceptors.
2. Some animals produce chemicals that produce very predictable, specific responses (often sexual) by other members of the species. These chemicals are known as
   a. perfumes.
   b. papillae.
   c. pheromones.
   d. endorphins.
3. Which is false?
   a. Taste receptor cells are located in the papillae.
   b. Most researchers believe there are four basic tastes.
   c. Taste and flavor mean the same thing.
   d. Taste receptors are not very selective and respond to more than one basic taste.

FROM THE PHYSICAL TO THE PSYCHOLOGICAL (PP. 177-180)

MASTERING THE VOCABULARY

Define or explain each of the following terms.

1. psychophysics
2. absolute threshold
3. signal detection
4. difference threshold
5. Weber's law
6. sensory adaptation

MASTERING THE CONCEPTS

Fill in the blanks to create a summary of the section.

Psychophysics studies the relationship between the physical stimulus and the psychological event. The [1] ____________ threshold is the intensity at which a stimulus is detected 50% of the time. Responses are influenced by both sensitivity and bias. The [2] ____________ technique is used to find the impact of bias by comparing rates of hits and [3] ____________ . Difference thresholds are the smallest detectable change, the just [4] ____________ difference. Weber's Law states that the difference threshold is a constant [5] ____________ of the standard stimulus. With continuous stimulation, sensory [6] ____________ occurs, reducing sensitivity.

EVALUATING YOUR PROGRESS

Select the best response. If you miss any questions, reread the relevant material before proceeding.

1. The field of psychophysics studies
   a. the relationship between the physical stimulus and the psychological experience.
   b. the way in which the stimulus stimulates the receptor organs.
   c. the neural pathway sensory information travels to the brain.
   d. the stability of perception in spite of changing stimulation.
2. The absolute threshold is
   a. the minimum stimulus energy that can be detected 50% of the time.
   b. the minimum amount of change in stimulus energy that can be detected 50% of the time.
   c. the maximum stimulus energy that does not produce pain sensations.
   d. the stimulus energy at which increases in intensity do not produce changes in perception.

3. Which of the following controls for the effect of strategies or bias in psychophysical research?
   a. the sensory adaptation approach
   b. Weber's Law
   c. transduction
   d. the signal detection technique

4. Sensitivity decreases with extended exposure to a stimulus. This represents
   a. Weber's Law.
   b. signal detection theory.
   c. sensory adaptation.
   d. perceptual constancy.

MAKING FINAL PREPARATIONS

Complete these sections without consulting your book or notes. For a more accurate estimate of how well you know this material, wait at least a day or two after studying the chapter before working on the questions. Some of the material you "know" immediately after working with the chapter will be quickly forgotten. Immediate tests will overestimate what you know well.

SHORT ESSAY QUESTIONS

Write a brief answer to each question.

1. Describe and explain the time course of dark adaptation.

   ____

   ____

2. Compare the characteristics and functions of the rods and cones.

   ____

   ____

3. Explain why expectancy is important and how it influences perception.

   ____

   ____

4. Define perceptual constancy and explain why it is adaptive.

   ____

   ____

5. Explain the relationship between depth perception and size perception.

____

____

6. Describe the place theory and frequency principle of pitch perception, and explain why both are needed to account for pitch discrimination.

____

____

7. Explain why you will have difficulty telling the direction from which an emergency vehicle is approaching if you drive with only your left windows open.

____

____

MATCHING

Select the correct definition or description for each item.

1. _______ optic chiasm
2. _______ pheromones
3. _______ lateral geniculate nucleus
4. _______ Weber's Law
5. _______ top-down processing
6. _______ basilar membrane
7. _______ acuity
8. _______ cold fibers
9. _______ olfactory bulb
10. _______ feature detectors
11. _______ semicircular canals
12. _______ blind spot
13. _______ transduction
14. _______ hit
15. _______ retina
16. _______ papillae

a. structure associated with auditory hair cells
b. point in the retina where the optic nerve exits
c. layer of tissue containing photoreceptors
d. brain structure that receives olfactory input
e. vestibular system structures
f. correctly detecting the presence of a stimulus
g. area of the thalamus that receives visual input
h. neurons that are activated by cooling of the skin
i. conversion of stimulus energy to neural activity
j. crossover point for visual system neurons
k. the ability to perceive fine detail
l. uses knowledge and expectancy to identify stimuli
m. neurons that respond to specific stimulus attributes
n. scents that produce a specific response
o. predicts difference thresholds
p. bumps on the tongue that contain taste buds

MULTIPLE CHOICE PRETEST 1

Select the one best response.

1. The two structures that focus the light are the lens and the
   a. retina.
   b. optic chiasm.
   c. iris.
   d. cornea.

2. The lens loses some of its flexibility in middle age. As a result
   a. dark adaptation is slower.
   b. receptive fields become smaller.
   c. accommodation is more difficult.
   d. acuity increases.

3. Which of the following is characteristic of rods?
   a. provide the best acuity
   b. are concentrated in the periphery (sides) of the retina
   c. work best in bright light
   d. give color vision

4. There is a "break" in the dark adaptation curve at about 8 minutes. This occurs because
   a. the rods and cones adapt at different rates.
   b. the pupil begins increasing in size again at that time.
   c. the optic chiasm begins to close.
   d. the last two cone photopigments begin to regenerate rapidly.

5. Each of the three cone photopigments responds most to different wavelengths of light. This fact best supports
   a. opponent process theory.
   b. trichromatic theory.
   c. frequency theory.
   d. top-down processing theory.

6. Biederman's recognition by components theory states that objects are recognized on the basis of
   a. the activity in single-cell feature detectors.
   b. top-down processing more than bottom-up processing.
   c. simple component forms called geons.
   d. binocular disparity information.

7. Small differences in the placement of images on the left and right retinas help create 3-dimensional perception. This depth cue is
   a. convergence.
   b. retinal disparity.
   c. linear perspective.
   d. accommodation.

8. Size perception is inaccurate in the Ames room and the Ponzo illusion because
   a. figure-ground relationships are not clear.
   b. stimulus distance is misjudged.
   c. binocular disparity is reversed.
   d. top-down processing is not possible.
9. Sequentially flashing lights make a wheel in a neon sign appear to turn. This is an example of
   a. convergence.
   b. sensory adaptation.
   c. the volley principle.
   d. the phi phenomenon.
10. Proximity, similarity, and closure are
   a. examples of top-down processing.
   b. determinants of pitch perception.
   c. monocular cues for depth.
   d. principles used to organize figure and ground.
11. The fact that different frequencies produce different movement patterns along the basilar membrane is most important for the
   a. place theory.
   b. gate control theory.
   c. trichromatic theory.
   d. frequency theory.
12. The frequency theory has difficulty accounting for pitch perception at high frequencies because
   a. the basilar membrane isn't long enough to allow different patterns of movement for high frequencies.
   b. there are not enough hair cells to correspond to the entire range of frequencies perceived.
   c. the maximum firing rate of neurons is not fast enough to represent the higher frequencies humans hear.
   d. many hair cells are activated at the same time for high frequencies.
13. We perceive cold only when
   a. the temperature of our skin is reduced.
   b. cold fibers fire at a specific rate.
   c. the stimulus is below 50 degrees.
   d. a papilla is stimulated intensely.
14. The sensory system whose receptors are associated with the muscles, tendons, and joints is the
   a. olfactory system.
   b. vestibular system.
   c. gustatory system.
   d. kinesthetic system.

15. If you are feeling dizzy or having trouble keeping your balance, you problem most like involves
    a. the semicircular canals and vestibular sacs.
    b. the cochlea and basilar membrane.
    c. the tympanic membrane and pinna.
    d. the lateral geniculate nucleus and occipital lobe.

16. If endorphins are released, we should expect the organism to
    a. feel less pain.
    b. be attracted to the source of the endorphins.
    c. experience dizziness or nausea.
    d. see color.

17. Which is false?
    a. Loss of the olfactory system would affect the flavor of food.
    b. The receptors for gustation are located in the taste buds.
    c. There are four specific types of olfactory receptors, corresponding to four basic smells.
    d. Olfactory signals are transmitted from receptor neurons to the olfactory bulb.

18. Neural information from the taste system is sent to
    a. the occipital lobe.
    b. olfactory bulb.
    c. the somatosensory cortex.
    d. the frontal lobe.

19. The dark adaptation curve is really a plot of ________ for vision as a function of time in the dark.
    a. Weber's Law
    b. false alarms
    c. absolute threshold
    d. difference threshold

20. In the signal detection technique a false alarm is recorded when the observer reports
    a. seeing a light when a light was presented.
    b. seeing a light when a light was not presented.
    c. seeing no light when a light was presented.
    d. seeing no light when no light was presented.

MULTIPLE CHOICE PRETEST 2

Select the one best response.

1. Hubel and Wiesel found that if they moved the electrode just to the side of a cell that responded only to lines at a 30-degree angle they usually found cells that responded to
    a. lines at a 20 degree angle.
    b. depth.
    c. movement.
    d. faces.

2. The Navy radar operator perceives the new radar image as a small submarine. The fisherman sees the same radar image and perceives it to be a large school of fish. This is explained best by
   a. recognition by components theory.
   b. top-down processing.
   c. Gestalt principles of perceptual organization.
   d. transduction.

3. The adaptive value of accommodation is that it
   a. allows the lens to focus light from objects located at different distances.
   b. allows the rods to regenerate their photopigment in order to provide better vision in the dark.
   c. allows the organization of the stimulus input into different objects.
   d. allows the brain to "fill in" the blind spot.

4. When the band marched in complete unison, they appeared as one large organism. When two members began leading with the opposite foot, they were perceived as a separate group and the unity was broken. This is an example of the Gestalt law of
   a. closure.
   b. good continuation.
   c. common fate.
   d. proximity.

5. Dana sees no glowing embers when she looks directly at the fireplace, but when she looks a little to the side, she can see a dimly glowing spot. What is the best explanation for this?
   a. Dark adaptation occurs faster outside the fovea.
   b. Rods produce more retinal disparity.
   c. Cones provide better acuity.
   d. Rods are more sensitive to light than cones.

6. Dick see yellow instead of red or green. Dick's common form of color blindness is due to
   a. having only one kind of rod.
   b. an optic nerve disorder.
   c. having no cones.
   d. lacking one type of cone photopigment.

7. The current view of the trichromatic theory and opponent-process theory of color is that
   a. trichromatic theory applies in the retina, and the opponent process theory applies at higher levels.
   b. opponent process theory applies in the retina, and the trichromatic theory applies at higher levels.
   c. trichromatic theory applies to primary colors, and opponent process theory applies to other colors.
   d. opponent process theory applies to primary colors, and trichromatic theory applies to other colors.

8. Ed lost one eye in an accident. His depth perception is slightly worse now because he can no longer use
   a. shading.
   b. common fate.
   c. linear perspective.
   d. convergence.

9. Marika is hearing-impaired because her auditory receptors and the structure in which they are located were damaged by a strange virus. The virus must have infected
   a. the pinna.
   b. the cochlea.
   c. the semicircular canals.
   d. the tympanic membrane.

10. Although both squares are at the same distance, depth cues make one square look farther away than another identical square. The "distant" square will be perceived as _________ than the other.
    a. more square
    b. less square
    c. larger
    d. smaller

11. Large portions of the basilar membrane are moved equally by low frequency stimuli, and as a result, many neurons are activated at the same time. This creates a problem for
    a. the frequency theory.
    b. the place theory.
    c. the opponent process theory.
    d. the gate control theory.

12. Which of the following is false?
    a. The auditory cortex contains cells that respond only to specific complex sounds.
    b. Neurons that process low frequency sounds are located in one area of the auditory cortex, whereas those that process high frequency sounds are located in another area.
    c. The auditory cortex is located primarily in the parietal lobes.
    d. Identification of a sound and auditory localization processing occur in two different brain regions.

13. Varying a sound's arrival time at each ear will change
    a. the perceived location of the sound.
    b. the pitch of the sound.
    c. the intensity of the sound.
    d. the comprehension (meaning) of the sound.

14. Which of the following is FALSE concerning the skin senses?
    a. The amount of cortex that processes input from the skin is proportional to the size of the body part.
    b. People are very good at identifying common articles by touch alone.
    c. "Warm" or "cold" is determined by changes in skin temperature, not an object's actual temperature.
    d. Different types of pressure-sensitive receptors respond to different types of touch stimulation.

15. During a battle for his life, the soldier did not notice the cuts he received from the rocks, but when you fell while rollerblading and received similar injuries, you felt significant pain. This is best explained by
    a. gate control theory.
    b. bottom-up processing.
    c. frequency theory.
    d. assuming you produced more endorphins.

16. The apparent role of olfaction in sexual behavior, feeding, and emotion is not surprising given that the olfactory neural path includes links to
    a. the olfactory bulb.
    b. the amygdala, hippocampus, and hypothalamus.
    c. the somatosensory cortex.
    d. the thalamus.

17. To increase profits, the cereal company wants to reduce the amount of raisins in each cup of cereal, but they don't want consumers to notice the change. To know how many raisins they can remove, they first need to obtain an estimate of the
    a. absolute threshold for raisins in a cup of cereal.
    b. difference threshold for raisins in a cup of cereal.
    c. signal detection threshold for raisins in a cup of cereal.
    d. hit rate for raisin detection in a cup of cereal.

18. Which is true concerning gustation?
    a. The neural code for a specific taste (e.g., sour) is based on which neurons are active.
    b. Most researchers accept that there are six basic tastes.
    c. Flavor involves more than taste.
    d. Input from taste receptors is processed in the somatosensory cortex.

19. Tom, 140 lb., Dick, 190 lb., and Harry, 240 lb., are beginning a weight-loss diet. According to Weber's Law (and assuming they all lose the same number of pounds per week) we should expect that
    a. Tom's weight loss will be noticeable first.
    b. Dick's weight loss will be noticeable first.
    c. Harry's weight loss will be noticeable first.
    d. a noticeable reduction in weight will occur at the same time for the three men.

20. What is the major advantage of using signal detection theory for studying sensory abilities?
    a. It measures absolute threshold and difference threshold simultaneously.
    b. It can be used with all senses, rather than just hearing and vision.
    c. It controls for the influence of bias or subject strategies.
    d. It determines the brain areas that are most active in a sensory task.

LANGUAGE DEVELOPMENT GUIDE

CORE TERMS

In the discussion of this chapter you are very likely to hear two expressions quite frequently: ***to distinguish between, to differentiate*** and ***to discriminate***. The last one is likely to be confusing the first time you hear it, because it has such a particular meaning in most people's minds (something close to 'prejudice').

Actually, the terms all mean very nearly the same thing -- to tell the difference between. And of course, the ability to tell the difference between things is important when we are discussing the senses.

Also, you will need to be comfortable with several Latin- and Greek-based words relating to the senses:

- ***vis*** or ***vid***, to see, becomes vision or video
- ***aud*** and ***acou***s, to hear, becomes auditory or acoustic (The word part ***son*** means sound)
- ***tact***, to touch, becomes tactile
- ***kinet***, to move, becomes kinesthetic
- ***olfac***, to smell, becomes olfactory
- ***gust***, to taste, becomes gustatory
- ***Vestibular***, as it turns out, is an exception to the rule. A 'vestibule' is a small entrance area like a lobby or, in anatomical terms, a chamber or channel that leads into another chamber or channel. To figure out why this sense is named as it is, you'll need to know where its sensory organ is located.

IDIOMS

p. 143	blink of an eye	very, very quickly; almost immediately
p. 144	cut across all	work in all cases; be relevant in all
p. 145	tackle the topic	address the subject; talk about
p. 159	three-dimensional	having height, length and depth
p. 159	plastered on	laid onto
p. 161	beckon us in	signals an invitation
p. 173	locus of such effects	the location, focus, or origin of the effects
p. 173	analgesic	pain-relieving
p. 173	acupuncture	a medical procedure from Asia that involves insertion of special needles into body parts
p. 179	strategic bias	a desire or way to achieve a certain goal

PRONUNCIATION

pupil (pew′-pul) *p. 146*
acuity (a-kew′-i-tee) *p. 148*
Gestalt (ge-stalt′) *p. 157*
tympanic (tim- pan′-ick) *p. 166*
cochlea (cock′-lee-a ; coke′-lee-a) *p. 166*
Weber (vay′-ber) *p. 179*

SOLUTIONS

PREVIEW & VISION: THE WORLD OF COLOR AND FORM (PP. 143-165)

MASTERING THE CONCEPTS

1. sensations (p. 144)
2. perception (p. 144)
3. neural (p. 145)
4. cornea (p. 146)
5. cones (p. 148)
6. acuity (p. 148)
7. Dark (p. 149)
8. thalamus (p. 150)
9. Feature (p. 150)
10. wavelengths (p. 153)
11. Trichromatic (p. 154)
12. blindness (p. 154)
13. Opponent (p. 155)
14. knowledge (p. 157)
15. perceptual organization (p. 157)
16. geons (p. 158)
17. retinal (p. 160)
18. phi (p. 161)
19. constancy (p. 161)
20. illusions (p. 162)

EVALUATING YOUR PROGRESS

1. A, Correct (p. 145)
   B. Wrong. Acuity is the ability to resolve fine details.
   C. Wrong. Brightness is associated with the intensity of a visual stimulus.
   D. Wrong. Accommodation is the adjustment of the lens to properly focus light on the retina.
2. C, Correct (p. 146)
   A. Wrong. The retina contains the receptor cells. It does not focus light.
   B. Wrong. The pupil is the opening for the light. It does not focus light.
   D. Wrong. The iris is the colored part of the eye. It does not focus light.
3. C, Correct (p. 148)
   A. Wrong. The lens is responsible for accommodation.
   B. Wrong. The rod photopigment allows operation in low light.
   D. Wrong. Cones have greater acuity than rods.
4. A, Correct (pp. 149-150)
   B. Wrong. Receptive field size is a function of neural connections, not light level.
   C. Wrong. The brain fills in information in the blind spot, but this doesn't relate to adaptation.
   D. Wrong. The cornea is involved in focusing light. It does not change size, only curvature.
5. D, Correct (p. 150)
   A. Wrong. This is not a cell. It's a rare disorder in which only unmoving objects can be seen.
   B. Wrong. The photoreceptors are not in the cortex, and they are selective only for wavelength.
   C. Wrong. Bipolar cells are in the retina and are not selective to specific stimuli.
6. A, Correct (p. 155)
   B. Wrong. Recognition by components theory is an object recognition theory, not a color theory.
   C. Wrong. Gestalt theory involves perceptual organization, not color vision.
   D. Wrong. Trichromatic theory proposes three types of cones, not opposite neural responses.
7. B, Correct (p. 158)
   A. Wrong. Depth cues do not include any of these. These guide perceptual organization.
   C. Wrong. Motion perception does not involve any of these to any great extent. These guide organization.
   D. Wrong. Center-surround receptive fields are determined by neural organization, not these laws.

8. C, Correct (p. 159)
   A. Wrong. Convergence is the degree to which the eyes turn inward to focus on near vs. far objects.
   B. Wrong. Retinal disparity is a depth cue that involves the differences in the images in each eye.
   D. Wrong. Common fate is a Gestalt principle involving uniform motion. It is not a depth cue.

9. B, Correct (p. 157)
   A. Wrong. Bottom-up emphasizes image features, not context or knowledge.
   C. Wrong. Opponent processing emphasizes opposite neural responses generated by certain colors.
   D. Wrong. Feature- or bottom-up processing relates to the image's features, not context or knowledge.

10. D, Correct (p. 161)
    A, B, C. Wrong. Phi is an illusion of motion, not color, depth, or size.

11. D, Correct (p. 161)
    A. Wrong. The Mueller-Lyer illusion is an illusion of size, but it does not involve changes in image size.
    B. Wrong. Recognition by components is a theory of object perception that does not involve changing image size.
    C. Wrong. Retinal disparity is a depth cue in which the image in each eye differs. Image size is not critical.

HEARING: IDENTIFYING AND LOCALIZING SOUNDS (PP. 166-170)

MASTERING THE CONCEPTS.

1. pitch (p. 166)
2. loudness (p. 166)
3. pinna (p. 166)
4. bones (p. 166)
5. cochlea (p. 166)
6. basilar (p. 167)
7. hair (p. 167)
8. opposite (p. 167)
9. far (p. 168)
10. oval window (p. 168)
11. place (p. 168)
12. frequency (p. 168)
13. volleys (p. 168)
14. temporal (169)
15. similarity (p. 169)
16. expectations (p. 169)

EVALUATING YOUR PROGRESS

1. B, Correct (p. 166)
   A. Wrong. Intensity relates to amplitude.
   C. Wrong. Location is signaled by inter-ear differences in the input.
   D. Wrong. A sound's purity is reflected in its waveform, not its frequency.

2. C, Correct (p. 166)
   A. Wrong. The semicircular canals contain vestibular receptors, not auditory receptors.
   B. Wrong. The tympanic membrane is the eardrum. It transmits sound but has no receptors.
   D. Wrong. The incus is one of the bones in the middle ear. It does not contain receptors.

3. C, Correct (p. 167)
   A. Wrong. The impulse is generated in the cochlea, not the eardrum (which has no neurotransmitters).
   B. Wrong. These push against the oval window of the cochlea, not the eardrum.
   D. Wrong. The fluid movement, not its chemistry, is involved in generating the impulse.

4. A, Correct (p. 166)

   B. Wrong. The membrane in the cochlea discussed in your text is the basilar membrane.

   C. Wrong. There are inner and outer hair cells, but not malleus hair cells, incus hair cells, etc.

   D. Wrong. The malleus, incus, and stapes are physical structures in the ear.

5. D, Correct (p. 168)

   A. Wrong. This corresponds to the frequency theory of pitch perception.

   B. Wrong. Impulses are all-or-none, remember? They vary in number, but not strength.

   C. Wrong. Number might relate to intensity, but not to pitch and the place theory.

6. C, Correct (p. 169)A, B, D. Wrong. These are true. However, top-down processing *is* very important in auditory perception.

7. A, Correct (p. 170)

   B, D. Wrong. Pitch (frequency) helps in auditory organization, but not in localization.

   C. Wrong. Top-down processing usually is not a major factor in auditory localization.

THE SKIN AND BODY SENSES: FROM TOUCH TO MOVEMENT (PP. 170-174)

MASTERING THE CONCEPTS

1. temperature (p. 171)
2. somatosensory (p. 171)
3. changes (p. 172)
4. pain (p. 172)
5. cognitive (p. 173)
6. spinal cord (p. 173)
7. endorphins (p. 173)
8. Kinesthesia (p. 173)
9. joints (p. 173)
10. vestibular (p. 174)
11. semicircular (p. 174)

EVALUATING YOUR PROGRESS

1. A, Correct (p. 171)

   B. Wrong. Electromagnetic energy is the stimulus for vision.

   C. Wrong. Endorphins are released in the brain, not the skin, and they reduce pain sensations.

   D. Wrong. Chemical changes are the stimuli for the chemical senses of taste and smell.

2. C, Correct (p. 173)

   A. Wrong. The free nerve endings often carry pain input, but they are not the location of the gate.

   B. Wrong. The tympanic membrane is part of the auditory system, not the pain system.

   D. Wrong. Pain input is processed in the somatosensory cortex, but it is not the gate's location.

3. B, Correct (p. 173)

   A. Wrong. No receptors are located in the cortex. The cortex does not contact the environment.

   C. Wrong. The semicircular canals have the receptors for the vestibular, not kinesthetic, system.

   D. Wrong. The cochlea contains the receptors for audition, not kinesthesia.

4. A, Correct (p. 174)

   B. Wrong. The semicircular canals are not touch receptors.

   C. Wrong. The semicircular canals signal movement, not temperature.

   D. Wrong. The semicircular canals are signal movement, not pain.

5. D, Correct (p. 174)

   A, B, C. Wrong. The semicircular canals are in the inner ear, very near the cochlea.

THE CHEMICAL SENSES: SMELL AND TASTE (PP. 174-177)

MASTERING THE CONCEPTS

1. chemoreceptors (p. 175)
2. olfactory bulb (p. 175)
3. sexual (p. 176)
4. taste buds (p. 176)
5. four (p. 176)

EVALUATING YOUR PROGRESS

1. C, Correct (p. 175)
   A. Wrong. Vestibular sacs are part of the vestibular system for motion and posture sensation.
   B. Wrong. Free nerve endings are usually associated with pain perception.
   D. Wrong. Mechanoreceptors respond to the mechanical stimuli for touch.
2. C, Correct (p. 176)
   A. Wrong. Perfumes do not necessarily have a predictable, specific effect on an organism.
   B. Wrong. Papillae are the bumps on the tongue that contain the taste buds.
   D. Wrong. Endorphins are brain chemicals that function as natural pain killers.
3. C, Correct (p. 176)
   A. Wrong. The receptors, taste cells, are found in taste buds, which are in the papillae.
   B. Wrong. Although some have argued for a fifth basic taste, four is the most widely accepted number.
   D. Wrong. Although a single receptor may respond more strongly to one taste than another, it does not respond exclusively to one.

FROM THE PHYSICAL TO THE PSYCHOLOGICAL (PP. 177-180)

MASTERING THE CONCEPTS

1. absolute (p. 178)
2. signal detection (p. 178)
3. false alarms (p. 178)
4. noticeable (p. 179)
5. proportion (p. 179)
6. adaptation (p. 180)

EVALUATING YOUR PROGRESS

1. A, Correct (p. 178)
   B. Wrong. Psychophysics focuses on stimulus energy and the perceptual result, not receptor activity.
   C. Wrong. Psychophysics focuses on stimulus energy and the perceptual result, not neural pathways.
   D. Wrong. This describes perceptual constancy, not psychophysics.
2. A, Correct (p. 178)
   B. Wrong. This is a definition of the difference threshold.
   C. Wrong. This is the pain threshold and involves a very intense stimulus.
   D. Wrong. Absolute threshold does not represent the upper range of perception.
3. D, Correct (p. 178)
   A. Wrong. Adaptation is reduced sensitivity due to constant stimulation. This does not address bias.
   B. Wrong. Weber's Law predicts just noticeable differences, not sensitivity vs. bias.
   C. Wrong. Transduction deals with production of neural activity, not psychophysical measurement.

4. C, Correct (p. 180)
   A. Wrong. Weber's Law involves difference thresholds, not changes in perceived intensity over time.
   B. Wrong. Signal detection theory considers sensitivity and bias in detection responses. It would not predict loss of sensitivity over time.
   D. Wrong. Perceptual constancy produces a constant perception, not a reduction in sensitivity.

MAKING FINAL PREPARATIONS

SHORT ESSAY QUESTIONS

1. Full dark adaptation requires approximately 20-25 minutes and involves regeneration of photopigments in the rods and cones. Cones adapt quickly, reaching their potential within 3-4 minutes. Adaptation does not increase further until eight minutes into the period when the sensitivity of rods equals and surpasses that of cones. This creates the "break" in the adaptation curve. Rods continue to adapt until 20-25 minutes into the adaptation period. (pp. 149-150)
2. Rods are long, slender visual receptors that are located outside the fovea. They are very sensitive to light but provide poor acuity and no color vision. Cones are short, thick, and pointed and are located in the fovea, and with less density in the periphery. They allow good acuity and are important for color perception, but require a relatively high level of light to operate. (p. 148)
3. Expectancy influences interpretation of the stimulus, especially in cases of incomplete or ambiguous sensory information. It provides a guide for organizing ambiguous input, as in the case of many auditory stimuli, or for identification of other ambiguous stimuli. (pp. 157; 169, 178)
4. Perceptual constancy is the unchanging perception of a stimulus even though the physical characteristics of the stimulus change. As an object moves away, its image shrinks. Instead of perceiving the object as shrinking, it is seen as a constant size due to the utilization of other information concerning size and distance. Constancy is adaptive. It prevents a constantly shifting world composed of unstable objects and relationships. (pp. 161-162)
5. The perception of size depends in part on depth perception. Image size, one cue to object size, changes depending on the distance of the object. Thus, in perceiving size, the image is evaluated in relation to the object's depth. If depth is misjudged, size perception is often inaccurate. (pp. 162-163)
6. Place theory states that different pitches stimulate neurons at different places along the basilar membrane. The frequency principle states that a high pitch causes neurons to fire very rapidly, whereas a low pitch produces a lower firing rate. Both are used because place information is not as specific as necessary, and the frequency principle is limited by the refractory period, creating problems for high frequency perception. (p. 168)

7. Auditory localization relies on inter-ear differences in stimulus intensity and arrival time. If only the left windows are open the sound will reach the left ear first and at greater intensity than the right because the sound will come in primarily through the left window, even if the source is to the right. This will result in localization of the sound source to the left in most cases. (p. 170)

MATCHING

1. j (p. 150)
2. n (p. 176)
3. g (p. 150)
4. o (p. 179)
5. l (p. 157)
6. a (p. 167)
7. k (p. 148)
8. h (p. 172)
9. d (p. 175)
10. m (p. 150)
11. e (p. 174)
12. b (p. 149)
13. i (p. 145)
14. f (p. 178)
15. c (p. 147)
16. p (p. 176)

MULTIPLE CHOICE PRETEST 1

1. D, Correct (p. 146)

   A. Wrong. The retina is the surface onto which light is focused. It doesn't focus the light itself.

   B. Wrong. The optic chiasm is a cross-over point in the neural pathway, not a structure in the eye.

   C. Wrong. The iris is the colored part of the eye. It does not focus light.

2. C, Correct (p. 146)

   A. Wrong. Dark adaptation is a function of photopigment production, and the lens is not involved.

   B. Wrong. The size of receptive fields is determined by neural connections, not the way light is focused.

   D. Wrong. Acuity, at least for near vision, *decreases* when the lens loses flexibility.

3. B, Correct (p. 148)

   A. Wrong. Cones provide the best acuity. Rods provide greater sensitivity to light.

   C. Wrong. Cones work best in bright light. Rods are most active in low light conditions.

   D. Wrong. Rods are not important for color vision; cones are.

4. A, Correct (p. 150)

   B. Wrong. The "break" is due to photopigment regeneration differences, not pupil size.

   C. Wrong. The optic chiasm is a location in the neural pathway. It does not open or close.

   D. Wrong. Cone photopigments fully adapt prior to the break. Rod photopigments continue, however.

5. B, Correct (p.154)

   A. Wrong. Opponent process theory emphasizes the opposite neural responses, not differences in photopigment response.

   C. Wrong. Frequency theory is a pitch perception theory, not a color vision theory.

   D. Wrong. Top-down processing refers to the use of knowledge or context for interpretation.

6. C, Correct (p. 158)

   A. Wrong. Biederman's theory is based on simple component structures, not feature detectors.

   B. Wrong. Biederman's theory is based on simple component structures, not context or knowledge.

   D. Wrong. Biederman's theory is based on simple component structures, not depth cues.

7. B, Correct (p. 160)

   A. Wrong. Convergence is the angle of the two eyes, not a difference in image location.

   C. Wrong. Linear perspective is a monocular cue, not a binocular cue like the one described.

   D. Wrong. Accommodation is a change in lens' shape that produces a focused image.

8. B, Correct (pp. 162-163)

   A. Wrong. These illusions reflect depth perception errors, not figure-ground ambiguity.

   C. Wrong. Binocular disparity is either unavailable (peephole view) or normal, not reversed.

   D. Wrong. Top-down processing contributes to the illusions (e.g., expect rectangular room).

9. D, Correct (p. 161)

   A. Wrong. Convergence is the angle of the eyes. The key here is motion from stationary flashing lights.

   B. Wrong. Sensory adaptation is reduced sensitivity to repeated stimulation, not a cue for motion.

   C. Wrong. The volley principle is related to pitch perception, not motion perception.

10. D, Correct (pp. 157-158)

    A. Wrong. These are Gestalt principles and are not dependent on knowledge or expectancy.

    B. Wrong. These are Gestalt principles of visual perception.

    C. Wrong. These are Gestalt principles of perceptual organization, not depth cues.

11. A, Correct (p. 168)

    B. Wrong. Gate control is a theory of pain. Basilar membrane movement relates to pitch perception.

    C. Wrong. Trichromatic theory is a color perception theory. Basilar membrane relates to hearing.

    D. Wrong. Frequency theory emphasizes the correspondence of firing rate and frequency, not different stimulation at different locations due to different movement patterns of the membrane.

12. C, Correct (p. 168)

    A. Wrong. In the frequency theory, neural firing rate is critical, not patterns of membrane movement.

    B. Wrong. Frequency theory does not propose certain hair cells respond only to certain frequencies.

    D. Wrong. Frequency theory emphasizes firing rate, not which or how many neurons are firing.

13. A, Correct (p. 172)

    B. Wrong. There is no specific firing rate for cold.

    C. Wrong. The key is changing skin temperature, not stimulus temperature.

    D. Wrong. Papillae are part of the taste system.

14. D, Correct (p. 173)

    A. Wrong. The olfactory receptors are in the nasal cavities.

    B. Wrong. The vestibular receptors are in the semicircular canals and vestibular sacs.

    C. Wrong. The gustatory receptors are in the tongue and mouth.

15. A, Correct (p. 174)

    B. Wrong. Problems with the cochlea or basilar membrane would affect hearing.

    C. Wrong. Problems with the tympanic membrane or pinna would affect hearing.

    D. Wrong. These are brain areas important for vision, not areas involved with the vestibular sense.

16. A, Correct (p. 173)

    B. Wrong. Pheromones produce a set response, such as approaching the source of the pheromone.

    C. Wrong. Abnormal stimulation of the vestibular system produces dizziness or nausea.

    D. Wrong. Endorphins are important in the body senses, not in vision.

17. C, Correct (pp. 175-176)

    A, B, D. Wrong. These are true, but there are over 1000 kinds of olfactory receptors, not four.

18. C, Correct (p. 177)

    A. Wrong. The occipital lobe receives visual input. Taste input goes to the somatosensory cortex.

    B. Wrong. The olfactory bulb receive olfactory (smell) input, not taste input.

    D. Wrong. The somatosensory area is in the parietal lobe and receives taste input.

19. C, Correct (p. 178)

    A. Wrong. Weber's Law predicts difference thresholds based on original stimulus intensity.

    B. Wrong. False alarms in signal detection theory represent cases in which a stimulus is "detected" even though no stimulus was presented.

    D. Wrong. The difference threshold is the minimum change in energy that can be detected.

20. B, Correct (p. 178)
    A. Wrong. This is a hit.
    C. Wrong. This is a miss.
    D. Wrong. This is a correct rejection.

MULTIPLE CHOICE PRETEST 2

1. A, Correct (p. 151)
   B, C, D. Wrong. Although there are feature detectors for these characteristics, they are not side by side with the line detectors. Line detectors vary by preferred orientation.
2. B, Correct (p. 157)
   A. Wrong. The key is the different expectations. Recognition by components doesn't address that.
   C. Wrong. The key is the different expectations, and that is not part of the Gestalt principles.
   D. Wrong. The key is the different expectations, not the translation of the stimulus to neural energy.
3. A, Correct (p. 146)
   B. Wrong. Accommodation is a change in lens thickness. This answer describes dark adaptation.
   C. Wrong. Accommodation is a change in lens thickness. This answer describes Gestalt laws.
   D. Wrong. Accommodation is a change in lens thickness. It has nothing to do with the blind spot.
4. C, Correct (p. 158)
   A. Wrong. Closure involves filling in gaps. The key here was the two moving differently than the rest.
   B. Wrong. Good continuation involves keeping intersected objects intact. The key here was the two moving differently than the rest.
   D. Wrong. Proximity involves grouping objects that are close to each other. The key here was the two moving differently than the rest.
5. D, Correct (p. 148)
   A. Wrong. Adaptation is slower for rods, which are all outside the fovea.
   B. Wrong. Retinal disparity is a depth cue and does not relate to sensitivity.
   C. Wrong. Acuity is better in the cone-dense fovea, but that is not relevant here. Sensitivity is key.
6. D, Correct (p. 154)
   A. Wrong. Having one type of rod is normal, and rods don't provide color vision anyway.
   B. Wrong. Color blindness of this sort is a receptor problem, not a neural one, in essentially all cases.
   C. Wrong. Having no cones at all would eliminate all color vision, not just red and green vision.
7. A, Correct (p. 156)
   B. Wrong. This is the opposite relationship.
   C, D. Wrong. Primary colors and other colors are processed and perceived in the same way.
8. D, Correct (pp. 157-160)
   A, C. Wrong. Monocular cues like these would be still be available. Ed lost the use of binocular cues.
   B. Wrong. Common fate is not a depth cue.
9. B, Correct (pp. 166-167)
   A. Wrong. The pinna is in the outer ear. Hair cells are in the cochlea.
   C. Wrong. The auditory receptors, hair cells, are located in the cochlea, not in the semicircular canals.
   D. Wrong. The tympanic membrane is the eardrum, whereas hair cells are in the cochlea.
10. C, Correct (p. 163)
    A, B. Wrong. Shape constancy is not involved (both are square). This involves size constancy.
    D. Wrong. A distant object must be larger than a near object in order to cast the same size image.

11. B, Correct (p. 168)
    A. Wrong. Frequency theory is based on firing rate, not which neurons are firing, so this is not a problem.
    C. Wrong. Opponent process theory involves color vision, not audition.
    D. Wrong. Gate control is a pain theory, not a theory of auditory perception.
12. C, Correct (p. 169)
    A, B, D. Wrong. These are all true, but the auditory cortex is located in the temporal, not parietal, lobes.
13. A, Correct (p. 170)
    B. Wrong. Pitch is a function of frequency, not inter-ear timing differences.
    C. Wrong. Intensity is a function of the sound wave's amplitude, not of inter-ear timing differences.
    D. Wrong. Meaning is influenced by the sound's physical characteristics and several top-down factors, but not by inter-ear timing differences.
14. A, Correct (p. 172)
    B, C, D. Wrong. These are all true. However, the size of the cortical area that processes input from the skin is proportional to the sensitivity of the body part, not its size.
15. A, Correct (p. 173)
    B. Wrong. Bottom-up processing emphasizes stimulus characteristics, so his pain should equal yours.
    C. Wrong. Frequency theory is a theory of pitch perception, not pain perception.
    D. Wrong. More endorphins would reduce pain more. The key here is cognitive or context factors.
16. B, Correct (p. 175)
    A. Wrong. The olfactory bulb processes olfactory input, but does not control emotion or motivation.
    C. Wrong. The somatosensory cortex is not involved in these motivational or emotional behaviors.
    D. Wrong. Olfaction is the only sense that does not include the thalamus in its neural path.
17. B, Correct (p. 179)
    A. Wrong. The absolute threshold would indicate the number of raisins detectable in cereal, not whether a change is detectable.
    C. Wrong. Signal detection theory does not use thresholds.
    D. Wrong. This relates to the detection of raisins, not the detection of differences in raisin number.
18. D, Correct (p. 176)
    A. Wrong. The neural code for taste is probably the activity profile across many neurons.
    B. Wrong. The idea of four basic tastes is most accepted, with some argument for a possible 5th.
    C. Wrong. Flavor involves taste, smell, and the entire psychological experience that accompanies eating.
19. A, Correct (p. 179)
    B, C, D. Wrong. Weber's law states that the just noticeable difference is a constant proportion of the magnitude of the original (standard) stimulus. That is, the greater the stimulus, the larger the absolute change required for detection. Tom weighs least, so he can lose fewer pounds than the others and the change will be noticed.
20. C, Correct (p. 178)
    A. Wrong. Signal detection theory does not measure absolute threshold or difference threshold.
    B. Wrong. Both signal detection and threshold procedures can be used in all senses.
    D. Wrong. Neither signal detection theory nor threshold methods involve finding active brain areas.

CHAPTER **6**

CONSCIOUSNESS

ESTABLISHING LEARNING GOALS

Use these learning goals as a preview of the chapter, a guide for active reading, and to evaluate your mastery of the material. Review the relevant goals as you begin and end your reading of each major section of the chapter.

I. Explain how priorities for mental functioning are established.

   A. Define attention and discuss its adaptive value.

   B. Explain how experiments on dichotic listening can be used to study attention.

   C. Describe automaticity and its effects on awareness.
      1. Explain how automaticity is identified.
      2. Define subliminal, and discuss whether subliminal messages affect behavior.

   D. Describe such disorders as visual neglect and attention deficit/hyperactivity disorder.

II. Describe the characteristics of sleep and sleep's adaptive function.

   A. Define biological rhythms, and discuss how they are controlled.

   B. Describe the various stages and characteristics of sleep.

   C. Discuss the function and adaptive significance of sleep.
      1. Differentiate the restorative and survival views of sleep.
      2. Describe the consequences of sleep deprivation.

   D. Discuss the function of REM sleep and theories of dreaming.
      1. Describe Freud's wish fulfillment theory of dreams.
      2. Describe the activation-synthesis hypothesis of dreams.

   E. Describe the various sleep disorders.

III. Discuss how consciousness can be altered biochemically.

   A. Compare neurotransmitters with psychoactive drugs.

   B. Discuss the different categories of psychoactive drugs, with examples of each.
      1. Describe the effects of each category of drug.
      2. Identify the method of action of each category of drug.

   C. Discuss the psychological factors that influence the effects of psychoactive drugs.

IV. Discuss how consciousness can be altered without drugs.

A. Describe the physiological and behavioral effects of hypnosis.

B. Discuss whether hypnosis can be used effectively to enhance memory.

C. Describe the dissociation and role-playing accounts of hypnosis.

D. Describe the physical, behavioral, and psychological effects of meditation.

MASTERING THE MATERIAL

PREVIEW & SETTING PRIORITIES FOR MENTAL FUNCTIONING: ATTENTION (PP. 187-196)

MASTERING THE VOCABULARY

Define or explain each of the following terms.

1. consciousness
2. attention
3. dichotic listening
4. cocktail party effect
5. automaticity
6. visual neglect
7. attention deficit/hyperactivity disorder

MASTERING THE CONCEPTS

Fill in the blanks to create a summary of the section.

Consciousness is the subjective [1] ____________ of internal and external events. By directing [2] ____________ to only some things, the organism sets priorities for mental function, protects mental resources and improves functioning. However, as the [3] ____________ effect and [4] ____________ listening experiments show, unattended input is monitored to some extent, and important input does affect behavior. One's name is recognized, and attention unconsciously follows a message continued in the unattended ear. Divided attention tasks show that [5] ____________ can develop for some highly practiced tasks, limiting conscious awareness of that task and freeing resources for other tasks. Stimuli that do not reach conscious awareness can influence behavior, but it is not clear whether the [6] ____________ (below threshold) messages supposedly embedded in advertising and self-help tapes even exist or are effective. In some cases, there is no evidence embedded messages are present, and controlled studies often find no influence of subliminal messages on behavior beyond that accounted for by a [7] ____________ effect.

Right (and sometimes left) parietal lobe damage can cause [8] ____________ , a disorder in which there is no conscious awareness of the left visual field, although input is processed. The inability to maintain or control attention, [9] ____________ disorder, affects many children. The cause is unknown, but the drug Ritalin often helps reduce the worst symptoms of the disorder. Nondrug treatments also can be beneficial, and there is concern that the disorder might be overdiagnosed.

EVALUATING YOUR PROGRESS

Select the best response. If you make any errors, reread the relevant material before proceeding.

1. In which procedure do subjects shadow (repeat) the message in one ear while ignoring the message in the other ear?
   a. visual neglect
   b. spotlighting
   c. dichotic listening
   d. subliminal embedding

2. The cocktail party effect and Treisman's "ear-switching" experiment demonstrate that
   a. right parietal lobe brain damage disrupts basic attentional mechanisms.
   b. highly practiced tasks require less attention than less well-practiced tasks.
   c. when more than one message is presented, neither message is understood well.
   d. an unattended message is monitored for important content.

3. A task that can be performed rapidly, effortlessly and without focused attention is considered a(n)
   a. automatic process.
   b. controlled process.
   c. split brain process.
   d. dissociated process.

4. A loss of awareness of the contents of one half of the visual field is known as
   a. visual neglect.
   b. attention deficit/hyperactivity disorder.
   c. hypnotic dissociation.
   d. split world disorder.

5. A subliminal message is a message that
   a. motivates you to behave in a certain way.
   b. is extremely appealing and pleasant.
   c. cannot be consciously detected.
   d. reduces your attention to the main message.

6. A disorder of attention commonly found in children and that involves an inability to maintain attention is
   a. ADHD.
   b. visual neglect.
   c. Ritalin deficit disorder.
   d. dichoticism.

SLEEPING AND DREAMING (PP. 197-207)

MASTERING THE VOCABULARY

Define or explain each of the following terms.

1. circadian rhythms
2. biological clocks
3. alpha waves
4. theta waves
5. delta activity
6. REM
7. REM rebound
8. manifest content
9. latent content
10. activation-synthesis hypothesis
11. dyssomnias
12. insomnia
13. hypersomnia
14. narcolepsy
15. parasomnias
16. nightmares
17. night terrors
18. sleepwalking

MASTERING THE CONCEPTS.

Fill in the blanks to create a summary of the section.

Sleep, an altered state of consciousness, is an example of a biological rhythm. Because sleep-waking has a 24-hour cycle, it is a [1] ____________ rhythm. The suprachiasmatic nucleus of the [2] ____________ may be the [3] ____________ clock for the sleep cycle, with light playing a key role in pacing the clock.

Brain EEG patterns vary in [4] ____________ , [5] ____________ , and regularity during sleep. Alpha waves are found during relaxation. Stage 1 sleep has mostly [6] ____________ waves. Irregular EEG patterns called sleep [7] ____________ and K-complexes occur in Stage 2 sleep. The deeper sleep of Stages 3 and 4 has slower, synchronous waves called [8] ____________ activity. The EEG of REM sleep has an irregular pattern similar to a waking state, but the person is deeply asleep. Thus, REM sleep is called [9] ____________ sleep. If awakened in REM sleep, people usually report they were [10] ____________ . Complete sleep cycles last about [11] ____________ and are repeated. The length of REM increases with each cycle. The function of sleep is unclear, but it may be restorative or a protective, adaptive response to light-dark cycles and past predators. Sleep deprivation leads to poor functioning.

The function of REM sleep is unclear. REM deprivation has only small psychological effects, but it does lead to REM [12] ____________ , increased REM sleep the next night, and it may impair learning. Freud proposed the dreams of REM sleep are a means for [13] ____________ fulfillment and reflect the contents of the unconscious mind. A dream's manifest content is the actual images of the dream, but the [14] ____________ content is its hidden meaning. According to the [15] ____________ -synthesis hypothesis, dreams are the brain's interpretation of random activity. REM sleep occurs in many species and in the prenatal period.

Sleep disorders are classified as dyssomnias or parasomnias. Dyssomnias, troubles in timing, quality, or quantity of sleep, include [16] ____________ , a problem getting to sleep or staying asleep, and hypersomnia, excessive sleepiness. In the rare disorder of [17] ____________ , there is a sudden onset of sleep and immediate entry into REM sleep. Parasomnias, abnormal events during sleep, include nightmares, [18] ____________ , and sleepwalking. Nightmares are REM dreams, but night terrors and sleepwalking occur in non-REM sleep.

EVALUATING YOUR PROGRESS

Select the best response. If you miss any questions, reread the relevant material before proceeding.

1. The suprachiasmatic nucleus of the hypothalamus is though to play an important role in
   a. the shift from REM to non-REM sleep.
   b. initiating sleepwalking.
   c. the control of circadian rhythms.
   d. regulating the sequence of the stages of sleep.

2. Based on EEG activity, researchers divide non-REM sleep into
   a. 2 stages.
   b. 3 stages.
   c. 4 stages.
   d. 5 stages.

3. REM sleep is called paradoxical sleep because
   a. it is the shortest stage of sleep, but it is the most necessary.
   b. dreams with complex plots are likely, but they are usually colorless.
   c. dreams are very likely to occur, but the brain waves are the slowest, highest amplitude type.
   d. the brain waves are similar to those of a waking state, but the person is very deeply asleep.

4. Which is true?
   a. Most people cycle through REM sleep about twice each night.
   b. More time is spent in REM sleep near morning than in the first hours of sleep.
   c. When people are awakened from REM sleep, they report dreaming about 30% of the time.
   d. REM stands for "restore energy mode."

5. The survival theory of why we sleep suggests that
   a. because we rely on vision, sleeping at night had the adaptive value of keeping us safe.
   b. without sleep our neurotransmitters would be depleted and we couldn't function.
   c. sleep is needed to restore psychological balance through dreaming.
   d. sleep is needed to resynchronize the various biological clocks so they do not drift.

6. Which of the following is classified as a parasomnia?
   a. insomnia
   b. night terrors
   c. narcolepsy
   d. hypersomnia

7. Freud proposed that we dream
   a. for wish fulfillment and to deal with highly disturbing desires.
   b. because we try to interpret the random brain activity generated during sleep.
   c. because we need to restore the supply of brain neurotransmitters.
   d. in order to solve the problems that arose during the day.

8. Night terrors usually
   a. indicate a serious psychological problem.
   b. indicate a serious medical problem.
   c. are most common in REM sleep.
   d. end by adolescence.

9. The inability to get to sleep or to stay asleep is
   a. hypersomnia.
   b. insomnia.
   c. sleep apnea.
   d. narcolepsy.

ALTERING AWARENESS: PSYCHOACTIVE DRUGS (PP. 207-213)

MASTERING THE VOCABULARY

Define or explain each of the following terms.

1. psychoactive
2. tolerance
3. drug dependency
4. withdrawal
5. depressants
6. stimulants
7. opiates
8. hallucinogens

MASTERING THE CONCEPTS

Fill in the blanks to create a summary of the section.

[1] ____________ drugs affect mental processes, consciousness, and behavior. These drugs mimic, block, or increase [2] ____________ activity. Long-term use may cause drug dependency, but the underlying cause is unclear. Drug [3] ____________ can develop, requiring higher doses for an effect, and if drug use ends, withdrawal occurs.

There are four categories of psychoactive drugs. [4] ____________ slow nervous system activity, and include alcohol, barbiturates, and tranquilizers. They increase GABA activity (also dopamine for alcohol), which reduces anxiety, but they can lead to dependency. [5] ____________ , like caffeine, nicotine, amphetamines, cocaine, and MDMA (Ecstasy), increase neural activity and improve alertness and mood temporarily. The effects of amphetamines and cocaine are due to increased norepinephrine and dopamine activity, with [6] ____________ key to producing positive feelings. [7] ____________ , including morphine, opium, and heroin, elevate mood by depressing nervous system activity, and are likely to cause dependence. [8] ____________ , or psychedelics, include LSD, mescaline, psilocybin, and [9] ____________ and are likely to produce alteration of perception. LSD seems to mimic serotonin. Side effects include "bad trips," "flashbacks," and impaired concentration or coordination. Drug effects depend on the user's environment, [10] ____________ , physical condition, and familiarity with the drug.

EVALUATING YOUR PROGRESS

Select the best response. If you miss any questions, reread the relevant material before proceeding.

1. With long-term use of some drugs, a higher dose is required to achieve the same effect as occurred initially. This describes
   a. withdrawal.
   b. dependency.
   c. rebound.
   d. tolerance.

2. Which drug is incorrectly assigned to a drug category?
   a. heroin---opiate
   b. diazepam (Valium)---depressant
   c. MDMA (Ecstasy)---hallucinogen
   d. alcohol---depressant

3. The neurotransmitter GABA is involved in the psychoactive effects of
   a. alcohol.
   b. heroin.
   c. amphetamines.
   d. LSD.

4. The effects of a psychoactive drug are determined by
   a. the user's expectations.
   b. how the drug affects brain neurotransmitters.
   c. the environment in which the drug is taken.
   d. all of the above.

ALTERING AWARENESS: INDUCED STATES (PP. 213-217)

MASTERING THE VOCABULARY

Define or explain each of the following terms.

1. hypnosis
2. hypnotic hypermnesia
3. hypnotic dissociation
4. meditation

MASTERING THE CONCEPTS

Fill in the blanks to create a summary of the section.

Hypnosis is a social interaction resulting in a heightened state of [1] ____________ . A technique is to suggest the person is getting very relaxed and [2] ____________ as the person fixates on an object. Hypnosis has assisted in ending unwanted habits and reducing [3] ____________ during medical procedures. Evidence that hypnosis produces hypermnesia, improved [4] ____________ , is poor.

Hilgard suggests that hypnosis involves hypnotic [5] ____________ , a splitting of consciousness into separate parts: a part that acts on the hypnotist's suggestions, and a [6] ____________ observer with normal awareness. An alternative is that hypnosis involves social [7] ____________ ; the subject simply tries to please the hypnotist and acts the hypnotized role. Simulated subjects research and the influence of the subject's expectations [8] ____________ about hypnosis support this view.

[9] ____________ , a way to self-induce shifts in awareness, is sometimes described as "pure thought" and often involves [10] ____________ paired with focused concentration on breathing or a mantra to help clear the mind. Research shows meditation reduces arousal and increases [11] ____________ brain waves, both common to relaxation, and it may help reduce anxiety.

EVALUATING YOUR PROGRESS

Select the best response. If you miss any questions, reread the relevant material before proceeding.

1. The individual credited with performing a form of hypnosis in 1783 was
   a. Ernest Hilgard.
   b. Timothy Leary.
   c. Sigmund Freud.
   d. Anton Mesmer.

2. Your text describes hypnosis as
   a. a sleep-like state of consciousness.
   b. a heightened state of suggestibility.
   c. "pure" thought
   d. self-induced state of focused concentration.

3. Hilgard's "hidden observer" experiments are used to provide evidence for
   a. age regression.
   b. social role playing.
   c. hypnotic hypermnesia.
   d. hypnotic dissociation.

4. The results of the simulated subjects research suggests
   a. meditation produces a unique physiological state.
   b. mediation is useful for reducing anxiety.
   c. hypnosis involves dissociation of consciousness.
   d. hypnosis involves role-playing.

5. The most positive benefit of meditation is its ability to
   a. enhance memory for long-forgotten events.
   b. produce a state of relaxation.
   c. increase physiological arousal.
   d. increase theta waves.

MAKING FINAL PREPARATIONS

Complete these sections without consulting your book or notes. For a more accurate estimate of how well you know this material, wait at least a day or two after studying the chapter before working on the questions. Some of the material you "know" immediately after working with the chapter will be quickly forgotten. Exercises done too soon after studying will overestimate what you know well.

SHORT ESSAY QUESTIONS

Write a brief answer to each question.

1. Discuss why the development of automaticity is adaptive.

2. Cite the data that show that unattended information is not completely ignored.

3. Describe the effects of sleep deprivation.

4. Explain why the effects of psychoactive drugs can vary from person to person or from time to time.

5. Cite the evidence supporting the social role playing view of hypnosis.

6. Discuss the idea that stimuli that do not reach conscious awareness can influence behavior.

MATCHING

Select the correct definition or description for each item.

1. _______ circadian rhythms
2. _______ dependency
3. _______ attention
4. _______ parasomnia
5. _______ manifest content
6. _______ alpha waves
7. _______ biological clock
8. _______ withdrawal
9. _______ dichotic listening task
10. _______ consciousness
11. _______ hypnotic hypermnesia
12. _______ K-complexes
13. _______ REM rebound
14. _______ mantra
15. _______ synesthesia
16. _______ dyssomnias

a. blending of sensory experiences
b. actual images and events in a dream
c. physical symptom caused by cessation of drug use
d. brain mechanism that controls bodily function cycles
e. brain waves found in Stage 2
f. biological cycles of approximately 24-hours
g. spending more time in REM after REM deprivation
h. particular sound or words used during meditation
i. selective attention task
j. internal process that sets mental function priorities
k. problems of timing or duration of sleep
l. subjective awareness of internal and external events
m. abnormal disturbances during sleep
n. brain waves associated with relaxed state
o. a physical or psychological need, often for a drug
p. memory enhancement with hypnosis

MULTIPLE CHOICE PRETEST 1

Select the one best response.

1. Automaticity is evaluated by comparing single task performance with a two-task situation known as a
   a. divided attention task.
   b. ear-switching task.
   c. dichotic listening task.
   d. hidden observer task.

2. When someone said your name across the room, your attention shifted immediately from the TV news you had been intently watching, to that conversation. This is most similar to
   a. shadowing.
   b. auditory neglect.
   c. the cocktail party effect.
   d. attentional rebound.

3. Zack appears to have no consciousness of anything that is in the left half of the visual field. Zack probably has brain damage located in
   a. the cerebellum.
   b. the occipital lobes.
   c. the hindbrain.
   d. the right hemisphere.

4. Based on the research of Vokey & Read (1985), what effect will subliminally embedded "sex" have on memory for pictures?
   a. Recognition memory will improve.
   b. Recognition memory will improve, but only if the pictures include people.
   c. Recognition memory will be reduced.
   d. Recognition memory will not differ.

5. Joe is impulsive, has difficulty sitting still, and switches from one activity to another without completing anything. Joe's behavior is most likely a result of
   a. attention deficit/hyperactivity disorder.
   b. narcolepsy.
   c. synesthesia.
   d. attentional neglect.

6. Which stage of sleep increases in length and frequency as the night progresses?
   a. REM
   b. Stage 2
   c. Stage 3
   d. Stage 4

7. REM sleep is associated with all of the following EXCEPT
   a. rapid eye movements.
   b. delta wave activity.
   c. dreaming.
   d. extremely relaxed muscle tone.

8. The EEG activity of Stage 2 sleep is characterized by
   a. fast, irregular waveforms.
   b. mostly delta waves.
   c. mostly alpha waves.
   d. K-complex waveforms.

9. Freud searched for the symbolic meaning of dreams. He described this symbolic aspect as
   a. the activation-synthesis hypothesis.
   b. the dissociation hypothesis.
   c. the dream's manifest content.
   d. the dream's latent content.

10. Su Chuen has sudden periods of extreme sleepiness when she will collapse and enter REM. This describes
    a. sleep apnea.
    b. insomnia.
    c. narcolepsy.
    d. hypermnesia.

11. The core idea in the activation-synthesis hypothesis is
    a. the interpretation of random brain activity.
    b. the splitting of consciousness into aware and unaware components.
    c. the adaptive value of restricting movements during dangerous periods.
    d. the brain or other physiological systems need time for repair or restoration.

12. Which of the following is an accurate summary of research on hypnosis and memory?
    a. All types of memory are improved by hypnosis, and this cannot be explained by other factors.
    b. Memory for recent events is improved by hypnosis, but memory for older events is not.
    c. Memory for very old events is improved by hypnosis, but memory for more recent events is not.
    d. There is little evidence from controlled research that indicates memory is enhanced by hypnosis.

13. Vic has used a drug that increases dopamine and enhances GABA activity. This drug probably is
    a. cocaine.
    b. heroin.
    c. alcohol.
    d. amphetamine.

14. Which of the following is most associated with opiate use?
    a. hallucinations
    b. pain reduction
    c. hypermnesia
    d. low risk of dependency

15. A rat will press a response bar hundreds of times if barpressing results in the administration of cocaine. Apparently the pleasurable and reinforcing aspects of the drug are due to cocaine's effect on
    a. endorphins.
    b. serotonin.
    c. dopamine.
    d. GABA.

16. Sid, a heroin addict, has not used heroin for over 24 hours. He is sweating, vomiting, and trembling. Sid's symptoms represent
    a. drug tolerance.
    b. drug dependency.
    c. withdrawal.
    d. synesthesia.

17. Meditation is defined as
    a. any form of social interaction that produces a heightened state of suggestibility.
    b. a blending of sensory experiences.
    c. self-induced manipulation of awareness.
    d. subjective awareness of internal and external events.

18. If Jill doesn't want to use drugs during childbirth, which of the following is another effective pain reduction technique she could try?
    a. meditation
    b. hypnosis
    c. REM deprivation therapy
    d. alpha wave therapy

MULTIPLE CHOICE PRETEST 2

Select the one best response.

1. The purpose of a dichotic listening task is to
    a. keep attention focused on one input.
    b. evaluate whether a behavior has reached automaticity.
    c. diagnose ADHD.
    d. test subliminal perception.

2. Which of the following is adaptive primarily because it establishes processing priorities?
    a. subliminal perception
    b. visual neglect
    c. attention
    d. activation-synthesis

3. The "burning house" research with visual neglect patients supports the idea that
    a. information not in consciousness may be processed and influence behavior.
    b. no processing occurs for even very important information if it is in the "neglected" region.
    c. automaticity develops with repeated exposure, even if presented in the "neglected" region.
    d. if important enough, stimuli in the neglected field will reach consciousness.

4. Keno was doing great in his driver's license road test until the officer started asking him questions. While replying, he scraped the curb and almost lost control. What conclusion is most likely?
    a. Keno probably has visual neglect.
    b. Keno probably has attention deficit disorder.
    c. Keno's driving is not yet automatic.
    d. The cocktail party effect may occur while driving.

5. Which is NOT an accurate summary of the subliminal perception research presented in your text?
   a. Stimuli that do not reach conscious awareness cannot influence behavior.
   b. The cause of the apparent success of subliminal self-help tapes is likely a placebo effect.
   c. Embedded words or images related to sex produce no improvements in memory or preferences.
   d. Some subliminal self-help tapes do not appear to have subliminal messages embedded in them.

6. REM sleep is often called "paradoxical" sleep because
   a. the sleeper's EEG is similar to that of a waking state, but the sleeper is very unresponsive.
   b. the sleeper's EEG is like that of deep sleep, but the sleeper is very responsive to external events.
   c. the eyes move rapidly during REM, but the heart rate and respiration rate are very low.
   d. research shows dreams are very common in REM, but the dreams are rarely remembered on awakening.

7. Jorge quits breathing and awakens gasping for breath many times each night. Jorge's problem is
   a. sleep apnea.
   b. narcolepsy.
   c. night terrors.
   d. insomnia.

8. The sleep spindles and K-complexes present in Lee's EEG a few minutes ago have been replaced by an increasing amount of delta activity. Lee has shifted from
   a. REM sleep to Stage 2 sleep.
   b. Stage 2 sleep to Stage 3 sleep.
   c. non-REM sleep to REM sleep.
   d. deep sleep to a near-waking state.

9. Which of the following is an accurate statement?
   a. Night terrors are the same as nightmares, but more intense.
   b. Night terrors typically occur in non-REM sleep.
   c. Night terrors are symptoms of significant psychological problems.
   d. Night terrors are most common after adolescence.

10. A rat's superchiasmic nucleus in the hypothlamus has been destroyed. What is a likely effect?
    a. attention deficit/hyperactivity disorder
    b. visual neglect
    c. problem with circadian rhythms
    d. hypermnesia

11. You dreamed about riding a train into a tunnel. Freud would most likely have suggested your dream
    a. is really about your need to fulfill an unacceptable wish or desire.
    b. is an attempt by your mind to solve a problem that arose during the last few days.
    c. is your brain's interpretation of the random neural activity generated during sleep.
    d. is an indication of a serious psychological disorder that should be treated.

12. Insomnia is an example of
    a. a circadian rhythm.
    b. parasomnia.
    c. dyssomnia.
    d. dissociation.

13. Which of the following is associated most with LSD use?
    a. pain reduction
    b. severe withdrawal symptoms
    c. very intense, but brief, effects
    d. synesthesia

14. Which of the following drugs is in the same general category as alcohol?
    a. barbiturates
    b. nicotine
    c. MDMA
    d. morphine

15. Frank is using a drug that increases the effectiveness of dopamine and norepinephrine. Fran most likely is using
    a. alcohol.
    b. heroin.
    c. LSD.
    d. an amphetamine.

16. Tito gets only a moderate effect from an amount of heroin that might kill a first-time user. This illustrates
    a. dependency.
    b. REM rebound.
    c. withdrawal.
    d. tolerance.

17. Ben feels his eyelids start to sag and he feels very relaxed as he stares at a coin on the table. He is willing to obey commands and might report reduced pain perception. Ben's highly suggestible state is due to
    a. hallucinogenic drugs.
    b. meditation.
    c. sleep deprivation.
    d. hypnosis.

18. If people are told prior to hypnosis that hypnosis causes rigidity of the arms, they are likely to show rigidity while hypnotized, even if rigidity is not part of any hypnotic suggestion. This supports the view that hypnosis is
    a. a dissociation of consciousness.
    b. due to an increase in alpha wave activity.
    c. a kind of social role playing.
    d. an acetylcholine (ACh) imbalance.

19. A hypnotized subject has submerged her hand in ice after being given the suggestion that she will feel little pain. Her "hidden observer" has been told to ring a bell to indicate what she (the hidden observer) feels. Based on Hilgard's research, if the person verbally reports a pain level of 4, the hidden observer will report a pain level of
    a. 0 -- hidden observers have no contact with the environment.
    b. 2 -- hidden observers react more strongly to hypnotic suggestions.
    c. 4 -- hidden observers perceive the same things the hypnotized person does.
    d. 8 -- hidden observers perceive what a non-hypnotized person perceives.

LANGUAGE DEVELOPMENT GUIDE

CORE TERMS

In the lectures on this chapter you may learn about ***illicit*** drugs -- that is, illegal drugs (the psychoactive drugs that are used to treat mental illnesses are discussed in chapter 15). You may learn about the ***deleterious*** (harmful) effects of these drugs on the brain, and about the effects of these drugs on a child ***in utero*** (in the uterus, before birth). You instructor might also share with you the ***prevalence*** of their use -- that is, how many people are thought to use them.

IDIOMS

p. 187	spring forth	suddenly appear
p. 189	heightened state of suggestibility	a state in which you are likely to do what you are told
p. 189	smorgasbord	a great feast or banquet; a wide and wonderful variety of choices
p. 190	a case in point	an example
p. 191	naïve	not sophisticated, not worldly or experienced
p. 192	in the realm of	within the world of; in the same area
p. 192	without a hitch	quite easily and without mistakes
p. 198	stay put	stay where they are
p. 198	play havoc with	make a mess of; badly confuse
p. 199	shrug off	not be affected by; take no notice of
p. 199	eavesdrop	to listen in secretly
p. 199	bears a striking similarity	seems very much like
p. 204	spontaneously activate	to start up completely on their own; suddenly
p. 209	is manifested	makes itself known; can be seen as

p. 211	particularly apt	especially appropriate
p. 212	euphoric	very happy and excited

PRONUNCIATION ASSISTANCE

dichotic (dy-kot′-ic) *p. 189*
circadian (sir-kay′-dee-in) *p. 197*
dyssomnia (dis-som′-nee-a) *p. 205*
hypnosis (hip-no′-sis) *p. 213*

SOLUTIONS

PREVIEW & SETTING PRIORITIES FOR MENTAL FUNCTIONING: ATTENTION (PP. 187-196)

MASTERING THE CONCEPTS

1. awareness (p. 187)
2. attention (p. 189)
3. cocktail party (p. 190)
4. dichotic (p. 189)
5. automaticity (p. 192)
6. subliminal (p. 193)
7. placebo (p. 194)
8. visual neglect (p. 194)
9. attention deficit (p. 195)

EVALUATING YOUR PROGRESS

1. C, Correct (p. 189)
   A. Wrong. Visual neglect is a neuropsychological disorder caused by parietal lobe damage.
   B. Wrong. Attention is often described as a spotlight, but there is no spotlight technique in research.
   D. Wrong. Subliminal refers to "below threshold." Input is not subliminal in the case described.
2. D, Correct (pp. 190-191)
   A. Wrong. The cocktail party and ear switching research deals with normal attention, not disorders.
   B. Wrong. This is true, but it does not relate to the selective attention experiments cited.
   C. Wrong. An attended message is well-processed, and the unattended message is at least monitored.
3. A, Correct (p. 192)
   B. Wrong. A controlled process requires controlled, conscious attention.
   C. Wrong. Automaticity does not imply that a single, isolated hemisphere is used for processing.
   D. Wrong. Dissociation is a splitting into parts. This is not required for automaticity.
4. A, Correct (p. 194)
   B. Wrong. Attention deficit disorder involves an inability to sustain or control attention.
   C. Wrong. Hypnotic dissociation is a splitting of consciousness with multiple forms of awareness.
   D. Wrong. Split world disorder is not an actual condition.
5. C, Correct (p. 192)
   A. Wrong. Subliminal does not relate to motivation, and such messages are not effective.
   B. Wrong. Subliminal does not relate to appeal. It relates to detection.
   D. Wrong. Subliminal does not relate to divided attention, and it does not reduce attention to a task.
6. A, Correct (p. 195)
   B. Wrong. Visual neglect, ignoring half of the visual field, is not common in children.
   C. Wrong. Ritalin is a drug used to treat ADHD. There is no Ritalin deficit disorder.
   D. Wrong. There is no disorder called dichoticism. A dichotic listening task is one way to study attention.

SLEEPING AND DREAMING (PP. 197-207)

MASTERING THE CONCEPTS.

1. circadian (p. 197)
2. hypothalamus (p. 197)
3. biological (p. 197)
4. height (p. 199)
5. frequency (p. 199)
6. theta (p. 199)
7. spindles (p. 200)
8. delta (p. 200)
9. paradoxical (p. 201)
10. dreaming (p. 201)
11. 90 minutes (p. 201)
12. rebound (p. 204)
13. wish (p. 204)
14. latent (p. 204)
15. activation (p. 204)
16. insomnia (p. 205)
17. narcolepsy (p. 206)
18. night terrors (p. 207)

EVALUATING YOUR PROGRESS

1. C, Correct (p. 197)
   A. Wrong. This nucleus is thought to help control circadian rhythms.
   B. Wrong. This nucleus is involved in circadian rhythms, not sleepwalking.
   D. Wrong. This nucleus is involved in circadian rhythms, not the stages of sleep.
2. C, Correct (p. 199)
   A., B., D. Wrong. There are 4 stages of non-REM sleep.
3. D, Correct (p. 201)
   A. Wrong. REM is not the shortest stage of sleep.
   B. Wrong. Dreams are likely, but the paradox of REM does not concern this or the vividness of dreams.
   C. Wrong. Delta waves are found in Stage 4 non-REM sleep, but the EEG pattern is important.
4. B, Correct (p. 201)
   A. Wrong. Most people cycle through four or five times.
   C. Wrong. Dreams are reported approximately 80% of the time.
   D. Wrong. REM stands for rapid eye movements.
5. A, Correct (p. 202)
   B, C, D. Wrong. These describe sleep as restorative or allowing repair of the system.
6. B, Correct (p. 207)
   A., C., D. Wrong. Insomnia, narcolepsy, and hypersomnia are all dyssomnias, not parasomnias.
7. A, Correct (p. 204)
   B. Wrong. This is Hobson & McCarley's activation-synthesis theory.
   C. Wrong. This is a restorative theory of sleep and dreams.
   D. Wrong. This is Cartwright's problem solving theory of dreams.
8. D, Correct (p. 207)
   A. Wrong. Most psychologists do not believe night terrors indicate serious psychological problems.
   B. Wrong. Most psychologists do not believe night terrors indicate serious medical problems.
   C. Wrong. Night terrors typically occur in non-REM (Stage 4) sleep, not in REM sleep.
9. B, Correct (p. 206)
   A. Wrong. Hypersomnia is excessive sleepiness, not difficulty sleeping.
   C. Wrong. Sleep apnea involves ceasing to breath during sleep, not an inability to get to sleep.
   D. Wrong. Narcolepsy is a disorder in which sleep (REM) onsets suddenly and at inappropriate times.

ALTERING AWARENESS: PSYCHOACTIVE DRUGS (PP. 207-213)

MASTERING THE CONCEPTS

1. Psychoactive (p. 208)
2. neurotransmitter (p. 208)
3. tolerance (p. 208)
4. Depressants (p. 209)
5. Stimulants (p. 210)
6. dopamine (p. 210)
7. Opiates (p. 210)
8. Hallucinogens (p. 211)
9. marijuana (p. 211)
10. expectations (p. 212)

EVALUATING YOUR PROGRESS

1. D, Correct (p. 208)
   A. Wrong. Withdrawal occurs when drug use is halted. Continued use often leads to tolerance.
   B. Wrong. Dependency develops with long term use, but it is a need for the drug, not a loss of strength.
   C. Wrong. The need to increase the dose with extended use is tolerance, not rebound.
2. C, Correct (p. 210)
   A, B, D. Wrong. These are correct pairings, but MDMA/Ecstasy is a stimulant, not a hallucinogen.
3. A, Correct (p. 209)
   B. Wrong. Heroin is an opiate and stimulates the same receptors as natural endorphins.
   C. Wrong. Amphetamines impact norepinephrine and dopamine systems.
   D. Wrong. LSD is associated with dopamine receptors.
4. D, Correct (p. 212)
   A, B, C. Wrong. These are all important determinants of the effect psychoactive drugs have.

ALTERING AWARENESS: INDUCED STATES (PP. 213-217)

MASTERING THE CONCEPTS

1. suggestibility (p. 213)
2. sleepy (p. 214)
3. pain (p. 215)
4. memory (p. 215)
5. dissociations (p. 216)
6. hidden (p. 216)
7. role playing (p. 216)
8. (p. 216)
9. Meditation (p. 217)
10. relaxation (p. 217)
11. alpha (p. 217)

EVALUATING YOUR PROGRESS

1. D, Correct (p. 213)
   A. Wrong. Hilgard, a contemporary psychologist, proposed the dissociation view of hypnosis.
   B. Wrong. Timothy Leary was a modern advocate of using LSD to expand consciousness.
   C. Wrong. Sigmund Freud, the 20th century psychoanalyst, did not originate hypnosis.
2. B, Correct (p. 213)
   A. Wrong. A sleepy feeling is sometimes part of hypnotic induction, but hypnosis is not like sleep.
   C. Wrong. "Pure" thought is a description sometimes given to meditation.
   D. Wrong. This is a possible definition of meditation, not hypnosis.
3. D, Correct (p. 216)
   A. Wrong. Hidden observer research usually deals with perceptual alterations, not age regression.
   B. Wrong. The expectancy effect experiments support the social role playing view.
   C. Wrong. Hidden observer research involves dissociation and pain perception, not memory.
4. D, Correct (p. 216)
   A. Wrong. This research involved hypnosis, and meditation does not produce a unique physiological state.
   B. Wrong. Meditation can reduce anxiety, but this research dealt with hypnosis, not meditation.
   C. Wrong. The hidden observer research supported dissociation. This research supported role-playing.
5. B, Correct (p. 217)
   A. Wrong. Meditation does not enhance memory.
   C. Wrong. Physiological arousal is decreased with meditation, not increased.
   D. Wrong. Meditation is associated with increased alpha, not theta, activity.

MAKING FINAL PREPARATIONS

SHORT ESSAY QUESTIONS

1. Automaticity involves rapid, effortless processing that requires little or no directed attention. Once a task is automatic, it is not a drain on limited mental resources. Other tasks can be performed at the same time without suffering a reduction in performance. (p. 192)
2. Dichotic listening experiments show that the unattended message does not reach awareness, but is processed. People respond to important information, such as their name, in an unattended message. Also, when the meaningful content of a message is switched to the unattended ear, shadowing switches to follow the meaning, rather than continuing with the "attended" ear. (pp. 189-192)
3. Sleep deprivation leads to poorer performance on complex tasks, including driving. When deprivation extends over several days, speech is slurred, mental ability declines and psychological disturbances such as paranoia or hallucinations may occur. Research on animals has shown that physiological systems are disrupted, and death occurs with deprivation lasting about three weeks. (pp. 202-204)
4. Several factors other than the chemical composition of a drug determine its effect. The physical condition of the user (e.g., tolerance) can modify drug effects. Also important are the mental set or expectations of the user and the environment in which the drug is taken. Expectancy can shape the reaction to a drug's effect or even create an effect where there is no drug. Likewise, the environment provides a context that interacts with the drug's actual effects. (p. 212)
5. First, people's behavior while hypnotized is influenced by their expectations or beliefs about hypnosis. They conform their behavior to fit their expectations, including the expectation that people who are hypnotized obey commands. Also, the suggestions made during hypnosis end when the subject believes they are no longer hypnotized, even if no modification of instructions are made by the hypnotist. Finally, most of the phenomena of hypnosis can be achieved by people "simulating" hypnosis (told to act hypnotized). (p. 216)
6. The cocktail party effect and "ear-switching" effect in dichotic listening research both show that unattended (but detectable) information is processed and can influence behavior, even though the "unattended" message usually doesn't reach conscious awareness. The research on subliminal (below threshold) stimuli, however, indicates that it has no effect on behavior other than possible placebo effects. Controlled studies of subliminal advertising and products have not obtained behavior that differed from that of the control group. (pp. 189-195)

MATCHING

1. f (p. 197)
2. o (p. 209)
3. j (p. 189)
4. m (p. 205)
5. b (p. 204)
6. n (p. 199)
7. d (p. 197)
8. c (p. 209)
9. i (p. 189)
10. l (p. 187)
11. p (p .215)
12. e (p. 200)
13. g (p. 204)
14. h (p. 217)
15. a (p. 211)
16. k (p. 205)

MULTIPLE CHOICE PRETEST 1

1. A, Correct (p. 192)
   B. Wrong. The ear-switching task examines selective attention, not automaticity.
   C. Wrong. A dichotic listening task examines selective attention, not automaticity.
   D. Wrong. The hidden observer task is a test of the dissociation view of hypnosis.
2. C, Correct (p. 190)
   A. Wrong. Shadowing is a technique in which a subject repeats a message as it is presented.
   B. Wrong. Auditory neglect is the lack of perception of sounds from certain locations in the environment.
   D. Wrong. Attentional rebound, if real, would be an increase in attention following inattention.
3. D, Correct (p. 194)
   A. Wrong. Attention is a higher cognitive process and involves the cerebral cortex, not the cerebellum.
   B. Wrong. Damage to the occipital lobe produces visual, not attention problems.
   C. Wrong. The hindbrain is responsible mostly for lower-level processes, not attention.
4. D, Correct (p. 193)
   A, B, C. Wrong. Having the word "sex" in the pictures generally does not influence memory.
5. A, Correct (p. 195)
   B. Wrong. Narcolepsy is a sleep disorder that causes sudden onset of sleep at unexpected times.
   C. Wrong. Synesthesia is a blending of the senses (e.g., hearing colors).
   D. Wrong. Visual neglect, being unaware of everything in one half of the environment, does not involve rapid shifts in attention and excessive activity.
6. A, Correct (p. 201)
   B, C, D. Wrong. These stages tend to become less frequent and briefer.
7. B, Correct (p. 201)
   A. Wrong. REM stands for rapid eye movements.
   C. Wrong. Dreams are most commonly reported in REM.
   D. Wrong. REM is accompanied by very relaxed muscles.
8. D, Correct (p. 200)
   A. Wrong. Fast, irregular waveforms are typical of brain activity when awake, not sleeping.
   B. Wrong. Delta waves are characteristic of Stage 3 and 4 sleep.
   C. Wrong. Alpha waves are characteristic of highly relaxed states, not sleep.
9. D, Correct (p. 204)
   A. Wrong. The activation-synthesis hypothesis is an alternative to Freud's theory of dreams.
   B. Wrong. The dissociation hypothesis proposes that consciousness splits during hypnosis.
   C. Wrong. The manifest content is the actual content and images of the dream, not their symbolism.
10. C, Correct (p. 206)
    A. Wrong. Sleep apnea is a disorder in which people quit breathing periodically while asleep.
    B. Wrong. Insomnia is a difficulty getting to sleep or staying asleep.
    D. Wrong. Hypermnesia is enhanced memory, not a sleep disorder.
11. A, Correct (p. 204)
    B. Wrong. This is the core idea in dissociation theory of hypnosis.
    C. Wrong. This is the core idea in the view that sleep is adaptive.
    D. Wrong. This is the core idea in that the purpose of sleep is restoration or repair.
12. D, Correct (p. 215)
    A. Wrong. Apparent memory enhancement can be accounted for by factors other than hypnosis.
    B. Wrong. Recent events are not recalled more accurately with hypnosis.
    C. Wrong. Old events are difficult to verify, so memory has not been shown to be better.
13. C, Correct (p. 209)
    A. Wrong. Cocaine impacts dopamine and norepinephrine, but not GABA.
    B. Wrong. Heroin impacts receptors that also respond to endorphins, not dopamine and GABA.
    D. Wrong. Amphetamine impacts dopamine and norepinephrine, but not GABA.

14. B, Correct (p. 210)
    A. Wrong. Hallucinations are not common with opiates. They are common with hallucinogenics like LSD.
    C. Wrong. Hypermnesia is improved memory. Opiates do not improve memory.
    D. Wrong. Opiates are very likely to produce dependency.
15. C, Correct (p. 210)
    A. Wrong. Endorphins are related to opiates, not cocaine. Dopamine is the key to cocaine's reinforcing effects.
    B. Wrong. Serotonin is affected by hallucinogens. Dopamine is the key to cocaine's effects.
    D. Wrong. Depressants affect GABA. Dopamine is the key to cocaine's effects.
16. C, Correct (p. 209)
    A. Wrong. Tolerance is the need for larger doses with continued drug use.
    B. Wrong. Dependency may lead to these symptoms, but it is not the symptoms themselves.
    D. Wrong. Synesthesia is a cross-sensory experience (e.g., "seeing" sounds).
17. C, Correct (p. 217)
    A. Wrong. This defines hypnosis.
    B. Wrong. This defines synesthesia.
    D. Wrong. This defines consciousness.
18. B, Correct (p. 215)
    A. Wrong. Meditation causes relaxation, but not pain reduction.
    C. Wrong. REM deprivation does not reduce pain perception.
    D. Wrong. Alpha waves are associated with relaxation, but not pain reduction.

MULTIPLE CHOICE PRETEST 2

1. A, Correct (p. 190)
   B. Wrong. A divided attention task, not a dichotic listening task, is used to evaluate automaticity.
   C. Wrong. ADHD is diagnosed through mostly behavioral evaluations, not including dichotic listening.
   D. Wrong. Both inputs in dichotic listening tasks are above threshold; subliminal perception isn't involved.
2. C, Correct (p. 189)
   A. Wrong. Subliminal perception involves stimuli that are below threshold, not setting priorities.
   B. Wrong. Visual neglect is not adaptive. It is an inability to attend to one half of the visual field.
   D. Wrong. Activation-synthesis is a theory of dreaming.
3. A, Correct (p. 195)
   B. Wrong. This research found that "neglected" stimuli are processed, but do not reach consciousness.
   C. Wrong. This research evaluated whether "neglected" input was processed, not automaticity.
   D. Wrong. The important stimuli did not reach consciousness, but it did influence behavior.
4. C, Correct (p. 192)
   A. Wrong. He'd never drive well if he lacked awareness of half of the visual field (visual neglect).
   B. Wrong. The key here is the addition of a second task, not a general inability to pay attention.
   D. Wrong. The cocktail party effect shows unattended input is processed. That is not the case here.
5. A, Correct (pp. 192-194)
   B., C., D. Wrong. These statements are accurate, but events below awareness can have an effect.
6. A, Correct (p. 201)
   B. Wrong. The opposite is true of REM sleep.
   C. Wrong. Heart rate and respiration are rapid, and this is not the origin of the term "paradoxical."
   D. Wrong. Dreams are often reported on awakening, and the paradoxical aspect relates to the EEG.

7. A, Correct (p. 206)

   B. Wrong. Narcolepsy is a tendency to fall asleep at inappropriate times.

   C. Wrong. Night terrors are feelings of extreme fear, not a tendency to quit breathing.

   D. Wrong. Insomnia is a difficulty getting to sleep or staying asleep.

8. B, Correct (p. 200)

   A. Wrong. Sleep spindles are found in Stage 2, not REM sleep.

   C. Wrong. Delta waves are not found in REM sleep.

   D. Wrong. Delta waves are associated with deep sleep, not being close to awakening.

9. B, Correct (p. 207)

   A. Wrong. Night terrors are different: They occur in a different stage of sleep, for one thing.

   C. Wrong. Night terrors are not signs of psychological problems. They occur in normal people.

   D. Wrong. Night terrors are most common in childhood. They tend to disappear by adolescence.

10. C, Correct (p. 197)

    A. Wrong. ADD is not due to superchiasmic nucleus damage. Other brain areas are more likely involved.

    B. Wrong. Visual neglect is associated with right parietal lobe damage.

    D. Wrong. Hypermensia is improved recall. This nucleus doesn't involve memory skills.

11. A, Correct (p. 204)

    B. Wrong. This would be a problem solving approach, not the activation-synthesis approach.

    C. Wrong. This would be an activation-synthesis view.

    D. Wrong. Freud's theory viewed dreams as helpful in diagnosing problems, but not that dreams always signal serious problems.

12. C, Correct (p. 205)

    A. Wrong. Circadian rhythms are 24-hour biological cycles. Insomnia is a sleep disorder.

    B. Wrong. Insomnia is a sleep disorder, but not a parasomnia.

    D. Wrong. Insomnia is a sleep disorder, not a splitting of consciousness.

13. D, Correct (p. 211)

    A. Wrong. Pain reduction is associated mostly with opiates.

    B. Wrong. LSD does not tend to produce dependency or withdrawal.

    C. Wrong. The effects of LSD last up to approximately 16 hours.

14. A, Correct (p. 209)

    B. Wrong. Nicotine is a stimulant; alcohol is a depressant.

    C. Wrong. MDMA is a stimulant; alcohol is a depressant.

    D. Wrong. Morphine is an opiate; alcohol is a depressant.

15. D, Correct (p. 210)

    A. Wrong. Alcohol tends to affect GABA, not norepinephrine.

    B. Wrong. Heroin mimics the activity of endorphins.

    C. Wrong. LSD affects serotonin receptors.

16. D, Correct (p. 208)

    A. Wrong. Dependency is a need for continued drug use.

    B. Wrong. REM rebound is a tendency to spend a more time in REM sleep if deprived on previous nights.

    C. Wrong. Withdrawal is the physical reaction to discontinuing drug use.

17. D, Correct (p. 214)

    A. Wrong. Hallucinogens do not increase suggestibility or reduce pain perception.

    B. Wrong. Meditation induces relaxation, but not heightened suggestibility.

    C. Wrong. Sleep deprivation causes sagging eyelids, but not pain reduction or suggestibility.

18. C, Correct (p. 216)

    A. Wrong. Hidden observer, not expectancy effect, experiments support the dissociation view.

    B. Wrong. The key aspect of the research is the subject's expectation, not brain waves.

    D. Wrong. This is not a view of hypnosis, and ACh has no relation to expectancy effects in hypnosis.

19. D, Correct (p. 216)

    A., B., C. Wrong. A hidden observer perceives reality and is not influenced by hypnotic suggestion.

CHAPTER **7**

LEARNING FROM EXPERIENCE

ESTABLISHING LEARNING GOALS

Use these learning goals as a preview of the chapter, a guide for active reading, and to evaluate your mastery of the material. Review the relevant goals as you begin and end your reading of each major section of the chapter.

I. Define learning.

II. Describe how organisms recognize and react appropriately to significant events.

- A. Describe and compare habituation and sensitization.

III. Describe how organisms recognize relationships between events and respond to them.

- A. Describe the basic elements of classical conditioning.
  1. Define conditioned stimulus, unconditioned stimulus, conditioned response and unconditioned response.
  2. Describe Pavlov's experiment, and identify the components of conditioning in that context.
- B. Discuss why and how conditioned responding develops.
  1. Discuss the evidence that suggests that conditioning is more than stimulus substitution.
  2. Discuss how taste aversions develop and explain how they are adaptive but troublesome.
- C. Differentiate among second-order conditioning, stimulus generalization and stimulus discrimination.
- D. Discuss extinction and conditioned inhibition.
  1. Describe the process of extinction and what spontaneous recovery indicates about extinction.
  2. Discuss the adaptive value of conditioned inhibition.

IV. Describe how organisms recognize the consequences of a behavior and respond to them.

- A. Define operant conditioning, and discuss the law of effect.
- B. Explain what we mean by discriminative stimulus.
- C. Define reinforcement and punishment, and distinguish between positive and negative forms.
  1. Provide examples of positive and negative reinforcement.
  2. Explain the response deprivation theory of reinforcement.
  3. Describe conditioned reinforcers.
  4. Provide examples of positive and negative punishment.

5. Discuss the limitations of punishment as a technique for eliminating a behavior.

D. Discuss and compare different schedules of reinforcement.

E. Explain how complex behaviors can be acquired through shaping.

F. Discuss how biological factors might limit the responses that can be learned.

V. Describe how organisms learn without being a direct participant.

A. Describe observational learning and the conditions that lead to effective modeling.

B. Explain why observational learning is adaptive, and discuss its practical effects.

MASTERING THE MATERIAL

PREVIEW & LEARNING ABOUT EVENTS: NOTICING AND IGNORING (PP. 223-227)

MASTERING THE VOCABULARY

Define or explain each of the following terms.

1. learning
2. orienting response
3. habituation
4. sensitization

MASTERING THE CONCEPTS

Fill in the blanks to create a summary of the section.

Learning is a change in [1] ____________, or potential to respond, resulting from [2] ____________. This chapter examines four major issues: How do people notice events? How do they learn about signaling properties of events? How do they learn about the consequences of behavior? How do they learn from others?

Novel stimuli cause [3] ____________ responses, a shift in attention toward the stimulus. [4] ____________, a reduction in responsiveness, occurs with repeated stimulation if the stimulus is without serious consequences. Habituation produces selective responding. For intense or punishing stimuli, sometimes [5] ____________ , an increase in responsiveness, occurs.

EVALUATING YOUR PROGRESS

Select the best response. If you make any errors, reread the relevant material before proceeding.

1. "A relatively permanent change in behavior, or potential behavior, that results from experience" is the basic definition of
   a. an orienting response.
   b. performance.
   c. learning.
   d. knowledge.
2. When a novel stimulus appears, attention automatically shifts to it. This describes
   a. modeling.
   b. an orienting response.
   c. spontaneous recovery.
   d. sensitization.
3. What has occurred if the orienting response increased when a stimulus was presented repeatedly?
   a. spontaneous recovery
   b. sensitization
   c. generalization
   d. habituation
4. Orienting responses often decrease over time when significant consequences do not follow the stimulus. This decrease in the orienting response is called
   a. habituation.
   b. sensitization.
   c. stimulus generalization.
   d. negative reinforcement.

LEARNING WHAT EVENTS SIGNAL: CLASSICAL CONDITIONING (PP. 227-237)

MASTERING THE VOCABULARY

Define or explain each of the following terms.

1. classical conditioning
2. unconditioned stimulus (US)
3. unconditioned response (UR)

4. conditioned stimulus (CS)
5. conditioned response (CR)
6. second-order conditioning
7. stimulus generalization
8. stimulus discrimination
9. extinction
10. spontaneous recovery
11. conditioned inhibition

MASTERING THE CONCEPTS.

Fill in the blanks to create a summary of the section.

Organisms learn to associate events through a process known as [1] ___________ conditioning. A Russian physiologist, [2] ___________ , developed the procedures of classical conditioning after noticing that the dogs in his digestion research began salivating before food was presented. Certain stimuli, [3] ___________ stimuli (USs), automatically lead to responses known as [4] ___________ responses (URs). No learning is required. Other stimuli that signal the US can acquire an ability to cause a [5] ___________ response (CR). These stimuli are called [6] ___________ stimuli (CSs). In Pavlov's experiments food is an unconditioned stimulus for the unconditioned response of salivation. The assistant's footsteps or a bell rung just before food presentation became conditioned stimuli and elicited a conditioned response of salivation.

To become a CS, a stimulus must provide reliable information about the US. CSs usually must come [7] ___________ the US (must signal the US) for conditioning to occur. The US usually must follow the CS closely in time. The CS must provide [8] ___________ information about the US. Other stimuli that accompany the CS will not become CSs if they provide no new information; [9] ___________ will occur.

The prevalent approach to classical conditioning today is the [10] ___________ view. This view stresses that conditioning involves the learning of complex relationships. This approach does not see the CS as a [11] ___________ for the US, eliciting a CR very similar to the UR, as did previous approaches.

Conditioned stimuli can be used to condition other stimuli, a process called [12] ____________ conditioning. In stimulus [13] ____________ new stimuli similar to the CS will elicit a CR. "Little Albert" was conditioned to cry when a rat was presented, but other furry items also elicited crying. In contrast, in stimulus [14] ____________ a new stimulus results in a different response, often after experience shows the new stimulus does not signal the US. If the CS is never again paired with the US, the CS loses its signaling characteristics and [15] ____________ , the loss of the CR, occurs. When previously extinguished CRs reappear, spontaneous [16] ____________ is said to have occurred. In conditioned [17] ____________ , the CS signals the absence of a US and leads to a reduction of the original response, or sometimes an opposite response.

Learning to predict events using signaling stimuli is adaptive. Conditioned taste [18] ____________ helps prevent consumption of dangerous foods. Organisms that become ill after eating a food, especially an unusual one, develop an aversion to that food and are unwilling to eat it again. In some cases, such as chemotherapy, conditioned taste aversions are not desirable, but can be prevented by giving a distinctive food as a "decoy" or by presenting bland foods unlikely to cause conditioned taste aversion.

EVALUATING YOUR PROGRESS

Select the best response. If you miss any questions, reread the relevant material before proceeding.

1. If a stimulus produces a response before training begins, that stimulus is
   a. a conditioned stimulus.
   b. an unconditioned stimulus.
   c. a discriminative stimulus.
   d. an associate stimulus.
2. At the end of the experiment, Little Albert cried when the rat was presented without the loud noise. At that time his crying was the
   a. unconditioned stimulus.
   b. unconditioned response.
   c. conditioned stimulus.
   d. conditioned response.
3. If new stimuli similar to the conditioned stimulus also produce the conditioned response, ______ has occurred.
   a. stimulus generalization
   b. spontaneous recovery
   c. stimulus discrimination
   d. conditioned inhibition

4. When extinction has occurred
   a. the conditioned response ceases.
   b. the conditioned stimulus is no longer presented.
   c. an opposite response is made to the conditioned stimulus.
   d. a conditioned response occurs when a new, but similar stimulus is presented.
5. For classical conditioning to occur the conditioned stimulus usually must be presented
   a. at the same time as the unconditioned stimulus.
   b. a little after the unconditioned stimulus.
   c. a little before the unconditioned stimulus.
   d. closely in time to the unconditioned stimulus, but the specific order is not important.
6. Even though a conditioned response has undergone extinction, it sometimes reappears later without any further training. This reappearance is known as
   a. spontaneous recovery.
   b. second-order conditioning.
   c. sensitization.
   d. generalization.
7. What occurs if a stimulus signals the absence of an unconditioned stimulus?
   a. backward conditioning
   b. conditioned inhibition
   c. stimulus discrimination
   d. blocking

LEARNING ABOUT THE CONSEQUENCES OF BEHAVIOR: OPERANT CONDITIONING (PP. 237-249)

MASTERING THE VOCABULARY

Define or explain each of the following terms.

1. operant conditioning (instrumental conditioning)
2. law of effect
3. discriminative stimulus
4. reinforcement
5. positive reinforcement
6. negative reinforcement
7. escape conditioning
8. avoidance conditioning
9. conditioned reinforcer

10. punishment
11. positive punishment
12. negative punishment
13. schedule of reinforcement
14. partial reinforcement schedule
15. fixed-ratio schedule
16. variable-ratio schedule
17. fixed-interval schedule
18. variable-interval schedule
19. shaping

MASTERING THE CONCEPTS

Fill in the blanks to create a summary of the section.

In classical conditioning, events signal outcomes, but in instrumental or [1] ____________ conditioning the organism's own actions *produce* outcomes. In the late 1800's, Thorndike proposed the law of [2] ____________ : Responses followed by pleasant consequence will be [3] ____________ ; responses followed by an unpleasant consequence will be [4] ____________ .

In the 20th century, Skinner proposed that [5] ____________ stimuli signal when a response will be rewarded. Stimulus [6] ____________ occurs when a response is made to stimuli that are similar to the original, and stimulus [7] ____________ occurs when responding occurs only to one stimulus.

The formal term for the situation in which a "pleasant" consequence "strengthens" a response is [8] ____________ , which is defined as consequences that increase the likelihood of response. [9] ____________ reinforcement is an event, that when presented after a response, increases the likelihood of that response. Response [10] ____________ theory states an event will be reinforcing if it allows a behavior that previously has been deprived. For negative reinforcement, the [11] ____________ of an event after a response increases the likelihood of the response occurring again. Negative reinforcement can involve [12] ____________ conditioning, in which a response ends an unpleasant event, and [13] ____________ conditioning, in which a response prevents the occurrence of an unpleasant event.

Note that "negative" refers to removing an event, not decreasing the response. All reinforcement increases response likelihood. Secondary, or [14] ____________ reinforcers have no direct value, but they have acquired reinforcing properties.

Consequences that [15] ____________ the likelihood of a response are called punishment. In positive punishment, an (aversive) event is [16] ____________ after a response. In negative punishment a positive event is [17] ____________ after a response. Problems with punishment include judging its strength, the fact that bad behavior is suppressed rather than a good behavior taught, and possibly resentment, aggression, and attempted escape.

The rules or [18] ____________ of reinforcement produce individual patterns of response. A [19] ____________ schedule of reinforcement reinforces every target response. A [20] ____________ reinforcement schedule reinforces only some responses. A [21] ____________ schedule requires a certain number of responses for reinforcement and produces steady responding, but a post-reinforcement [22] ____________ can occur with large ratios. If the number of required responses varies around an average, a [23] ____________ schedule is in effect, and the response rate will be high and steady. [24] ____________ schedules require a certain amount of time to pass before another response will be reinforced and produces low rates of responding with a scalloped appearance. If the time interval varies, the schedule is a variable interval schedule and produces steady responding.

When reinforcement is no longer given, [25] ____________ begins, and the organism eventually quits responding. The schedule of reinforcement influences how long responding will continue. Continuous schedules produce faster extinction than partial schedules, and fixed schedules result in [26] ____________ extinction than variable schedules, apparently due to differences in the [27] ____________ of reinforcement in the different schedules.

The method of successive approximations, or [28] ____________ , is used to train an organism to make a desired response. Responses that approximate the desired response are reinforced, and the standards for reinforcement are increased gradually until the final form of the response is required. Accidental or adventitious reinforcement can also modify behavior. This is one cause of [29] ____________ behavior. Biological constraints also influence learning. Some responses are not easily learned.

EVALUATING YOUR PROGRESS

Select the best response. If you miss any questions, reread the relevant material before proceeding.

1. Responses followed by pleasant consequences are strengthened; responses followed by unpleasant consequences are weakened. This represents
   a. extinction.
   b. the law of effect.
   c. shaping.
   d. observational learning.
2. "Response consequences that increase the likelihood of the response occurring again" describes
   a. shaping.
   b. punishment.
   c. reinforcement.
   d. discrimination.
3. A specific low-pitched tone was used to signal when pressing the bar would result in access to food, but now the rat presses the bar whenever any low-pitched tone occurs. This describes
   a. shaping.
   b. extinction.
   c. generalization.
   d. spontaneous recovery.
4. The "positive" and "negative" in positive and negative reinforcement refer to whether
   a. the reinforced response increases or decreases in frequency.
   b. the reinforcer is presented before or after the response.
   c. a stimulus or event is presented or removed when a response is made.
   d. the reinforcer has intrinsic value or acquired value.
5. A consequence that decreases a response is
   a. reinforcement.
   b. punishment.
   c. shaping.
   d. generalization.
6. A stimulus or event that has acquired it reinforcing properties is
   a. an adventitious reinforcer.
   b. a primary reinforcer.
   c. a negative reinforcer.
   d. a conditioned reinforcer.
7. The situation in which reinforcement is no longer given following the trained response is called
   a. extinction.
   b. conditioned inhibition.
   c. a post-reinforcement pause.
   d. shaping.

8. The Brelands' research with raccoons and pigs demonstrated that
   a. animals learn better with reinforcement than with punishment.
   b. animals learn better with punishment than with reinforcement.
   c. with enough time and patience, any response can be conditioned.
   d. biological tendencies make teaching some responses almost impossible.
9. Trish's basketball coach began by praising her every time she shot the ball. Later, she was praised only if the shot at least hit the rim, and finally, only if she made the basket. The technique her coach used is best described as
   a. shaping.
   b. primary reinforcement.
   c. a variable ratio schedule.
   d. partial reinforcement.
10. A reinforcement schedule that reinforces the first response made after 1 minute has elapsed is known as a
    a. fixed ratio schedule.
    b. variable ratio schedule.
    c. fixed interval schedule.
    d. variable interval schedule.
11. A pigeon is still pecking the key at a steady, rapid pace, even though no reinforcement has been given for a long time. The pigeon probably was trained on a
    a. continuous reinforcemet schedule.
    b. fixed ratio schedule.
    c. fixed interval schedule.
    d. variable ratio schedule.

LEARNING FROM OTHERS: OBSERVATIONAL LEARNING (PP. 250-252)

MASTERING THE VOCABULARY

Define or explain each of the following terms.

1. observational learning
2. modeling

MASTERING THE CONCEPTS

Fill in the blanks to create a summary of the section.

Organisms do not have to be directly involved in behavior to learn about its consequences. Much is learned through [1] ____________, or social, learning. Here, the organism observes the behavior of others and imitates, or [2] ____________ it. Observing others being reinforced or punished for a behavior can result in modification of the observer's behavior due to [3] ____________ reinforcement or punishment. Bandura has shown that children who watched an adult hitting a doll were more likely to hit the doll than children watching an adult play nonviolently. This research raises questions about the impact of TV violence.

EVALUATING YOUR PROGRESS

Select the best response. If you miss any questions, reread the relevant material before proceeding.

1. Children learn many things by watching other people's behavior. This type of learning is called
   a. instrumental learning.
   b. indirect learning.
   c. higher-order learning.
   d. social learning.

2. The natural tendency to imitate the behavior of significant others in one's surrounding is
   a. shaping.
   b. modeling.
   c. generalization.
   d. discrimination.

3. Which is FALSE?
   a. Observational learning is found only in humans.
   b. An attractive or likeable model increases the likelihood of observational learning.
   c. An observer's self-efficacy influences observational learning.
   d. The consequences of the model's behavior is important.

4. Modeling is more likely if the person being observed is reinforced for their behavior. Watching someone be reinforced is called
   a. accidental reinforcement.
   b. vicarious reinforcement.
   c. partial reinforcement.
   d. secondary reinforcement.

MAKING FINAL PREPARATIONS

Complete these sections without consulting your book or notes. For a more accurate estimate of how well you know the material, wait at least a day or two after studying the chapter before working on the questions. Some of the material you "know" immediately after working with the chapter will be quickly forgotten. Exercises done too soon after studying will overestimate what you know well.

MATCHING

Select the correct definition or description for each item.

1. _______ conditioned inhibition
2. _______ sensitization
3. _______ post-reinforcement pause
4. _______ Thorndike
5. _______ Watson & Raynor
6. _______ spontaneous recovery
7. _______ modeling
8. _______ Pavlov
9. _______ Bandura
10. _______ second-order conditioning
11. _______ discriminative stimulus
12. _______ shaping
13. _______ escape conditioning
14. _______ orienting response
15. _______ instrumental conditioning

a. did a famous experiment on observational learning
b. imitation of observed behavior
c. developed principles of classical conditioning
d. proposed the law of effect
e. successive approximations to a response are reinforced
f. automatic shift of attention to a novel stimulus
g. a new CS produces a CR after being paired with an established CS
h. increased responsiveness to a repeated event
i. response delay after reinforcement in a fixed ratio schedule
j. a negative reinforcement situation
k. did "little Albert" study of conditioned fear
l. reappearance of formerly extinguished CR
m. learn an event signals the absence of the US
n. operant conditioning
o. signals when a response will be reinforced

SHORT ESSAY QUESTIONS

Write a brief answer to each question.

1. Compare habituation and classical conditioning extinction.

____

____

2. Explain why stimulus generalization might be adaptive, and give an example.

____

____

3. Explain why conditioned taste aversions develop. Identify the US, CS, UR, and CR.

____

____

4. Explain why variable schedules of reinforcement produce greater resistance to extinction than fixed and continuous schedules.

____

____

5. Discuss the limitations of punishment as a means of behavior modification.

____

____

6. Explain the adaptive value of observational learning.

____

____

7. Describe fixed interval and variable interval schedules of reinforcement. Compare their effects.

____

____

MULTIPLE CHOICE PRETEST 1

Select the one best response.

1. An orienting stimulus produced sensitization instead of habituation. The stimulus probably
   a. rarely occurred.
   b. was visual.
   c. was weak.
   d. was intense.

2. Classical conditioning is a process by which organisms learn
   a. by observing the actions of others.
   b. the consequences of their voluntary actions.
   c. what stimuli signal or predict.
   d. to direct attention to a novel stimulus.

3. In Pavlov's experiments, the bell was the
   a. unconditioned stimulus.
   b. conditioned stimulus.
   c. discriminative stimulus.
   d. blocking stimulus.

4. In the Little Albert experiment, Little Albert cried when a loud noise was presented. Crying in this situation is an example of
   a. an unconditioned response.
   b. a conditioned response.
   c. generalization.
   d. discrimination.

5. Which of the following is least important for producing strong conditioning?
   a. The two stimuli must be presented closely in time.
   b. The CS must come before the US.
   c. The CS and US must be as strong as the US.
   d. The CS must provide new information about the US.

6. A shock is given shortly after a buzzer sounds, but not if the light is also flashing. A rat will act normally if the light and buzzer are presented, but it will freeze if only the buzzer is presented. This is an example of
   a. the law of effect.
   b. conditioned inhibition.
   c. escape conditioning.
   d. avoidance conditioning.

7. Burt got sick with a stomach flu shortly after eating sardines. The conditioned taste aversion he developed involved not only sardines, but also most other fish. This is best explained in terms of
   a. second-order conditioning.
   b. negative punishment.
   c. simultaneous conditioning.
   d. generalization.

8. After months of work, Phil's conditioned fear of flying finally disappeared. However, his fear suddenly reappeared. His renewed fear probably represents
   a. conditioned inhibition.
   b. second-order conditioning.
   c. spontaneous recovery.
   d. extinction.

9. Operant conditioning differs from classical conditioning because in operant conditioning
   a. an organism's behavior produces outcomes, but in classical conditioning events signal outcomes.
   b. an organism is learning something, but in classical conditioning no learning occurs.
   c. the principles apply only to animals, but in classical conditioning the principles apply to humans.
   d. discrimination and generalization do not occur, but in classical conditioning they do.

10. A stimulus or event that, when removed following a response, decreases the likelihood the response will be made again is a
    a. positive reinforcer.
    b. negative reinforcer.
    c. positive punishment.
    d. negative punishment.

11. Randy had to write an essay and discuss it with his teacher because he said an obscene word in class. His teacher was frustrated when Randy's use of obscenity became more frequent in spite of being made to write an essay and talk to the teacher each time. In this example, writing the essay and talking to the teacher must be
    a. positive reinforcement.
    b. negative reinforcement.
    c. positive punishment.
    d. negative punishment.

12. A response increased in frequency because it allowed the rat to escape or avoid a shock. This represents
    a. positive reinforcement.
    b. negative reinforcement.
    c. positive punishment.
    d. negative punishment.

13. Whenever Bhavin left his homework at school, he lost his computer privileges for two days. Bhavin forgets his homework much less often now. Losing computer privileges is an example of
    a. positive reinforcement.
    b. negative reinforcement.
    c. positive punishment.
    d. negative punishment.

14. Slot machines are set to pay off after some average number of plays (let's guess 150), but a machine might pay off after 30 plays one time and after 270 plays another time. This is an example of a
    a. fixed ratio schedule of reinforcement.
    b. fixed interval schedule of reinforcement.
    c. variable ratio schedule of reinforcement.
    d. variable interval schedule of reinforcement.

15. The small helmet decals given to a football player who has had an outstanding performance are examples of
    a. variable reinforcers.
    b. primary reinforcers.
    c. negative reinforcers.
    d. conditioned reinforcers.

16. The key peck record from the pigeon shows long periods of few responses followed by brief periods of very rapid responses, creating a scalloped effect. This bird probably was reinforced on a
    a. fixed ratio schedule.
    b. variable ratio schedule.
    c. fixed interval schedule.
    d. variable interval schedule.

17. Which of the following is most related to reinforcement of successive approximations of the response?
    a. shaping
    b. partial reinforcement
    c. discrimination
    d. sensitization

18. Marta wasn't surprised that her first driving experience went well. "After all, I've been a passenger for 15 years!" she explained. Marta seems to attribute her initial driving skill to
    a. positive reinforcement of driving responses.
    b. classical conditioning of driving responses.
    c. second-order conditioning of driving responses.
    d. observational learning of driving responses.

MULTIPLE CHOICE PRETEST 2

Select the one best response.

1. Damon's dorm room is next door to the bathroom. At the beginning of the term, Damon found his attention captured by each flush of a toilet. His behavior is an example of
    a. sensitization.
    b. learning.
    c. an orienting response.
    d. habituation.

2. Kim lives near the hospital. At first, the ambulance sirens woke her several times each night, but after a few weeks, she hardly noticed them anymore. This change can be explained as
    a. habituation.
    b. sensitization.
    c. observational learning.
    d. spontaneous recovery.

3. Little Albert was conditioned to fear a white rat. He also acted afraid of rabbits or other small animals, even though they never were paired with the loud noise. This is best explained by
    a. spontaneous recovery.
    b. discrimination.
    c. second-order conditioning.
    d. generalization.

4. Niko was hit by a line drive, and afterward he would duck whenever he heard the crack of a bat hitting a baseball. After hearing that sound many times without ever getting hit again by a ball, Niko no longer ducks at the sound of a hit. This is best explained by
   a. spontaneous recovery.
   b. observational learning.
   c. extinction.
   d. conditioned inhibition.

5. After a tone became the conditioned stimulus for a conditioned eye blink response, a red light was presented just before the tone. Soon the red light alone produced an eye blink. This is an example of
   a. habituation.
   b. blocking.
   c. second-order conditioning.
   d. generalization.

6. The term "instrumental conditioning" is interchangeable with
   a. operant conditioning.
   b. classical conditioning.
   c. avoidance conditioning.
   d. escape conditioning.

7. A few seconds before your new clock radio sounds its alarm, it makes a tiny click. You've recently noticed that you wake up right after the click and before the alarm even though you previously never woke up to anything but the alarm itself. The click is acting as a(n)
   a. unconditioned stimulus.
   b. conditioned stimulus.
   c. positive reinforcer.
   d. blocking stimulus.

8. Thorndike's law of effect is most similar to what B.F. Skinner would describe as
   a. stimulus discrimination and stimulus generalization.
   b. operant conditioning and classical conditioning.
   c. reinforcement and punishment.
   d. habituation and sensitization.

9. Gia has learned that if the TV is tuned to a football game, asking her father to take her to the park always results in the answer "No." If the TV is off, her father almost always answers "Yes." The status of the TV is an example of
   a. a shaping stimulus.
   b. negative reinforcement.
   c. a conditioned stimulus.
   d. a discriminative stimulus.

10. Pat screamed until his mother gave him the cookie he wanted. Now Pat screams any time he wants something. His mother's behavior (giving Pat a cookie) is an example of
    a. positive reinforcement.
    b. negative reinforcement.
    c. positive punishment.
    d. negative punishment.
11. At first, Tom's father cheered every time Tom swung the bat. He gradually required Tom to make good swings before cheering, and eventually only a hit got a cheer. Tom's father used
    a. social learning.
    b. shaping.
    c. a fixed ratio schedule.
    d. modeling.
12. Response deprivation theory is concerned with
    a. why superstitious behavior develops.
    b. why partial reinforcement resists extinction.
    c. when social learning is most likely to occur.
    d. when an event will be reinforcing.
13. You called the radio station and won a CD. You can't win again for 30 days. In your case, calling the radio station is controlled by a
    a. fixed ratio schedule of reinforcement.
    b. fixed interval schedule of reinforcement.
    c. variable ratio schedule of reinforcement.
    d. variable interval schedule of reinforcement.
14. Sara's cold water in her shower almost disappears if the toilet is flushed. When Sara hears the toilet flush, she quickly jumps out of the water so she doesn't get burned. This situation represents
    a. avoidance conditioning.
    b. a conditioned reinforcer.
    c. observational learning.
    d. positive reinforcement.
15. Workers hired by a candidate were paid $1 for every valid signature they obtained on a petition. This is most similar to
    a. a variable interval schedule.
    b. a variable ratio schedule.
    c. a fixed interval schedule.
    d. a fixed ratio schedule.
16. Who will continue to respond the longest after extinction begins?
    a. Alice, who was previously on a continuous reinforcement schedule.
    b. Bill, who was previously on a variable ratio schedule of reinforcement.
    c. Carl, who was previously on a fixed ratio schedule of reinforcement.
    d. Diedre, who was previously on a fixed interval schedule of reinforcement.

17. A post-reinforcement pause is usually associated with
    a. a variable interval schedule.
    b. a fixed interval schedule.
    c. a variable ratio schedule.
    d. a fixed ratio schedule.

18. Seth watched the two shoplifters taken out of the store by the police. He put the CD he had planned to steal back on the shelf and never again tried to take anything without paying. This example illustrates
    a. vicarious punishment.
    b. extinction.
    c. conditioned inhibition.
    d. accidental reinforcement.

19. Much of the concern about the effects that violence on TV may have on children's behavior is based on Bandura's research on
    a. adventitious (accidental) reinforcement.
    b. orienting responses.
    c. primary vs. secondary reinforcement.
    d. social learning.

LANGUAGE DEVELOPMENT GUIDE

CORE TERMS

There are a few terms your instructor is likely to use without necessarily defining them first. The first is ***elicit***, which means "to call forth." If I elicit a response from you, I am doing something that causes you to respond. Next, your instructor may use the term ***contingent upon***. This means "dependent upon"; you might receive a job offer contingent upon graduation from college by a certain date. Finally, you might hear the term ***temporal***, as in, "The temporal relationship of the stimulus and the response is important." That means their relation in time -- which comes first, and how close together they happen -- is important.

IDIOMS

p. 225	whose fate has already been sealed	who are headed for a sure and bad end
p. 226	modest in intensity	fairly quiet or of moderate intensity
p. 227	turn of the century	near the beginning of a new century; here, the period from the 1890s - 1910s
p. 232	metronome	device that produces a regular sound to indicate tempo

p. 243	principal's office	the office of the head of a school, where children who misbehave sometimes are sent
p. 244	haphazard	disorganized; carelessly arranged
p.250	trial and error	trying different things to see what works

PRONUNCIATION

reinforcement (ree-in-force′-ment) *p. 240*

extinction (ex-stink′-shun) *p. 234*

SOLUTIONS

PREVIEW & LEARNING ABOUT EVENTS: NOTICING AND IGNORING (PP. 223-227)

MASTERING THE CONCEPTS

1. behavior (p. 224)
2. experience (p. 224)
3. orienting (p. 225)
4. Habituation (p. 226)
5. sensitization (p. 226)

EVALUATING YOUR PROGRESS

1. C, Correct (p. 224)
   A. Wrong. An orienting response is an inborn tendency to shift attention toward a novel stimulus.
   B. Wrong. Performance is any overt behavior, not a change in behavior.
   D. Wrong. Knowledge is a by-product of learning.
2. B, Correct (p. 225)
   A. Wrong. Modeling is imitation of other people's actions and is not relevant here.
   C. Wrong. Spontaneous recovery is the reappearance of a CR after extinction has occurred.
   D. Wrong. Sensitization is an increase in responsiveness to a stimulus that has been repeated.
3. B, Correct (p. 226)
   A. Wrong. Spontaneous recovery is the reappearance of a CR after extinction has occurred.
   C. Wrong. Stimulus generalization is responding to stimuli that are similar to the original stimulus
   D. Wrong. Sensitization increases the orienting response. Habituation decreases it.
4. A, Correct (p. 226)
   B. Wrong. Sensitization increases the orienting response. Habituation decreases it.
   C. Wrong. Stimulus generalization is responding to stimuli that are similar to the original stimulus.
   D. Wrong. Reinforcement increases a response.

LEARNING WHAT EVENTS SIGNAL: CLASSICAL CONDITIONING (PP. 227-237)

MASTERING THE CONCEPTS.

1. classical (p. 227)
2. Pavlov (p. 227)
3. unconditioned (p. 227)
4. unconditioned (p. 227)
5. conditioned (p. 228)
6. conditioned (p. 227)
7. before (p. 228)
8. new (p. 229)
9. blocking (p. 231)
10. cognitive (p. 231)
11. substitute (p. 231)
12. second-order (p. 232)
13. generalization (p. 233)
14. discrimination (p. 233)
15. extinction (p. 234)
16. recovery (p. 234)
17. inhibition (p. 236)
18. aversion (p. 230)

EVALUATING YOUR PROGRESS

1. B, Correct (p. 227)
   A. Wrong. A conditioned stimulus produces a response after training has occurred.
   C. Wrong. A discriminative stimulus indicates whether a response will be reinforced or not.
   D. Wrong. Associate stimulus is not a term used in learning and conditioning.
2. D, Correct (p. 228)
   A. Wrong. The unconditioned stimulus was the loud noise.
   B. Wrong. The unconditioned response was Little Albert's crying in response to the noise.
   C. Wrong. The conditioned stimulus was the rat.
3. A, Correct (p. 233)
   B. Wrong. Spontaneous recovery occurs when a previously extinguished response reappears.
   C. Wrong. Stimulus discrimination occurs if only the original conditioned stimulus yields a response.
   D. Wrong. Conditioned inhibition occurs with a stimulus signals the absence of an unconditioned stimulus.
4. A, Correct (p. 234)
   B. Wrong. The unconditioned stimulus is no longer presented.
   C. Wrong. An opposite response occurs with conditioned inhibition. In extinction no response occurs.
   D. Wrong. This describes stimulus generalization, not extinction.
5. C, Correct (p. 228)
   A. Wrong. Simultaneous conditioning usually produces little or no conditioning. Signaling can't occur.
   B. Wrong. Backward conditioning usually produces little or no conditioning. Signaling can't occur.
   D. Wrong. Order is important, too. The conditioned stimulus needs to signal the unconditioned stimulus.
6. A, Correct (p. 234)
   B. Wrong. Second-order conditioning uses a CS to condition another CS. There is no extinction.
   C. Wrong. Sensitization is an increase in an orienting response, not a return of a CR.
   D. Wrong. Generalization involves a CR to a new stimulus, not the return of an extinguished CR.
7. B, Correct (p. 236)
   A. Wrong. Backward conditioning is presenting the CS after the US; it doesn't signal an absence.
   C. Wrong. Stimulus discrimination involved a refinement of which stimuli produce a CR.
   D. Wrong. Blocking occurs when a new stimulus provides no new information about the US.

LEARNING ABOUT THE CONSEQUENCES OF BEHAVIOR: OPERANT CONDITIONING (PP. 237-249)

MASTERING THE CONCEPTS

1. operant (p. 237)
2. effect (p. 238)
3. strengthened (p. 238)
4. weakened (p. 238)
5. discriminative (p. 239)
6. generalization (p. 239)
7. discrimination (p. 239)
8. reinforcement (p. 240)
9. Positive (p. 240)
10. deprivation (p. 240)
11. removal (p. 240)
12. escape (p. 240)
13. avoidance (p. 240)
14. conditioned (p. 242)
15. decrease (p. 242)
16. presented (p. 242)
17. removed (p. 242)
18. schedules (p. 244)

19. continuous (p. 244)
20. partial (p. 244)
21. fixed ratio (p. 244)
22. pause (p. 244)
23. variable ratio (p. 244)
24. Fixed interval (p. 246)
25. extinction (p. 245)
26. faster (p. 245)
27. predictability (p. 245)
28. shaping (p. 247)
29. superstitious (p. 248)

EVALUATING YOUR PROGRESS

1. B, Correct (p. 238)

   A. Wrong. Extinction is the elimination of a response by ending reinforcement or ending the US.

   C. Wrong. Shaping (method of successive approximations) is a method for teaching a response.

   D. Wrong. Observational learning is learning by observing the responses of others.

2. C, Correct (p. 240)

   A. Wrong. Shaping involves reinforcing responses that are increasingly similar to the target response.

   B. Wrong. Punishment would decrease the likelihood of the response.

   D. Wrong. Discrimination involves signals concerning when a response will produce reinforcement.

3. C, Correct (p. 239)

   A. Wrong. Shaping is a method of training a response, not the generalization of responses.

   B. Wrong. Extinction is the elimination of a response when reinforcement or a US is terminated.

   D. Wrong. Spontaneous recovery is the reemergence of a formerly extinguished response.

4. C, Correct (p. 240)

   A. Wrong. Response increase or decrease determines reinforcement vs. punishment.

   B. Wrong. Reinforcers always come after the response. They're the consequences of a response.

   D. Wrong. Intrinsic vs. acquired value differentiates primary and secondary (acquired) reinforcement.

5. B, Correct (p. 242)

   A. Wrong. Reinforcement increases the response. Punishment decreases it.

   C. Wrong. Shaping is a method used to teach a response.

   D. Wrong. Generalization occurs when a response is made to stimuli other than the original one.

6. D, Correct (p. 242)

   A. Wrong. Adventitious reinforcement is accidental reinforcement, not a reinforcer that has acquired reinforcing properties.

   B. Wrong. Primary reinforcers have direct, unlearned reinforcing properties, but conditioned reinforcers have acquired theirs.

   C. Wrong. Negative reinforcement involves removal of a stimulus. Acquired vs. unlearned properties are not relevant.

7. A, Correct (p. 245)

   B. Wrong. In conditioned inhibition, a stimulus signals when a US will not occur.

   C. Wrong. A post-reinforcement pause is a period after reinforcement when no responses are made.

   D. Wrong. Shaping is the reinforcing of responses that are increasingly similar to the desired response.

8. D, Correct (p. 248)

   A., B., C. Wrong. Their experiences addressed the interaction of natural tendencies and learned relationships, making some relationships easier to learn than others.

9. A, Correct (p. 247)

   B. Wrong. Praise is usually considered a secondary reinforcer. The key here is the change in the response that was reinforced.

   C. Wrong. The number of shots made was not critical. Of importance is the change in the requirements for reinforcement.

   D. Wrong. The key here is the changing nature of the response required for reinforcement. That is not what defines partial reinforcement.

10. C, Correct (p. 246)
    A., B. Wrong. Ratio schedules are based on the number of responses, not the time between responses.
    D. Wrong. Variable interval schedules are based on an average interval, not a specific (e.g., 1 minute) interval.

11. D, Correct (p. 244)
    A. Wrong. Continuous reinforcement does not produce great resistance to extinction.
    B, C. Wrong. Fixed schedules, ratio or interval, aren't resistant to extinction, and usually do not produce steady responding.

LEARNING FROM OTHERS: OBSERVATIONAL LEARNING (PP. 250-252)

MASTERING THE CONCEPTS

1. observational (p. 250)
2. models (p. 250)
3. vicarious (p. 251)

EVALUATING YOUR PROGRESS

1. D, Correct (p. 250)
   A., B., C. Wrong. Learning by observing other is known as observational or social learning.
2. B, Correct (p. 250)
   A. Wrong. Shaping is reinforcement of responses increasingly like a desired response, not imitation.
   C. Wrong. Generalization occurs if responses are made to similar stimuli. Imitation is not involved.
   D. Wrong. Discrimination occurs when responses become increasingly selective. No imitation occurs.
3. A, Correct (p. 250)
   B. Wrong. Attractiveness, likeability, status, etc. are influential in observational learning.
   C. Wrong. If a person doesn't believe he/she can imitate the act, observational learning is not likely.
   D. Wrong. Vicarious reinforcement or punishment influence observational learning.
4. B, Correct (p. 251)
   A. Wrong. Accidental reinforcement is reinforcement that follows a response by chance rather than intent.
   C. Wrong. Partial reinforcement involves reinforcing only some, not all, appropriate responses.
   D. Wrong. Secondary reinforcement uses a reinforcer with acquired value, rather than intrinsic value.

MAKING FINAL PREPARATIONS

MATCHING

1. m (p. 236)
2. h (p. 226)
3. i (p. 244)
4. d (p. 238)
5. k (p. 233)
6. l (p. 234)
7. b (p. 250)
8. c (p. 227)
9. a (p. 251)
10. g (p. 232)
11. o (p. 239)
12. e (p. 247)
13. j (p. 240)
14. f (p. 225)
15. n (p. 237)

SHORT ESSAY QUESTIONS

1. Habituation is a reduction of an orienting response after a stimulus has occurred repeatedly without significant consequences. Extinction is a reduction of a conditioned response due to repeated absence of the unconditioned stimulus. For both, responses are reduced when stimuli no longer signal notable consequences. (pp. 226, 234)
2. Stimulus generalization is adaptive because what is learned with one specific stimulus is transferred to other similar stimuli. Learning is not required for all stimulus variations. This improves interaction with the environment because every variation doesn't require new learning. To open a door with a slightly different knob doesn't require a separate trial and error procedure. Rather than approaching a black snake to see if it bites like the brown one did, the organism can use prior learning to avoid a potentially dangerous situation. (pp. 233, 239)
3. Nausea that occurs following eating or drinking becomes associated with whatever was ingested, particularly new or distinctive items. The illness (US) actually produces the nausea/taste aversion (UR). The food or drink becomes a conditioned stimulus for the conditioned response of nausea/taste aversion. That is: food (CS) ->illness (US) -> nausea (UR), then food (CR) -> nausea/taste aversion (CR). (p. 230)
4. The varying time interval or number of responses involved in variable schedules makes extinction more difficult for the organism to identify than when the intervals and responses are constant, as in fixed schedules. (pp. 245-246)
5. Although punishment can quickly eliminate a response, it has limitations. These include failing to teach an appropriate response (it teaches what not to do, not what to do), being difficult to gauge in terms of intensity, and may cause anger, aggression, and resentment. (p. 243)
6. Observational learning allows learning without the organism directly participating. The organism can quickly, and perhaps more safely, learn the consequences of a behavior. It can learn from the mistakes and success of others and more effectively interact with the environment. (p. 250)
7. An FI schedule reinforces the first response made after some set time interval has passed since reinforcement. A VI schedule is similar, but it varies the interval required. FI schedules produce low levels of response in a scalloped pattern, due to the tendency to respond only near the end of the interval. A VI schedule produces a higher and more consistent rate of response. The VI schedule is also more resistant to extinction. (pp. 245-246)

MULTIPLE CHOICE PRETEST 1

1. D, Correct (p. 226)

   A., B., C. Wrong. Sensitization occurs for repeated, intense stimuli, regardless of sensory system.

2. C, Correct (p. 227)

   A. Wrong. This answer describes observational learning.

   B. Wrong. This answer describes respondent (operant) conditioning.

   D. Wrong. Although not learned, this answer describes an orienting response.

3. B, Correct (p. 228)

   A. Wrong. The unconditioned stimulus was the food.

   C. Wrong. A discriminative stimulus indicates when reinforcement is available. The bell was the CS.

   D. Wrong. Blocking occurs when a new stimulus is added but does not provide new information. The bell was the CS.

4. A, Correct (p. 233)

   B. Wrong. Crying when the rat was presented was a conditioned response. The noise produced an unconditioned response.

   C. Wrong. Generalization occurred when Albert cried in response to furry objects other than the rat.

   D. Wrong. Discrimination wasn't tested, but would have occurred if Albert cried only to the rat, but not to other furry objects.

5. C, Correct (pp. 228-229)

   A. Wrong. Close timing makes it easier to make an association. Equal strength is not important.

   B. Wrong. The order of events is important because the CS must predict the US. Equal strength is not important.

   D. Wrong. When no new information is provided, conditioning doesn't occur. Equal strength is not important.

6. B, Correct (p. 236)

   A. Wrong. The law of effect involves response consequences, not a signal that a stimulus won't appear.

   C. Wrong. Escape conditioning requires a response that ends an event. The rat's response doesn't.

   D. Wrong. Avoidance conditioning requires a response to prevent a stimulus. The rat's response doesn't.

7. D, Correct (p. 233)

   A. Wrong. The other fish were not paired with the sardines as required by second-order conditioning.

   B. Wrong. Conditioned taste aversions involve classical conditioning. Punishment relates to operant conditioning.

   C. Wrong. Simultaneous conditioning involves presenting the CS and US simultaneously.

8. C, Correct (p. 234)

   A. Wrong. If inhibition had occurred, fear would have been inhibited.

   B. Wrong. Second-order conditioning uses an established CS to condition a new CS.

   D. Wrong. The disappearance, not the reappearance, of the fear would represent extinction.

9. A, Correct (p. 237)

   B. Wrong. Both types of conditioning involve learning.

   C. Wrong. Both types of conditioning apply to animals and humans.

   D. Wrong. Discrimination and generalization occur in operant conditioning.

10. D, Correct (p. 242)

    A., B. Wrong. The response here decreases, so no reinforcement of either type is involved.

    C. Wrong. The decrease in response means punishment occurred, but something is added in positive punishment.

11. A, Correct (p. 240)

    B. Wrong. It's reinforcement, but something is added (essay requirement), not removed.

    C., D. Wrong. The response (using obscenity) increased, so it isn't punishment.

12. B, Correct (p. 240)

    A. Wrong. Positive reinforcement involves presenting something, not taking something away or avoiding something.

    C., D. Wrong. The response increased; no punishment occurred. Escape and avoidance relate to negative reinforcement.

13. D, Correct (p. 242)

    A., B. Wrong. The response (forgetting homework) was reduced, so reinforcement isn't involved.

    C. Wrong. No aversive event was added as required by positive punishment. A desired event (computer access) was removed.

14. C, Correct (p. 244)

    A. Wrong. Because the requirements for reinforcement are variable, it isn't a fixed schedule.

    B. Wrong. Payoffs are based on number of plays, not time. The number isn't constant, so it's not FI.

    D. Wrong. Payoffs are based on number of plays (responses), not time, so it isn't an interval schedule.

15. D, Correct (p. 252)

    A. Wrong. There is no variable reinforcer. Were you thinking of variable schedule of reinforcement?

    B. Wrong. Primary reinforcers have intrinsic value, like food or water. Helmet decals must acquire value.

    C. Wrong. Decals are given; an aversive event is not eliminated if they perform well.

16. C, Correct (p. 246)

    A, B, D. Wrong. A scalloped pattern is characteristic of a fixed interval schedule.

17. A, Correct (p. 247)

    B. Wrong. Partial reinforcement is reinforcing some responses, not changing the required response.

    C. Wrong. Discrimination involves responding only when a signal indicates reinforcement is possible.

    D. Wrong. Sensitization is an increase in an orienting response to a stimulus that is repeated.

18. D, Correct (p. 250)

    A, B, C. Wrong. The key here is her previous experience observing drivers drive.

MULTIPLE CHOICE PRETEST 2

1. C, Correct (p. 225)

   A. Wrong. There was no increase in the sound's ability to capture his attention.

   B. Wrong. Damon's behavior did not develop due to experience.

   D. Wrong. There was no decrease in the sound's ability to capture his attention.

2. A, Correct (p. 226)

   B. Wrong. Sensitization would have increased her response to the elevator bell.

   C. Wrong. Observational learning is learning by watching others. She didn't do this.

   D. Wrong. Spontaneous recovery is the reappearance of an extinguished conditioned response.

3. D, Correct (p. 233)

   A. Wrong. Spontaneous recovery is the reappearance of an extinguished CR. A new CS doesn't occur.

   B. Wrong. Discrimination would require the CR to occur only to the rat.

   C. Wrong. The other animals have not been paired with the rat, so this isn't second-order conditioning.

4. C, Correct (p. 234)

   A. Wrong. Spontaneous recovery is the reappearance of a previously extinguished CR.

   B. Wrong. Niko didn't learn by observing the behavior of other people.

   D. Wrong. No stimulus is mentioned that signals when a ball won't hit him, as required by conditioned inhibition.

5. C, Correct (p. 232)

   A. Wrong. Habituation is the lessening of an orienting response, not the conditioning of a new stimulus.

   B. Wrong. When a newly added stimulus doesn't become a conditioned stimulus, blocking has occurred.

   D. Wrong. Generalization occurs if stimuli similar to the CS produce a response. No similarity was involved here.

6. A, Correct (p. 237)

   B. Wrong. Instrumental relates to behavior impacting outcomes; in classical conditioning outcomes are signaled, not impacted.

   C. Wrong. Avoidance conditioning is a specific type of instrumental conditioning, but the two terms are not interchangeable.

   D. Wrong. Escape conditioning is a specific type of instrumental conditioning, but the two terms are not interchangeable.

7. B, Correct (p. 228)

   A. Wrong. The alarm is the unconditioned stimulus for the response of waking up.

   C. Wrong. A positive reinforcer is a stimulus that, when presented after a response, increases the likelihood of that response occurring again.

   D. Wrong. Blocking occurs when a second stimulus fails to give new signaling information and fails to become a conditioned stimulus.

8. C, Correct (pp. 239-242)

   A. Wrong. The law of effect involves the results of an action influencing future action, not signaling events prior to a response.

   B. Wrong. The law of effect involves operant principles, but not classical conditioning.

   D. Wrong. Habituation and sensitization don't relate to the results of a response, as in the law of effect.

9. D, Correct (p. 239)

   A. Wrong. Shaping is a method for teaching a response, not a sign that reinforcement is possible.

   B. Wrong. Negative reinforcement is an event that, if removed after a response, increases responding.

   C. Wrong. This is not a classical conditioning scenario. It is an operant conditioning scenario.

10. A, Correct (p. 240) B. Wrong. A response (screaming) led to the *presentation of* an event (cookie) and an increased likelihood of the response.

    C, D. Wrong. A response (crying) increased, not decreased, so punishment isn't involved.

11. B, Correct (p. 247)

    A. Wrong. Social learning is learning by observation, not changing the reinforcement requirements.

    C. Wrong. An FR schedule is based on the number of responses, not the form of the responses.

    D. Wrong. Tom's father didn't imitate or demonstrate. The key here is the changing requirements.

12. D, Correct (p. 240)

    A. Wrong. Response deprivation theory explains why reinforcement occurs, not the impact of accidental reinforcement.

    B. Wrong. Response deprivation theory explains why reinforcement occurs, not resistance to extinction.

    C. Wrong. Social learning theory does include the impact of reinforcement, but the emphasis is on observation.

13. B, Correct (p. 245)

    A. Wrong. The key determinant of when reinforcement (winning a CD) will occur is based on time, not number of responses.

    C. Wrong. The key determinant is a set time period, so it would be a fixed schedule and an interval, not ratio, schedule.

    D. Wrong. The required interval is fixed, not variable.

14. A, Correct (p. 240)

    B. Wrong. A conditioned reinforcer acquired its reinforcing characteristics. Pain avoidance is naturally reinforcing.

    C. Wrong. Sara's response wasn't learned by observing others.

    D. Wrong. Positive reinforcement adds something after a response. Here, the response terminates an aversive event.

15. D, Correct (p. 244)

    A, C. Wrong. An interval schedule is based on the time since reinforcement, not the number of responses (signatures).

    B. Wrong. Variable schedules reinforce after a variable (average) number of responses.

16. B, Correct (p. 245)

    A. Wrong. Continuous reinforcement produces the fastest extinction.

    C, D. Wrong. Extinction is faster after fixed schedules than after variable schedules.

17. D, Correct (p. 244)

    A, C. Wrong. Variable schedules produce relatively continuous response patterns.

    B. Wrong. A fixed interval schedule is characterized by a scalloped response pattern, not a brief pause following reinforcement.

18. A, Correct (p. 251)

    B. Wrong. Reinforcement did not occur and then end. The key is observational learning.

    C. Wrong. Conditioned inhibition occurs when a stimulus signals a US won't occur. There is no US.

    D. Wrong. Accidental reinforcement follows a behavior but is not a result of that behavior.

19. D, Correct (p. 251)

    A. Wrong. Adventitious reinforcement relates to superstitious behavior, not modeling research.

    B. Wrong. Orienting responses involve shifts of attention to novel stimuli, not effects of violence.

    C. Wrong. Bandura's research involved modeling, not the issue of natural vs. learned reinforcers.

CHAPTER **8**

MEMORY

ESTABLISHING LEARNING GOALS

Use these learning goals as a preview of the chapter, a guide for active reading, and to evaluate your mastery of the material. Review the relevant goals as you begin and end your reading of each major section of the chapter.

I. Define memory, and describe the role of encoding, storage, and retrieval.

II. Discuss how information is remembered over the short term.

   A. Discuss how visual and auditory sensory memories can be measured.
      1. Define sensory memory and distinguish it from short-term memory.
      2. Describe Sperling's research on iconic memory, and discuss its conclusions.
      3. Identify the type of code and the duration of echoic memory.
      4. Discuss the adaptive value of sensory memory.

   B. Describe how information is represented, maintained, and forgotten over the short term.
      1. Describe the nature of short-term memory and the working memory model.
      2. Evaluate the question of whether mental images are the same as perceptual images.
      3. Discuss short-term forgetting and evaluate the role of rehearsal.
      4. Discuss why short-term memory has a limited capacity and explain how chunking may help.

III. Discuss how information is stored for the long term.

   A. Define episodic, semantic, and procedural memories.

   B. Explain why it is important to form an elaborate and distinctive memory record.

   C. Describe some simple mnemonic techniques.
      1. Describe the method of loci, pegword techniques, and linkword systems.
      2. Discuss flashbulb memories.

IV. Discuss how information is retrieved from memory.

   A. Discuss the importance of retrieval cues in remembering.
      1. Discuss the idea that forgetting is mostly cue-dependent.
      2. Explain the importance of the encoding-retrieval match and transfer-appropriate processing.

   B. Explain the role of schemas in reconstructive memory.
      1. Provide evidence that long-term memory is reconstructive.

2. Explain both the adaptive value and the costs of memory schemas.

C. Discuss the differences between explicit and implicit memory.

V. Discuss how memory is updated and managed.

A. Discuss the contributions of Ebbinghaus, and explain why forgetting is often adaptive.

B. Describe the mechanisms that cause forgetting, including decay and retroactive and proactive interference.

C. Discuss motivated forgetting and the case for repression.

D. Describe retrograde and anterograde amnesia, and explain where memories might be stored in the brain.

MASTERING THE MATERIAL

PREVIEW & REMEMBERING OVER THE SHORT TERM (PP. 257-267)

MASTERING THE VOCABULARY

Define or explain each of the following terms.

1. memory
2. encoding
3. storage
4. retrieval
5. sensory memory
6. short-term memory
7. iconic memory
8. echoic memory
9. rehearsal
10. memory span
11. chunking

MASTERING THE CONCEPTS

Fill in the blanks to create a summary of the section.

Memory is the capacity to [1] ____________ and [2] ____________ information. Memory involves three processes: [3] ____________ , storage, and [4] ____________ . This chapter considers four issues: How do we remember over the short term? How do we store information for the long term? How is information recovered appropriately? How do we keep memory current?

[5] ____________ memory retains a replica of the stimulus for a few seconds to assist perceptual processing. Visual sensory memory is [6] ____________ memory. Using a [7] ____________ report procedure, Sperling concluded iconic memory is brief (.5 sec). [8] ____________ memory for audition has a duration of less than a second, although some data suggest 5-10 seconds.

Short-term memory, or working (p. 261) memory, briefly stores and manipulates information. Information is mostly coded in an acoustic (p. 262) form, or inner voice, but other codes are possible. Errors often sound like the original input. Imagery has properties of both memory and perception. Detail is incomplete, as in memory, but neurological data suggest processes used in perception are also used in imagery.

If short-term memories are not [9] ____________ they are lost within 1-2 seconds (older estimates suggested 10-15 sec) due to [10] ____________ , interference from new input, or both. Short-term memory span is 7 units, plus or minus 2, and represents memory's [11] ____________ . The time needed to rehearse input might limit the span; memory span is lower for input that takes longer to say. [12] ____________ , rearranging input into meaningful groups, speeds rehearsal and increases memory span. The [13] ____________ memory model is a common approach to short-term memory. It includes several mechanisms, including a phonological loop, a visuospatial sketchpad, and a central [14] ____________ , and it helps explain memory problems.

EVALUATING YOUR PROGRESS

Select the best response. If you make any errors, reread the relevant material before proceeding.

1. A psychologist who is studying how memories are formed and represented is studying the process of
   a. encoding.
   b. storage.
   c. retrieval.
   d. interference.

2. Iconic memory is an example of
   a. short-term memory.
   b. auditory memory.
   c. sensory memory.
   d. repressed memory.

3. Recall from iconic memory is limited because
   a. iconic memory has a limited capacity.
   b. the information fades before all of it can be processed and reported.
   c. vocal responses interfere with the operation of the inner voice.
   d. information is stored using only simple rehearsal.

4. Information in short-term memory can be encoded in several forms, but the most common code is
   a. acoustic.
   b. visual.
   c. abstract (not related to any sense).
   d. episodic.

5. To keep information in short-term memory for more than a few seconds requires
   a. retrieval cues.
   b. chunking.
   c. rehearsal.
   d. partial report.

6. When chunking occurs
   a. short term memory capacity is increased.
   b. recall often is reduced due to interference.
   c. memory span decreases.
   d. a visual code becomes more likely than an acoustic code.

7. A common estimate of the short-term memory span is
   a. 1-5 items.
   b. 5-9 items.
   c. 9-15 items.
   d. more than 20 items.

8. A popular view of short-term memory is the idea of
   a. iconic memory.
   b. working memory.
   c. echoic memory.
   d. whole report memory.

STORING INFORMATION FOR THE LONG TERM (PP. 267-273)

MASTERING THE VOCABULARY

Define or explain each of the following terms.

1. long-term memory
2. episodic memory
3. semantic memory
4. procedural memory
5. elaboration
6. distinctiveness
7. flashbulb memories
8. visual imagery
9. distributed practice
10. primacy effect
11. recency effect
12. mnemonic devices
13. method of loci
14. peg-word method

MASTERING THE CONCEPTS.

Fill in the blanks to create a summary of the section.

Long-term memory maintains information for extended periods. Long-term memories can be [1] ____________ memories, which are memories of personal events, [2] ____________ memories, factual memories not related to personal events, or [3] ____________ memories, memories about how to do something.

Several techniques improve long-term memory. [4] ____________ links new items to existing memories, forming connections that act as retrieval cues. Elaboration is encouraged by thinking about meaning, using [5] ____________ processing, noting distinctiveness of input, and using visual [6] ____________ . Using [7] ____________ rather than massed practice creates rich retrieval cues that aid memory. An item's place in a list also affects its recall, producing a [8] ____________ curve. The first and last items are recalled best, the primacy and [9] ____________ effects. Being more distinctive might produce these effects. Emotional content influences memory. [10] ____________ memories are detailed memories of emotionally significant events. People confidently recall many details, but these memories are not always very accurate.

Many [11] ____________ devices or memory aids emphasize imagery, thus increasing distinctiveness and retrieval cues. In the [12] ____________ technique items are imaged along a path which later acts as a retrieval cue. The [13] ____________ method uses imagery to link items to memory cues, or pegs, such as a familiar rhyme. The [14] ____________ system for learning foreign vocabulary uses imagery to link a foreign word with a rhyming known word.

EVALUATING YOUR PROGRESS

Select the best response. If you miss any questions, reread the relevant material before proceeding.

1. Episodic memory includes
   a. events in one's personal history.
   b. information about how to do something.
   c. the contents of working memory.
   d. basic factual information such as "Austin is the capital of Texas."

2. Distributed practice is beneficial because
   a. it increases the type of retrieval cues created.
   b. rehearsal is not interrupted by other events that cause interference.
   c. it involves the use of imagery.
   d. it relates to-be-remembered items to previously established memory cues.

3. Forming images of the to-be-remembered items associated with a nursery rhyme similar sequence (e.g., one is a bun, two is a shoe...) describes
   a. the pegword method.
   b. the chunking method.
   c. the linkword method.
   d. the method of loci.

4. The recency effect in memory is improved recall for items
   a. at the beginning of a list.
   b. at the end of a list.
   c. given relational processing.
   d. that have emotional content.

5. Distributed practice is beneficial because it
   a. increases the types of retrieval cues created.
   b. avoids interference effects.
   c. involves the use of imagery.
   d. ensures transfer-appropriate processing.

6. Especially vivid memories of emotionally-charged events are known as
   a. repressed memories.
   b. flashbulb memories.
   c. iconic memories.
   d. procedural memories.

RECOVERING INFORMATION FROM CUES (PP. 274-281)

MASTERING THE VOCABULARY

Define or explain each of the following terms.

1. free recall
2. cued recall
3. transfer-appropriate processing
4. schema
5. implicit memory
6. explicit memory

MASTERING THE CONCEPTS

Fill in the blanks to create a summary of the section.

Retrieval is guided by internal or external [1] ____________ . If retrieval cues are presented externally, as in a [2] ____________ task, recall is better than if no external cues are given, as in free recall. Researchers believe most [3] ____________ is due to inadequate or inaccessible retrieval cues, not loss of input. To be effective, a cue needs to match at [4] ____________ and at retrieval. This is most likely to occur with [5] ____________ -appropriate proccssing, usiug the same processes at learning as at testing.

Memories are [6] ____________ , not replayed, and [7] ____________ , clusters of related facts, are used to fill in gaps in memory. Although adaptive, this can distort memory. Research also shows memories are influenced by the form of the [8] ____________ used in testing. Thus, eyewitness memories can be influenced by the interview itself.

Not all memories are conscious, or [9] ____________ , memories. Remembering without conscious awareness is [10] ____________ memory. Picture or word fragment completion tests show implicit memory influences behavior, but without the person's awareness. Retrieval cues are important for both types of memory, but conscious strategies are not effective for implicit memory. Déjà vu and the false [11] ____________ effect may be effects of implicit memories.

EVALUATING YOUR PROGRESS

Select the best response. If you miss any questions, reread the relevant material before proceeding.

1. Which of the following best supports the idea that most memory failure is due to inadequate retrieval cues?
   a. the false fame effect
   b. eyewitness memory research by Loftus and Palmer
   c. comparison of free recall and cued recall test performance
   d. comparison of implicit and explicit memory test performance
2. Transfer-appropriate processing involves
   a. studying in one long session.
   b. studying in short, spaced periods.
   c. using the same processes to learn material that will be used to test memory for the material.
   d. using memory tests that do not ask for direct recall, but instead, that test memory indirectly.
3. Organized clusters of facts assist recall from long-term memory when actual memories are limited. These knowledge structures are called
   a. the inner voice.
   b. schemas.
   c. episodic memories.
   d. working memories.
4. Loftus and Palmer's research on memories for accident details clearly demonstrates that
   a. people usually can recall minor details with high accuracy because of the visual nature of events.
   b. people realize what they know about an accident and what they don't know about an accident.
   c. free recall produces more accurate and more extensive recall than cued recall.
   d. the way questions about memories are asked significantly influences the memories reported.

5. Remembering without conscious awareness or willful intent is
   a. explicit memory.
   b. implicit memory.
   c. schematic memory.
   d. reconstructive memory.

6. Remembering is not a literal replay of past events. Instead, it is partly a creative process that blends information from schemas with memories about the event. In other words, long-term memory is
   a. reconstructive.
   b. distinctive.
   c. transfer-appropriate.
   d. primarily iconic.

UPDATING MEMORY (PP. 282-288)

MASTERING THE VOCABULARY

Define or explain each of the following terms.

1. forgetting
2. decay
3. retroactive interference
4. proactive interference
5. repression
6. amnesia
7. retrograde amnesia
8. anterograde amnesia

MASTERING THE CONCEPTS.

Fill in the blanks to create a summary of the section.

Forgetting, the loss in [1] ____________ of stored material, is adaptive because it reduces memory "clutter." By testing relearning after various delays, the [2] ____________ method, Ebbinghaus developed a "forgetting curve." Most forgetting occurs [3] ____________ after initial learning and continues gradually.

Forgetting was first attributed to [4] ____________ , a loss due to the passage of time, but current theories emphasize [5] ____________ , disruption caused by other material. When new material disrupts old material, [6] ____________ interference occurs. When old material disrupts new material, [7] ____________ interference occurs. Interference theory suggests material is not necessarily eliminated but becomes harder to access.

Forgetting can occur for emotionally adaptive or motivated reasons. [8] ____________ , a defense mechanism proposed by Freud in which memories are pushed out of consciousness, may reduce anxiety. Repression's scientific validity is unclear. Apparent cases of repression might be due to reconstructive memory, differential rehearsal, or other factors.

[9] ____________ is forgetting caused by physical problems. Head injuries can lead to a loss of memory for events that occurred before the injury, [10] ____________ amnesia. Brain damage also can lead to the loss of memory for events after the injury, [11] ____________ amnesia. Implicit memory tests show memories might be formed but not consciously accessible. One cause of this amnesia is [12] ____________ syndrome, due to alcoholism. The [13] ____________ is critical for memory, but so are other brain areas.

EVALUATING YOUR PROGRESS

Select the best response. If you make any errors, reread the relevant material before proceeding.

1. Ebbinghaus' forgetting curve shows that forgetting occurs
   a. very slowly at first, and then rapidly after a week.
   b. very rapidly at first, and then continues gradually for a long time.
   c. very rapidly at first, but then stops quickly.
   d. at about the same moderate pace for at least the first six months, then stops.
2. If newly learned material disrupts memory for previously learned material _______ has occurred.
   a. retrograde amnesia
   b. anterograde amnesia
   c. retroactive interference
   d. proactive interference
3. The decay theory of forgetting proposes
   a. simply the passage of time is responsible for forgetting.
   b. newly learned material covers up or disturbs memories.
   c. neurotransmitter changes are responsible for forgetting.
   d. brain injury leads to tissue death, which disrupts memory.

4. Anxiety-producing memories may be pushed into the unconscious, according to Freud. This is known as
   a. anterograde amnesia.
   b. retroactive interference.
   c. Korsakoff's syndrome.
   d. repression.

5. The loss of memory for events that occurred just before a brain injury is known as
   a. cryptomnesia.
   b. retrograde amnesia.
   c. anterograde amnesia.
   d. proactive amnesia.

6. Recent research on anterograde amnesia suggests that the amnesia occurs because
   a. new input is not passed from sensory memory to short-term memory.
   b. the memory span of working memory is reduced drastically, preventing learning.
   c. the storage processes of long-term memory are destroyed, preventing any learning.
   d. new input is stored in long-term memory, but direct conscious retrieval is not possible.

7. Normal memory function is very dependent on having a healthy
   a. occipital lobe.
   b. parietal lobe.
   c. pons.
   d. hippocampus.

MAKING FINAL PREPARATIONS

Complete these sections without consulting your book or notes. For a more accurate estimate of how well you know this material, wait at least a day or two after studying the chapter before working on the questions. Some of the material you "know" immediately after working with the chapter will be quickly forgotten. Exercises done too soon after studying will overestimate what you know well.

SHORT ESSAY QUESTIONS

Write a brief answer to each question.

1. What is the adaptive value of sensory memory?

   ____

   ____

2. Compare the characteristics and functions of sensory memory and short-term memory.

   ____

   ____

3. Nick spent the entire day before each multiple choice test reading and rereading the text but failed the tests. Give at least two responses his instructor might make that are based on principles of memory.

____

____

4. Compare the two types of amnesia discussed in your text and discuss what aspect of memory (encoding, storage, retrieval) seems to be defective.

____

____

5. Explain why memory is described as "reconstructive," and the advantages and disadvantages of this.

____

____

MATCHING

Select the correct definition or description for each item.

1. _______ Ebbinghaus
2. _______ chunking
3. _______ Sperling
4. _______ memory span
5. _______ memory schema
6. _______ echoic memory
7. _______ phonological loop
8. _______ Peterson & Peterson
9. _______ mnemonic device
10. _______ free recall
11. _______ repression
12. _______ Loftus & Palmer
13. _______ partial report task
14. _______ savings method
15. _______ sensory memory
16. _______ procedural memory

a. must recall items without explicit retrieval cues
b. studied sensory memory
c. short-term memory capacity
d. must report cued row of stimulus array
e. determined forgetting curve
f. technique to improve retrieval, e.g., pegword
g. compares time to learn with time to relearn
h. studied duration of short-term memory
i. auditory sensory memory
j. system that very briefly retains a replica of input
k. component of working memory
l. studied the influence the question has on memory
m. "how to" memory
n. reorganizing input into meaningful units
o. motivated forgetting
p. clusters of related facts that supplement memory

MULTIPLE CHOICE PRETEST 1

Select the one best response.

1. Memory is the capacity to preserve and recover information. Information is recovered through
   a. transduction processes.
   b. encoding processes.
   c. storage processes.
   d. retrieval processes.

2. Which of the following is a type of sensory memory?
   a. implicit memory
   b. working memory
   c. echoic memory
   d. reconstructive memory

3. Mistakes in short-term memory are likely to involve responses that sound like one of the original items, even if the items were presented visually. From this, researchers conclude that short-term memory
   a. mostly uses an inner voice to code information.
   b. retains information for 1-2 seconds.
   c. has a limited capacity of 5 to 9 items.
   d. can be disrupted by either decay or interference.

4. Although recent studies suggest a shorter duration, the Peterson & Peterson distractor experiment originally was interpreted to mean the duration of short-term memory (without rehearsal) is
   a. 1-2 seconds.
   b. 10-15 seconds.
   c. 30-40 seconds.
   d. 1-2 minutes.

5. Carlos formed an image of the to-be-remembered items at specific places along a familiar path. When he needed to recall the items, he mentally walked the path and retrieved the stored images. This illustrates
   a. the method of loci.
   b. a pegword method.
   c. the inner voice.
   d. a distributed practice method.

6. Chuck listened carefully as the technician described the seven steps required to set up his new computer system, but afterward, Chuck realized he could remember only the last few steps. This pattern of recall is most like
   a. flashbulb memory.
   b. the recency effect.
   c. the partial report effect.
   d. proactive interference.

7. In a short-term memory task, chess masters organized a view of a chess board in terms of recognizable patterns rather than individual pieces. The technique being used is
   a. chunking.
   b. method of loci.
   c. transfer appropriate processing.
   d. distributed practice.

8. You don't really remember what you did at Thanksgiving two years ago, but you can give a fairly close description by using general information about holiday traditions, where you lived, and other schemas. This illustrates the __________ nature of long-term memory.
   a. cue-dependent
   b. transfer-appropriate
   c. reconstructive
   d. distributed

9. After the phone call inviting her to the party, Marta repeated, "238 Elm, 238 Elm, 238 Elm," until she found a pen and paper. Marta was keeping the address in short term memory by using
   a. rehearsal.
   b. cued recall.
   c. elaboration.
   d. implicit memory.

10. Which mechanism in working memory controls how processing is allocated?
    a. the visuospatial sketch pad
    b. the phonological loop
    c. the dichotic control
    d. the central executive

11. Recent research suggests that memory span is determined not so much by space limitations, but by
    a. the distinctiveness of the information being placed in memory.
    b. the number of retrieval cues that are developed at input.
    c. the emotional content of the items being placed in memory.
    d. the rate at which items can be rehearsed in the inner voice.

12. To answer the question, "Who is the President of the United States?" requires primarily
    a. episodic memory.
    b. procedural memory.
    c. semantic memory.
    d. flashbulb memory.

13. The feature the method of loci, the pegword method, and the linkword method have in common is the use of
    a. imagery.
    b. distributed practice.
    c. episodic memory.
    d. rhymes.

14. The camp counselor realized that once she learned the names of the July campers, she couldn't remember the names of the June campers. This is an example of
    a. motivated forgetting.
    b. retroactive interference.
    c. proactive interference.
    d. anterograde amnesia.

15. An example of an implicit memory test is
    a. Sperling's partial report test.
    b. Sperling's whole report test.
    c. a cued recall test.
    d. a word fragment test.

16. Following a rape, the victim had no memory of the rape, but became very anxious if approached by a man. According to Freud's concept of defense mechanisms and memory, this would be a case of
    a. anterograde amnesia.
    b. proactive interference.
    c. Korsakoff's syndrome.
    d. repression.

17. Drivers who suffer a head injury in an accident often have no memory of the events just prior to the accident. This memory loss would be considered
    a. repression.
    b. Korsakoff's syndrome.
    c. retrograde amnesia.
    d. anterograde amnesia.

18. Helen reports she has a very detailed, vivid memory of what happened when she was robbed at gunpoint. This is an example of
    a. repression.
    b. the primacy effect.
    c. iconic memory.
    d. flashbulb memory.

19. The current view of forgetting emphasizes
    a. decay.
    b. interference.
    c. repression.
    d. physical problems.

20. Korsakoff's syndrome includes
    a. repression.
    b. anterograde amnesia.
    c. retrograde amnesia.
    d. exceptionally good memory, with some synesthesia (blending of sensations).

MULTIPLE CHOICE PRETEST 2

Select the one best response.

1. Why did Sperling conclude that the entire stimulus display is represented in sensory memory?
   a. Immediate partial report performance was very accurate.
   b. Errors tended to sound like the actual stimulus.
   c. Cues that occurred after 1 second did not improve performance.
   d. Recall was better if the stimuli could be pronounced quickly.

2. The adaptive value of sensory memory is that it
   a. allows past experiences to influence current ones.
   b. helps develop distinctive retrieval cues.
   c. provides additional processing time after a stimulus has ended.
   d. increases the capacity of working memory.

3. Gwen continues to hear the tone a second or so after it has ended. This "phantom" tone probably represents
   a. an implicit memory.
   b. an echoic memory.
   c. proactive interference.
   d. a memory schema.

4. Students who slept after studying remembered more than those who did other things during that period. This supports the importance of
   a. encoding specificity.
   b. transfer-appropriate processing.
   c. decay processes.
   d. interference from other input.

5. Evidence that mental imagery is similar to normal visual perception includes all of the following EXCEPT:
   a. Large objects are easier to "see" in images than small objects.
   b. Similar brain areas are active in visual perception and visual imagery.
   c. Partial report patterns are found in both visual perception and imagery.
   d. Brain damaged people sometimes show deficits in both normal perception and imagery.

6. Zelda was presented the list, "hat, dog, rock, pen, hair, lake, cloud, rug, and sheet" in a short-term memory experiment. Her most likely error would be
   a. saying "pear" instead of "hair."
   b. saying "pond" instead of "lake."
   c. forgetting "sheet" entirely.
   d. forgetting "hat" entirely.

7. One way to increase the amount of information held in short term memory is to use
   a. repression.
   b. partial report.
   c. chunking.
   d. the method of loci.

8. Which of the following is false concerning Baddeley's model of working memory?
   a. Visual and spatial information is processed in a different system than verbal information.
   b. Short-term memory and long-term memory are controlled by the same mechanisms.
   c. The effects of certain types of brain damage are explained.
   d. A central executive controls and coordinates processing.

9. To help ensure a good encoding-retrieval match, learners should use
   a. distributed practice.
   b. chunking.
   c. memory schemas.
   d. transfer-appropriate processing.

10. After studying most of the morning, Gil took the practice test and got every multiple-choice question right. To his surprise, he did poorly on the multiple-choice exam the next day. Which of the following can best account for this difference in performance?
    a. the difference in implicit and explicit memory tests
    b. failing to use transfer appropriate processing
    c. the use of distributed practice
    d. Ebbinghaus' forgetting curve

11. Research on flashbulb memories confirms all of the following EXCEPT:
    a. Flashbulb memories usually concern emotional or surprising events.
    b. Flashbulb memories are reported with great confidence, even after significant time.
    c. Flashbulb memories are highly accurate because they are like a picture of the event.
    d. Flashbulb memories include vivid details about the event.

12. Elaboration is important because it promotes
    a. a distinctive memory record.
    b. a strong recency effect.
    c. a strong primacy effect.
    d. efficient storage.

13. Knowing how to tie your shoes depends most on
    a. episodic memory.
    b. semantic memory.
    c. iconic memory.
    d. procedural memory.

14. Chris is having trouble learning the new arrangement of the song. She often finds herself shifting to the old arrangement in the middle. This is an example of
    a. memory overwriting.
    b. repression.
    c. proactive interference.
    d. retroactive interference.

15. You are on the jury in a trial involving a fight in a bar. Based on what you know about the research conducted by Loftus and Palmer, as you listen to the various eyewitnesses you would be wise to
    a. accept their memories of the event as trustworthy and highly accurate.
    b. accept their memories as highly accurate as long as they are very confident about their memories.
    c. believe absolutely nothing they say because eyewitness testimony is never correct.
    d. listen very carefully to the questions that are asked of each person.

16. The emergency services personnel initially read about the procedures to be used in a large scale disaster. To complete the learning process, they took part in a mock disaster and rescued and treated "victims" as they would in a real disaster. This approach is based on the principle of
    a. reconstructive remembering.
    b. transfer-appropriate processing.
    c. proactive interference.
    d. cue-dependent forgetting.

17. If your recognition of the mugger is influenced by the clothes, race, or "attitude" of the people in a line-up because they fit your idea of "criminal" you are demonstrating the role of _________ in memory.
    a. schemas
    b. elaboration
    c. interference
    d. encoding specificity

18. Pat can only remember the events up to the time of his serious brain infection. He can't recall anything that has happened since. If given a word to remember and then distracted for a few seconds, Pat can't remember the word. He forgets what he had for dinner minutes afterward. Pat's problem is
    a. anterograde amnesia.
    b. retrograde amnesia.
    c. flashbulb memory.
    d. cue-dependent forgetting.

19. Damage to which brain area is most strongly associated with anterograde amnesia?
    a. the hypothalamus
    b. the hippocampus
    c. the parietal lobe
    d. the cerebellum

LANGUAGE DEVELOPMENT GUIDE

CORE TERMS

In this chapter, your instructor will probably talk about the ***practical applications*** of what we know about memory -- that is, how you can use the information day-to-day. And then they might use the term ***pragmatic***. That's another term that means, "to focus on uses of something." You could say that a pragmatic person looks for practical applications. You might also hear the term ***implications***, as in, "So what are the implications of this research finding?" That means something like, "What does this mean in the real world? How can these findings be applied? What further ideas do they lead to?"

A pragmatic person is likely to be interested in ***strategies*** -- ways to actually use something. In a lecture on learning strategies, you are likely to hear three words: **rote**, ***repetition*** and ***simple rehearsal***. As you can probably guess, they all have to do with practicing something over and over. Those terms will be contrasted with ***elaboration***, which means adding detail. It's ***counterintuitive*** (not what you'd expect), but the more detail you add to what you want to remember, the better you will remember it. But the key is that the details have to be interesting. So the practical application here is that if you are studying, the more interesting details and examples you can pay attention to, the better you will remember the material!

IDIOMS

p. 258	devoid of	without any
p. 259	fleeting snapshot	quick picture or photograph; quick impression
p. 259	internal repetition	saying it over and over in your mind
p. 263	indefinitely	for an unknown, perhaps long, period of time
p. 269	an involved sequence	a complicated series
p. 271	mediocre at best	only average, or even worse
p. 278	undergraduates	college students
p. 278	just prior to	just before
p. 283	cardiopulmonary resuscitation	CPR, a lifesaving technique during heart attacks
p. 284	conceivable that	it could be that
p. 285	retain the capacity	keep the ability to
p. 285	in the conventional sense	the usual meaning or approach
p. 286	cast themselves in a positive light	make themselves seem as good as possible

PRONUNCIATION

iconic (eye-kon′-ick) *p. 259*
echoic (eh-ko′-ick) *p. 260*
mnemonic (nee-mon′-ick) *p. 272*
schema (skee′-muh) *p. 277*
anterograde (an-tair′-o-grade’) *p. 286*

SOLUTIONS

PREVIEW & REMEMBERING OVER THE SHORT TERM (PP. 257-267)

MASTERING THE CONCEPTS

1. preserve (p. 257)
2. recover (p. 257)
3. encoding (p. 258)
4. retrieval (p. 258)
5. Sensory (p. 259)
6. iconic (p. 259)
7. partial p. 261)
8. Echoic (p. 261)
9. rehearsed (p. 263)
10. decay (p. 264)
11. capacity (p. 265)
12. Chunking (p. 266)
13. working (p. 266)
14. executive (p. 266)

EVALUATING YOUR PROGRESS

1. A, Correct (p. 258)
   B. Wrong. Storage involves maintenance, not recovery.
   C. Wrong. Retrieval involves the recovery of memories, not forming them.
   D. Wrong. Interference is a process by which information is "forgotten."
2. C, Correct (p. 259)
   A. Wrong. Iconic memory is a sensory memory.
   B. Wrong. Iconic memory is visual, not auditory.
   D. Wrong. Repressed memories have been hidden in the unconscious. Iconic memory is accessible.
3. B, Correct (p. 260)
   A. Wrong. Capacity isn't the problem. All the information is represented, but it fades too quickly.
   C. Wrong. The inner voice is involved in short-term memory, and vocal responses do not interfere.
   D. Wrong. Rehearsal is not involved in iconic memory; rehearsal is important for short- and long-term memory.
4. A, Correct (p. 262)
   B. Wrong. Iconic memory has a visual code; STM is acoustic.
   C. Wrong. STM errors are acoustic, not abstract/semantic.
   D. Wrong. Episodic relates to time-linked memories in LTM, not a STM code.
5. C, Correct (p. 263)
   A. Wrong. Retrieval accesses memories; it doesn't help retain them.
   B. Wrong. Chunking improves storage efficiency, not memory duration.
   D. Wrong. Partial report is a memory test, not a way to maintain memories longer.
6. A, Correct (p. 266)
   B. Wrong. Chunking usually increases recall.
   C. Wrong. Chunking usually increases memory span.
   D. Wrong. Chunking does not influence the most likely code; it influences capacity or memory span.
7. B, Correct (p. 265)
   A, C, D. Wrong. Most people can recall 7, plus or minus 2, items.
8. B, Correct (p. 266)
   A. Wrong. Iconic memory is visual sensory memory, not short-term memory.
   C. Wrong. Echoic memory is auditory sensory memory, not short-term memory.
   D. Wrong. Whole report is one of the recall tasks used in Sperling's sensory memory research.

STORING INFORMATION FOR THE LONG TERM (PP. 267-273)

MASTERING THE CONCEPTS.

1. episodic (p. 267)
2. semantic (p. 268)
3. procedural (p. 268)
4. Elaboration (p. 269)
5. relational (p. 269)
6. imagery (p. 270)
7. distributed (p. 271)
8. serial position (p. 270)
9. recency (p. 270)
10. Flashbulb (p. 270)
11. mnemonic (p. 272)
12. method of loci (p. 272)
13. pegword (p. 272)
14. linkword (p. 273)

EVALUATING YOUR PROGRESS

1. A, Correct (p. 267)

   B. Wrong. This describes procedural memory.

   C. Wrong. Episodic memory is a type of long-term memory; working memory is short-term memory.

   D. Wrong. This describes semantic memory.
2. A, Correct (p. 271)

   B. Wrong. Distributed practice does not involve an unbroken period of rehearsal.

   C. Wrong. Distributed practice refers when practice occurs, not the form the rehearsal takes.

   D. Wrong. Elaboration improves memory, but distributed practice doesn't necessarily involve elaboration.
3. A, Correct (p. 272)

   B. Wrong. Chunking involves regrouping into meaningful units, not imagery.

   C. Wrong. Linkword methods use imagery to link an unfamiliar item with a familiar one.

   D. Wrong. The method of loci employs imagery of different locations, not rhymes.
4. B, Correct (p. 271)

   A. Wrong. This is the primacy effect.

   C. Wrong. The recency effect relates to serial position, not elaboration.

   D. Wrong. The recency effect relates to serial position, not emotionally-charged memories.
5. A, Correct (p. 271)

   B. Wrong. Because other events intervene between practice sessions, interference is possible.

   C. Wrong. Distributed practice doesn't necessarily involve imagery. It relates to the timing of practice.

   D. Wrong. Spacing practice sessions doesn't mean processing at encoding and retrieval will be similar.
6. B, Correct (p. 270)

   A. Wrong. Repressed memories are pushed out of consciousness and not easily retrieved.

   C. Wrong. Iconic memories are sensory memories that are very, very brief.

   D. Wrong. Procedural memories are "how to" memories, not memories of events.

RECOVERING INFORMATION FROM CUES (PP. 274-281)

MASTERING THE CONCEPTS

1. retrieval cues (p. 274)
2. cued recall (p. 274)
3. forgetting (p. 275)
4. encoding (p. 276)
5. transfer (p. 276)
6. reconstructed (p. 277)
7. schemas (p. 277)
8. questions (p. 278)
9. explicit (p. 280)
10. implicit (p. 280)
11. fame (p. 281)

EVALUATING YOUR PROGRESS

1. C, Correct (p. 274)
   A. Wrong. The false fame effect illustrates an effect of implicit memory, not the importance of retrieval cues.
   B. Wrong. Eyewitness memory research deals with the impact of schema and how information is tested.
   D. Wrong. Implicit and explicit memory tests demonstrate the influence of information not in conscious awareness, not the importance of retrieval cues.
2. C, Correct (p. 276)
   A. Wrong. This describes massed practice, not transfer-appropriate processing.
   B. Wrong. This describes spaced practice, not transfer-appropriate processing.
   D. Wrong. This describes an implicit memory test, not transfer-appropriate processing.
3. B, Correct (p. 277)
   A. Wrong. The inner voice relates to short-term memory encoding, not long-term memory retrieval.
   C. Wrong. Episodic memories relate to personal events, not knowledge structures.
   D. Wrong. Working memory is a short-term memory concept, not a long-term memory concept.
4. D, Correct (pp. 278-279)
   A. Wrong. Long-term memory is not highly visual. Loftus's work emphases its reconstructive aspect.
   B. Wrong. Loftus showed that people could be made to think they saw something they didn't.
   C. Wrong. Cued recall produces better recall, and Loftus and Palmer did not focus on cued versus free recall.
5. B, Correct (p. 280)
   A. Wrong. Explicit memory involves conscious, strategic memory processes.
   C. Wrong. Schemas are information structures. The key here is "without willful intent."
   D. Wrong. Reconstructive means constructed from memories and schemas. The key here is "unconscious" or unintentional.
6. A, Correct (p. 277)
   B. Wrong. Distinctiveness relates to which information is recalled, but not the description given here.
   C. Wrong. Transfer-appropriate processing is learning material in a way similar to the way it will be recalled. This does not relate to the current description.
   D. Wrong. Iconic refers to sensory memory, not long-term memory.

UPDATING MEMORY (PP. 282-288)

MASTERING THE CONCEPTS.

1. accessibility (p. 282)
2. savings (p. 283)
3. soon (p. 283)
4. decay (p. 283)
5. interference (p. 283)
6. retroactive (p. 284)
7. proactive (p. 284)
8. Repression (p. 285)
9. Amnesia (p. 286)
10. retrograde (p. 286)
11. anterograde (p. 286)
12. Korsakoff's (p. 287)
13. hippocampus (p. 287)

EVALUATING YOUR PROGRESS

1. B, Correct (pp. 282-283)
   A, C, D. Wrong. Forgetting is very rapid initially, then slows to a very gradual loss.
2. C, Correct (p. 284)
   A, B. Wrong. Amnesia is not due to the influence of other learning. It is physically determined.
   D. Wrong. In proactive interference, old material interferes with newly learned material.
3. A, Correct (p. 283)
   B. Wrong. Interference, described in this answer, assumes factors other than time.
   C. Wrong. Decay theory proposes forgetting due to time passing, not neurotransmitter problems.
   D. Wrong. Time, not tissue damage, is the focus of decay theory.

4. D, Correct (p. 285)

   A. Wrong. Anterograde amnesia is due to brain damage, not psychological trauma.

   B. Wrong. Retroactive interference is not a defense mechanism. It involves poor memory for older items because of the formation of newer memories.

   C. Wrong. Korsakoff's syndrome is amnesia caused by brain damage from alcoholism.

5. B, Correct (p. 286)

   A. Wrong. Cryptomnesia is unintentional plagiarism, an effect that might involve implicit memory.

   C. Wrong. Anterograde amnesia is a loss of memory for events that occur *after* the injury.

   D. Wrong. There is no such thing. Proactive interference involves old memories interfering with newer memories.

6. D, Correct (p. 287)

   A, B, C. Wrong. Indirect memory tests show new input is stored in long-term memory. The problem is one of direct, conscious retrieval of new input, not storage failure.

7. D, Correct (p. 287)

   A. Wrong. The occipital lobe is important for visual processing, not memory.

   B. Wrong. The parietal lobe is important for touch and spatial relations, not memory.

   C. Wrong. The pons is responsible for some life support systems and arousal, not memory.

MAKING FINAL PREPARATIONS

SHORT ESSAY QUESTIONS

1. Sensory memory retains a fairly complete replica of the original sensory input for a short period after the stimulus ends. This allows more time for initial processing and thus, allows more complete processing. Sensory memory may be very important for audition, where stimuli (e.g., speech) must be integrated over time. (pp. 260-261)
2. Sensory memory contains the original sensory input, its duration is less than a second for vision (perhaps a little longer for audition), and it holds the entire stimulus display. Short term memory contains processed information, mostly encoded acoustically, it has a longer duration (1-2 sec), although older estimates suggest it might be only 15-30 sec), and is limited in its capacity. (pp. 260-266)
3. The amount of time studied is not always as important as when you study and how you study. First, you should study for shorter periods throughout the entire period before the exam, not just at the end. This is distributed practice, which is better than massed practice (cramming). Second, most forgetting occurs soon after initial learning. What you knew the night before the exam overestimates what you will know the next day. Third, you need to use elaboration to form the rich, distinctive retrieval cues you'll need for the exam; don't just read. Fourth, you should use transfer-appropriate processing--learn the material using the processes you'll use to retrieve it: Practice with multiple-choice questions. (pp. 268-276, 282-284)
4. Retrograde amnesia involves the inability to recall information that was learned prior to the onset of the amnesia. This type of amnesia commonly follows a head injury. Because the memories are often regained, retrieval would be the defective process. In cases in which the memories are not regained, it is possible that storage was disrupted, although research on a second form of amnesia, anterograde amnesia, suggests caution in attributing amnesia to storage deficits. In anterograde amnesia, memories for events that occur after injury cannot be recalled. Although this might suggest that storage processes are defective, implicit memory tests show that memories are present, but unable to be retrieved with conscious intent – a retrieval failure. (pp. 286-287)

5. Long-term memories are not exact versions of the original material. They contain the general idea, but specific details are reconstructed based on memories, expectations, and schema. This is beneficial because to permanently store all information would require massive capacity and retrieval probably would be both difficult and slow. Schema-based reconstruction allows rapid responses and responses to new environments. However, reconstruction can introduce inaccuracies in memory. (pp. 277-280)

MATCHING

1. e (p. 282)
2. n (p. 266)
3. b (p. 260)
4. c (p. 265)
5. p (p. 277)
6. i (p. 260)
7. k (p. 266)
8. h (p. 264)
9. f (p. 272)
10. a (p. 274)
11. o (p. 285)
12. l (p. 278)
13. d (p. 261)
14. g (p. 283)
15. j (p. 259)
16. m (p. 268)

MULTIPLE CHOICE PRETEST 1

1. D, Correct (p. 258)
   A. Wrong. Transduction is the transformation of physical energy into neural activity.
   B. Wrong. Encoding is the initial formation of memories, not their recovery.
   C. Wrong. Storage processes maintain, rather than recover, information.
2. C, Correct (p. 259)
   A. Wrong. Implicit memory is not consciously accessible. Sensory memory is accessible.
   B. Wrong. Working memory is a conceptualization of short term memory.
   D. Wrong. Reconstructive is a term used to describe long-term memory.
3. A, Correct (p. 262)
   B, C, D. Wrong. Although true concerning STM, these are not conclusions from the data cited.
4. B, Correct (p. 264)
   A. Wrong. This is the more recent estimate of the duration of short term memory.
   C. Wrong. This is longer than any short-term memory estimate.
   D. Wrong. This is longer than any short-term memory estimate.
5. A, Correct (p. 272)
   B. Wrong. Pegword methods use a rhyme or other series of words as retrieval cues.
   C. Wrong. The inner voice relates to short-term memory encoding, not mnemonic techniques.
   D. Wrong. Distributed practice refers to spacing practice, rather than massing it all at once.

6. B, Correct (p. 271)
   A. Wrong. Flashbulb memories are detailed memories about emotionally important events.
   C. Wrong. Partial report is a technique used in sensory memory experiments. This is a STM situation.
   D. Wrong. Proactive interference would cause the last items to be forgotten, not the first.
7. A, Correct (p. 266)
   B. Wrong. The method of loci uses imagery involving familiar places, not meaningful patterns.
   C. Wrong. The chess masters are not matching encoding and retrieval processes.
   D. Wrong. Distributed practice is spaced practice.
8. C, Correct (p. 277)
   A. Wrong. A "memory" is created (constructed) here, in spite of having no direct retrieval cues.
   B. Wrong. A "memory" is created (constructed) here. Learning vs. testing processes are not key here.
   D. Wrong. Distributed means spaced, which does not relate to schema.
9. A, Correct (p. 263)
   B. Wrong. Marta is rehearsing. Cued recall is a type of memory test in which cues are presented.
   C. Wrong. Elaboration involves forming connections to other items. Marta isn't doing that.
   D. Wrong. Implicit memory is remembering without conscious awareness or intent.
10. D, Correct (p. 266)
    A. Wrong. The visuospatial sketch pad maintains and processes visual input.
    B. Wrong. The phonological loop maintains and processes acoustic input.
    C. Wrong. The dichotic task is not a working memory mechanism.
11. D, Correct (p. 265)
    A, B, C. Wrong. Recent research centers on the length of time required to rehearse the items. The longer it takes to say an item, the smaller the memory span seems to be.
12. C, Correct (p. 268)
    A. Wrong. Episodic memory involves events in one's personal history.
    B. Wrong. Procedural memory is "how to" memory.
    D. Wrong. Flashbulb memories are highly detailed memories of emotionally charged events.
13. A, Correct (p. 272)
    B. Wrong. Distributed practice refers to spacing practice rather than massing it all at once.
    C. Wrong. Method of loci and pegword methods often are used to improve episodic memory, but the linkword method is frequently used to improve semantic memory, instead.
    D. Wrong. Pegwords use rhymes, but the method of loci doesn't.
14. B, Correct (p. 284)
    A. Wrong. Motivated forgetting, like repression, is not likely without anxiety involved.
    C. Wrong. If proactive, the counselor would have trouble with the new names due to the old names.
    D. Wrong. Even if the counselor had brain damage, the pattern fits retrograde, not anterograde amnesia.
15. D, Correct (p. 280)
    A, B, C. Wrong. These all require conscious, willful use of memory; they are explicit tests.
16. D, Correct (p. 285)
    A. Wrong. Anterograde amnesia isn't a defense mechanism. It is caused by brain injury.
    B. Wrong. Proactive interference isn't a defense mechanism. It is old memories interfering with new ones.
    C. Wrong. Korsakoff's syndrome isn't a defense mechanism. It is an amnesia caused by alcoholism.
17. C, Correct (p. 286)
    A. Wrong. Repression is due to emotional trauma, not physical trauma to the brain.
    B. Wrong. Korsakoff's syndrome is due to alcoholism and involves problems forming new memories.
    D. Wrong. Anterograde amnesia is loss of memory for events after the injury, not those before.
18. D, Correct (p. 270)
    A. Wrong. Repression is the inability to remember traumatic events.
    B. Wrong. The primacy effect is improved memory for the first items in a list.
    C. Wrong. Iconic memory is a type of sensory memory, not a type of long-term memory.

19. B, Correct (p. 283)
    A. Wrong. Decay is given much less emphasis, although some researchers do not rule it out.
    C. Wrong. Repression is a special case of forgetting, and its scientific validity is questioned.
    D. Wrong. Physical problems certainly affect memory, but not the usual forgetting.

20. B, Correct (p. 286)
    A. Wrong. Korsakoff's syndrome produces physically-induced amnesia, not motivated forgetting.
    C. Wrong. Korsakoff's syndrome usually involves anterograde amnesia, not retrograde.
    D. Wrong. Korsakoff's syndrome produces amnesia, not good memory.

MULTIPLE CHOICE PRETEST 2

1. A, Correct (p. 261)
   B. Wrong. This leads to the conclusion that short-term memory is encoded in the inner voice.
   C. Wrong. This would indicate the duration of sensory memory is about 1 second.
   D. Wrong. This is evidence that suggests short-term memory span is determined by the speed of rehearsal.
2. C, Correct (p. 260)
   A. Wrong. Sensory memory doesn't involve recall of previous events. It involves processing current ones.
   B. Wrong. Sensory memory doesn't influence retrieval cues. It just transfers input to STM.
   D. Wrong. Sensory memory is a separate stage of memory than working memory, so it can't increase capacity.
3. B, Correct (p. 261)
   A. Wrong. Implicit memory is not available to conscious awareness.
   C. Wrong. Proactive interference involves prior memories interfering with new memories.
   D. Wrong. Memory schema are important in long term memory, not the sensory memory involved here.
4. D, Correct (p. 284)
   A. Wrong. The key is what occurred during a period of time, not differences in encoding.
   B. Wrong. The difference is in the activity during a period of time, not how encoding and testing corresponded.
   C. Wrong. The time interval was the same, so decay processes would be the same.
5. C, Correct (p. 263)
   A, B, D. Wrong. These are true.
6. A, Correct (p. 262)
   B. Wrong. This would be a typical error in a long-term memory experiment.
   C. Wrong. "Sheet" was the last item, so the recency effect would tend to *improve* recall for "sheet."
   D. Wrong. "Hat" was the first item, so the primacy effect would tend to *improve* recall for "hat."
7. C, Correct (p. 266)
   A. Wrong. Repression prevents access to long term memories. It doesn't increase STM capacity.
   B. Wrong. Partial report is a type of test used to explore sensory memory.
   D. Wrong. The method of loci provides retrieval cues for long-term memories. It doesn't increase capacity.
8. B, Correct (p. 266)
   A, C, D. Wrong. These are true, but this model proposes different mechanisms for STM and LTM.

9. D, Correct (p. 275)

   A. Wrong. Distributed practice improves memory, but it doesn't ensure encoding-retrieval matches.

   B. Wrong. Chunking improves STM capacity, but doesn't make encoding match retrieval.

   C. Wrong. Memory schemas provide useful information, but don't influence encoding-retrieval match.

10. D, Correct (p. 282)

   A. Wrong. Both the practice test and the exam were explicit memory tests.

   B. Wrong. Both the practice test and the exam were multiple-choice, so this probably wasn't the problem.

   C. Wrong. Distributed practice improves memory, and Gil studied in one block, so he used massed practice.

11. C, Correct (p. 270)

   A, B, D. Wrong. These are all true statements. Flashbulb memories are not necessarily accurate.

12. A, Correct (p. 269)

   B. Wrong. The recency effect is improved recall for the last items in a list. Elaboration isn't involved.

   C. Wrong. The primacy effect is improved recall for the first items in a list. Elaboration isn't involved.

   D. Wrong. Elaboration doesn't necessarily lead to efficient storage. It produces distinctiveness.

13. D, Correct (p. 268)

   A. Wrong. Episodic memory involves personal events, not "how to."

   B. Wrong. Semantic memory involves word meanings, not "how to."

   C. Wrong. Iconic memory is sensory memory, not "how to" memory.

14. C, Correct (p. 284)

   A. Wrong. In overwriting, new material overwrites (obscures) old memories, the opposite of here.

   B. Wrong. Repression makes unpleasant memories inaccessible. It doesn't involve interference, as here.

   D. Wrong. Retroactive interference would be the new arrangement wiping out the old arrangement.

15. D, Correct (p. 278)

   A. Wrong. Although not completely inaccurate, they can be far from correct.

   B. Wrong. Confidence does not ensure accuracy of memory.

   C. Wrong. Although far from perfect, the memories are not entirely inaccurate.

16. B, Correct (p. 276)

   A. Wrong. Reconstructive memory suggests memories are constructed, not just replayed. The key here, though, is learning using the processes to be used during testing, a disaster.

   C. Wrong. Proactive interference is memory disruption caused by previously learned items. The key here, though, is learning using the processes to be used during testing, a disaster.

   D. Wrong. Cue-dependent forgetting occurs when items are in memory but appropriate retrieval cues are not available. The key here is learning that uses the same processes that will be used for testing, a disaster.

17. A, Correct (p. 277)

   B. Wrong. Elaboration is the expansion of to-be-remembered items to improve later recovery.

   C. Wrong. Interference is a possible cause of forgetting.

   D. Wrong. Encoding specificity relates the cues at encoding with the effective cues for retrieval.

18. A, Correct (p. 286)

   B. Wrong. Retrograde amnesia disrupts retrieval of old memories, not forming new ones.

   C. Wrong. Flashbulb memories are detailed memories of an emotionally-charged event.

   D. Wrong. Cue-dependent forgetting is forgetting due to having inappropriate retrieval cues.

19. B, Correct (p. 287)

   A, C, D. Wrong. Damage here doesn't usually cause amnesia. Damage to the hippocampus does.

CHAPTER **9**

LANGUAGE AND THOUGHT

ESTABLISHING LEARNING GOALS

Use these learning goals as a preview of the chapter, a guide for active reading, and to evaluate your mastery of the material. Review the relevant goals as you begin and end your reading of each major section of the chapter.

I. Discuss how we communicate with others.

   A. Understand the structure of language.
      1. Define phoneme, morpheme, phonology, syntax, and semantics.
      2. Differentiate the surface structure and deep structure of language.

   B. Isolate the factors that contribute to language comprehension.

   C. Identify the major milestones of language development.

   D. Assess language in nonhuman species.
      1. Describe the language skills of the animals studied.
      2. Discuss the criticisms of the claims that nonhuman species learned a language.

   E. Evaluate the possibility that language is an adaptation.

II. Discuss how objects are classified or categorized.

   A. Understand how category and category membership are defined.
      1. Discuss the idea that categories have defining features.
      2. Discuss the idea that categorization is based on family resemblance.

   B. Distinguish between prototype and exemplar views of categorization.

   C. Explain the hierarchical organization of categories.

III. Discuss how problems are solved effectively.

   A. Distinguish between well- and ill-defined problems.

   B. Describe the pitfalls of problem representation.
      1. Explain what is meant by problem representation.
      2. Define functional fixedness, and explain its adaptive value.

   C. Compare algorithms and heuristics.
      1. Describe the means-ends heuristic.

2. Describe the working backward heuristic.
3. Describe the searching for analogies heuristic and when analogies will be recognized.

D. Describe the Aha! Moment in problem solving.

IV. Discuss how effective decisions are made.

A. Understand how "framing" alternatives influences decision making.

B. Identify some common decision-making biases.

C. Describe the common decision-making heuristics.
1. Explain the role of base rate and conjunction errors in the representativeness heuristic.
2. Describe how the availability and anchoring and adjustment heuristics influence decisions.

D. Evaluate the pros and cons of using heuristics.

MASTERING THE MATERIAL

PREVIEW & COMMUNICATING WITH OTHERS (PP. 293-304)

MASTERING THE VOCABULARY

Define or explain each of the following terms.

1. thinking
2. grammar
3. phonology
4. syntax
5. semantics
6. phonemes
7. morphemes
8. surface structure
9. deep structure
10. pragmatics

MASTERING THE CONCEPTS

Fill in the blanks to create a summary of the section.

Thinking involves mentally manipulating knowledge. This chapter examines four issues concerning thinking: How do individuals communicate? How do they categorize things? How do people solve problems? How do people make decisions?

Language and thought are related. The linguistic [1] ____________ hypothesis suggests language influences both thought and perception. To be a language, the communication system must have [2] ____________ , rules for combining symbols to convey meaning. Grammar involves three parts: [3] ____________ , the rules for combining sounds, [4] ____________ , the rules for combining words, and semantics, the rules for meaning. Words are composed of [5] ____________ , the smallest speech sounds, and morphemes, the smallest units of [6] ____________ . Words are combined using syntax to form phrases and sentences. Language can be ambiguous because one surface structure can have multiple [7] ____________ structures. These meanings are evaluated by top-down processes, including [8] ____________ , the practical knowledge used to judge a speaker's intent.

The universal stages of development suggest language is not entirely determined by [9] ____________ . Babies coo at 3-5 weeks, [10] ____________ by 4-6 months, produce single words by 1 year, and multiple words by 2 years. Environment affects language after [11] ____________ , shaping accent and specific words. Early speech is described as [12] ____________ speech because it omits all unimportant words ("Give cup."), but it has syntax. The tendency to [13] ____________ ("runned") may indicate children automatically learn language production rules, and supports the idea of natural preparedness for language development. Nonhuman primates have learned to communicate with [14] ____________ language or plastic symbols. Not all researchers agree this is [15] ____________ . The fact that there are specialized language areas in the brain, a specialized vocal tract, a rapid rate of development, and the universal tendency to make certain errors suggests language is an [16] ____________ .

EVALUATING YOUR PROGRESS

Select the best response. If you make any errors, reread the relevant material before proceeding.

1. Morphemes are
   a. the smallest unit of sound.
   b. the smallest unit of language that carries meaning.
   c. the rules for combining sounds to make words.
   d. the underlying representation of meaning in language.

2. People use practical knowledge in addition to the specific words spoken to comprehend the intention of the speaker. This describes the concept of
   a. grammar.
   b. semantics.
   c. pragmatics.
   d. phonology.

3. Which is NOT a part of grammar?
   a. semantics
   b. syntax
   c. prototypes
   d. phonology

4. The meaning of a sentence corresponds to its
   a. phonology.
   b. linguistic relativity.
   c. surface structure.
   d. deep structure.

5. The smallest speech sounds are
   a. phonemes.
   b. morphemes.
   c. the surface structure.
   d. the deep structure.

6. Which of the following is false concerning language development?
   a. Many psychologists believe humans are born ready to learn language.
   b. The sequence of language development varies from language to language.
   c. Syntax is present in the telegraphic speech stage.
   d. Children learn the rules for language without systematic instruction.

7. At about 12 months of age, most children begin
   a. babbling.
   b. making overgeneralization errors.
   c. using single words.
   d. using telegraphic speech.

8. Telegraphic speech omits
   a. articles.
   b. verbs.
   c. nouns.
   d. intonation or stress ("?," "!").

9. A major criticism of the idea that chimpanzees can acquire language is that
   a. chimps don't put multiple words together.
   b. too much of the evidence for language in chimps is anecdotal.
   c. chimps can only use gestures or plastic symbols to communicate.
   d. chimps learn only nouns.

CLASSIFYING AND CATEGORIZING (PP. 304-308)

MASTERING THE VOCABULARY

Define or explain each of the following terms.

1. category
2. defining features
3. family resemblance
4. prototypes
5. category exemplars
6. basic-level categories

MASTERING THE CONCEPTS.

Fill in the blanks to create a summary of the section.

A [1] ____________ is a class of objects that belong together and allows inferences about members' characteristics and predictions about the future. Categories are defined in terms of [2] ____________ features and family [3] ____________ . Using fixed features can work poorly for [4] ____________ categories with fuzzy [5] ____________ . Members of natural categories have features that are characteristic, not [6] ____________ . In a family resemblance approach, members share many, but not all, of a set of critical features.

Psychologists differentiate the idea of [7] ____________ , an ideal representative of a category, and category [8] ____________ , examples of the category, as means for assigning category membership.

The exemplar view suggests all members of the category are stored and used for comparison. The prototype view suggests items are compared to a stored prototype, not the actual members of the category. Because more information is available than [9] ____________ would predict, researchers tend to favor the [10] ____________ view.

Categories are structured in [11] ____________ . [12] ____________ categories are the first to be learned and give the most useful information. Higher categories, [13] ____________ , are less descriptive.

EVALUATING YOUR PROGRESS

Select the best response. If you miss any questions, reread the relevant material before proceeding.

1. The defining features and family resemblance approaches differ because the defining features approach
   a. requires the object to have all the defining features, but family resemblance doesn't.
   b. uses prototypes, but family resemblance uses category exemplars to assign membership.
   c. is used best with natural concepts, but family resemblance is used best with math concepts.
   d. applies to non-living objects, but family resemblance applies to living objects.
2. Prototype theory proposes that new objects are classified based on a comparison to
   a. each of the individual examples of members of the category.
   b. a list of critical features that define the category.
   c. the abstract "best" example of a category.
   d. the superordinate characteristics of the category.
3. The category level that generates the most useful information, is used most, and is learned first is the
   a. prototype.
   b. superordinate.
   c. fuzzy.
   d. basic-level.

SOLVING PROBLEMS (PP. 309-315)

MASTERING THE VOCABULARY

Define or explain each of the following terms.

1. well-defined problem
2. ill-defined problem
3. functional fixedness
4. algorithms
5. heuristics

6. means-ends analysis
7. working backward
8. searching for analogies
9. mental sets
10. insight

MASTERING THE CONCEPTS

Fill in the blanks to create a summary of the section.

Problems are situations in which there is some uncertainty about how to reach a goal. [1] ____________ defined problems have a clear goal, a starting point, and a way to evaluate success. [2] ____________ defined problems do not have clear goals, starting points, or ways to evaluate the outcome. Problem [3] ____________ is critical, but prior beliefs and habits can distort the process. For example, people treat objects and their functions in a fixed and typical way in functional [4] ____________ .

Strategies for solving problems include [5] ____________ , step-by-step rules that guarantee a solution, and [6] ____________ , "rules of thumb" which are helpful but do not guarantee success. Algorithms are useful only for certain [7] ____________ problems. Heuristics can be inaccurate, but they allow rapid, logical, decisions. One heuristic is [8] ____________ analysis, in which actions are chosen to reduce distance to the goal. This often includes breaking a larger problem down into [9] ____________ . The working [10] ____________ heuristic begins at the goal and works toward the start. In the searching for [11] ____________ heuristic, similar past problems guide the solution. Mental [12] ____________ may cause reliance on old strategies and can be a problem. [13] ____________ is the process of suddenly seeing a solution to a problem.

EVALUATING YOUR PROGRESS

Select the best response. If you miss any questions, reread the relevant material before proceeding.

1. Which is not required in a well-defined problem?
   a. a clear starting point
   b. a well-stated goal
   c. defined subgoals
   d. an easy way to tell when a solution is correct

2. A tendency to rely on particular strategies that were successful in the past is
   a. mental set.
   b. insight.
   c. the working backward heuristic.
   d. the means-ends heuristic.

3. Which of the following represents an obstacle to accurate problem representation?
   a. functional fixedness
   b. algorithms
   c. means-end analysis
   d. insight

4. Finding a similar problem and using its solution as a guide for solving a new problem is
   a. incubation.
   b. the availability heuristic.
   c. the working backward heuristic.
   d. the searching for analogies heuristic.

5. An algorithm is
   a. a step-by-step rule that guarantees a correct solution.
   b. a general guideline or strategy for solving a problem.
   c. a sudden solution to a difficult problem.
   d. the quickest solution to a problem.

6. If you suddenly see the solution to a problem, you have
   a. displayed functional fixedness.
   b. solved an ill-defined problem.
   c. used an algorithm.
   d. experienced insight.

7. Selecting actions to reduce the gap between the current starting point and the desired goal describes
   a. the representativeness heuristic.
   b. the availability heuristic.
   c. the means-ends heuristic.
   d. the searching for analogies heuristic.

8. The incubation effect occurs if a solution to a problem is found suddenly or more easily when
   a. the searching for analogies heuristic is used.
   b. the problem is set aside for a period of time.
   c. an ill-defined problem becomes a well-defined problem.
   d. the working backward heuristic is used.

MAKING DECISIONS (PP. 315-320)

MASTERING THE VOCABULARY

Define or explain each of the following terms.

1. decision making
2. framing
3. confirmation bias
4. belief persistence
5. representativeness heuristic
6. availability heuristic
7. conjunction error
8. anchoring and adjustment

MASTERING THE CONCEPTS

Fill in the blanks to create a summary of the section.

Decision making, choosing from among a set of alternatives, is affected by beliefs and perceptions. How alternatives are presented, their [1] ____________ , is important. Selection is not necessarily rational. Personal interpretation of the situation and biases, rather than objective information is critical. For example [2] ____________ bias and [3] ____________ persistence are biases that tend to cause people to make decisions that maintain pre-existing ideas.

Heuristics can lead to inaccurate evaluations. The [4] ____________ heuristic, in which alternatives are compared to a prototype, causes decisions that disregard objective facts. Base rates are often ignored. This also causes the [5] ____________ error, in which a combination of traits is judged more common than a single trait (A+B > A). In the [6] ____________ heuristic, estimates are inflated if many examples of the concept can be generated easily. In the anchoring and [7] ____________ heuristic, the starting point is influential. Low starting values lead to [8] ____________ estimates. Heuristics can distort decisions, but they allow [9] ____________ , often effective, decisions using incomplete information.

EVALUATING YOUR PROGRESS

Select the best response. If you miss any questions, reread the relevant material before proceeding.

1. When treatment outcomes are described in terms of deaths, doctors make different decisions than if treatment outcomes are described in terms of survival. In other words, the decision is influenced by
   a. framing.
   b. the representativeness heuristic.
   c. the availability heuristic.
   d. conjunction errors.

2. Which heuristic involves comparing the similarity of an event to the average or prototypical situation?
   a. the availability heuristic
   b. the anchoring and adjustment heuristic
   c. the means-ends heuristic
   d. the representativeness heuristic

3. The tendency to seek out and use only information that supports an initial belief is
   a. the conjunction error.
   b. confirmation bias.
   c. belief persistence.
   d. the anchoring and adjustment heuristic.

4. People tend to overestimate the likelihood of an event if they can easily recall a similar event. This reflects
   a. confirmation bias.
   b. anchoring and adjustment.
   c. the representativeness heuristic.
   d. the availability heuristic.

5. The value of an initial reference point often impacts estimates. This represents
   a. belief persistence.
   b. the representativeness heuristic.
   c. anchoring and adjustment.
   d. confirmation bias.

MAKING FINAL PREPARATIONS

Complete these sections without consulting your book or notes. For a more accurate estimate of how well you know this material, wait at least a day or two after studying the chapter before working on the questions. Some of the material you "know" immediately after working with the chapter will be quickly forgotten. Exercises done too soon after studying will overestimate what you know well.

SHORT ESSAY QUESTIONS

Write a brief answer to each question.

1. Cite some reasons why many researchers believe humans come prepared to learn language.

2. Summarize the language capabilities of nonhuman species.

3. Compare the prototype and category exemplar theories of categorization, and explain why researchers tend to favor the exemplar theory.

4. Why are mental sets such as functional fixedness generally adaptive?

5. Define heuristics and discuss their limitations and adaptive value.

MATCHING

Select the correct definition or description for each item.

1. _______ algorithm
2. _______ exemplars
3. _______ thinking
4. _______ mental sets
5. _______ framing
6. _______ semantics
7. _______ decision making
8. _______ insight
9. _______ prototype
10. _______ anchors
11. _______ syntax
12. _______ defining features
13. _______ heuristics
14. _______ phonology

a. the "Aha!" moment in problem solving
b. rules used in language to communicate meaning
c. rules of thumb or general strategies
d. most representative member of category
e. rules for how sounds combine to form words
f. processes of mental manipulation of knowledge
g. rules for how words are combined
h. step-by-step rules that guarantee a correct solution
i. processes used to choose from among alternatives
j. specific category members stored in memory
k. well-established habits of perception and thought
l. manner in which a problem is presented
m. characteristics required to be in a category
n. starting points that influence decisions or estimates

MULTIPLE CHOICE PRETEST 1

Select the one best response.

1. The Welsh language allows letter and sound sequences that English does not (e.g., drwy, llwytho). This represents a difference in the two languages'
   a. phonology.
   b. syntax.
   c. semantics.
   d. pragmatics.

2. How many morphemes are in the word *undone*?
   a. 2
   b. 3
   c. 4
   d. 5

3. At approximately what age do children's vocalizations begin to show the phonology and "accent" of their native language?
   a. about 4 months
   b. about 8 months
   c. about 1 year
   d. about 18-24 months

4. The speaker's actual intent is not always clear from the specific words used, but listeners use their practical knowledge to accurately comprehend the intent and to reply appropriately. This practical knowledge represents
   a. syntax.
   b. prototypes.
   c. pragmatics.
   d. defining features.

5. "Mommy give cookie Tommy?" is an example of
   a. babbling.
   b. pragmatics.
   c. telegraphic speech.
   d. overgeneralization.

6. Which of the following is not evidence that supports the idea that language is an adaptation?
   a. Language is learned very quickly without systematic instruction.
   b. There are inherited tendencies to make certain grammatical errors.
   c. Fossil records show evidence of language evolution.
   d. Specific brain areas process language.

7. Which of the following is true concerning attempts to teach nonhuman species language?
   a. A few chimps have learned spoken language, although their pronunciation is poor.
   b. Chimps have learned to use single words, but they cannot progress to the two-word stage.
   c. Chimps can use symbols to communicate only if the symbols look like the objects they represent.
   d. Researchers have reported that chimps can learn language by observing other chimps.

8. If wings, feathers, and a beak are required for something to be a bird, category membership is based on
   a. family resemblance.
   b. a prototype.
   c. exemplars.
   d. defining features.

9. The linguistic relativity hypothesis suggests
   a. the speed of language acquisition relates to the richness of language in the environment.
   b. language influences thought and perception.
   c. good language requires being informative, truthful, relevant, and clear.
   d. language is highly correlated with intelligence.

10. Basic level categories
    a. are at the lowest level of the category hierarchy.
    b. include the most general type of information ("living thing").
    c. provide the most useful information.
    d. begin to be used by children at about age 4.

11. An example of a well-defined problem would be
    a. getting a vase to your mother by her birthday.
    b. understanding the meaning of life.
    c. selecting the best college to attend.
    d. finding the person who will be a good spouse.

12. Ann looked at the rocks near the top of the rock wall and visually followed the series of footholds from the top, until she had an idea about which way she should start climbing up the wall. Ann used the problem solving approach known as
    a. means-ends analysis.
    b. searching for analogies.
    c. anchoring and adjustment.
    d. working backward.

13. All of the following are true concerning algorithms EXCEPT:
    a. They guarantee a correct solution if properly followed.
    b. They are step-by-step rules or procedures for solving a problem.
    c. They guarantee the most rapid solution to a problem.
    d. They are more useful with well-defined problems than with ill-defined problems.

14. Jonas always looks for evidence that supports his theory, but he never tries to find evidence that contradicts his theory. Jonas' research approach illustrates
    a. confirmation bias.
    b. the representativeness heuristic.
    c. the working backwards, heuristic.
    d. belief persistence.

15. Giving up on a nasty programming problem, Flo went to the movies. When she returned and looked at her program, she realized she knew the solution. This is an example of
    a. functional fixedness.
    b. an incubation effect.
    c. belief persistence.
    d. a framing effect.

16. People usually decide that coin tosses of HHHTTT are less likely than HTHTTH because HHHTTT doesn't seem like an outcome that could be a typical random sequence. This demonstrates
    a. the availability heuristic.
    b. the representativeness heuristic.
    c. functional fixedness.
    d. anchoring and adjustment.

17. Because the news report of a plane crash was fresh in her mind, Lara decided flying was just too risky. Her risk estimate appears to have been influenced by
    a. a framing effect.
    b. functional fixedness.
    c. the representativeness heuristic.
    d. the availability heuristic.

18. In the anchoring and adjustment heuristic, the "anchor" is the
    a. initial estimate or starting point.
    b. end goal.
    c. the ease of recalling a similar situation.
    d. how well the information fits existing views.

MULTIPLE CHOICE PRETEST 2

Select the one best response.

1. The cat chased the lizard. The lizard was chased by the cat. These two sentences share the same. These sentences have the same
    a. surface structure.
    b. deep structure.
    c. phonemic content.
    d. mnemonics.

2. Vic said, "The cat catched the mouses." This illustrates
    a. ambiguous deep structure.
    b. telegraphic speech.
    c. the linguistic relativity effect.
    d. overgeneralization.

3. Fred just started using single words to communicate. If Fred's language development is typical, how old is he?
    a. 6 months
    b. 8 months
    c. 1 year
    d. 2 years

4. Which of the following is false concerning research on the language abilities of chimpanzees?
    a. Chimps have created new word combinations.
    b. Chimps have been taught to use sign language, but they can't understand spoken English.
    c. Chimps have learned language by observing other chimps.
    d. Chimps can learn to manipulate symbols that represent words.

5. Overgeneralization demonstrates that
   a. language development is strongly influenced by the environment.
   b. children develop language by imitating their parents.
   c. children have a natural inclination to acquire the rules of language.
   d. language development is not as universal as the genetic view of language development requires.

6. Features associated with birds include flying, laying eggs, and having a beak. Penguins do not fly, but most people still categorize them as birds. This suggests they are categorizing penguins based on
   a. the family resemblance approach.
   b. the defining features approach.
   c. a hierarchical approach.
   d. the superordinate approach.

7. Sean compares a new dog to his ideal images of different breeds in order to identify the new dog's breed. Sean seems to base categorization on
   a. category exemplars.
   b. prototypes.
   c. defining features.
   d. basic-level categories.

8. Research on categorization suggests all of the following are true EXCEPT:
   a. Identifying defining features for natural categories is difficult.
   b. In general conversation, basic level categories are used most often.
   c. Basic level categories are the first used by children.
   d. Categorization might be handled in other ways, but prototypes seem to be used most often.

9. Brina has broken her job search problem into subgoals that will move her toward her goal: prepare resumé, sign up at placement center, practice interviews, research companies, and so on. This problem solving approach is most similar to
   a. means-ends analysis.
   b. searching for analogies.
   c. working backward.
   d. the framing effect.

10. The chess instructor told his student, "To win, control the center of the board." His instructions represent
   a. a heuristic.
   b. mental set.
   c. a framing effect.
   d. an algorithm.

11. Cassie knew that her radio only worked if it was by her window in her high-rise apartment. When her cell phone wasn't getting a signal in a big office building, she tried moving to the window to improve reception. Cassie's problem solving strategy is characteristic of
    a. the working backward heuristic.
    b. the availability heuristic.
    c. the searching for analogies heuristic.
    d. a means-ends analysis.

12. The recipe gives step-by-step instructions for making brownies, and if followed accurately, the brownies will be excellent. Thus, the recipe is an example of
    a. a heuristic.
    b. an analogy.
    c. an algorithm.
    d. a prototype.

13. The adaptive value of heuristics is that they
    a. always produce rational, highly accurate decisions.
    b. allow reasonable, quick decisions from limited facts.
    c. keep decision-making objective and fact-oriented.
    d. provide step-by-step instructions that reduce cognitive demands.

14. Bhavin had struggled for hours trying to figure out how to finance his spring break trip. He was just about to give up, when the solution suddenly was obvious. This pattern of problem solving is characteristic of
    a. means-ends analysis.
    b. the incubation effect.
    c. insight.
    d. the prototype approach.

15. You expect a class will be hard if the instructor says 35% of the class will get Ds or Fs, but not if the instructor says 65% will get a C or higher. Your expectations illustrate the importance of
    a. the availability heuristic.
    b. belief persistence.
    c. framing.
    d. mental set.

16. People were surveyed about how much TV they watch each day. When the options were 0-2 hours, 2-4 hours, 4-6 hours, and more than 6 hours, the most common response was 2-4 hours. When the options were 2-4 hours, 4-6 hours, 6-8 hours, and more than 8 hours, the most common response was 4-6 hours. This result is best explained by
    a. the anchoring and adjustment heuristic.
    b. the means-ends heuristic.
    c. the representativeness heuristic.
    d. the availability heuristic.

17. Jibu is out of sand and salt to use on his icy driveway. The 10 lbs of birdseed he has in his garage would be a good substitute, but he doesn't consider that possibility. Jibu's thinking illustrates
    a. the availability heuristic.
    b. a framing effect.
    c. means-ends analysis.
    d. functional fixedness.

18. Dave has played guitar since he was 12, has long hair, and can be found in a nightclub several times a week. You decided Dave is more likely to be a member of a rock band and under age 30 than only under age 30. Your decision illustrates
    a. the conjunction error.
    b. functional fixedness.
    c. a framing effect.
    d. confirmation bias.

19. The coach told Bob's father, "He can't dribble, shoot, defend or even keep his shoes tied!" and showed him the year's statistics. Even so, Bob's father still thinks Bob has a career in professional basketball. This represents
    a. confirmation bias.
    b. a framing effect.
    c. the incubation effect.
    d. belief persistence.

LANGUAGE DEVELOPMENT GUIDE

CORE TERMS

In discussing thought, your instructor may talk about ***logic***, and how illogical some of our thinking is. We often commit logical ***fallacies*** -- errors in clear thinking, such as making unfounded assumptions. You may be urged to think ***critically.*** That means questioning your own assumptions as well as those of others.

In discussing language your instructor may use the terms ***bilingual*** or ***multilingual***. The word part *bi* means two, and the word part *multi* means many, so a *bilingual* person speaks two languages, and a *multilingual* person speaks many. Your instructor might also use the term ***non-native***, meaning someone who was not born or raised in the country that they are now in.

IDIOMS

p. 293	rationales	reasons
p. 294	knack	special talent or skill

p. 294	homo sapiens	human beings
p. 298	nuances	subtle clues or details that provide information
p. 298	to bolster	to increase the support for something
p. 299	trivial	of little importance
p. 301	fine-tune their articulation skills	get better at speaking clearly
p. 301	arbitrary symbols	symbols chosen more or less randomly
p. 302	surrogate children	adopted children
p. 302	effectively mute	unable to speak
p. 303	the jury is still out	it has not yet been definitely decided
p. 303	follow rigid scripts	follow very specific rules about how to behave
p. 311	an arsenal of problem strategies	a collection of ways to attack a problem
p. 313	ticket scalping	buying tickets, and then selling them for a higher price

PRONUNCIATION

linguistic (lin-gwis′-tick) *p. 295*
phonology (fone-ol′-o-gee) *p. 2996*
morphemes (mor′-feem) *p. 297*
algorithms (al′-go-ri-thums) *p. 311*
heuristics (hure-is′-ticks) *p. 312*
anchoring (ang′-kor-ing) *p. 318*

SOLUTIONS

PREVIEW & COMMUNICATING WITH OTHERS (PP. 293-304)

MASTERING THE CONCEPTS

1. relativity (p. 295)
2. grammar (p. 596)
3. phonology (p. 296)
4. syntax (p. 296)
5. phonemes (p. 296)
6. meaning (p. 297)
7. deep (p. 308)
8. pragmatics (p. 308)
9. experience (p. 300)
10. babble (p. 300)
11. 6 months (p. 300)
12. telegraphic (p. 301)
13. overgeneralize (p. 301)
14. sign (p. 302)
15. language (p. 303)
16. adaptation (p. 303)

EVALUATING YOUR PROGRESS

1. B, Correct (p. 297)

   A. Wrong. This describes phonemes, not morphemes.

   C. Wrong. This describes phonology, not morphemes.

   D. Wrong. This describes deep structure, not morphemes.

2. C, Correct (p. 299)

   A. Wrong. The rules of language = grammar. Grammar is not practical knowledge.

   B. Wrong. Semantics are the rules for communicating meaning, but do not include practical knowledge.

   D. Wrong. The rules for combining sounds = phonology. This is not practical knowledge.

3. C, Correct (p. 296)

   A. Wrong. Semantics, rules used to communicate meaning, is a part of grammar.

   B. Wrong. Syntax, rules for combining words, is a part of grammar.

   D. Wrong. Phonology, rules for combining sounds, is a part of grammar.

4. D, Correct (p. 298)

   A. Wrong. Phonology relates to the rules for combining sounds to make words, not the meaning of a sentence.

   B. Wrong. The linguistic relativity hypothesis proposes that language influences perception.

   C. Wrong. Surface structure is the word order of a sentence. Meaning is conveyed through deep structure.

5. A, Correct (p. 296)

   B. Wrong. Morphemes are the smallest units of meaning. Phonemes are sound units.

   C, D. Wrong. These are grammatical characteristics of sentences, not speech sounds.

6. B, Correct (p. 300)

   A, C, D. Wrong. These are all true.

7. C, Correct (p. 300)

   A. Wrong. Babbling begins between 4 and 6 months.

   B. Wrong. Overgeneralization occurs during the preschool years.

   D. Wrong. Telegraphic speech begins around age 2.

8. A, Correct (p. 301)

   B, C, D. Wrong. Telegraphic speech has nouns, verbs, and intonation, but no articles or prepositions.

9. B, Correct (p. 303)

   A. Wrong. Chimps do use multiple words. This isn't a problem.

   C. Wrong. Speaking isn't required in the definition of language. Sign language is a language.

   D. Wrong. Chimps learn verbs, adjectives, etc.

CLASSIFYING AND CATEGORIZING (PP. 304-308)

MASTERING THE CONCEPTS.

1. category (p. 304)
2. defining (p. 305)
3. resemblance (p. 305)
4. natural (p. 305)
5. boundaries (p. 305)
6. defining (p. 305)
7. prototypes (p. 306)
8. exemplars (p. 306)
9. prototypes (p. 307)
10. exemplar (p. 307)
11. hierarchies (p. 308)
12. Basic-level (p. 308)
13. superordinates (p. 308)

EVALUATING YOUR PROGRESS

1. A, Correct (p. 305)
   B. Wrong. Defining features give a clear definition, so prototypes (and exemplars) are not relevant.
   C. Wrong. Defining features are not very appropriate for natural categories (with fuzzy boundaries).
   D. Wrong. Defining features are inappropriate for natural categories, including non-living ones.
2. C, Correct (p. 306)
   A. Wrong. This describes exemplar theory. A prototype is the "best" example.
   B. Wrong. This describes the critical features definition of categories. "Best" = prototype.
   D. Wrong. Superordinate is the most general category. A prototype is the "best" example.
3. D, Correct (p. 308)
   A. Wrong. A prototype is not a category. It is the most representative member of a category.
   B. Wrong. Superordinate categories are high level categories that are less useful.
   C. Wrong. Fuzzy is not a category level. It is a description of a type of boundary.

SOLVING PROBLEMS (PP. 309-315)

MASTERING THE CONCEPTS

1. Well- (p. 309)
2. Ill- (p. 309)
3. representation (p. 310)
4. fixedness (p. 323)
5. algorithms (p. 311)
6. heuristics (p. 312)
7. well-defined (p. 311)
8. means-ends (p. 312)
9. subgoals (p. 312)
10. backward (p. 312)
11. analogies (p. 313)
12. sets (p. 313)
13. Insight (p. 313)

EVALUATING YOUR PROGRESS

1. C, Correct (p. 309)
   A, B, D. Wrong. These are all required in a well-defined problem. Defined subgoals are not required.
2. A, Correct (p. 313)
   B. Wrong. Insight is suddenly seeing a solution to a problem.
   C. Wrong. Working backward involves starting at the goal, rather than at the beginning of a problem.
   D. Wrong. The means-ends heuristic establishes subgoals that move the person closer to the goal.
3. A, Correct (p. 311)
   B. Wrong. Algorithms are step-by-step plans that ensure a solution. They don't influence representation.
   C. Wrong. Means-end analysis is a strategy for solving a problem. It comes after representation.
   D. Wrong. Insight involves suddenly seeing a solution, so it can't influence representation.

4. D, Correct (p. 313)
   A. Wrong. Incubation involves taking a break from working on a difficult problem.
   B. Wrong. The availability heuristic is to use ease of recalling examples, not to look for similar cases.
   C. Wrong. Working backward from a goal is not mentioned.
5. A, Correct (p. 311)
   B. Wrong. This answer describes heuristics.
   C. Wrong. This describes insight.
   D. Wrong. Algorithms are sometimes very time consuming.
6. D, Correct (p. 313)
   A. Wrong. Functional fixedness is seeing objects in a stereotypical way.
   B. Wrong. Sudden solutions may occur for either well-defined or ill-defined problems.
   C. Wrong. Algorithms don't necessarily produce a sudden solution. They can be very slow.
7. C, Correct (p. 312)
   A. Wrong. The representativeness heuristic uses ideas of the "representative" case to make decisions.
   B. Wrong. The availability heuristic involves basing estimates on the ease of generating examples.
   D. Wrong. Searching for analogies involves considering how similar problems were solved in the past.
8. B, Correct (p. 314)
   A. Wrong. Searching for analogies helps solve problems, but it doesn't relate to the incubation effect. Incubation relates to a waiting period, or period of development.
   C. Wrong. The incubation effect occurs for both well-defined and ill-defined problems. Incubation relates to a waiting period, or period of development.
   D. Wrong. Working backward helps solve problems, but it doesn't relate to the incubation effect. Incubation relates to a waiting period, or period of development.

MAKING DECISIONS (PP. 315-320)

MASTERING THE CONCEPTS

1. framing (p. 315)
2. confirmation (p. 317)
3. belief (p. 317)
4. representativeness (p. 317)
5. conjunction (p. 318)
6. availability (p. 318)
7. adjustment (p. 318)
8. lower (p. 318)
9. economical (p. 320)

EVALUATING YOUR PROGRESS

1. A, Correct (p. 315)
   B. Wrong. The key to this question is the wording of the outcomes, not how representative they are.
   C. Wrong. The key here is the wording of the outcomes, not how easily an example is generated.
   D. Wrong. The key to this question is the wording of the outcomes, not misestimating a conjunction.
2. D, Correct (p. 317)
   A. Wrong. The availability heuristic involves the ease of thinking of a similar example.
   B. Wrong. The anchoring and adjustment heuristic involves the impact of a starting level on estimates.
   C. Wrong. The means-ends heuristic is a problem-solving heuristic involving subgoals, not a decision-making heuristic involving resemblance to some prototype.
3. B, Correct (p. 317)
   A. Wrong. The conjunction error is thinking the probability of two events is larger that either component.
   C. Wrong. Belief persistence involves ignoring disconfirming evidence, rather than looking only for confirming evidence.
   D. Wrong. Anchoring and adjustment involves the impact of an initial reference point on estimates.

4. D, Correct (p. 318)
   A. Wrong. Confirmation bias involves seeking out only confirming information.
   B. Wrong. In anchoring and adjustment initial events, not the ease of recall, effect estimates.
   C. Wrong. Representativeness involves similarity to a prototype, not ease of recall of a similar event.

5. C, Correct (p. 318)
   A. Wrong. Belief persistence involves ignoring information that does not match prior beliefs.
   B. Wrong. The representativeness heuristic involves comparison to a prototype, not the impact of a reference point.
   D. Wrong. Confirmation bias involves seeking out only information that will confirm one's prior beliefs.

MAKING FINAL PREPARATIONS

SHORT ESSAY QUESTIONS

1. Language development occurs in the same sequence and at approximately the same rate across the world, as predicted by a biological component. The grammar of children differs from adults' and would not be predicted from an environmental view. Overgeneralization of rules occurs, causing the production of word forms that would not have been reinforced. Development also occurs very rapidly. (pp. 300-301, 303)
2. Chimps and other nonhuman primates have been taught to use sign language or plastic symbol keys to communicate. Some have developed significant vocabularies, produced multiple-word constructions, perhaps have generated novel constructions, and have learned language by watching other chimps. The process is difficult and slow, and the anecdotal nature of the data, cause some to question whether their communication should be considered true language. (pp. 301-303)
3. Prototype theory proposes that new items are compared to a prototype, an ideal example of the category. The category exemplar theory proposes that all the members of the category are stored in memory and are used to compare to new items. Researchers favor the exemplar theory because people seem to have more information available about the category than prototype theory would predict. (pp. 306-307)
4. Mental sets develop as a result of experience in the world. They reflect the way the world often works. Thus, they provide a rapid, and usually accurate, means of representing information. (pp. 310-311, 313)
5. Heuristics are "rules of thumb" or general strategies used in reasoning and problem solving. They give guidance, not explicit instructions, and though they often lead to good answers, they don't guarantee success. People don't always have time to evaluate all possible strategies. Heuristics afford a means for making economical, rapid, and fairly accurate responses even with incomplete information. (pp. 312-313, 317-320)

MATCHING

1. h (p. 311)
2. j (p. 306)
3. f (p. 293)
4. k (p. 313)
5. l (p. 315)
6. b (p. 296)
7. i (p. 315)
8. a (p. 313)
9. d (p. 306)
10. n (p. 318)
11. g (p. 296)
12. m (p. 305)
13. c (p. 312)
14. e (p. 296)

MULTIPLE CHOICE PRETEST 1

1. A, Correct (p. 296)

   B. Wrong. Syntax regulates word combinations.

   C. Wrong. Semantics are rules for communicating meaning.

   D. Wrong. Pragmatics involve practical knowledge used to guide language comprehension.
2. A, Correct (p. 297)

   B, C, D. Wrong. There are only 2 morphemes here. The morphemes are "un" and "done."
3. B, Correct (p. 300)

   A. Wrong. Babbling begins at about 4 months. It is some time before babbling resembles the native language.

   C. Wrong. Children begin to use single words at about 1 year.

   D. Wrong. Children begin to put words together at about 18-24 months.
4. C, Correct (p. 299)

   A. Wrong. Syntax is rules for combining words, not practical knowledge used in comprehension.

   B. Wrong. Prototypes are ideal representation of category members, not aspects of comprehension.

   D. Wrong. Defining features is an approach to categorization, not language comprehension.
5. C, Correct (p. 301)

   A. Wrong. Babbling does not include words.

   B. Wrong. Pragmatics, use of practical knowledge, might be needed here, but this doesn't represent pragmatics.

   D. Wrong. Overgeneralization is applying rules of grammar too broadly, not omitting function words.
6. C, Correct (p. 303)

   A, B, D. Wrong. These all support an adaptation view. There is no fossil evidence, however.
7. D, Correct (pp. 301-303)

   A. Wrong. This is false. Attempts to teach spoken language were totally unsuccessful.

   B. Wrong. This is false. Washoe and others do combine "words."

   C. Wrong. This is false. The symbols can be abstract (triangle = banana).
8. D, Correct (p. 305)

   A. Wrong. Family resemblance does not require all attributes to be present.

   B. Wrong. A prototype is an ideal member, but other members don't have to have all attributes.

   C. Wrong. Exemplars are the particular members of a category, not really a way to define it.
9. B, Correct (p. 295)

   A. Wrong. The linguistic relativity hypothesis doesn't involve language acquisition.

   C. Wrong. This relates to pragmatics, not linguistic relativity.

   D. Wrong. Linguistic relativity doesn't relate language and intelligence; it relates language and perception.
10. C, Correct (p. 308)

    A. Wrong. Basic level categories are at an intermediate level in the hierarchy.

    B. Wrong. Basic level categories provide the most useful, not the most general type of information.

    D. Wrong. Basic-level categories are the first type of categories children use, and this occurs before age 4.
11. A, Correct (p. 309)

    B, C, D. Wrong. These have no easily defined or evaluated goal.
12. D, Correct (p. 312)

    A. Wrong. Ann worked backward from the goal. She did not use subgoals.

    B. Wrong. There were no analogous problems here. She worked backward from the goal.

    C. Wrong. Anchoring and adjustment is an estimation procedure. There were no estimates required.

13. C, Correct (p. 311)
    A, B, D. Wrong. These are true. Algorithms don't always give quick solutions, only correct ones.
14. A, Correct (p. 331729)
    B. Wrong. He is not basing a decision on a "typical" example. Key here is looking only for one type of information.
    C. Wrong. He is not working backwards from a goal. He is seeking only facts that fit his ideas.
    D. Wrong. He is not ignoring disconfirming evidence, because he is not even looking for it.
15. B, Correct (p. 328314
    A. Wrong. Functional fixedness involves seeing items only in their usual functions or roles.
    C. Wrong. Belief persistence involves maintaining a belief in spite of contradictory evidence.
    D. Wrong. Framing effects occur when wording impacts decision making or problem representation.
16. B, Correct (p. 317)
    A. Wrong. Availability is based on ease of generating examples, not similarity to a typical outcome.
    C. Wrong. The key here is the comparison to typical randomness, not an object's usual function.
    D. Wrong. Starting points are not relevant; comparison to a typical situation is.
17. D, Correct (p. 318)
    A. Wrong. Framing effects involve the influence of wordings. This decision was influenced by a recent example of a bad outcome.
    B. Wrong. Functional fixedness involves not seeing new uses. The key here is the recent bad outcome.
    C. Wrong. The representativeness heuristic involves decisions based on similarity to a standard example. Key here is the recent example of a bad outcome.
18. A, Correct (p. 318)
    B, C, D. Wrong. An initial estimate or starting point is the anchor. Adjustments are made from there.

MULTIPLE CHOICE PRETEST 2

1. B, Correct (p. 298)
   A. Wrong. Each has a different word order (surface structure) but the same meaning (deep structure).
   C. Wrong. Each has different phonemes (speech sounds).
   D. Wrong. Mnemonics are devices or techniques that assist memory. Word order relates to surface structure.
2. D, Correct (p. 301)
   A. Wrong. There is only one meaning here, so deep structure is not ambiguous.
   B. Wrong. Telegraphic speech doesn't include articles such as "the."
   C. Wrong. The key here is the incorrect word forms, not how language influences perception. .
3. C, Correct (p. 300)
   A. Wrong. Babbling, not word use, usually begins at about 4-6 months.
   B. Wrong. Babbling resembles a particular language at 8 months, but no words are used.
   D. Wrong. Children begin using two words together by age 2.
4. B, Correct (p. 302)
   A, C, D. Wrong. These are all true, but some chimps can understand spoken English.
5. C, Correct (p. 301)
   A, B. Wrong. Environmental reinforcement models for overgeneralization are not likely.
   D. Wrong. Overgeneralization is used to support the natural predisposition for language.
6. A, Correct (p. 305)
   B. Wrong. Defining features requires all features be present.
   C. Wrong. There is no mention of hierarchies. Key is accepting the category in spite of missing features.
   D. Wrong. Superordinate categories are high in the hierarchy and include very general features.
7. B, Correct (p. 306)
   A. Wrong. Using exemplars requires comparing the object to all memories of each dog he's seen.
   C. Wrong. Defining features compares the object to a list of specific features, not to an ideal example.
   D. Wrong. Basic-level categories describe a level in the hierarchy, not a way to assign categories.

8. D, Correct (p. 307)
   A, B, C. Wrong. These are true, but using exemplars appears to be the most common strategy.
9. A, Correct (p. 312)
   B. Wrong. There is no consideration of analogous problems. The key here was attacking subgoals.
   C. Wrong. Brina worked from "start" toward a goal, not the reverse. The key here are the subgoals.
   D. Wrong. Framing is the way a problem is stated. The key here are the subgoals.
10. A, Correct (p. 312)
   B. Wrong. Problem solving isn't being based on the approach used frequently in the past.
   C. Wrong. The wording isn't critical. The key here is the general nature of the instructions.
   D. Wrong. The instructions are not precise, and probably do not guarantee success.
11. C, Correct (p. 313)
   A. Wrong. She didn't begin at the goal; she used a similar problem as a guide to the solution.
   B. Wrong. The availability heuristic concerns frequency estimates when examples are easily remembered.
   D. Wrong. There were no subgoals.
12. C, Correct (p. 311)
   A. Wrong. Heuristics are rules of thumb, not detailed instructions. The key here is "step-by-step."
   B. Wrong. Analogies are similarities between problems. The key here is "step-by-step."
   D. Wrong. Prototypes are ideal members of a category. The key here is "step-by-step."
13. B, Correct (p. 312)
   A. Wrong. Heuristics do not always produce rational or highly accurate decisions.
   C. Wrong. Heuristics involve subjective factors (memory, interpretation, "typical").
   D. Wrong. Heuristics don't give step-by-step instructions.
14. C, Correct (p. 313)
   A. Wrong. There were no subgoals. The key here is the sudden solution.
   B. Wrong. There was no inactive period breaking up the problem solving attempt.
   D. Wrong. Prototypes are ideal members of a category. The key here is the sudden solution.
15. C, Correct (p. 315)
   A. Wrong. There is no difference in the ability to generate examples. The key here is the wording.
   B. Wrong. An opinion wasn't maintained in spite of contradictory facts. The key here is the wording.
   D. Wrong. Habits are not relevant. The key here is the different wording of the outcomes.
16. A, Correct (p. 318)
   B. Wrong. There were no subgoals. The key here was the starting value given as choices.
   C. Wrong. The decision wasn't influenced by typical representations. The key was the starting value given.
   D. Wrong. Being able to easily remember an example wasn't involved. The key was the starting value given.
17. D, Correct (p. 311)
   A. Wrong. The question involved a restricted view of an object's function, not ease of recalling events.
   B. Wrong. Wording is not an issue. Seeing only the usual function of an object is the key here.
   C. Wrong. No subgoals were involved. Seeing only the usual function of an object is the key here.
18. A, Correct (p. 318)
   B. Wrong. Representing something in terms of its usual function was not involved.
   C. Wrong. Wording is not an issue. The key here is thinking two things will be more common than one.
   D. Wrong. Searching only for confirming evidence wasn't involved.
19. D, Correct (p. 317)
   A. Wrong. He is ignoring contradictory information, not just failing to look for it.
   B. Wrong. The key in this question is ignoring contradictory facts, not the specific way information was given.
   C. Wrong. The key to this question is ignoring contradictory facts, not a break from problem solving.

CHAPTER 10

INTELLIGENCE

ESTABLISHING LEARNING GOALS

Use these learning goals as a preview of the chapter, a guide for active reading, and to evaluate your mastery of the material. Review the relevant goals as you begin and end your reading of each major section of the chapter.

I. Discuss the definition of intelligence.

A. Understand the psychometric approach to conceptualizing intelligence, including Spearman's two-factor theory.
1. Describe how Galton applied the psychometric approach in measuring intelligence.
2. Explain Spearman's two-factor theory, and discuss its contribution.
3. List Thurstone's primary mental abilities and how they were identified.

B. Distinguish between fluid intelligence and crystallized intelligence.

C. Explain how the speed of neural transmission might influence intelligence.

D. Evaluate the various theories of multiple intelligences.
1. Describe and evaluate Gardner's theory of multiple intelligences.
2. Describe and evaluate Sternberg's triarchic theory of intelligence.

II. Discuss how individual differences are measured.

A. Understand the components of a good test.

B. Understand and evaluate IQ.
1. Describe the purpose of Binet and Simon's IQ test and how IQ is computed.
2. Define deviation IQ, and discuss its advantages.

C. Define mental retardation and giftedness.
1. Describe the behavioral characteristics of individuals with high IQ scores.
2. Describe the behavioral characteristics of individuals with low IQ scores.

D. Assess the validity of IQ tests and the effects of labeling.
1. Describe how the validity of intelligence tests is evaluated and the outcome of the evaluation.
2. Discuss labeling effects and why they occur.

E. Contrast creativity, emotional intelligence, and tacit knowledge.

III. Discuss the sources of intelligence.

A. Understand how IQ changes with age.
B. Explain how twin studies are used to evaluate genetic contributions to intelligence.
   1. Discuss the evidence for a genetic influence in intelligence.
   2. Explain heritability, and describe the heritability of intelligence.
C. Understand environmental influences on intelligence, and how they interact with genetic influences.
   1. Discuss the evidence that environment influences intelligence.
   2. Identify factors that might account for group differences in intelligence test scores.

MASTERING THE MATERIAL

PREVIEW & CONCEPTUALIZING INTELLIGENCE (PP. 327-336)

MASTERING THE VOCABULARY

Define or explain each of the following terms.

1. intelligence
2. psychometrics
3. factor analysis
4. g (general intelligence)
5. s (specific intelligence)
6. fluid intelligence
7. crystallized intelligence
8. multiple intelligences
9. triarchic theory

MASTERING THE CONCEPTS

Fill in the blanks to create a summary of the section.

Intelligence is a concept used to account for individual [1] ____________ in mental test performance. This chapter considers three issues: How should intelligence be conceptualized? How can it be measured? What are the sources of intelligence?

The [2] ____________ approach analyzes performance on mental tests to understand intelligence. [3] ____________ first proposed that some single intellectual ability causes similar performance across a variety of psychological and physical tests. [4] ____________ is a mathematical technique to find relationships between scores on several tests. [5] ____________ concluded two factors explain test performance: g, or [6] ____________ intelligence, and s, or [7] ____________ abilities. Spearman's [8] ____________ analysis has been criticized, with Thurstone proposing seven "[9] ____________ mental abilities" instead. Modifications of general intelligence include hierarchical models, with [10] ____________ at the top and sub-factors, such as Cattell and Horn's [11] ____________ and crystallized intelligence, at lower levels. Fluid and crystallized intelligence help explain differences in intelligence due to culture and [12] ____________ .

[13] ____________ transmission speed also has been proposed as a determinant of mental ability. Faster speed means faster processing and more efficient resource allocation. The latency of the [14] ____________ signal correlates with intelligence test scores.

Gardner's theory of [15] ____________ intelligences proposes eight different intelligences, rather than one general intelligence. Based on [16] ____________ studies of exceptional talents, it includes traditional types of intelligence (e.g., logical-mathematical) that are measured by conventional tests and others (e.g., bodily-kinesthetic, musical, intrapersonal, naturalist) that are not. Although many agree with a [17] ____________ view of intelligence, some see Gardner's theory as a study of talents, not intelligence, and criticize its lack of scientific support.

Sternberg's [18] ____________ theory proposes three major components and includes not only information processing activities, but also creative and practical components. [19] ____________ intelligence refers to analytical skills and information processing, the skills measured by most psychometric tests. [20] ____________ intelligence applies to coping with new tasks. [21] ____________ intelligence involves the ability to adapt to the environment, or "street smarts." Triarchic theory is limited by the difficulty of measuring the practical and creative components.

EVALUATING YOUR PROGRESS

Select the best response. If you make any errors, reread the relevant material before proceeding.

1. In the psychometric approach to studying intelligence, the main focus is on
   a. neural transmission and processing speed.
   b. performance on mental tests.
   c. adaptation to the environment.
   d. the interaction of mental ability, creativity, and adaptability.
2. The two-factor theory of Spearman suggests intelligence can be accounted for by
   a. general intelligence and a test-specific factor.
   b. fluid intelligence and crystallized intelligence.
   c. verbal intelligence and spatial intelligence.
   d. analytical intelligence and practical intelligence.
3. Verbal comprehension, verbal fluency, numerical ability, spatial ability, memory, perceptual speed, and reasoning make up
   a. different types of crystallized intelligence.
   b. the subparts of Sternberg's practical intelligence.
   c. Gardner's multiple intelligences.
   d. Thurstones primary mental abilities.
4. Problem solving, reasoning, and memory skills that are not greatly influenced by experience are part of
   a. fluid intelligence.
   b. crystallized intelligence.
   c. interpersonal intelligence.
   d. practical intelligence.
5. Researchers who use the P100 signal believe intelligence is related to
   a. the dominant hemisphere of the brain.
   b. the efficiency of muscle contractions.
   c. the speed of neural processing.
   d. the size of the brain area activated by mental tests.
6. Bodily-kinesthetic intelligence and intrapersonal intelligence are included in
   a. Thurstone's primary mental abilities theory of intelligence.
   b. Sternberg's triarchic theory of intelligence.
   c. Gardner's multiple intelligences theory.
   d. Spearman's two-factor theory of intelligence.
7. Factor analysis of performance on several mental tests has shown positive correlations between many of the tests. This finding led to the development of
   a. Gardner's multiple intelligences theory.
   b. Spearman's two factor theory.
   c. Sternberg's triarchic theory.
   d. Cattell's concept of fluid and crystallized intelligence.

8. According to the triarchic theory, a person who deals well with new tasks is high in
   a. general intelligence.
   b. practical intelligence.
   c. analytical intelligence.
   d. creative intelligence.

MEASURING INDIVIDUAL DIFFERENCES (PP. 337-347)

MASTERING THE VOCABULARY

Define or explain each of the following terms.

1. achievement tests
2. aptitude tests
3. reliability
4. validity
5. standardization
6. intelligence quotient (IQ)
7. mental age
8. deviation IQ
9. mental retardation
10. gifted
11. creativity
12. emotional intelligence
13. tacit knowledge

MASTERING THE CONCEPTS.

Fill in the blanks to create a summary of the section.

Psychological tests measure individual differences. Some, [1] ____________ tests, measure current competence. Others, [2] ____________ tests, measure the ability to learn. Regardless of what is measured, all good tests need [3] ____________ , [4] ____________ , and standardization. Reliability is a measure of [5] ____________ and often is evaluated in terms of [6] ____________ reliability, the correlation of scores from two separate testings. Validity is a measure of whether the test measures what it is supposed to measure. [7] ____________ validity evaluates whether the test provides a broad measure of the characteristic. [8] ____________ validity evaluates how well the test predicts future behavior. [9] ____________ validity measures how well the test relates to a theoretical view or concept. Standardization is the use of [10] ____________ procedures on all occasions.

The most famous index of intelligence is the intelligence [11] ____________ or IQ. Binet and Simon developed an intelligence test to identify children who would have difficulty in school. A child's [12] ____________ was determined based on a comparison of his or her performance with the performance of children of specific ages. A child with a mental (not actual) age of 8 performs as well as an average 8-year-old. Later, Terman developed the formula, ([13] ____________ age / chronological age) X 100 = IQ, which creates an "average" score of [14] ____________ .

Modern tests compute a [15] ____________ IQ, based on a score's location in the distribution for others of the same age, to avoid problems created by comparisons based on mental age. Most people have IQs between [16] ____________ . Scores below 70 suggest mental [17] ____________ ; scores above 130 suggest [18] ____________ . Mental retardation is caused by both genetic and environmental influences and varies from mild to profound. Giftedness is associated with many aspects of success. People who have extreme abilities in one area are called [19] ____________ .

Major intelligence tests (Stanford-Binet, WAIS, etc.) are valid for predicting [20] ____________ success. Because of criticisms that previous tests failed to broadly sample intelligence, [21] ____________ items were included in the Weschler tests. Testing dangers include [22] ____________ effects and misinterpretation.

[23] ____________ is the ability to generate original, useful ideas. Creativity is not highly correlated with traditional IQ scores. [24] ____________ intelligence is the ability to perceive, understand, and express emotion in useful ways, and might be a better predictor of social or career success than IQ.

Standard intelligence assessments focus on well-defined, academic material, and do not predict job success well. Wagner & Sternberg suggest job performance can be predicted by evaluating [25] ____________ knowledge, unspoken practical "know how" that is rarely taught, but is gained through [26] ____________ people's behavior. Criticisms of the tacit knowledge concept include questions about whether it differs from job knowledge.

EVALUATING YOUR PROGRESS

Select the best response. If you miss any questions, reread the relevant material before proceeding.

1. If a test gives approximately the same result from one administration to the next, the test is said to be
   a. standardized.
   b. tacit.
   c. reliable.
   d. valid.

2. Binet's original IQ test was designed to
   a. quantify the genetic determinant of intelligence.
   b. quantify the environmental determinants of intelligence.
   c. predict job success in adulthood.
   d. identify children who would do poorly in traditional schools.

3. A test has validity if
   a. it measures what it is supposed to measure.
   b. it is administered and scored the same way each time.
   c. it gives a similar score when a person is retested.
   d. the score is compared to a group norm.

4. The average IQ score is
   a. 70.
   b. 80.
   c. 100.
   d. 110.

5. Deviation IQ is used because of problems caused by
   a. defining IQ as a ratio.
   b. the mathematical complexity of the original IQ computation.
   c. difficulty getting good predictive validity scores with the original IQ format.
   d. lack of standardization.

6. To be classified as mentally retarded, a person's IQ score must be below
   a. 100.
   b. 90.
   c. 70.
   d. 50.

7. A person who has a good understanding of unspoken rules and strategies of a job would be said to be high in
   a. emotional intelligence.
   b. analytical intelligence.
   c. tacit knowledge.
   d. creativity.
8. Creativity
   a. is highly correlated with IQ.
   b. was added as a sub-part to the Stanford-Binet test to improve construct validity.
   c. requires novel ideas be useful.
   d. is thought by many psychologists to be the best predictor of personal success.
9. The concept of emotional intelligence
   a. is thought to be a very good predictor of career and social success.
   b. is negatively correlated with traditional measures of intelligence.
   c. applies primarily to controlling one's own emotions.
   d. has been dismissed by most psychologists as invalid and unscientific.

DISCOVERING THE SOURCES OF INTELLIGENCE (PP. 348-355)

MASTERING THE VOCABULARY

Define or explain each of the following terms.

1. The Flynn effect
2. Heritability

MASTERING THE CONCEPTS

Fill in the blanks to create a summary of the section.

Strong genetic determinants predict stable intelligence, whereas strong environmental determinants predict changing intelligence. Some evidence suggests fast [1] ____________ in infancy relates to intelligence, but reliable measurements of intelligence cannot be obtained until age [2] ____________ . A longitudinal study found [3] ____________ in IQ throughout adulthood, but a decline begins at age 60. [4] ____________ intelligence, basic information processing, declines but crystallized intelligence, acquired knowledge, remains constant or increases. The [5] ____________ , a general increase in IQ test performance over the past 70 years, is usually explained in terms of changes in [6] ____________ .

Twin studies suggest that genetic factors are important determinants of intelligence. [7] ____________ twins have the most similar IQs, even if reared apart. Twin studies indicate [8] ____________ , the amount of the variation in IQ scores within a population that is due to genetics, may be 50 - 70%. Still, separated twins have less similar IQs than twins reared together, showing that [9] ____________ influences intelligence.

Racial differences in IQ occur, but why is unclear. They reflect average IQs, and cannot be applied to individuals. Economic differences exist and these environmental factors are hard to separate from genetic factors. Test [10] ____________ can contribute to the difference, but it does not account for all of it. Studies of minority children adopted into advantaged homes find higher IQs than the racial average, supporting an [11] ____________ factor. Most see IQ resulting from an [12] ____________ of genetics and environment. Genetics may establish a range in which IQ is pushed up or down by environmental factors.

EVALUATING YOUR PROGRESS

Select the best response. If you miss any questions, reread the relevant material before proceeding.

1. The Seattle Longitudinal study suggests intelligence is relatively stable until about age
   a. 40.
   b. 50.
   c. 60.
   d. 70.

2. The best evidence for a strong genetic determinant of intelligence would be to find high positive correlations for the IQ scores of
   a. fraternal twins who were raised together.
   b. fraternal twins who were raised apart.
   c. identical twins who were raised together.
   d. identical twins who were raised apart

3. The Flynn Effect is
   a. the higher heritability estimate found for certain ethnic groups.
   b. the decrease in IQ scores sometimes found when stereotypes produce negative expectations.
   c. the change in an IQ score that is due to test bias.
   d. an increase in the typical IQ scores over the past several decades.

4. The extent to which IQ differences in a population can be accounted for by genetic factors is
   a. the genotype of intelligence.
   b. the heritability of intelligence.
   c. the genetic concordance of intelligence.
   d. the inheritance quotient for intelligence.
5. Results of research with African American children adopted into white homes best supports the idea that racial differences in IQ test scores
   a. are the result of stereotype threat.
   b. are not the result of test bias in the major intelligence tests.
   c. are due almost entirely to genetic influences.
   d. are significantly influenced by environmental conditions.

MAKING FINAL PREPARATIONS

Complete these sections without consulting your book or notes. For a more accurate estimate of how well you know this material, wait at least a day or two after studying the chapter before working on the questions. Some of the material you "know" immediately after working with the chapter will be quickly forgotten. Exercises done too soon after studying will overestimate what you know well.

SHORT ESSAY QUESTIONS

Write a brief answer to each question.

1. Explain what is meant by general intelligence (g) and why Spearman proposed this concept.

   ____

   ____

2. Discuss the contributions and limitations of the multiple intelligences theory and the triarchic theory.

   ____

   ____

3. Explain why standardization is necessary in a good test.

   ____

   ____

4. Define validity, and discuss the apparent validity of intelligence tests.

   ____

   ____

5. Discuss the possible dangers of IQ labeling.

____

____

6. Discuss the stability of intelligence in adulthood, including the roles of fluid and crystallized intelligence.

____

____

7. Summarize the current thought concerning the role of genes and the environment as determinants of intelligence, citing evidence relevant to each factor.

____

____

MATCHING

Select the correct definition or description for each item.

1. ________ Sternberg
2. ________ achievement test
3. ________ crystallized intelligence
4. ________ Galton
5. ________ heritability
6. ________ aptitude test
7. ________ fluid intelligence
8. ________ test-retest reliability
9. ________ tacit knowledge
10. ________ Spearman
11. ________ Thurstone
12. ________ practical intelligence
13. ________ Terman
14. ________ mental age
15. ________ norm group
16. ________ Gardner

a. used for standard comparison of scores
b. proposed 7 primary mental abilities instead of g
c. intelligence based on acquired knowledge
d. actual age that best fits a child's test performance
e. unspoken practical knowledge
f. proposed the triarchic theory
g. basic reasoning & information processing skill
h. proposed multiple intelligences theory
i. index of trait variability in a group due to genetics
j. similarity of scores on two administrations of a test
k. proposed the two-factor theory
l. one of first to use the psychometric approach
m. revised Binet's test and developed IQ formula
n. measures current status of knowledge
o. "street smarts" in the triarchic theory
p. measures ability to learn

MULTIPLE CHOICE PRETEST 1

Select the one best response.

1. Spearman studied the relationships between scores on several types of mental tests to develop a theory of intelligence. This approach is known as
   a. the multiple intelligences approach.
   b. the mental aptitudes approach.
   c. the psychometric approach.
   d. the deviation IQ technique.

2. Thurstone's theory of primary mental abilities suggests
   a. a high score on one primary mental ability will be accompanied by high scores on the others.
   b. that differences in intelligence are best described by three factors or abilities.
   c. the primary mental abilities are fairly independent abilities.
   d. emotional intelligence is the most critical primary mental ability.

3. Fluid intelligence is best described as
   a. the natural ability to solve problems and reason.
   b. the ability to adapt to an environment ("street smarts").
   c. the ability to infer other people's moods and motivations.
   d. knowledge and mental ability acquired from experience.

4. The P100 signal has been proposed as a way to predict intelligence. This approach is based on
   a. the idea that differences in left and right hemisphere function predict intelligence test scores.
   b. the idea that a specific region of the brain is responsible for intelligence.
   c. the high heritability of intelligence.
   d. the idea that faster neural transmission is associated with higher intelligence test scores.

5. Spearman's two-factor theory of intelligence proposes
   a. verbal intelligence and mathematical intelligence.
   b. fluid intelligence and crystallized intelligence.
   c. analytical intelligence and practical intelligence.
   d. general intelligence and specific abilities.

6. Gardner's theory of multiple intelligences has been criticized for all of the following except:
   a. It is primarily descriptive.
   b. It really deals with talents, not intelligences.
   c. It is supported by little scientific evidence.
   d. It broadens the way intelligence is conceptualized.

7. In Sternberg's triarchic theory, which type of intelligence best predicts performance on traditional intelligence tests?
   a. analytical
   b. practical
   c. tacit
   d. creative

8. When Dr. Askew gave his new personality test to a group of people on three separate occasions, he found that the scores were very similar each time. This suggests the test is
   a. reliable.
   b. standardized.
   c. unbiased.
   d. valid.

9. Eve didn't go to college and she was never trained to run a business, but with experience she developed great management skills and understands how to make a business prosper. Eve would score well on a test of
   a. tacit knowledge.
   b. general intelligence (g).
   c. analytical intelligence.
   d. fluid intelligence.

10. Daria is 10 and scored as well as the average 8-year-old. Terman would compute her IQ score to be
    a. 60.
    b. 80.
    c. 90.
    d. 125.

11. Dr. Fort is comparing an 8-year-old's intelligence test score to the average score of 8-year-olds. Dr. Fort is
    a. finding the standardized score.
    b. checking the reliability of the intelligence test.
    c. determining the deviation IQ score.
    d. evaluating the predictive validity of the intelligence test.

12. To evaluate the construct validity of a new test for depression, a psychologist might check to see if
    a. it predicts who will develop depression within the next six months.
    b. its scores tend to vary the way an accepted theory of depression would predict.
    c. it samples a wide range of behaviors associated with depression.
    d. it gives about the same result if taken twice in a relatively short period of time.

13. Which is false regarding mental retardation?
    a. The diagnosis of mental retardation is based on more than an IQ score.
    b. Approximately 85% of cases of mental retardation fall in the moderately to profoundly retarded ranges.
    c. The use of alcohol or other drugs during pregnancy may cause low IQ.
    d. Many people with mental retardation lead independent lives.

14. Most psychologists would agree that the most widely used intelligence tests
    a. have good predictive validity for academic performance.
    b. are valid for differentiating fluid and crystallized intelligence.
    c. have high validity for predicting creativity.
    d. are not valid because they are seriously racially biased.

15. Most psychologists agree that a reliable assessment of intelligence can't be obtained until the person is
    a. at least 9 months to 1 year old.
    b. 2 and 3 years old.
    c. 4 to 7 years old.
    d. 8 to 10 years.

16. Although some researchers give heritability estimates of 70%, the most common estimate is approximately
    a. 30%.
    b. 50%.
    c. 80%.
    d. 90%.

17. Although Winner has reported contradictory findings, most research suggests that gifted children
    a. are unskilled socially.
    b. become "ordinary" adults.
    c. have no more successful careers than other people.
    d. are emotionally stable.

18. The idea of emotional intelligence is most similar to
    a. tacit knowledge.
    b. Sternberg's creative intelligence.
    c. Gardner's interpersonal intelligence.
    d. crystallized intelligence.

MULTIPLE CHOICE PRETEST 2

Select the one best response.

1. When people take several very different mental abilities tests, their scores across tests are often similar or positively correlated. This best supports
    a. Spearman's two-factor theory of intelligence.
    b. Gardner's multiple intelligences theory.
    c. Sternberg's triarchic theory of intelligence.
    d. Cattell's concept of crystallized and fluid intelligence.

2. How do most modern psychologists perceive the concept of general intelligence?
    a. It is a totally worthless concept without support from any data.
    b. It is at the top of a hierarchy of factors that are involved in intelligence.
    c. It is one of three equally important factors that are involved in intelligence.
    d. It is the sole factor determining differences in performance on mental tests.

3. All of the following are true EXCEPT:
    a. Crystallized intelligence is probably determined primarily by genetic factors.
    b. Crystallized intelligence helps explain cultural differences in mental test performance.
    c. Crystallized intelligence is influenced significantly by experience.
    d. Crystallized intelligence declines less than fluid intelligence after age 60.

4. Holly graduated last in her law school class, but she is the first in her class to make partner in a big firm. Her success was due to her ability to evaluate how things work in the firm, and to adapt her behavior accordingly. According to the triarchic theory of intelligence, Holly is probably high in
    a. analytical intelligence.
    b. creative intelligence.
    c. practical intelligence.
    d. intrapersonal intelligence.

5. The Psychology Subject Test required by some graduate schools tests a person's knowledge of psychology. This test is an example of
    a. an aptitude test.
    b. an achievement test.
    c. an intelligence test.
    d. an analogies test.

6. Using deviation IQ is preferred today because it
    a. increases the reliability of intelligence tests.
    b. avoids problems created by using mental age to compute IQ.
    c. allows separate scores for verbal and nonverbal components of intelligence.
    d. reduces the likelihood of errors when computing IQ.

7. To allow fair comparisons of scores across individuals, a test must be
    a. high in predictive validity.
    b. high in content validity.
    c. an aptitude test.
    d. standardized.

8. Concerns about using the P100 signal to evaluate intelligence include all of the following EXCEPT:
    a. The relationship is a correlation.
    b. Differences in the P100 signal account for a small part of the differences in intelligence scores.
    c. The P100 might correlate with IQ scores, but not be directly related to intelligence.
    d. People differ in the amount of time required for the P100 signal to appear.

9. Mike is a skilled therapist, partly because he is very good at perceiving his clients' moods, temperaments, and motivations. Based on this, we should expect him to score high in
    a. bodily-kinesthetic intelligence.
    b. naturalist intelligence.
    c. interpersonal intelligence.
    d. intrapersonal intelligence.

10. Although Terman's study found general benefits of being gifted, recent research has suggested an increased emotional problems and social isolation for a subgroup of the gifted population. This subgroup is primarily
    a. the moderately gifted (IQ = 130-150).
    b. the profoundly gifted (IQ > 180).
    c. female.
    d. from high socioeconomic backgrounds.

11. The most popular intelligence tests include exercises of several types in an attempt to test the different aspects of intelligence. This broad approach should increase the test's
    a. content validity.
    b. construct validity.
    c. standardization.
    d. reliability.

12. Binet's intelligence test originally was intended to
    a. identify children who would not do well in standard schools.
    b. identify adults who were not mentally fit to enter the army.
    c. measure "natural" or inherited intelligence.
    d. test Spearman's concept of general intelligence (g).

13. Research shows that children identified as smart get more respect from teachers and are given more educational opportunities than other children. This difference in how they are treated is an example of'
    a. stereotype threat.
    b. the labeling effect.
    c. the Flynn effect.
    d. the Mozart effect.

14. Jess can think of many new and useful ways to use duct tape. Jess probably would score high on a test of
    a. practical intelligence.
    b. tacit knowledge.
    c. creativity.
    d. fluid intelligence.

15. African Americans perform worse when they believe they are taking an intelligence test than when they think the test has some other purpose. This has been explained in terms of
    a. racial bias in test content.
    b. the Flynn effect.
    c. the heritability of intelligence.
    d. stereotype threat.

16. Suppose the IQ scores of fraternal twins raised together were as highly correlated as those of identical twins raised together. This would support
    a. the high heritability for intelligence.
    b. the different basis of fluid and crystallized intelligence.
    c. a strong environmental determinant of intelligence.
    d. a strong genetic determinant of intelligence.

17. During adulthood, fluid intelligence usually __________, and crystallized intelligence __________.
    a. stays the same or increases; stays the same or increases
    b. stays the same or increases; decreases
    c. decreases; decreases
    d. decreases; stays the same or increases

18. The Mozart effect most likely is due to
    a. changes in brain development.
    b. activation of brain areas related to spatial reasoning.
    c. improved mood or arousal.
    d. a placebo effect.

19. Most psychologists believe that intelligence is determined by
    a. genetics, almost exclusively.
    b. the environment, almost exclusively.
    c. a significant interaction of genetics and environment.
    d. some yet-to-be-discovered factor.

LANGUAGE DEVELOPMENT GUIDE

CORE TERMS

One of the central questions about intelligence is whether it is one thing or many things, and you are likely to hear terms like ***comprehensive***, ***multifaceted***, and ***multimodal***. A *comprehensive* test covers all the relevant material, so a comprehensive intelligence test would have many questions of different kinds. *Multifaceted* and *multimodal* are very similar; a multifaceted test would have many different parts, and a multimodal one would measure something in many different ways

Your instructor may talk about various levels of education using unfamiliar terms. ***Primary*** school is from kindergarten to about 6th grade. ***Secondary*** school is 7th through 12th grade. ***Higher education*** is all that follows graduation from high school. ***Undergraduates*** are college students seeking bachelor's degrees. ***Graduate*** students are pursuing master's degrees or doctorates, and we would say that they are in graduate school. ***Postgraduate*** work is academic work done after receiving a doctorate.

IDIOMS

p. 327	cocky grin	a smile that says that he is very self-confident
p. 327	furrowed brows	wrinkled foreheads, suggesting worry or concentration
p. 327	secret caches	valuable things hidden away in various spots
p. 329	cartography school	a school for map-makers
p. 329	granted that	given that; let's assume that
p. 330	in a more rigorous way	with more standardization, more careful control, etc.
p. 330	mathematically inclined	very good at and interested in math
p. 333	socioeconomic classes	your social level, based upon your income
p. 334	savant	short for idiot savant, a person with low mental ability except in one spectacular area
p. 340	appropriate curriculum adjustments	helpful changes in what is being taught
p. 342	bookworm	someone who reads a lot
p. 343	pass with flying colors	perform very well
p. 347	cut and dried	easy to understand; clear and simple
p. 347	intuitively plausible	possible, based on common sense
p. 348	airtight	perfect; impossible to damage
p. 348	battery of tests	group of tests
p. 351	irrespective	no matter which one

PRONUNCIATION

triarchic (try-ark′-ick) *p. 335*
quotient (kwo′-shint) *p. 339*
tacit (ta′-sit) *p. 347*
heritability (hair-i-ta-bil′-i-ty) *p. 351*

SOLUTIONS

PREVIEW & CONCEPTUALIZING INTELLIGENCE (PP. 327-336)

MASTERING THE CONCEPTS

1. differences (p. 329)
2. psychometric (p. 329)
3. Galton (p. 330)
4. Factor analysis (p. 330)
5. Spearman (p. 330)
6. general (p. 331)
7. specific (p. 331)
8. two-factor (p. 331)
9. primary (p. 331)
10. g (p. 332)
11. fluid (p. 332)
12. age (p. 333)
13. Neural (p. 333)
14. P100 (p. 333)
15. multiple (p. 334)
16. case (p. 334)
17. broad (p. 335)
18. triarchic (p. 335)
19. Analytical (p. 335)
20. Creative (p. 335)
21. Practical (p. 336)

EVALUATING YOUR PROGRESS

1. B, Correct (p. 329)

   A. Wrong. Biological measures are not usually considered part of the psychometric approach.

   C. Wrong. This is closer to Sternberg's Triarchic approach.

   D. Wrong. This describes Sternberg's Triarchic approach.

2. A, Correct (p. 331)

   B. Wrong. These are Cattell and Horn's units of intelligence.

   C. Wrong. These are two of Gardner's seven multiple intelligences.

   D. Wrong. These are two of the three types of intelligence in the triarchic theory.

3. D, Correct (p. 331)

   A. Wrong. The abilities mentioned are mostly fluid intelligence abilities.

   B. Wrong. Sternberg's analytical intelligence is a closer match than practical intelligence.

   C. Wrong. Gardner's multiple intelligences are much broader in scope than these mental abilities describe.

4. A, Correct (p. 332)

   B. Wrong. Crystallized intelligence is significantly influenced by experience.

   C. Wrong. Interpersonal intelligence involves the ability to evaluate other people's mood or behavior.

   D. Wrong. Practical intelligence is "street smarts."

5. C, Correct (p. 333)

   A. Wrong. The P100 doesn't indicate the dominant hemisphere.

   B. Wrong. The P100 is an electrical waveform generated by the brain.

   D. Wrong. The P100 does not reflect the size of an active brain area.

6. C, Correct (p. 334)

   A. Wrong. Thurstone's primary abilities are traditional mental skills.

   B. Wrong. Sternberg proposes similarly unique dimensions, but not these.

   D. Wrong. Spearman proposed g and s, not these.

7. B, Correct (p. 331)

   A. Wrong. The fact that many tests are correlated suggests a single main intelligence factor, not multiple ones.

   C. Wrong. This finding suggests a single factor, and doesn't lead to broadening of the types of intelligence.

   D. Wrong. This finding led to the idea of general intelligence, not the subdivision of that factor by Cattell.

8. D, Correct (p. 335)

   A. Wrong. General intelligence is not part of the triarchic theory. It is part of Spearman's 2-factor theory.

   B. Wrong. Practical intelligence is the ability to adapt to the environment or "street smarts."

   C. Wrong. Analytical intelligence involves information processing and reasoning – standard mental abilities.

MEASURING INDIVIDUAL DIFFERENCES (PP. 337-347)

MASTERING THE CONCEPTS.

1. achievement (p. 337)
2. aptitude (p. 337)
3. reliability (p. 337)
4. validity (p. 338)
5. consistency (p. 337)
6. test-retest (p. 337)
7. Content (p. 338)
8. Predictive (p. 338)
9. Construct (p. 338)
10. the same (p. 338)
11. quotient (p. 339)
12. mental age (p. 340)
13. mental (p. 340)
14. 100 (p. 340)
15. deviation (p. 340)
16. 85 and 115 (p. 341)
17. retardation (p. 341)
18. giftedness (p. 342)
19. savants (p. 343)
20. academic (p. 343)
21. nonverbal (p. 343)
22. labeling (p. 344)
23. Creativity (p. 345)
24. Emotional (p. 345)
25. tacit (p. 347)
26. observing (p. 347)

EVALUATING YOUR PROGRESS

1. C, Correct (p. 337)

   A. Wrong. Standardized involves using the same procedures each time.

   B. Wrong. Tacit knowledge is unspoken job knowledge.

   D. Wrong. Validity related to whether the test measures what it is supposed to measure.

2. D, Correct (p. 339)

   A, B, C. Wrong. The French government wanted to identify "dull" children who needed a different academic experience.

3. A, Correct (p. 338)

   B. Wrong. This describes standardization.

   C. Wrong. This describes reliability.

   D. Wrong. Using norms doesn't relate to validity. Validity involves testing what you mean to test.

4. C, Correct (p. 340)

   A, B. Wrong. These are too low.

   D. Wrong. This is too high.

5. A, Correct (p. 340)

   B. Wrong. The original IQ is a simple ratio.

   C. Wrong. Deviation IQ is used with the same test format, and does not really impact predictive validity.

   D. Wrong. The change was computational, and did not involve improving standardization.

6. C, Correct (p. 341)

   A, B. Wrong. Mental retardation is assigned when IQ is below 70. IQ of 70-130 is normal.

   D. Wrong. An IQ of 50 indicates retardation, but below 70 is the basic standard. IQ of 70-130 is normal.

7. C, Correct (p. 347)

   A. Wrong. Emotional intelligence may predict career success, but it doesn't involve unspoken job knowledge.

   B. Wrong. Analytical intelligence corresponds to traditional components of intelligence, not job knowledge.

   D. Wrong. Creativity is the ability to produce new ideas, not job knowledge.

8. C, Correct (p. 345)

   A. Wrong. Creativity is not highly correlated with IQ.

   B. Wrong. Creativity is not measured by the Stanford-Binet or any of the major standard intelligence tests.

   D. Wrong. Creativity is not viewed as a strong predictor of personal success.

9. A, Correct (p. 345)

   B. Wrong. No such correlation has been found.

   C. Wrong. Emotional intelligence involves perceiving other people's emotions, too.

   D. Wrong. Although research is limited, many psychologists have positive views of emotional intelligence.

DISCOVERING THE SOURCES OF INTELLIGENCE (PP. 348-355)

MASTERING THE CONCEPTS

1. habituation (p. 348)
2. 4 - 7 years (p. 348)
3. stability (p. 349)
4. Fluid (p. 349)
5. Flynn effect (p. 349)
6. the environment (p. 349)
7. Identical (p. 350)
8. heritability (p. 351)
9. environment (p. 352)
10. bias (p. 352)
11. environmental (p. 354)
12. interaction (p. 354)

EVALUATING YOUR PROGRESS

1. C, Correct (p. 349)

   A, B, D. Wrong. Intelligence is quite stable until about age 60, when a decline begins.
2. D, Correct (p. 350)

   A. Wrong. These have the same environment, but not genes, so similarity would favor an environmental view.

   B. Wrong. Because both genes and environment differ, an explanation would be rather difficult.

   C. Wrong. Because both genes and environment are the same, either factor could be responsible.
3. D, Correct (p. 349)

   A. Wrong. The Flynn effect relates to change in the population's mean IQ over time, not heritability.

   B. Wrong. This answer describes stereotype threat.

   C. Wrong. The Flynn effect relates to change in the population's mean IQ over time, not test bias.
4. B, Correct (p. 351)

   A. Wrong. A genotype represents the pattern of genes a person has.

   C. Wrong. Concordance is the degree to which two scores or traits match.

   D. Wrong. There is an intelligence quotient (IQ) that represents test performance, but not inheritance quotient.
5. D, Correct (p. 354)

   A. Wrong. This research did not address stereotype threat. It investigated the influence of the environment.

   B. Wrong. This research didn't deal directly with this issue, although test bias isn't viewed as the primary problem.

   C. Wrong. The children adopted into white homes performed better, so genetics is not the key.

MAKING FINAL PREPARATIONS

SHORT ESSAY QUESTIONS

1. Discuss the contributions and limitations of the multiple intelligences theory and the triarchic theory. (pp. 330-331)
2. Both Gardner's and Sternberg's theories broadened what intelligence is conceptualized to be. They included aspects of behavior which previous theories had not, and they extended intelligence to include interpersonal and "real world," nonacademic abilities. These additions are difficult to define or test scientifically, and critics ask whether they are part of intelligence or only specific talents. (pp. 333-336)
3. Standardization, maintaining the same procedures for all administrations of the test, is needed if scores are to be compared across individuals or groups. If procedures differ, differences in IQ scores could be due to the procedural differences rather than individual differences in intelligence. (pp. 338-339)
4. Validity is an assessment of how well a test measures what it is supposed to measure. Intelligence tests are considered to be valid, at least relating to academic performance. They predict academic performance well, giving them good predictive validity. Researchers have questioned their content validity, but the Weschler tests added performance scales so that a broader range of activities are sampled. (pp. 338, 343)
5. Labels of "smart" or "slow" are difficult to change and lead to different treatment. Teachers treated "smart" children with more respect and expose them to more opportunities than "slow" children, further delaying possible advancement of the "slow" children. Mislabeling due to misuse of IQ tests resulted in immigration laws designed to keep out "defective" groups early in the 20th century. (p. 344)
6. The Seattle Longitudinal study suggests that IQ remains quite steady throughout adulthood, with only a slight decline after age 60. Individual differences are large in later years, possibly due to physical problems. Fluid intelligence seems to decline, but crystallized intelligence remains constant or increases. (pp. 349)
7. Intelligence is determined by an interaction of genes and environment. Genetic factors are supported by twin studies that show genetic similarity predicts IQ similarity. Even if environments differ, identical twins have more similar IQs than same-sex fraternal twins reared together. Adoption studies of minority children reared in "advantaged" homes find they have higher IQs than average, supporting environmental factors. (pp. 350-355)

MATCHING

1. f (p. 335)
2. n (p. 337)
3. c (p. 332)
4. l (p. 330)
5. i (p. 351)
6. p (p. 337)
7. g (p. 332)
8. j (p. 337)
9. e (p. 347)
10. k (p. 330)
11. b (p. 331)
12. o (p. 336)
13. m (p. 340)
14. d (p. 340)
15. a (p. 340)
16. h (p. 334)

MULTIPLE CHOICE PRETEST 1

1. C, Correct (p. 329)
   A. Wrong. Multiple intelligences is a theory of intelligence proposed by Gardner.
   B. Wrong. Using mental tests as a foundation for a theory of intelligence is the psychometric approach.
   D. Wrong. Deviation IQ is a way to measure intelligence, not a way of studying it via mental tests.
2. C, Correct (p. 331)
   A. Wrong. The factors are fairly independent, so one doesn't predict another.
   B. Wrong. Thurstone proposed 7 primary mental abilities, not 3.
   D. Wrong. Emotional intelligence is not one of the primary mental abilities.
3. A, Correct (p. 332)
   B. Wrong. This is Sternberg's practical intelligence.
   C. Wrong. This is emotional intelligence, or Gardner's interpersonal intelligence.
   D. Wrong. This is crystallized intelligence, as opposed to fluid intelligence.
4. D, Correct (p. 333)
   A. Wrong. The P100 doesn't measure this, and this idea is not valid.
   B. Wrong. Intelligence is not thought to originate in one brain area.
   C. Wrong. The use of P100 implies faster transmission equals better processing. Heritability isn't relevant.
5. D, Correct (p. 331)
   A. Wrong. Spearman emphasized the general nature of intelligence, rather than breaking it down by "subject," although he did recognize specific abilities exist, too.
   B. Wrong. These were proposed by Cattell and Horn and represent components of Spearman's *g*.
   C. Wrong. These are two of Sternberg's three proposed types of intelligence.
6. D, Correct (p. 335)
   A, B, C. Wrong. These are all points of criticism.
7. A, Correct (p. 335)
   B. Wrong. Practical intelligence is not measured well by traditional intelligence tests.
   C. Wrong. Tacit knowledge is not part of Sternberg's model. Practical intelligence, which it resembles, is not measured well by traditional intelligence tests.
   D. Wrong. Creative intelligence is not reflected by traditional intelligence test scores.
8. A, Correct (p. 337)
   B. Wrong. A test is standardized if it is administered the same way for all people, every time.
   C. Wrong. Similar scores on multiple occasions doesn't address bias.
   D. Wrong. A test is valid if it tests what it purports to test; similar scores when repeated shows reliability.
9. A, Correct (p. 347)
   B. Wrong. These are tacit knowledge skills, which do not relate to g.
   C. Wrong. Analytical intelligence involves standard intelligence skills.
   D. Wrong. Intrapersonal intelligence is insight about one's own feelings and emotions.
10. B, Correct (p. 340)
    A, C, D. Wrong. IQ = (mental age/chronological age) X 100 = (8/10) X 100 = 80.
11. C, Correct (p. 340)
    A. Wrong. Standardization relates to procedures, not a comparison of scores. He's computing deviation IQ.
    B. Wrong. Reliability involves consistency from one administration to another, not between test takers.
    D. Wrong. Predictive validity involves being able to predict performance on some future performance.
12. B, Correct (p. 338)
    A. Wrong. This answer describes predictive validity.
    C. Wrong. This answer describes content validity.
    D. Wrong. This answer describes reliability.
13. B, Correct (p. 342)
    A, C, D. Wrong. These are all true, but about 85% of the mentally retarded or only mildly affected.

14. A, Correct (p. 343)

    B. Wrong. Intelligence tests were designed for, and currently are evaluated in terms of predicting academic performance. They do not differentiate fluid and crystallized intelligence abilities well.

    C. Wrong. Intelligence tests were designed for, and currently are evaluated in terms of predicting academic performance. They do not predict creativity well.

    D. Wrong. Intelligence tests are valid for predicting academic success. Although not completely unbiased, most psychologists feel bias is not a major problem.

15. C, Correct (p. 348)

    A, B, D. Wrong. Reliability is poor in infancy and toddlerhood, but good by early school-age.

16. B, Correct (p. 351)

    A, C, D. Wrong. The most common estimate is 50%.

17. D, Correct (p. 342)

    A, B, C. Wrong. Terman found they were generally emotionally healthy, socially adept, and highly successful.

18. C, Correct (p. 345)

    A. Wrong. Tacit knowledge is untaught work-related knowledge, not the ability to read and control emotions.

    B. Wrong. Creative intelligence is the ability to deal well with novel tasks, not to read and control emotions.

    D. Wrong. Crystallized intelligence is based on acquired knowledge. It doesn't involve understanding emotion.

MULTIPLE CHOICE PRETEST 2

1. A, Correct (p. 331)

   B, C. Wrong. Such a correlation supports a single factor view. These are multifactor.

   D. Wrong. This correlation would have nothing to say about the fluid vs. crystallized issue.

2. B, Correct (p. 332)

   A. Wrong. General intelligence hasn't been discarded or accepted totally.

   C. Wrong. Triarchic theory proposes three aspects of intelligence, but none is g.

   D. Wrong. General intelligence hasn't been discarded or accepted totally.

3. A, Correct (p. 332)

   B, C, D. Wrong. These are all true, but fluid, not crystallized, intelligence, probably is genetically influenced.

4. C, Correct (p. 336)

   A. Wrong. Analytical intelligence involves traditional mental skills and reasoning.

   B. Wrong. Creative intelligence involves learning novel tasks quickly.

   D. Wrong. Intrapersonal intelligence is not part of the triarchic theory.

5. B, Correct (p. 337)

   A. Wrong. Aptitude tests examine your potential ability to learn something, not your current knowledge.

   C. Wrong. Intelligence tests mostly evaluate mental processes, not acquired knowledge.

   D. Wrong. Tests that focus on current knowledge are achievement tests. Analogies are not a likely focus.

6. B, Correct (p. 340)

   A. Wrong. How IQ is computed doesn't determine reliability. The consistency of result determines reliability.

   C. Wrong. Deviation IQ compares performance to that of other people the same age; the components of the test are not relevant.

   D. Wrong. Computing deviation IQ is not simpler than computing Terman's IQ score.

7. D, Correct (p. 338)

   A. Wrong. Comparisons could be fair, but the test would not be useful for predicting anything.

   B. Wrong. Comparison could be fair, but the test would not provide a good measure of the attribute.

   C. Wrong. Aptitude tests are not the only tests that allow comparisons across people.

8. D, Correct (p. 333)
   A, B, C. Wrong. These are all reasons for caution in using the P100 signal to predict intelligence. The fact that individual differences occur in P100 is the reason it might be useful.
9. C, Correct (p. 334)
   A. Wrong. Bodily-kinesthetic intelligence involves control of the body, or athletic skills.
   B. Wrong. Naturalist intelligence involves the ability to interact with a wide variety of species.
   D. Wrong. Intrapersonal intelligence involves insight into one's own emotions, not other people's.
10. B, Correct (p. 342)
   A. Wrong. Moderately gifted people had no greater problems than "normals."
   C. Wrong. No sex differences are reported in your text.
   D. Wrong. High socioeconomic background has been proposed as a reason for greater success.
11. A, Correct (pp. 338, 343)
   B. Wrong. Construct validity is evaluated by seeing how well the results match predictions of theories of the concept involved (e.g., intelligence).
   C. Wrong. Standardization involved the methods used to administer tests, not the content of the tests.
   D. Wrong. Reliability involves whether the test gives the same general answer on separate occasions.
12. A, Correct (p. 339)
   B. Wrong. It was originally designed for predicting academic success.
   C. Wrong. The origin of intelligence wasn't the issue; identifying "slow" kids was.
   D. Wrong. It doesn't allow differentiation of different views of intelligence.
13. B, Correct (p. 344)
   A. Wrong. Stereotype threat involves changes in behavior do to one's own expectations.
   C. Wrong. The Flynn effect is the increase in IQ scores over the past 50 or more years.
   D. Wrong. The Mozart effect is the increase in IQ scores following listening to classical music.
14. C, Correct (p. 345)
   A. Wrong. Although duct tape is practical, the ability to generate new ideas is creativity.
   B. Wrong. Tacit knowledge is untaught knowledge, typically about work.
   D. Wrong. Fluid intelligence corresponds to basic mental processes. This is creativity.
15. D, Correct (p. 353)
   A. Wrong. Self-perceptions don't determine test content.
   B. Wrong. The Flynn effect is an increase in scores over several decades.
   C. Wrong. The impact of self-perceptions are not genetic.
16. C, Correct (pp. 350, 352)
   A. Wrong. Heritability involves genetic influence, but environment is key in this scenario.
   B. Wrong. There's no differentiation of fluid and crystallized intelligence here.
   D. Wrong. Fraternal twins' genes differ, so the similarity must be due to the shared environment.
17. D, Correct (p. 349)
   A, B, C. Wrong. Fluid intelligence decreases, while crystallized intelligence remains stable.
18. C, Correct (p. 346)
   A. Wrong. The effect is produced even in adults when development isn't impacted.
   B. Wrong. There is no evidence of this, and there is evidence consistent with an alternative.
   D. Wrong. Expectations are not critical.
19. C, Correct (p. 354)
   A, B, D. Wrong. Data clearly show both environment and genes influence intelligence.

CHAPTER **11**

MOTIVATION AND EMOTION

ESTABLISHING LEARNING GOALS

Use these learning goals as a preview of the chapter, a guide for active reading, and to evaluate your mastery of the material. Review the relevant goals as you begin and end your reading of each major section of the chapter.

I. Discuss the activation of behavior.

A. Compare instinct and drive and their roles in activating behavior.

B. Understand incentive motivation and its role in activating behavior.

C. Compare achievement motivation and intrinsic motivation.

D. Describe Maslow's hierarchy of needs.

II. Discuss how the biological need for food is met.

A. Understand how internal and external factors influence the desire to eat.
1. Describe the role of glucose and insulin levels in hunger and eating.
2. Discuss the role of the hypothalamus and other brain areas in the control of eating.

B. Explain how body weight is regulated.

C. Distinguish between anorexia nervosa and bulimia nervosa.

III. Discuss how the biological need for sexual activity is met.

A. Describe the human sexual response cycle.

B. Consider the role of hormones in sexual behavior.

C. List external influences on sexual behavior.

D. Understand factors that influence mate selection.

E. Discuss factors that may determine sexual orientation.

IV. Discuss how emotion is expressed and experienced.

A. Examine the evidence for and against basic emotions.
1. Discuss the cross-cultural research concerning facial expressions and emotion.
2. Explain the facial-feedback hypothesis.

B. Understand the role of arousal in emotional experience.

C. Describe the subjective experiences of anger, happiness, and disgust.

D. Differentiate among the James-Lange, Cannon-Bard, and two-factor theories of emotion.

   1. Describe Schachter & Singer's research and the resulting conclusions.
   2. Critique each theory.

MASTERING THE MATERIAL

PREVIEW & ACTIVATING BEHAVIOR (PP. 361-369)

MASTERING THE VOCABULARY

Define or explain each of the following terms.

1. motivation
2. emotions
3. instincts
4. drive
5. homeostasis
6. incentive motivation
7. achievement motive
8. intrinsic motivation
9. need hierarchy

MASTERING THE CONCEPTS

Fill in the blanks to create a summary of the section.

Motivation, the set of factors that initiate and [1] ____________ behavior toward a goal, and emotion are closely linked. Emotions include a [2] ____________ reaction, a [3] ____________ experience, and an expressive reaction. Four major issues are discussed: What factors activate behavior? What factors create hunger and control eating? What factors promote sexual behavior? How and why do emotions occur?

Motivation is the result of both internal and external events. [4] ____________ , unlearned characteristic responses, are internal motivators that influence animal, and possibly human, behavior. The concept of [5] ____________ , an internal state, is an alternative to the idea of instincts. Drives maintain [6] ____________ , but unlike instincts, drives are flexible in format.

[7] ____________ motivation involves the value of an external factor. Internal and external factors interact, as in the case of [8] ____________ motivation, a drive for success or accomplishment. Experience with failure, cultural attitudes, and other external factors influence achievement behaviors.

[9] ____________ motivation, self-motivated behavior without external reward or homeostatic influence, can be reduced by rewards. Explanations include a loss of [10] ____________ when rewarded and the possibility the [11] ____________ is perceived to be the source of motivation. This occurs only if rewards are [12] ____________ , so the promise of reward might be critical, not the reward itself.

Maslow proposed a [13] ____________ that prioritizes needs. [14] ____________ and safety needs are most basic, and [15] ____________ , reaching one's full potential, is the final need. Maslow's theory is criticized for its lack of scientific rigor, but it has had wide impact.

EVALUATING YOUR PROGRESS

Select the best response. If you make any errors, reread the relevant material before proceeding.

1. Unlearned, characteristic patterns of responding that are controlled by the environment are called
   a. drives.
   b. incentives.
   c. motivations.
   d. instincts.
2. An internal psychological state that arises in response to a need is
   a. drive.
   b. an instinct.
   c. an emotion.
   d. homeostasis.
3. Incentives differ from drives because
   a. incentives involve physiological needs, but drives do not.
   b. incentives "pull" behavior, but drives "push" behavior.
   c. incentives are unlearned, but drives are learned.
   d. incentives are internal, but drives are external.

4. Homeostasis is
   a. an internal drive or need for success.
   b. goal-directed behavior that seems to be entirely self-motivated.
   c. an internal state that arises in response to a physiological need.
   d. the process through which the body maintains a steady state.
5. Working hard to complete a task or to accomplish something is most associated with
   a. instinct.
   b. high achievement motivation.
   c. self-actualization.
   d. intrinsic motivation.
6. Marla spent all afternoon hitting a tennis ball against the side of the house, simply because she enjoys it. This behavior is best explained in terms of
   a. self-actualization.
   b. homeostasis.
   c. drive.
   d. intrinsic motivation.
7. The most important and most accepted aspect of Maslow's hierarchy of needs is
   a. the idea that need for self-actualization is the most important need of all.
   b. the clear definitions given for newly proposed needs.
   c. the idea that some needs are more important or basic than others.
   d. the suggestion that need for achievement is the most important need of all.
8. What need is at the top of Maslow's hierarchy?
   a. self-esteem
   b. physiological need
   c. safety needs
   d. self-actualization

MEETING BIOLOGICAL NEEDS: HUNGER AND EATING (PP. 369-375)

MASTERING THE VOCABULARY

Define or explain each of the following terms.

1. glucose
2. insulin
3. leptin
4. ventromedial hypothalamus
5. lateral hypothalamus

6. set point
7. obesity
8. anorexia nervosa
9. bulimia nervosa

MASTERING THE CONCEPTS.

Fill in the blanks to create a summary of the section.

Internal conditions, including stomach contents, are monitored to control eating. Receptors monitor blood [1] ____________ , a sugar required for energy production, and [2] ____________ , a pancreatic hormone required for glucose utilization. The glucose-insulin interaction is critical, but leptin levels might also be important.

The [3] ____________ is important in the control of eating. Damage to the [4] ____________ hypothalamus results in overeating; stimulation of this area inhibits eating. Damage to the [5] ____________ hypothalamus inhibits eating; stimulation initiates eating. These areas were once considered the satiety and initiation centers for eating, but recent data suggest the situation is more complex. Other brain areas, the [6] ____________ and [7] ____________ , also may be involved in eating behavior. Eating is also influenced by learned eating [8] ____________ , the presence of food cues, and other external factors.

Both internal and external factors impact weight regulation. The [9] ____________ theory states individuals have a natural weight the body tries to maintain. [10] ____________ factors may control the number of fat cells and [11] ____________ rate to establish a set point. Excessive body fat, [12] ____________ , is not just a matter of poor willpower. Metabolic rate, set point, cultural habits, and stress also influence eating and weight.

Culturally-influenced "ideal" weights and inaccurate body images affect eating. [13] ____________ nervosa, in which an abnormally low weight is maintained, can include the perception of being fat even while starving. In [14] ____________ nervosa, [15] ____________ eating is followed by purging.

Both disorders have serious medical consequences and are most common in women with an obsessive desire to be thin.

EVALUATING YOUR PROGRESS

Select the best response. If you miss any questions, reread the relevant material before proceeding.

1. Feeling hungry is most strongly associated with a low level of
   a. estrogen.
   b. glucose.
   c. insulin.
   d. leptin.

2. Destruction of a rat's ventromedial hypothalamus typically results in
   a. greatly reduced food intake and subsequent weight loss.
   b. greatly increased food intake and subsequent weight gain.
   c. greatly reduced food intake, but no subsequent weight loss.
   d. greatly increased food intake, but no subsequent weight gain.

3. After eating a meal of sweet foods, sweet foods lose their appeal, but foods of other flavors do not. Psychologists explain this effect in terms of
   a. glucose-insulin interaction.
   b. a set point.
   c. homeostasis.
   d. sensory-specific satiety.

4. The set point is
   a. the fixed amount of glucose needed for cellular activity.
   b. the natural weight the body tries to maintain.
   c. the insulin level that stimulates a desire to eat.
   d. the weight that is viewed as ideal in a specific culture.

5. Bulimia nervosa is an eating disorder
   a. most common in young men.
   b. in which the person eats massive quantities of food at one time.
   c. often accompanied by cessation of the menstrual cycle.
   d. is found in all parts of the world.

MEETING BIOLOGICAL NEEDS: SEXUAL BEHAVIOR (PP. 376-382)

MASTERING THE VOCABULARY

Define or explain each of the following terms.

1. excitement phase
2. plateau phase
3. orgasmic phase
4. resolution phase
5. sexual scripts
6. sexual orientation

MASTERING THE CONCEPTS

Fill in the blanks to create a summary of the section.

Sexual behavior ensures continuation of the species and may lead to companionship, love and protection. The sexual response follows a fixed sequence. In the [1] ____________ phase, physiological arousal begins, leading to erection in men and lubrication in women. In the [2] ____________ phase, these processes continue to develop, but slowly. Sexual release occurs during the [3] ____________ phase, and then arousal returns to normal in the [4] ____________ phase. Men have a [5] ____________ period in which further sexual response is impossible.

Animals' sexual behavior is controlled by [6] ____________ and often limited to a period of fertility. Human sexual behavior is mostly under the control of the [7] ____________ , although estrogens and androgens are influential. Loss of sex hormones does not necessarily eliminate all sexual motivation in humans. Touch and other external stimuli affect human sexual behavior. Animals respond to certain scents or [8] ____________ , but little evidence supports an effect on sexual desire.

Exactly how, when, and why people have sex is influenced by [9] ____________ , learned tendencies and attitudes. Some sex differences in sexual scripts are cross-cultural. Men do not link sex and marriage, are more likely to engage in [10] ____________ strategies, and prefer young, attractive partners, not financially secure partners. Some of these behaviors may be adaptations.

A person's sexual [11] ____________ involves whether the same or different sex is found sexually and emotionally attractive. [12] ____________ are predominantly attracted to the same sex; [13] ____________ are predominantly attracted to the opposite sex. Orientation should be considered a continuum, rather than distinct categories. Homosexuality once was thought to be caused by a dominant mother and passive father. Recent research refutes this and suggests [14] ____________ factors influence orientation. Differences in the [15] ____________ have been found. Twin studies support a [16] ____________ factor, and a "gay gene" has been proposed. However, the data are [17] ____________, which complicates interpretation, and genetic factors clearly are not the entire story.

EVALUATING YOUR PROGRESS

Select the best response. If you miss any questions, reread the relevant material before proceeding.

1. The role of sex hormones in the sexual behavior of humans can be described as
   a. highly important. They strictly determine when people seek sexual activity.
   b. moderately important. They are more important than most things, but they don't have total control.
   c. minimally important. Hormones have some influence, but the individual maintains control.
   d. totally unimportant. Hormones have no influence on sexual behavior.

2. The first phase in the human sexual response is the
   a. plateau phase.
   b. orgasmic phase.
   c. resolution phase.
   d. excitement phase.

3. Cross-cultural studies show that in most cultures
   a. men are more likely than women to pursue long-term sexual strategies.
   b. men place more value on their long-term partner's attractiveness than women do.
   c. women place less value on the financial status of a prospective partner than men do.
   d. men are less concerned than women with having a young sexual partner.

4. Pheromones are
   a. sexual odor-producing chemicals.
   b. sex hormones.
   c. tactile (touch) stimuli that produce arousal.
   d. a biological determinant of sexual orientation.

5. The learned programs that instruct people on how, why, and what to do in their sexual interactions are
   a. sexual menus.
   b. sexual orientations.
   c. sexual instincts.
   d. sexual scripts.

6. Recent research suggests that homosexuality is at least partially determined by
   a. sexual molestation during early childhood.
   b. having a domineering mother and passive father.
   c. single parent families with no father or other role model present.
   d. biological factors.

EXPRESSING AND EXPERIENCING EMOTION (PP. 382-391)

MASTERING THE VOCABULARY

Define or explain each of the following terms.

1. facial-feedback hypothesis
2. James-Lange theory
3. Cannon-Bard theory
4. two-factor theory

MASTERING THE CONCEPTS

Fill in the blanks to create a summary of the section.

Emotions involve a [1] ____________ reaction, an expressive reaction, and [2] ____________ experience. Ekman found six basic emotions (fear, happiness, [3] ____________ , sadness, anger, and disgust/contempt) associated with cross-cultural [4] ____________ expressions, suggesting a genetic origin of the expression of emotion. The facial [5] ____________ hypothesis suggests input from facial muscles influence emotion. Others view basic emotions as shared components of many emotions.

Physiological arousal prepares the body to make a response, performance [6] ____________ at very low and high levels of arousal. Events such as being restrained or having expectations violated are linked to [7] ____________ . Happiness is influenced by social [8] ____________ and adaptation level. The emotion of [9] ____________ is often food-related, but also relates to contamination. Disgust is universal, but not innate.

Different theories of emotion handle the three components of emotion differently. The common sense view states a stimulus causes an emotion, which causes physical changes. The [10] ____________ theory states a stimulus causes physical changes, and these changes determine an emotion. This theory requires different patterns for each emotion and a [11] ____________ of emotion if feedback about physical changes is eliminated. Some research confirms these predictions. The [12] ____________ theory states a stimulus independently produces both the emotional experience and physical changes. The [13] ____________ theory, currently the most accepted theory, states the stimulus causes physical changes, but the emotion is the result of cognitive appraisal or interpretation of the physical changes in context. This is supported by Schachter & Singer's data showing expectations affect emotion.

EVALUATING YOUR PROGRESS

Select the best response. If you miss any questions, reread the relevant material before proceeding.

1. Which is not a standard component of emotion?
   a. social comparison
   b. expressive reaction
   c. subjective experience
   d. physiological arousal

2. Some facial expressions are recognized across cultures and occur in early infancy. This supports
   a. the facial feedback hypothesis.
   b. the James-Lange theory of emotion.
   c. a genetic origin for expressions of emotion.
   d. the two-factor theory of emotion.

3. The facial feedback hypothesis states that
   a. information from facial muscles to the brain influences what emotion is experienced.
   b. people evaluate the emotional impact they have on someone by noting facial expressions.
   c. people tend to adopt the facial expressions shown by the people around them.
   d. the experience of an emotion determines facial expression.

4. As arousal increases,
   a. performance increases.
   b. performance decreases.
   c. performance decreases and then increases.
   d. performance increases and then decreases.

5. Seth said, "After I saw the F on my grade report, my heart started racing, and then I felt overwhelming anxiety." This type of sequencing supports
   a. the commonsense view of emotion.
   b. the James-Lange theory of emotion.
   c. the social comparison theory of emotion.
   d. the two-factor theory of emotion.

6. The two-factor theory is very different from other approaches because it
   a. adds a cognitive component to the experience of emotion.
   b. places more emphasis on specific physiological patterns than other theories.
   c. proposes emotion precedes any physiological changes.
   d. proposes that emotions are independent of physiological changes.

7. Which of the following is false?
   a. Happiness is influenced by social comparisons.
   b. Anger often results from a violation of expectations.
   c. Disgust reactions are partly learned.
   d. Expressing anger reduces the likelihood of expressing anger in the future.

MAKING FINAL PREPARATIONS

Complete these sections without consulting your book or notes. For a more accurate estimate of how well you know this material, wait at least a day or two after studying the chapter before working on the questions. Some of the material you "know" immediately after working with the chapter will be quickly forgotten. Exercises done too soon after studying will overestimate what you know well.

MATCHING

Select the correct definition or description for each item.

1. _______ Cannon-Bard
2. _______ incentive motivation
3. _______ refractory period
4. _______ James-Lange
5. _______ sexual orientation
6. _______ Eckman
7. _______ intrinsic motivation
8. _______ instinct
9. _______ homeostasis
10. _______ anorexia nervosa
11. _______ bulimia nervosa
12. _______ Maslow
13. _______ plateau phase
14. _______ motivation
15. _______ Schachter & Singer

a. set of factors that initiate and direct behavior
b. unlearned behaviors controlled by triggering stimuli
c. eating disorder in which binge eating occurs
d. external factor that exerts a pulling effect on actions
e. did cross-cultural research on emotion
f. proposed need hierarchy
g. self-motivated goal directed behavior
h. added cognitive evaluation to the emotion sequence
i. proposed body reactions precede and drive emotion
j. eating disorder associated with very low weight
k. physical and emotional responses are independent
l. process used to maintain a steady state
m. sexual/emotional attraction to same or different sex
n. second stage in sexual response cycle
o. time when stimulation can't result in sexual arousal

SHORT ESSAY QUESTIONS

Write a brief answer to each question.

1. Compare incentive motivation and drive.

____

____

2. Describe how external factors influence eating behavior.

____

____

3. Compare the determinants of sexual behavior for animals and humans.

____

____

4. Describe the three basic components of all emotions.

____

____

5. Discuss how expectations and adaptation level influence happiness.

____

____

MULTIPLE CHOICE PRETEST 1

Select the one best response.

1. For human behavior, the concept of drive has replaced the concept of
   a. incentive.
   b. intrinsic motivation.
   c. instinct.
   d. emotion.

2. Steve had eaten a large breakfast right before coming to work, but he couldn't resist taking one of the doughnuts a co-worker brought to share with the office. His behavior is an example of the power of
   a. drives.
   b. instincts.
   c. incentives.
   d. needs.

3. Children will be most likely to show high achievement motivation and attempt to accomplish a task if
   a. they have a history of failing at the task, driving up their need to achieve.
   b. their parents show they value the task.
   c. they are never rewarded for their effort.
   d. they are working at the lowest levels of Maslow's hierarchy.

4. Scott has always volunteered to walk his neighbor's dog because he thinks it is fun. Before the neighbor went on vacation, he said he'd pay Scott to walk the dog each day. According to research on intrinsic motivation, it is likely that when expecting to be paid, Scott found walking the dog to be
   a. more fun than before.
   b. as fun as before.
   c. less fun than before.
   d. less fun for a week, then more fun than before.

5. Deanna's parents are worried about her refusal to eat. She weighs 80 lbs., but still thinks she is too fat for a 5 ft-6 inch 17-year-old. A health professional should advise her parents that
   a. Deanna probably has anorexia nervosa, a serious eating disorder.
   b. Deanna probably has bulimia nervosa, a serious eating disorder.
   c. Deanna will begin eating again when she reaches her normal set point.
   d. Deanna is just going through a growth spurt that is nothing to worry about.

6. Frieda is ethically sensitive, spontaneous, and open to experiences. These characteristics are associated with
   a. high achievement motivation.
   b. strong incentives.
   c. high self-esteem.
   d. self-actualization.

7. Stimulation of which brain area causes an animal to begin eating?
   a. hippocampus
   b. brainstem
   c. lateral hypothalamus.
   d. ventromedial hypothalamus

8. A chemical found in high levels in the obese and that may regulate the storage of energy in fat cells is
   a. leptin.
   b. androgen.
   c. estrogen.
   d. glucose.

9. When at a reception that offered many different types of hors d'oeuvres, you ate 10 pieces. At a reception in which only one type was served, you were content with eating only 5 pieces. This difference in eating behavior illustrates the concept of
   a. food habits.
   b. set point.
   c. hyperphagia.
   d. sensory-specific satiety.

10. A person's set point probably is determined by
    a. cultural attitudes.
    b. willpower.
    c. food preferences.
    d. genetics.

11. According to Masters and Johnson, arousal continues to slowly increase during
    a. the orgasmic phase.
    b. the resolution phase.
    c. the excitement phase.
    d. the plateau phase.

12. For humans, sexual motivation is best described as
    a. a hormone-based drive.
    b. incentive motivation.
    c. a process of self-actualization.
    d. a physiological need.

13. Research on homosexuality has found
    a. the structure of the hypothalamus differs in heterosexual and homosexual men.
    b. if one identical twin is homosexual, there is an 80% chance the other twin is homosexual.
    c. a dysfunctional home environment is a major factor associated with homosexuality.
    d. approximately 20% of the population is homosexual.

14. What role does do pheromones play in human sexual behavior?
    a. Pheromones are responsible for differences in brain development in the two sexes.
    b. Pheromones produced by females produce sexual frenzy of desire in males.
    c. Pheromones produced by males produce a dramatic increase in sexual desire in females.
    d. Pheromones do not seem to impact humans greatly, but odors do influence sexual behavior.

15. Dot's friend tells her, "Smile. You'll feel better." Her advice is consistent with the
    a. Cannon-Bard theory.
    b. the two-factor theory.
    c. the facial feedback hypothesis.
    d. the James-Lange theory.

16. The reason that many psychologists believe there are 4-6 basic emotions is that
    a. twins show identical emotional reactions to a stimulus.
    b. all babies show emotions very early.
    c. facial expressions representing those emotions are accurately recognized in many cultures.
    d. those emotions are represented by specific words in every language, unlike other emotions.

17. Firecrackers exploded behind Kim. To explain Kim's fear, the Cannon-Bard theory would suggest
    a. the firecrackers made Kim feel afraid, and being afraid makes her heart beat rapidly.
    b. the firecrackers made Kim feel afraid and made her heart beat rapidly.
    c. Kim felt afraid because she appraised the situation as dangerous.
    d. Kim was afraid because her heart was beating rapidly.

18. In the Schachter and Singer study, which participants were most likely to adopt the mood of the accomplice?
    a. those who were aroused and expected arousal
    b. those who were aroused and did not expect arousal
    c. those who were not aroused and expected no arousal
    d. those who were not aroused and expected arousal

19. Recent research has found differences in the physiological responses and brain activity patterns associated with different emotions. This is most crucial for
   a. the James-Lange theory.
   b. the Cannon-Bard theory.
   c. the two-factor theory.
   d. the commonsense view.

MULTIPLE CHOICE PRETEST 2

Select the one best response.

1. Newly hatched turtles immediately begin to crawl to the sea. This unlearned characteristic behavior is an example of
   a. incentive motivation.
   b. a drive.
   c. an instinct.
   d. homeostasis.

2. Tad hasn't eaten in 12 hours. The internal state that will cause him go to the pantry for food is
   a. a need.
   b. incentive motivation.
   c. a drive.
   d. intrinsic motivation.

3. A lizard moves into the sunlight when its body temperature drops too low, and moves back into the shade when its body temperature gets too warm. This is best explained in terms of
   a. incentive motivation.
   b. instinct.
   c. set point.
   d. homeostasis.

4. Research suggests that the critical determinant of the effect reward has on intrinsic motivation is
   a. the size of the reward.
   b. whether the reward is expected.
   c. the amount of time since the last reward.
   d. the age or sex of the person providing the reward.

5. Mona worked very hard to get As in school, practiced daily to become an expert pianist, and successfully ran for class President. Mona's internal drive to succeed best represents strong
   a. incentive motivation.
   b. basic needs.
   c. need for homeostasis.
   d. achievement motivation.

6. School breakfast programs make sure children aren't hungry so that they will be interested and able to focus on learning and academic achievement. The view of motivation that is most similar to this is
   a. incentive motivation theory.
   b. Schachter & Singer's two-factor theory.
   c. Maslow's hierarchy of needs.
   d. intrinsic motivation theory.

7. Destruction of a rat's ventromedial hypothalamus usually produces
   a. an increase in sexual behavior.
   b. a decrease in sexual behavior.
   c. a decrease in eating and weight loss.
   d. an increase in eating and weight gain.

8. Tom has weighed 250 lbs. all of his adult life. He lost 20 lbs. while sick one time, but was back up to 250 lbs. within a few weeks of getting well. Tom's experience is best explained by
   a. overjustification.
   b. Maslow's need hierarchy.
   c. the two-factor theory.
   d. set point theory.

9. Mandy frequently eats a half-gallon of ice cream, two bags of cookies, a bucket of fried chicken, half a cake and three bags of potato chips in one evening. Afraid of gaining weight, but unable to stop eating, she vomits and uses laxatives to get rid of the food. Mandy's behavior is characteristic of
   a. a lateral hypothalamic lesion or tumor.
   b. diabetes, an insufficiency of insulin.
   c. anorexia nervosa.
   d. bulimia nervosa.

10. When May studied abroad, she found that some sexual behaviors her home culture considered unacceptable were very accepted in her new culture. These differences are best explained in terms of different
    a. evolutionary adaptations.
    b. genes.
    c. sexual scripts.
    d. sexual orientations.

11. Ten minutes after he reached orgasm, Chuck is mentally responding to his partner's sexual advances, but his body isn't responding. Chuck's limitation is probably due to the fact that he
    a. is in the plateau phase of sexual response.
    b. is in the resolution phase of sexual response.
    c. is in the pre-excitement phase of sexual response.
    d. has depleted his testosterone supply.

12. Brain and twin studies are consistent with the idea that sexual orientation is partially determined by biological or genetic factors, but a cause-effect relationship has not been established because
    a. the brain and twin studies data are correlational.
    b. the brain and twin studies do not match other recent data that show no biological factor.
    c. not all of the identical twins have the same orientation.
    d. sexual orientation is too difficult to classify.

13. Which is LEAST likely to represent a male's sexual attitudes?
    a. Attractiveness is highly valued in the choice of a long-term partner.
    b. Sexual intercourse with someone known only briefly is not appealing.
    c. Younger mates are preferred.
    d. Short-term relationships are acceptable or desirable.

14. Bert, Cal, and Joe all had the same knowledge when they took the final exam, but they differed in their level of arousal. Bert had a very low level of arousal, Cal had a moderate level of arousal, and Joe had a very high level of arousal. Which student probably got the highest score on the exam?
    a. Bert
    b. Cal
    c. Joe
    d. Everybody probably scored the same. Arousal doesn't influence performance.

15. Babies show a wide range of emotional expressions, and emotional facial expressions are identified across cultures. These data support the idea that
    a. there are 10 basic emotions.
    b. the expression of emotion has a biological or genetic component.
    c. cognitive appraisal is an important part of the emotional experience.
    d. feedback from facial muscles is used to interpret an emotional experience.

16. The facial feedback hypothesis is most similar to
    a. the James-Lange theory.
    b. the two-factor theory.
    c. the Cannon-Bard theory.
    d. the social comparison concept.

17. Juan meets a woman as he emerges from climbing three flights of stairs. According to the two-factor theory, Juan will be most likely to report the emotion of sexual attraction or "love at first sight" if
    a. his physiological pattern is specific to love rather than exercise.
    b. he attributes his increased heart rate to the woman, rather than to the stairs.
    c. he receives feedback that he is smiling.
    d. he expects his heart rate to increase as a result of climbing the stairs.

18. Although Mia made a 60 on her paper, she is happy because other people made 50s. This supports the idea that happiness is influenced by
    a. adaptation level.
    b. social comparison.
    c. the relationship between arousal and performance.
    d. a need hierarchy.

19. The greatest contribution of the two-factor theory and the supporting research is that
    a. the independence of physiological arousal and emotion was established.
    b. different patterns of physiological responses associated with each emotion were established.
    c. the early appearance of emotional response was explained.
    d. the importance of cognitive factors was recognized and incorporated.

LANGUAGE DEVELOPMENT GUIDE

CORE TERMS

This chapter will approach the subject of emotions and motivation ***objectively***; that is, it will not refer to individual experiences, but to what people in general experience. Psychologists are interested in the ***universality*** of motivation and emotions -- the behaviors, facial expressions, and so on that are common to people all around the world. You will probably find yourself comparing what you read about emotions with your ***subjective***, personal experience.

IDIOMS

p. 361	meltdown	step-by-step breakdown with dangerous results
p. 361	needle tracks	marks from injections, usually of illegal drugs
p. 361	"fix"	a dose of an drug
p. 362	junkies	drug addicts
p. 363	shy away	move away to avoid
p. 370	optimal level	best level for good performance
p. 385	rates skyrocket	rates go up very high quickly
p. 386	blowing off steam	expressing anger, such as yelling
p. 387	Holy Grail	a very valuable thing that is sought but not often found (refers to the cup Christ used at the Last Supper, which legendary knights went on quests to find)
p. 388	have no conception	have no idea

PRONUNCIATION

homeostasis (home-ee-o-stay′-sis) *p. 364*

ventromedial (ven-tro-mee′-dee-al) *p. 370*

obese (o-bees′) *p. 370*

plateau (pla-toh’′) *p. 377*

SOLUTIONS

PREVIEW & ACTIVATING BEHAVIOR (PP. 361-369)

MASTERING THE CONCEPTS

1. direct (p. 362)
2. physiological (p. 362)
3. subjective (p. 362)
4. Instincts (p. 363)
5. drive (p. 364)
6. homeostasis (p. 364)
7. Incentive (p. 364)
8. achievement (p. 365)
9. Intrinsic (p. 366)
10. control (p. 367)
11. reward (p. 367)
12. expected (p. 367)
13. hierarchy (p. 368)
14. Biological (p. 368)
15. self-actualization (p. 368)

EVALUATING YOUR PROGRESS

1. D, Correct (p. 363)

   A. Wrong. Drives are internal states that arise in response to a need.

   B. Wrong. Incentives are external rewards that pull and guide behavior.

   C. Wrong. Motivations are sets of factors that initiate and direct behavior, usually toward a goal.

2. A, Correct (p. 364)

   B. Wrong. Instincts are unlearned, characteristic patterns of behavior, not an internal state.

   C. Wrong. Emotions are not responses to internal physiological needs.

   D. Wrong. Homeostasis is the process by which the body maintains a steady state.

3. B, Correct (p. 364)

   A. Wrong. Drives involve physiological needs, incentives do not.

   C. Wrong. Incentives can be learned, and drives are usually unlearned.

   D. Wrong. Incentives are external, and drives are usually internal.

4. D, Correct (p. 364)

   A. Wrong. This is a definition of achievement motivation.

   B. Wrong. This is a definition of intrinsic motivation.

   C. Wrong. This is a definition of drive.

5. B, Correct (p. 365)

   A. Wrong. Instinct is a characteristic behavioral response to an external stimulus.

   C. Wrong. Self-actualization involves fulfilling your ultimate potential in life.

   D. Wrong. Intrinsic motivation is self-motivated behavior, such as painting a picture for pleasure.

6. D, Correct (p. 366)

   A. Wrong. Self-actualization involves reaching one's potential.

   B. Wrong. There is no physiological imbalance here.

   C. Wrong. Drives are psychological states resulting from physiological needs.

7. C, Correct (p. 368)

   A. Wrong. Self-actualization and its position are not entirely accepted.

   B. Wrong. Critics complain about the lack of clear definition and testability.

   D. Wrong. Achievement is not given as the most important need in the hierarchy.

8. D, Correct (p. 368)

   A. Wrong. Self-esteem needs are only relatively high in the hierarchy.

   B. Wrong. Physiological needs are at the bottom of the hierarchy.

   C. Wrong. Safety needs are near the bottom of the hierarchy.

MEETING BIOLOGICAL NEEDS: HUNGER AND EATING (PP. 369-375)

MASTERING THE CONCEPTS.

1. glucose (p. 370)
2. insulin (p. 370)
3. hypothalamus (p. 370)
4. ventromedial (p. 370)
5. lateral (p. 370)
6. brainstem (p. 371)
7. hippocampus (p. 371)
8. habits (p. 371)
9. set point (p. 373)
10. Genetic (p. 373)
11. metabolic (p. 373)
12. obesity (p. 373)
13. Anorexia (p. 375)
14. bulimia (p. 375)
15. binge (p. 375)

EVALUATING YOUR PROGRESS

1. B, Correct (p. 370)
   A, C, D. Wrong. Glucose levels are critical for controlling hunger.
2. B, Correct (p. 370)
   A. Wrong. This occurs when the lateral hypothalamus is destroyed.
   C. Wrong. Both reduced intake and weight loss occurs when the *lateral* hypothalamus is destroyed.
   D. Wrong. Both increased intake and weight gain occurs.
3. D, Correct (p. 372)
   A. Wrong. A glucose-insulin interaction influences eating, but it doesn't produce this effect.
   B. Wrong. A set point might influence the amount eaten, but it doesn't produce this effect.
   C. Wrong. Homeostasis, the process of maintaining a steady state, is not related to this effect.
4. B, Correct (p. 373)
   A., C., D. Wrong. Set point refers to a weight the body tries to maintain.
5. B, Correct (p. 375)
   A. Wrong. Bulimia is most common in young women.
   C. Wrong. Menstrual disruptions occur with the low food intake of anorexia nervosa.
   D. Wrong. Bulimia is rarely found in parts of the world without Western influence.

MEETING BIOLOGICAL NEEDS: SEXUAL BEHAVIOR (PP. 376-382)

MASTERING THE CONCEPTS

1. excitement (p. 377)
2. plateau (p. 377)
3. orgasmic (p. 377)
4. resolution (p. 377)
5. refractory (p. 377)
6. hormones (p. 378)
7. individual (p. 378)
8. pheromones (p. 379)
9. sexual scripts (p. 379)
10. short-term (p. 380)
11. orientation (p. 380)
12. Homosexuals (p. 380)
13. Heterosexuals (p. 380)
14. biological (p. 381)
15. hypothalamus (p. 381)
16. genetic (p. 382)
17. correlational (p. 382)

EVALUATING YOUR PROGRESS

1. C, Correct (p.378)
   A. Wrong. Even the absence of sex hormones does not necessarily prevent sexual behavior.
   B. Wrong. For humans, sexual behavior is primarily determined by personal control.
   D. Wrong. Hormone levels can reduce sexual behavior in some cases or increase it.
2. D, Correct (p. 377)
   A. Wrong. The plateau phase is the second phase.
   B. Wrong. The orgasmic phase is the third phase.
   C. Wrong. The resolution phase is the last phase.
3. B, Correct (p. 380)
   A., C., D. Wrong. These are all opposite from the actual data.
4. A, Correct (p. 379)
   B. Wrong. Pheromones are odor-producing chemicals, not hormones.
   C. Wrong. Pheromones are odor-producing chemicals, not tactile stimuli.
   D. Wrong. Pheromones may be a biological influence of sexual behavior, but not of orientation.
5. D, Correct (p. 379)
   A. Wrong. Sexual menu is not a relevant term.
   B. Wrong. Sexual orientations involve the type (sex) of sexual partner selected.
   C. Wrong. Instincts are not learned.
6. D, Correct (p. 381)
   A., B., C. Wrong. Recent research does not confirm these hypotheses.

EXPRESSING AND EXPERIENCING EMOTION (PP. 382-391)

MASTERING THE CONCEPTS

1. physiological (p. 382)
2. subjective (p. 382)
3. surprise (p. 383)
4. facial (p. 383)
5. feedback (p. 383)
6. declines (p. 385)
7. anger (p. 386)
8. comparisons (p. 386)
9. disgust (p. 387)
10. James-Lange (p. 388)
11. reduction (p. 388)
12. Cannon-Bard (p. 390)
13. two-factor (p. 390)

EVALUATING YOUR PROGRESS

1. A, Correct (p. 382)
   B, C, D. Wrong. These are all standard components of emotion. Social comparison is not standard.
2. C, Correct (p. 383)
   A. Wrong. This hypothesis deals with influences on emotion, not with recognizing facial expressions.
   B. Wrong. This theory states physiological responses determine the emotion. Recognizing facial expressions is not relevant.
   D. Wrong. The 2-factor theory requires an interpretation of a physiological reaction, but not cross-cultural similarity in facial expression.
3. A, Correct (p. 383)
   B, C, D. Wrong. These do not represent the facial feedback hypothesis, which states feedback from facial muscles is used to interpret the emotion being experienced.
4. D, Correct (p. 385)
   A. Wrong. At high levels of arousal, performance decreases.
   B. Wrong. Performance decreases only at high levels of arousal; it increases otherwise.
   C. Wrong. This is backward.

5. B, Correct (p. 388)
   A. Wrong. Commonsense view would say stimulus → emotion → physical changes.
   C. Wrong. There is no comparison to what is happening to other people, thus no social comparison.
   D. Wrong. The two-factory theory includes a cognitive evaluation, which is absent here.
6. A, Correct (p. 390)
   B. Wrong. The James-Lange theory places most emphasis on physical change.
   C. Wrong. Two-factor theory has emotion following physical change.
   D. Wrong. This is the Cannon-Bard theory, not two-factor theory.
7. D, Correct (p. 386)
   A, B, & C. Wrong. These are all true, but expressing anger increases future expressions of anger.

MAKING FINAL PREPARATIONS

MATCHING

1. k (p. 390)
2. d (p. 364)
3. o (p. 377)
4. i (p. 388)
5. m (p. 380)
6. e (p. 383)
7. g (p. 366)
8. b (p. 363)
9. l (p. 364)
10. j (p. 375)
11. c (p. 375)
12. f (p. 368)
13. n (p. 377)
14. a (p. 362)
15. h (p. 390)

SHORT ESSAY QUESTIONS

1. A drive is a psychological state that arises in response to an internal physiological need and pushes the organism into action. Incentive motivation is an external factor that exerts a pulling effect on action. Thus, they differ both in origin and method of activation of behavior. (pp. 364-365)
2. External factors include food cues, eating habits, cultural influences, and social factors. Food cues may provide an incentive to eat even when physiological signals do not indicate hunger. Similarly, eating habits influence when and what we eat, and these are influenced by cultural and social factors. Eating is associated with social situations, and culture determines many attitudes about food. (pp. 371-372)
3. Hormones control animal sexual behavior but only minimally influence humans. Many animals mate during fertile periods, and their sexual behavior is highly specific in form, both determined by hormones. Some animals respond to pheromones, scents which activate sexual behavior. For humans, if hormones are absent, sexual activity often declines, but the normal rhythm of hormones exerts minimal changes in sexual activity. Humans control the timing and form of their sexual behavior. Pheromones exert no clear effect. (pp. 378-380)
4. Emotions involve (1) physiological reaction, an arousal manifest in changes in heart rate, blood pressure, etc.; (2) expressive reactions, such as facial expressions, postures, or vocalization; and (3) subjective reaction, internal thoughts and feelings of fear, sadness, etc. (pp. 382, 385-388)
5. Happiness can be produced when expectations are exceeded, or can be eliminated when expectations are not met. How high one's expectations are affects the likelihood of being happy. People also become used to certain conditions, and deviations from that adaptation level produce changes in happiness. (pp. 386-387)

MULTIPLE CHOICE PRETEST 1

1. C, Correct (pp. 363-364)

   A. Wrong. Incentive is a concept in current use to explain human behavior.

   B. Wrong. Intrinsic motivation is a concept in use to explain human behavior.

   D. Wrong. Emotions can act as motivators, but they did not replace the concept of drive.

2. C, Correct (p. 364)

   A. Wrong. Steve isn't hungry; there is no physiological need to eat.

   B. Wrong. Humans don't have a characteristic, unlearned response to doughnuts.

   D. Wrong. Needs are states of deprivation. Steve has just eaten and has no need for more food.

3. B, Correct (p. 365)

   A. Wrong. This reduces the chance they will try, even if they have high achievement motivation.

   C. Wrong. Rewards can reduce intrinsic motivation, but they can act as incentives for achievement.

   D. Wrong. The lowest levels concern bodily needs, not achievement.

4. C, Correct (p. 366)

   A, B, D. Wrong. Expectation of rewards reduces intrinsic motivation.

5. A, Correct (p. 375)

   B. Wrong. Bulimia is characterized by relatively stable weight, but binge eating and purging.

   C. Wrong. Refusal to eat, excessive weight loss, and distorted body image describe anorexia.

   D. Wrong. Refusal to eat, excessive weight loss, and distorted body image describe anorexia.

6. D, Correct (p. 368)

   A. Wrong. Achievement motivation involves working hard to accomplish something.

   B. Wrong. Incentives are not personal characteristics. They are external events or stimuli.

   C. Wrong. High self-esteem is not associated with these traits. These describe self-actualization.

7. C, Correct (p. 370)

   A. Wrong. The hippocampus is important in regulating eating, but stimulating it doesn't produce eating.

   B. Wrong. The brainstem is important in regulating eating, but stimulating it doesn't produce eating.

   D. Wrong. Stimulating the ventromedial hypothalamus is more likely to cause eating to stop.

8. A, Correct (p. 370)

   B. Wrong. Androgen is a male sex hormone.

   C. Wrong. Estrogen is a female sex hormone.

   D. Wrong. Glucose is important in hunger, but it doesn't regulate storage of energy.

9. D, Correct (p. 372)

   A. Wrong. This is not a difference in food habit. The key here is eating more when variety is available.

   B. Wrong. A set point is an ideal or target weight that the body supposedly tries to maintain.

   C. Wrong. Hyperphagia is the condition produced by destroying the ventromedial hypothalamus.

10. D, Correct (p. 373)

    A, B, C. Wrong. These influence eating patterns, but not the set point.

11. D, Correct (p. 377)

    A. Wrong. This is the phase in which orgasm occurs, not when arousal is developing.

    B. Wrong. During resolution, arousal subsides to normal. This is the last phase.

    C. Wrong. The excitement phase is the first phase, during which arousal increases significantly.

12. B, Correct (p. 379)

    A., D. Wrong. There is no real physiological need for sex, and hormones are not critical.

    C. Wrong. Self-actualization does not involve sexual behavior.

13. A, Correct (pp. 381-382)

    B. Wrong. The concordance rate is 50%, not 80%.

    C. Wrong. The families of homosexual and heterosexual men are very similar.

    D. Wrong. The highest estimate given frequently is 10%, and some estimates are 1%-2%.

14. D, Correct (p. 379)
    A. Wrong. Hormones, not pheromones influence brain development.
    B, C. Wrong. The effect of pheromones is much, much more limited than this.
15. C, Correct (p. 383)
    A. Wrong. The key here is the idea that one's expression affects subjective experience of emotion, not that physiological and subjective components are simultaneous and independent.
    B. Wrong. The key here is the idea that one's expression affects subjective experience, not that physiological responses are cognitively interpreted to yield a particular emotion.
    D. Wrong. The key here is the idea that one's expression affects subjective experience, not that specific patterns of physiological activity identify an emotion.
16. C, Correct (p. 383)
    A., B. Wrong. Data such as these would only support a biological origin, not 4-6 basic emotions.
    B. Wrong. The age at which emotional expressions appear doesn't relate to the number of emotions.
    D. Wrong. Some languages do not include individual words for these emotions.
17. B, Correct (p. 390)
    A. Wrong. This is the commonsense view.
    C. Wrong. This is the two-factor view.
    D. Wrong. This is the James-Lange view.
18. B, Correct (p. 390)
    A. Wrong. These people would attribute the arousal to the drug, not to emotion.
    C, D. Wrong. Without the arousal component, any emotion is unlikely.
19. A, Correct (p. 388)
    B. Wrong. This theory does not propose emotion is determined by specific physiological patterns.
    C. Wrong. Here, different physiological reactions are less important than the interpretation of those reactions in context.
    D. Wrong. This view has physiological reactions follow emotional experience, so these data are not important.

MULTIPLE CHOICE PRETEST 2

1. C, Correct (p. 363)
   A. Wrong. Incentive motivation doesn't produce the same response on all occasions.
   B. Wrong. Drives are responses to internal physiological needs. There is no need here.
   D. Wrong. Homeostasis is a process by which the body maintains a steady state.
2. C, Correct (p. 364)
   A. Wrong. A need (food deprivation) causes the drive (an internal state) that gets him to look for food.
   B. Wrong. Incentive motivation is an external factor "pulling" behavior, not a psychological state.
   D. Wrong. He seeks food because of a biological need. Intrinsic motivation isn't a response to a need.
3. D, Correct (p. 364)
   A. Wrong. There is no external pull on the behavior. Key here is maintaining an acceptable state.
   B. Wrong. There is no external stimulus controlling the behavior.
   C. Wrong. Set point relates to weight control, not body temperature.
4. B, Correct (p. 367)
   A. Wrong. Size of reward isn't critical. Whether it is expected is.
   C. Wrong. Time since being rewarded isn't critical. Whether reward is expected is.
   D. Wrong. The type of person giving the reward isn't critical. Whether reward is expected is.

5. D, Correct (p. 365)
   A. Wrong. Incentive motivation depends on external factors, but Mona's need to succeed is internal.
   B. Wrong. Basic needs include food, water, safety, not a need to succeed.
   C. Wrong. Homeostasis is a process of maintaining a steady state, not a need to succeed.
6. C, Correct (p. 368)
   A., D. Wrong. Incentive and intrinsic motivation do not emphasize satisfying basic needs first.
   B. Wrong. Two-factor theory relates to emotion. Prioritizing needs is Maslow's idea.
7. D, Correct (p. 350)
   A., B. Wrong. The ventromedial hypothalamus is associated with eating, not sex.
   C. Wrong. Damage to the lateral hypothalamus is associated with weight loss.
8. D, Correct (p. 373)
   A. Wrong. Overjustification relates to the effect of reward on intrinsic motivation, not weight control.
   B. Wrong. Maslow's hierarchy proposes motives are prioritized, but doesn't involve weight control.
   C. Wrong. The 2-factor theory is Spearman's theory of intelligence or Schachter & Singer's theory of emotion, not a theory of weight control.
9. D, Correct (p. 375)
   A. Wrong. Damage to the lateral hypothalamus would more likely cause her to quit eating.
   B. Wrong. Diabetes would keep glucose high, leading to less hunger and less eating.
   C. Wrong. Anorexia nervosa involves self-starvation.
10. C, Correct (p. 379)
    A. Wrong. Differences across cultures are unlikely to be evolutionary adaptations.
    B. Wrong. Genes do not determine sexual attitudes.
    D. Wrong. Sexual orientation relates to heterosexuality or homosexuality, not habits like these.
11. B, Correct (p. 377)
    A. Wrong. Stimulation produces arousal during the plateau phase. The key here is the recent orgasm.
    C. Wrong. This is not a true phase of sexual response. The key here is the recent orgasm.
    D. Wrong. Sexual activity does not deplete testosterone. The key here is the recent orgasm.
12. A, Correct (p. 382)
    B., C., D. Wrong. The brain and twin studies were correlational and can't prove cause-effect. Data for other factors wouldn't eliminate biological factors as partial determinants.
13. B, Correct (p. 380)
    A., C., D. Wrong. These are all characteristic of male sexual attitudes.
14. B, Correct (p. 385)
    A. Wrong. Low levels of arousal are associated with less than optimum performance.
    C. Wrong. High levels of arousal are associated with less than optimum performance.
    D. Wrong. Arousal *does* influence performance.
15. B, Correct (p. 383)
    A. Wrong. These data don't support a certain number of basic emotions, and 4-6, not 10, is accurate.
    C. Wrong. These data don't relate to the two-factor theory. Cognitive factors are not involved here.
    D. Wrong. These data don't relate to facial feedback hypothesis. No mention of feedback is made.
16. A, Correct (p. 388)
    B. Wrong. There is no cognitive appraisal in the facial feedback hypothesis.
    C. Wrong. Physiological information does not determine emotion in the Cannon-Bard theory.
    D. Wrong. Facial feedback doesn't involve comparisons to other people.
17. B, Correct (p. 390)
    A. Wrong. Two-factor theory doesn't require different physical patterns for different emotions.
    C. Wrong. Two-factor theory isn't based on facial expression feedback.
    D. Wrong. Here, the heart rate would be attributed to the stairs, rather than attraction to a woman.
18. B, Correct (p. 386)
    A. Wrong. The issue isn't the frequency of getting low grades, but how the other people did.
    C. Wrong. Arousal was not an issue. The relationship of her grade to other people's was key.
    D. Wrong. Need hierarchies do not involve comparison with other people.

19. D, Correct (p. 390)

    A. Wrong. Emotion is not independent of physiological arousal in this theory.

    B. Wrong. Research that established different responses was not related to the two-factor theory.

    C. Wrong. This theory didn't address the innate aspects of emotion.

CHAPTER **12**

PERSONALITY

ESTABLISHING LEARNING GOALS

Use these learning goals as a preview of the chapter, a guide for active reading, and to evaluate your mastery of the material. Review the relevant goals as you begin and end your reading of each major section of the chapter.

I. Discuss how personality is conceptualized and measured.
   - A. Discuss how factor analysis is used to identify basic personality traits.
     1. Describe Cattell's source traits and Eysenck's superfactors.
     2. Describe the Big Five and explain why this approach is popular.
   - B. Distinguish among cardinal, central, and secondary traits.
   - C. Describe self-report inventories and projective personality tests.
     1. Describe three self-report inventories, how they are used, and their strengths and weaknesses.
     2. Compare projective tests to self-report inventories and identify their strengths and weaknesses.

II. Discuss how personality develops.
   - A. Describe Freud's psychodynamic theory of personality and mind.
     1. Define conscious, preconscious, and unconscious mind, and describe their roles.
     2. Define id, ego, and superego, and describe their relationship to each other and to behavior.
     3. Describe repression, denial, projection, sublimation, and reaction formation.
     4. Describe each psychosexual stage, and discuss the concept of fixation.
     5. Describe Jung's, Horney's, Adler's, and the current view of psychodynamic theory.
   - B. Summarize and evaluate humanistic approaches to personality.
     1. Compare the humanistic and psychodynamic approaches.
     2. Describe Roger's theory, and discuss the self-concept, positive regard, and congruence.
     3. Describe Maslow's theory, and discuss the role of self-actualization.
     4. Discuss the criticisms of the humanistic approach to personality.
   - C. Describe social-cognitive theories of personality.
     1. Explain the role of classical and instrumental conditioning and observational learning.
     2. Describe how expectations and beliefs influence behavior or personality.
     3. Discuss the criticisms of the social-cognitive approach.

III. Discuss how the person-situation debate may be resolved.

A. Define the person-situation debate, and discuss its components.
   1. Discuss the research on situational consistency.
   2. Discuss self-monitoring behavior.
B. Discuss how genetic factors influence personality.

MASTERING THE MATERIAL

PREVIEW & CONCEPTUALIZING AND MEASURING PERSONALITY (PP. 397-405)

MASTERING THE VOCABULARY

Define or explain each of the following terms.

1. personality
2. trait
3. trait theories
4. Big Five
5. cardinal traits
6. central traits
7. secondary traits
8. self-report inventories
9. projective personality test

MASTERING THE CONCEPTS

Fill in the blanks to create a summary of the section.

[1] ____________ is one's distinguishing pattern of psychological characteristics. Personality [2] ____________ , tendencies to behave in a particular way, establish an identity. Trait theories, systems for assessing individual [3] ____________ , use a psychometric approach in which responses on questionnaires are used to identify traits. [4] ____________ analysis identifies related behaviors that reflect a disposition or trait. Cattell identified 16 [5] ____________ traits that vary between two opposites (e.g., reserved-outgoing). Eysenck proposed three superfactors: extroversion, how sociable one is;

[6] ____________ , how moody or anxious; and psychoticism, how uncaring or cruel. Most psychologists support the [7] ____________ traits: extroversion, [8] ____________ , conscientiousness, neuroticism, and openness to experience. Allport, studying individuals rather than group data, proposed three levels of traits. [9] ____________ traits are very dominant traits. Central traits are less dominant but enduring. [10] ____________ traits are mostly situation-specific.

There are two main types of personality tests. [11] ____________ inventories are paper-and-pencil tests involving true-false questions or ratings. These include the 16 Personality Factor, which measures Cattell's 16 primary factors, the NEO-PI-R, which measures the Big 5, and the very popular [12] ____________ , which is also used to diagnose disorders. Self-report inventories are [13] ____________ tests whose strengths are reliability, standardization, validity and ease of scoring. [14] ____________ tests, such as the Rorschach test and the [15] ____________ , allow unrestricted responses, often to an ambiguous stimulus. Critics of projective tests cite poor reliability and validity. Critics of inventories cite the problem of potential subject bias.

EVALUATING YOUR PROGRESS

Select the best response. If you make any errors, reread the relevant material before proceeding.

1. Cattell proposed 16 basic personality traits (timid--venturesome, relaxed--tense) he called
   a. cardinal traits.
   b. central traits.
   c. source traits.
   d. secondary traits.
2. In Eysenck's trait approach, a person strong in psychoticism is likely to
   a. be anxious and moody.
   b. sociable and outgoing.
   c. shy and withdrawn.
   d. rude or cruel to other people.
3. Currently, the most popular trait theory is
   a. the Big 5 traits.
   b. Eysenck's three superfactors.
   c. Allport's trait theory.
   d. Cattell's 16 factor theory.

4. In Allport's theory, traits that dominate a person's behavior are called
   a. secondary traits.
   b. source traits.
   c. central traits.
   d. cardinal traits.
5. Allport's trait theory was developed based on
   a. the factor analysis of tests from large groups of people.
   b. cross-cultural testing of groups of people with many languages.
   c. comparing the Rorschach test results of normal and disturbed groups.
   d. detailed studies of particular individuals.
6. All of the following are self-report inventories EXCEPT
   a. the MMPI.
   b. the NEO-PI-R.
   c. the Rorschach test.
   d. the 16 Personality Factor test.
7. Projective personality tests
   a. have very high validity and reliability.
   b. use a true-false or rating scale format in most cases.
   c. use an unstructured or ambiguous stimulus in most cases.
   d. use an objective scoring technique.

DETERMINING HOW PERSONALITY DEVELOPS (PP. 406-419)

MASTERING THE VOCABULARY

Define or explain each of the following terms.

1. psychodynamic theory
2. conscious mind
3. preconscious mind
4. unconscious mind
5. id
6. superego
7. ego
8. defense mechanisms
9. repression
10. denial

11. rationalization
12. projection
13. reaction formation
14. sublimation
15. oral stage
16. anal stage
17. phallic stage
18. latency period
19. genital stage
20. collective unconscious
21. humanistic psychology
22. self-concept
23. positive regard
24. conditions of worth
25. incongruence
26. self-actualization
27. social-cognitive theories
28. locus of control
29. self-efficacy
30. reciprocal determinism

MASTERING THE CONCEPTS.

Fill in the blanks to create a summary of the section.

Freud's [1] ____________ theory proposes behavior is influenced by unconscious forces, and that the mind includes the conscious mind, holding current thoughts, and the [2] ____________ mind, containing memories, urges, and conflicts that are inaccessible, but that still influence behavior. Items in the unconscious are revealed in the symbolic or latent content of [3] ____________ .

Freud suggested personality has three parts. The [4] ____________ , residing in the unconscious, is driven by innate urges and the need for immediate gratification. It operates by the [5] ____________ principle, without regard to morals. The [6] ____________ contains morals defined by parents and society and acts as a conscience. It follows an [7] ____________ principle. The [8] ____________ operates by the [9] ____________ principle. It tries to satisfy the id while staying within the limits set by the superego.

To reduce anxiety, the ego uses [10] ____________ mechanisms. The most important is [11] ____________ , burying uncomfortable, often sexual, thoughts in the unconscious. In denial, a person refuses to believe anxiety-producing facts, and rationalization explains away those facts. In [12] ____________ unacceptable ideas are attributed to others. Reaction formation involves transforming anxiety-producing thoughts into an [13] ____________ form of behavior (e.g., hate to floods of affection). In [14] ____________ unacceptable behaviors are channeled into socially acceptable forms.

Freud proposed [15] ____________ stages of development, each associated with an erogenous zone of the body. In the first year, the [16] ____________ stage, pleasure is obtained by the mouth. The second year begins the [17] ____________ stage, and pleasure is obtained by passing feces. The [18] ____________ stage begins at age 3 and is focused on the genitals. At this time sexual feelings are directed toward the opposite sex parent, which causes the conflict of the [19] ____________ complex (boys) or Electra complex (girls). Failure to resolve this conflict causes later sexual problems. After age 5 and until puberty, sexuality is suppressed, and the [20] ____________ stage focuses on friendships. At puberty, sexuality reemerges in an adult form in the [21] ____________ stage. Failure to satisfy the needs of a stage (or overindulgence) leads to a [22] ____________ and adult behavior characteristic of that childhood stage. An oral fixation retains excessive oral activities (e.g., smoking); anal fixation results in excessive neatness or messiness.

Adler, Jung, and Horney, disagreed with Freud's emphasis on sexuality. Adler viewed feelings of [23] ____________ as the force behind behavior. Jung replaced sexuality with a general life force and added the idea of a [24] ____________ unconscious that contains [25] ____________ , symbols passed down through generations. Horney argued against the concept of penis envy and for a balanced view of women. Freud's theory has lost much of its influence, although some basic ideas, such as the impact of the conflict between personal and societal demands still are accepted. Criticisms include a lack of scientific rigor and testability, and continued concern about his view of women.

The [26] ____________ approach stresses people's positive qualities and potential for growth. Actions are influenced by the environment and a person's [27] ____________ of reality. Rogers stressed the need for a [28] ____________ self-concept, which develops when [29] ____________ is given without conditions of worth. Maslow believed personality reflects the person's position in the need hierarchy. Inappropriate behavior results from being unable to satisfy basic needs and self- actualization. Critics argue humanistic theories are vague, incomplete, based on subjective data, and too optimistic, but this approach remains popular.

The social-[30] ____________ approach emphasizes experience and cognitive factors. Classically or operantly conditioned behaviors become "traits." Modeling theories say traits come from [31] ____________ others' behavior. The social-cognitive view also considers people's beliefs. Some people see outcomes as based on chance, an [32] ____________ locus of control, while others feel they control the outcome, an [33] ____________ locus of control. Feelings of competence or [34] ____________ also effect behavior. These factors interact, which Bandura describes as [35] ____________ determinism. Critics argue social-cognitive theories are insufficient and focus too much on the situation and too little on biological factors and the whole person.

EVALUATING YOUR PROGRESS

Select the best response. If you miss any questions, reread the relevant material before proceeding.

1. Freud proposed that anxiety-producing ideas are pushed into the
   a. preconscious mind.
   b. conscious mind.
   c. unconscious mind.
   d. collective unconscious mind.

2. According to Freud, the superego
   a. operates according to the reality principle.
   b. operates according to the pleasure principle.
   c. contains society's rules about right and wrong.
   d. desires immediate, total satisfaction of needs.

3. The purpose of defense mechanisms is to
   a. reduce anxiety.
   b. satisfy the demands of the id.
   c. satisfy the demands of the superego.
   d. act as a conscience.

4. Each of Freud's stages of development are based on the
   a. body region that provides pleasure or sexual gratification.
   b. defense mechanism that the ego tends to employ the most.
   c. part of the personality that is dominant at that time (ego, id, superego).
   d. level of congruence that has been achieved for the self-concept at that time.

5. Jung's archetypes are
   a. a general life force.
   b. mystical, inherited concepts.
   c. defense mechanisms.
   d. located in the personal unconscious.

6. Which of the following is false?
   a. Freud's theory has steadily gained influence during the past several decades.
   b. Many of the important and unique concepts in Freud's theory lack scientific rigor.
   c. Many of the important and unique concepts in Freud's theory are almost impossible to test.
   d. Freud's theory is very male-oriented and views women as weaker psychologically.

7. The humanistic theory of personality stresses
   a. biological urges and needs.
   b. reinforcement and other experiences.
   c. self-efficacy and locus of control.
   d. the potential for growth and self-awareness.

8. According to Carl Rogers, a humanistic theorist, psychological health requires
   a. an external locus of control.
   b. reciprocal determinism.
   c. a congruent self-concept.
   d. conditions of worth.

9. The social-cognitive approach to personality emphasizes
   a. self-actualization.
   b. biological urges that drive behavior.
   c. learning and expectations.
   d. the innate goodness of human nature.

10. People who believe luck or fate determines what happens to them
    a. are fixated at the anal period.
    b. have high self-efficacy.
    c. are self-actualized.
    d. have an external locus of control.

RESOLVING THE PERSON-SITUATION DEBATE (PP. 419-423)

MASTERING THE VOCABULARY

Define or explain each of the following terms.

1. person-situation debate
2. self-monitoring

MASTERING THE CONCEPTS

Fill in the blanks to create a summary of the section.

The person-situation debate involves the question of whether behavior is [1] ____________ across situations, as a definition of personality based on enduring traits requires. Mischel found behavior was fairly [2] ____________ across situations. Within similar situations, Hartshorne & May found consistent behavior. Apparent inconsistency might be due to the number of observations, or it might reflect a personality trait, [3] ____________ . Those high in this trait monitor the situation and change their behavior to fit it; those low in the trait act consistently regardless of the context. Self-monitoring may be associated with good [4] ____________ performance and position in social networks. Most psychologists assume both the situation and the person interact to produce behavior. Certain situations compel inconsistency; others allow consistency.

Twin studies of personality traits support a [5] ____________ factor. Although the environment is influential, genetic influences are also very important, at least for some traits. This allows enduring traits.

EVALUATING YOUR PROGRESS

Select the best response. If you miss any questions, reread the relevant material before proceeding.

1. The person-situation debate involves the basic question of whether
   a. behavior is consistent across situations.
   b. personality is innate or learned.
   c. self-monitoring is a genetic trait or a learned trait.
   d. personality tests reflect the conscious or unconscious aspects of the mind.

2. High self-monitors
   a. act very consistently across situations.
   b. modify their behavior to fit the particular situation they encounter.
   c. are aware of their own behavior, but are not aware of what goes on around them.
   d. provide evidence that supports a genetic influence in personality.

3. Twin studies suggest that personality traits measured by the MMPI are determined
   a. entirely by genetics.
   b. entirely by the environment or experience.
   c. by both the environment and genetics, but genetics probably play a greater role.
   d. by both the environment and genetics, with each equally important.

MAKING FINAL PREPARATIONS

Complete these sections without consulting your book or notes. For a more accurate estimate of how well you know this material, wait at least a day or two after studying the chapter before working on the questions. Some of the material you "know" immediately after working with the chapter will be quickly forgotten. Exercises done too soon after studying will overestimate what you know well.

SHORT ESSAY QUESTIONS

Write a brief answer to each question.

1. Compare source traits and superfactors.

___

___

2. Compare projective personality tests and self-report inventories.

___

___

3. Compare the psychodynamic and humanistic views of personality.

___

___

4. Explain Ron's very quiet personality in terms of operant conditioning and modeling.

___

___

5. Discuss the criticism of the social-cognitive approach to personality and behavior.

____

____

6. Explain how psychologists resolve the person-situation debate.

____

____

MATCHING

Select the correct definition or description for each item.

1. _______ Karen Horney
2. _______ Raymond Cattell
3. _______ Gordon Allport
4. _______ Alfred Adler
5. _______ Hans Eysenck
6. _______ Carl Jung
7. _______ Walter Mischel
8. _______ self-efficacy
9. _______ Abraham Maslow
10. _______ Carl Rogers
11. _______ Sigmund Freud
12. _______ Rorschach
13. _______ Electra complex
14. _______ positive regard
15. _______ reciprocal determinism
16. _______ conditions of worth

a. found 16 source traits of personality
b. stressed observational learning and self-efficacy
c. proposed cardinal, central, & secondary traits
d. added collective unconscious
e. beliefs about our own ability
f. expectations people believe others place on them
g. girl's anxiety over sexual attraction to father
h. beliefs, behavior, environment affect what's learned
i. idea that people value others' approval
j. found three trait superfactors of personality
k. stressed the self-concept
l. found inconsistency of behavior across situations
m. proposed fixation and psychosexual stages
n. projective personality test
o. argued against idea of penis envy in women
p. proposed inferiority complex

MULTIPLE CHOICE PRETEST 1

Select the one best response.

1. Zack completed a personality test based on the Big 5 trait theory. The test probably was
   a. Rorschach test.
   b. 16 Personality Factor test.
   c. MMPI (Minnesota Multiphasic Personality Inventory).
   d. NEO-PI-R.

2. Critics of self-report inventories such as the MMPI have complained that
   a. subjects can bias their answers to make themselves look good.
   b. the scoring procedures are much too subjective.
   c. they are not well standardized.
   d. they allow too much freedom in the person's response.

3. Cattell referred to the personality factors he found as
   a. the Big 5.
   b. source traits.
   c. superfactors.
   d. central traits.

4. An advantage of projective personality tests is that
   a. they are highly objective and can be scored by computer.
   b. they are not standardized.
   c. they help people open up and talk about themselves.
   d. the interpretation of the results is very reliable and valid.

5. Max is anxious all the time, and he has no idea why. Freud probably would say the cause of Max's anxiety has been hidden in his
   a. preconscious mind.
   b. unconscious mind.
   c. superego.
   d. reaction formation.

6. Al has always struggled with aggressive desires. Today, Al works in a slaughterhouse and spends all day killing cattle. Freud might suggest Al's choice of occupations is an example of the defense mechanism
   a. projection.
   b. reaction formation.
   c. repression.
   d. sublimation.

7. According to Freud, the id
   a. uses defense mechanisms to reduce anxiety produced by the superego.
   b. seeks immediate satisfaction of animalistic urges.
   c. follows the idealistic principle.
   d. develops from experience with parents and society.

8. When the needs of a stage of psychosexual development are not met, the person will continue to act in ways representative of that stage. This describes
   a. fixation.
   b. self-efficacy.
   c. sublimation.
   d. an Oedipal or Electra complex.

9. The psychosexual stage in which sexual feelings are mostly suppressed and forming friendships is emphasized is the
   a. anal stage.
   b. phallic stage.
   c. genital stage.
   d. latency stage.

10. Adler proposed that the important factor in abnormal personality development is
    a. developing irrational, rather than rational, beliefs.
    b. developing incongruence and conditions of worth during childhood.
    c. how people deal with a basic sense of inferiority.
    d. having many models of unhealthy personalities during childhood.

11. Jung proposed that certain enduring concepts are inherited and reside in the collective unconscious. These concepts are called
    a. archetypes.
    b. fixations.
    c. ego ideals.
    d. latent concepts.

12. The humanistic theorist, Carl Rogers, suggested that a person's self concept is greatly influenced by other people because of a need for
    a. external locus of control.
    b. positive regard.
    c. reciprocal determinism.
    d. conditions of worth.

13. Maslow, a humanistic theorist, proposed that negative personality traits reflect
    a. an inferiority complex.
    b. experience with reinforcement for negative behaviors.
    c. a failure to satisfy basic needs.
    d. fixation at an early psychosexual stage of development.

14. The humanistic view of personality and behavior has been criticized for all of the following EXCEPT
    a. proposing humans have control over their behavior, rather than being driven by animalistic urges.
    b. the fact that many of the concepts in their theories are vague and not clearly developed.
    c. the problem of testing a theory that emphasizes subjective experiences.
    d. the highly optimistic view that all humans will achieve lofty goals if not blocked in their pursuit.

15. Mia believes her successes and failures are the result of her own actions, not luck or fate. Mia
    a. has reached self-actualization.
    b. has a congruent self-concept.
    c. has an internal locus of control.
    d. has an external locus of control.

16. The idea that beliefs, behavior, and the environment interact to shape what is learned from experience is
    a. self-efficacy.
    b. self-actualization.
    c. reciprocal determinism.
    d. conditions of worth.

17. The view that personality traits are influenced by genetic factors is supported by higher correlations on the MMPI for
    a. identical twins reared together than for identical twins reared apart.
    b. identical twins reared apart than for fraternal twins reared together.
    c. fraternal twins reared together than for fraternal twins reared apart.
    d. fraternal twins reared apart than for identical twins reared apart.

18. Based on Hartshorne and May's research on dishonesty, if Kim stole a dollar from a classmate
    a. Kim will probably steal money from another classmate if given the opportunity.
    b. Kim will probably steal again and is likely to cheat on tests at school.
    c. Kim will show dishonest behavior in all aspects of life from childhood to adulthood.
    d. Kim is no more likely to steal again or show dishonesty in any aspect of life than anybody else.

19. Self-monitoring behavior may help explain
    a. whether genetic background or experience is most critical in personality development.
    b. patterns of behavioral consistency or inconsistency.
    c. why different theorists propose very different numbers of personality traits.
    d. why mental disorders develop.

MULTIPLE CHOICE PRETEST 2

Select the one best response.

1. Marisha is competitive in every aspect of her life. She had to be first in her class, go to the best school, win every game, and have the nicest car. She feels badly if anybody beats her at anything. Marisha's competitiveness is characteristic of Allport's concept of
    a. a primary trait
    b. a secondary trait.
    c. a cardinal trait.
    d. a central trait.

2. "How can you use that test?" Ed asked. "Don't you know that two psychologists are probably going to give two different interpretations, and the validity is questionable?" The test probably is
    a. the 16 Personality Factor.
    b. the Rorschach test.
    c. the NEO-PI-R.
    d. the MMPI.

3. Martha is always anxious, and most people describe her as moody. Eysenck would describe her as high in
   a. extroversion.
   b. neuroticism.
   c. conscientiousness.
   d. psychoticism.

4. Cross-cultural studies of personality traits are most commonly interpreted to support
   a. Allport's trait theory.
   b. Cattel's source trait approach.
   c. Eysenck's superfactors approach.
   d. the Big 5 approach.

5. Tom is taking a test that consists of hundreds of true-false questions that will be used to help diagnose his psychological problems. This test probably is
   a. the Thematic Apperception Test.
   b. the Rorschach test.
   c. the MMPI.
   d. the NEO-PI-R.

6. Sociopaths are sometimes described as having no conscience or morality. Freud would say that sociopaths lack
   a. an ego.
   b. an id.
   c. a superego.
   d. a fixation.

7. Claire was sexually abused 10 years ago. She hasn't thought about it in years. However, she can describe what happened if asked a question about it. Claire's memory of her abuse was kept in her
   a. unconscious mind.
   b. preconscious mind.
   c. collective unconscious.
   d. reaction formation.

8. Roy, age 4, has unconscious sexual feelings for his mother. Roy is currently in Freud's
   a. phallic stage.
   b. oral stage
   c. genital stage.
   d. anal stage.

9. Jung proposed that the collective unconscious contains
   a. all the forbidden desires and traumas accumulated over the person's life.
   b. the ego and its defense mechanisms.
   c. a driving force to overcome inferiority and to achieve superiority.
   d. archetypes, symbols of enduring concepts passed from one generation to the next.

10. When attempting to satisfy the needs of the id and superego, the ego follows
    a. the pleasure principle.
    b. the reality principle.
    c. the principle of reciprocal determinism.
    d. the principle of self-efficacy.

11. Leo frequently brings up the topic of academic dishonesty, saying how terrible it is that everybody cheats on exams and plagiarizes papers. In reality, Leo is the real cheater. Freud might suggest Leo is dealing with the anxiety his cheating produces by using the defense mechanism of
    a. sublimation.
    b. rationalization.
    c. repression.
    d. projection.

12. Tanisha has undergone a peak experience that has allowed her to clearly understand her place in the universe and the meaning of her existence. Maslow would say she has
    a. developed strong conditions of worth.
    b. reached an internal locus of control.
    c. attained self-actualization.
    d. found her collective unconscious.

13. All his life, Ted's parents have wanted him to be an engineer and have discourage him any time he expressed his interest in art, the one thing he has always enjoyed. Ted decided to major in engineering, but he is unhappy and anxious. According to Roger's humanistic theory of personality, Ted's problem is
    a. an incongruent self-concept.
    b. an external locus of control.
    c. fixation at the phallic stage.
    d. high self-monitoring.

14. Pat believes that personality is determined by an interaction of conditioning, modeling, and personal interpretation of one's experiences. Pat's beliefs are most similar to
    a. Freudian psychodynamic approach.
    b. Adler's psychodynamic approach.
    c. the social-cognitive approach.
    d. the humanistic approach.

15. Lisa is a "neat freak." Her dorm room is always spotless, and everything is painfully orderly. She even gets mad when anybody fails to maintain her perfectly organized shelf of CDs. According to psychodynamic theory, Lisa's behavior might be characteristic of
    a. an unresolved Electra complex.
    b. anal fixation.
    c. projection.
    d. repression.

16. Nina got a bad grade on her first exam. This led her to think she could never understand the material or pass the class. As a result, she quit going to class, and of course, failed. Bandura calls this interaction of belief, experience, and behavior
    a. self-efficacy.
    b. self-monitoring.
    c. reciprocal determinism.
    d. conditions of worth.

17. The person-situation debate is important for personality theory because
    a. personality is defined in terms of enduring (consistent) psychological characteristics.
    b. none of the current theories have a component that suggests consistent behavior should occur.
    c. personality theories propose factors that supposedly apply to all people, not just a few.
    d. personality theories should explain individual differences, not behavior common to everyone.

18. May believes business success is determined by how hard people work. May has
    a. low self-efficacy.
    b. high self-efficacy.
    c. internal locus of control.
    d. external locus of control.

19. Lester is very nervous about attending an Ivy League school. He isn't sure he can handle the work required. Lester seems to have
    a. low self-efficacy.
    b. high self-efficacy.
    c. an internal locus of control.
    d. an external locus of control.

20. The social-cognitive theory has been criticized because it
    a. overemphasizes the role of biological and genetic determinants of personality.
    b. tends to neglect the individual as a whole and emphasizes the reactions to specific situations.
    c. doesn't consider the role of operant and classical conditioning as a determinant of personality.
    d. is essentially scientifically untestable.

21. Fiona modifies her behavior to fit each situation. She is an example of
    a. low self-efficacy.
    b. high self-efficacy.
    c. low self-monitoring.
    d. high self-monitoring.

LANGUAGE DEVELOPMENT GUIDE

CORE TERMS

In the lectures on this chapter and those that follow, you are likely to hear several related terms that all have to do with a way of organizing ideas. First of all, this process of organizing and classifying ideas can be called 'creating a ***taxonomy***.' A familiar taxonomy might be the one that you learned in biology class, classifying different organisms into species. To explain complex concepts like personality (or intelligence or development) we construct a ***model*** -- a tentative description that shows all the parts we know about and how they relate. There are different kinds of models. One kind is a ***hierarchy***, a sort of pyramid or stair-step which has the most basic element at the bottom, and climbs to the more rare or special elements. A second common kind of model is a ***matrix***. A matrix is a set of boxes arranged in rows and columns -- you might call it a chart. The matrix has a vertical ***axis*** and a horizontal axis, and it allows you to neatly classify things in relation to one another; you just sort them into the cell to which they belong. Imagine a chart that has 'height' along one side and 'weight' along the bottom. You could put each of your friends into a box between those lines, depending upon their height and weight. The plural of axis is axes, and they are also sometimes called ***dimensions***.

IDIOMS

p. 397	thesis	main idea
p. 397	dark side of their nature	unpleasant, evil, or animal-like part of their personality
p. 399	brooding	worrying, especially for a long time, without action
p. 400	an opposing pole	an opposite
p. 406	the nineteenth century	the 1800s
p. 408	rears its ugly head	shows itself
p. 408	dark recesses	back corners; hidden places
p. 408	harboring	keeping, holding
p. 408	anti-Semite	one who hates Jews
p. 411	coining	making for the first time
p. 411	intellectual heir	someone who will carry on one's ideas
p. 419	strikes at the core of	gets at the most important part of
p. 420	chameleon-like	able to change one's appearance; able to change one's behavior to fit in or meet expectations (refers to a lizard that can change its body color for camouflage)

PRONUNCIATION

ego (ee′-go) *p. 407*

efficacy (eff′-i-kuh-see) *p. 417*

SOLUTIONS

PREVIEW & CONCEPTUALIZING AND MEASURING PERSONALITY (PP. 397-405)

MASTERING THE CONCEPTS

1. Personality (p. 398)
2. traits (p. 398)
3. differences (p. 399)
4. Factor (p. 399)
5. source (p. 400)
6. neuroticism (p. 400)
7. Big 5 (p. 400)
8. agreeableness (p. 400)
9. Cardinal (p. 402)
10. Secondary (p. 402)
11. Self-report (p. 403)
12. MMPI (p. 403)
13. objective (p. 403)
14. Projective (p. 404)
15. TAT (p. 404)

EVALUATING YOUR PROGRESS

1. C, Correct (p. 400)
   A., B., D. Wrong. These are Allport's types of traits.
2. D, Correct (p. 400)
   A. Wrong. These traits relate to the neuroticism factor.
   B, C. Wrong. These traits relate to the extroversion factor.
3. A, Correct (p. 400)
   B., C., D. Wrong. These are not the most popular. The Big 5 have greater acceptance.
4. D, Correct (p. 402)
   A. Wrong. Secondary traits are limited to specific situations.
   B. Wrong. Source traits are Cattell's idea.
   C. Wrong. Central traits are "representative" traits.
5. D, Correct (p. 402)
   A., B., C. Wrong. Allport used an ideographic (case study) approach, not group data.
6. C, Correct (p. 404)
   A., B., D. Wrong. These are self-report inventories; the Rorschach is a projective test.
7. C, Correct (pp. 404-405)
   A. Wrong. The validity and reliability have been questioned.
   B. Wrong. Self-report personality inventories (objective tests) use these formats, not projective tests.
   D. Wrong. Self-report inventories are scored objectively. Projective tests use subjective scoring.

DETERMINING HOW PERSONALITY DEVELOPS (PP. 406-419)

MASTERING THE CONCEPTS.

1. psychodynamic (p. 406)
2. unconscious (p. 406)
3. dreams (p. 407)
4. id (p. 407)
5. pleasure (p. 407)
6. superego (p. 407)
7. idealistic (p. 407)
8. ego (p. 407)
9. reality (p. 407)
10. defense (p. 408)
11. repression (p. 408)
12. projection (p. 408)
13. opposite (p. 408)
14. sublimation (p. 408)
15. psychosexual (p. 408)
16. oral (p. 410)
17. anal (p. 410)
18. phallic (p. 410)
19. Oedipus (p. 410)
20. latency (p. 410)
21. genital (p. 410)
22. fixation (p. 410)
23. inferiority (p. 411)
24. collective (p. 411)
25. archetypes (p. 411)
26. humanistic (p. 412)
27. interpretation (p. 412)
28. congruent (p. 413)
29. positive regard (p. 413)
30. cognitive (p. 415)
31. modeling (p. 416)
32. external (p. 416)
33. internal (p. 416)
34. self-efficacy (p. 417)
35. reciprocal (p. 417)

EVALUATING YOUR PROGRESS

1. C, Correct (p. 408)
   A. Wrong. The preconscious contains information that is not in consciousness, but can be retrieved.
   B. Wrong. The conscious mind has active, current thoughts.
   D. Wrong. The collective unconscious is Jung's idea, and it is inaccessible.
2. C, Correct (p. 407)
   A. Wrong. This answer describes the ego.
   B., D. Wrong. These answers describe the id.
3. A, Correct (p. 408)
   B, C. Wrong. Although some defense mechanisms help satisfy the demands of the id or superego, not all do, and this is not their central purpose.
   D. Wrong. This is reaction formation. Repression pushes forbidden desires into the unconscious.
4. A, Correct (p. 410)
   B., C., D. Wrong. Freud proposed psychosexual stages, based on the part of the body from which sexual pleasure is derived at a particular time.
5. B, Correct (p. 411)
   A. Wrong. Jung preferred a general life force to Freud's sexual one, but archetypes are not a life force.
   C. Wrong. Defense mechanisms are strategies for reducing anxiety. Archetypes are symbolic concepts.
   D. Wrong. Archetypes are found in the collective unconscious, not the personal unconscious.
6. A, Correct (pp. 411-412)
   B., C., D. Wrong. These are all true, but Freud's theory has lost influence.
7. D, Correct (p. 412)
   A. Wrong. The psychodynamic theory stresses biological urges. Humanistic theory stresses growth.
   B. Wrong. Social-cognitive theory stresses reinforcement. Humanistic theory stresses growth.
   C. Wrong. Social-cognitive theory stresses self-efficacy and locus of control. Humanistic theory stresses growth.
8. C, Correct (p. 413)
   A. Wrong. This is a social-cognitive concept, not humanistic, and is not required for mental health.
   B. Wrong. This describes an interaction of experience, perception, and behavior, and is not humanistic.
   D. Wrong. Conditions of worth lead to an incongruent self-concept, an unhealthy situation.
9. C, Correct (p. 415)
   A., D. Wrong. These are stressed in humanistic theories.
   B. Wrong. This is a Freudian view.
10. D, Correct (p. 416)
    A. Wrong. Anal fixation typically involves neatness or sloppiness, not belief in luck or fate.
    B. Wrong. Self-efficacy is a belief in one's ability or competency.
    C. Wrong. Self-actualized people do not necessarily believe in luck or fate.

RESOLVING THE PERSON-SITUATION DEBATE (PP. 419-423)

MASTERING THE CONCEPTS

1. consistent (p. 419)
2. inconsistent (p. 420)
3. self-monitoring (p. 420)
4. job (p. 421)
5. genetic (p. 422)

EVALUATING YOUR PROGRESS

1. A, Correct (p. 419)
   B. Wrong. The person-situation debate involves behavioral consistency and does not involve the issue of genetic vs. learned influences.
   C. Wrong. Self-monitoring has been suggested as a concept that might help explain inconsistency of behavior, but it is not the basic issue in the debate.
   D. Wrong. The person-situation debate involves behavioral consistency, not levels of consciousness.
2. B, Correct (p. 420)
   A. Wrong. High self-monitors act inconsistently.
   C. Wrong. They are very aware of the environment, and pattern their behavior accordingly.
   D. Wrong. Because they act inconsistently, a genetic influence is not supported.
3. C, Correct (pp. 422-423)
   A. Wrong. Fraternal twins reared apart were less similar than fraternal twins reared together.
   B. Wrong. Identical twins reared apart were more similar than fraternal twins reared together.
   D. Wrong. For some traits at least, identical twins were no less similar if raised apart.

MAKING FINAL PREPARATIONS

SHORT ESSAY QUESTIONS

1. Cattell's source traits are 16 trait dimensions that account for individual differences in behavior. Eysenck, using a different version of factor analysis found 3 superfactors (neuroticism, psychoticism, and extroversion) that he felt described the basics of personality. Source traits provide a finer analysis than superfactors. (pp. 399-400)
2. Projective tests do not constrain the possible answers and often involve ambiguous stimuli, allowing the unconscious to project its contents onto the answer. Interpretation of responses is partly subjective. Self-report inventories ask the individual to rate themselves. Questions are direct and involve limited response options (true-false, etc.). Scoring is objective, but subjects may bias their answers to look good. (pp. 403-405)
3. The psychodynamic view is based on negative, animalistic biological urges, conflicts, and anxiety. Unconscious sexuality and aggression battle the need to be moral. The humanistic view is a positive view of people that stresses their innate goodness, control over their behavior, self-awareness, and potential for growth. In this view, people strive to achieve their full potential. (pp. 406-414)
4. An instrumental conditioning view of personality would suggest that Ron often had been reinforced when quiet in the past. A modeling (observational learning) approach would add that he might have observed another person's quiet behavior and its consequences. In both cases, he learned that the consequence of being quiet is reinforcement, so he developed and maintained his quiet ways. An instrumental conditioning view of personality would suggest that Ron often had been reinforced when quiet in the past. A modeling (observational learning) approach would add that he might have observed another person's quiet behavior and its consequences. In both cases, he learned that the consequence of being quiet is reinforcement, so he developed and maintained his quiet ways. (pp. 415-416)

5. The social-cognitive approach has been criticized as being insufficient. By focusing on what is learned about particular situations, this approach ignores the person as a whole. Also, biological influences are neglected. (pp. 417-419)

6. Psychologists solve the debate by assuming that both the person and the situation must be considered because people interact with situations. Current conditions will influence behavioral traits, causing some traits to appear in one context and not in others. Also, some situations can force modification of behavior. (pp. 421-422)

MATCHING

1. o (p. 411)
2. a (p. 400)
3. c (p. 402)
4. p (p. 411)
5. j (p. 400)
6. d (p. 411)
7. l (p. 420)
8. b (p. 417)
9. e (p. 414)
10. k (p. 412)
11. m (p. 406)
12. n (p. 404)
13. g (p. 410)
14. i (p. 413)
15. h (p. 417)
16. f (p. 413)

MULTIPLE CHOICE PRETEST 1

1. D, Correct (p. 403)

   A. Wrong. The Rorschach is a projective test, not a personality inventory.

   B. Wrong. The 16 Personality Factor test is based on Cattel's source traits.

   C. Wrong. The MMPI often is used to diagnose disorders, and it doesn't address the dimensions listed.

2. A, Correct (p. 403)

   B. Wrong. Self-report tests are objectively scored, often by computer. Projective test scoring is fairly subjective.

   C. Wrong. Objective tests are standardized. This is not a problem.

   D. Wrong. Self-report tests limit responses (e.g., true/false). Projective tests are open-ended.

3. B, Correct (p. 400)

   A. Wrong. Cattell found 16 factors, which he called source traits.

   C. Wrong. Superfactors are what Eysenk's 3 traits or dimensions of personality are called.

   D. Wrong. Central traits refer to Allport's trait theory.

4. C, Correct (p. 405)

   A. Wrong. Projective tests are scored rather subjectively and computer scoring is not usual.

   B. Wrong. This wouldn't be an advantage, and there is some degree of standardization involved.

   D. Wrong. Projective tests are often criticized for problems with reliability and validity.

5. B, Correct (p. 407)

   A. Wrong. The conscious and preconscious are accessible. The unconscious is not.

   C. Wrong. The superego defines and strives for ideal behavior. It does not contain hidden conflicts.

   D. Wrong. Reaction formation is a defense mechanism, not a storehouse for conflicts.

6. D, Correct (p. 408)

   A. Wrong. Nothing is being attributed to another person. The key here is a socially acceptable outlet for his urges.

   B. Wrong. There is no opposite behavior. The key here is the socially acceptable outlet for his urges.

   C. Wrong. There is no forgetting. The key here is the socially acceptable outlet for his urges.

7. B, Correct (p. 407)
   A. Wrong. The ego uses defense mechanisms.
   C. Wrong. The superego follows the idealistic principle.
   D. Wrong. The id is innate. The superego develops with experience.
8. A, Correct (p. 410)
   B. Wrong. Self-efficacy is a feeling of competence described by Bandura.
   C. Wrong. Sublimation is a defense mechanism in which unacceptable urges are channeled into acceptable ones.
   D. Wrong. The Oedipal and Electra complexes are conflicts that arise in the phallic period.
9. D, Correct (p. 410)
   A. Wrong. During the anal stage, pleasure is focused on the anal region. Friendships are the focus of the latency stage.
   B. Wrong. The phallic stage contains the Oedipal/Electra complex, which involve sexual feelings.
   C. Wrong. The genital stage following puberty, involves the emergence of mature sexual feelings.
10. C, Correct (p. 411)
    A. Wrong. This is Horney's view. Adler stressed overcoming inferiority.
    B. Wrong. This is Roger's humanistic view. Adler stressed overcoming inferiority.
    D. Wrong. This is a social learning view. Adler stressed overcoming inferiority.
11. A, Correct (p. 411)
    B. Wrong. Fixations involve behavior characteristic of an earlier stage, due to unresolved issued in that stage.
    C. Wrong. The ego ideal is a term associated with the superego. It is not a Jungian term for inherited concepts.
    D. Wrong. Latent content (not concepts) refers to the symbolic content of dreams in Freud's theory.
12. B, Correct (p. 413)
    A. Wrong. Rogers didn't discuss locus of control, and an external locus is not needed.
    C. Wrong. This is a social-cognitive theory concept and doesn't involve something people need.
    D. Wrong. These are not needs, although they do influence the self concept and may lead to incongruence.
13. C, Correct (p. 414)
    A. Wrong. Inferiority complex is one of Adler's a psychodynamic concepts, not a humanistic one.
    B. Wrong. Reinforcement is more characteristic of social-cognitive theories.
    D. Wrong. Psychosexual fixation is a Freudian psychodynamic concept.
14. A, Correct (pp. 414-415)
    B., C., D. Wrong. These are all points of criticism. Personal control is well accepted.
15. C, Correct (p. 416)
    A. Wrong. Self-actualization doesn't require this belief. Such belief is an internal locus of control.
    B. Wrong. A congruent self-concept doesn't necessarily require an internal locus of control.
    D. Wrong. An external locus of control gives emphasis to luck or fate.
16. C, Correct (p. 417)
    A. Wrong. Self-efficacy is the belief a person holds about their own ability to perform a task.
    B. Wrong. Self-actualization is the ingrained desire to reach one's true potential.
    D. Wrong. Conditions of worth are the expectations that people believe others place on them.
17. B, Correct (p. 422)
    A., C. Wrong. These are accurate data, but they support an environmental component.
    D. Wrong. These are inaccurate data, and they would not really favor either view.
18. A, Correct (p. 420)
    B., C. Wrong. Dishonesty is likely to reoccur in similar situations, but not in different situations.
    D. Wrong. Dishonesty is likely to reoccur in similar situations.
19. B, Correct (pp. 420-421)
    A. Wrong. Self-monitoring, modifying behavior to fit a situation, says little about the nature-nurture issue.
    C. Wrong. Self-monitoring, modifying behavior to fit a situation, says little about factor analysis.
    D. Wrong. Self-monitoring, modifying behavior to fit a situation, does not relate to psychopathology.

MULTIPLE CHOICE PRETEST 2

1. C, Correct (p. 402)

   A. Wrong. Allport did not propose "primary" traits.

   B. Wrong. Secondary traits are traits that occur occasionally, not in all aspects of behavior.

   D. Wrong. Central traits are characteristic of the person but are not evident in all aspects of behavior.

2. B, Correct (pp. 404-405)

   A., C., D. Wrong. These are criticisms of projective tests (Rorschach), not self-report inventories.

3. B, Correct (p. 400)

   A. Wrong. Extroversion relates to sociability.

   C. Wrong. This is the Big 5 trait, not Eysenck's, showing dependability, productivity, etc.

   D. Wrong. Low psychoticism would include being sensitive, caring, and kind.

4. D, Correct (p. 401)

   A, B, C. Wrong. Cross-cultural research generally found the Big 5 traits common to most cultures.

5. C, Correct (p. 403)

   A. Wrong. The TAT involves a series of rather ambiguous pictures, not true-false questions.

   B. Wrong. The Rorschach test is a series of inkblots, not true-false questions.

   D. Wrong. The NEO-PI-R is not used to diagnose psychological problems and doesn't involve hundreds of true-false questions.

6. C, Correct (p. 407)

   A. Wrong. The ego does not involve the conscience or morality. It is the mediator or executive.

   B. Wrong. The id does not have a conscience or morality. It follows the pleasure principle.

   D. Wrong. Fixation involves an unresolved psychosexual stage of development, not the absence of morality.

7. B, Correct (p. 406)

   A. Wrong. Things in the unconscious are not directly accessible.

   C. Wrong. The collective unconscious contains ancestral, not personal memories.

   D. Wrong. Reaction formation is a defense mechanism characterized by behavior opposite to one's true feelings.

8. A, Correct (p. 410)

   B., C., D. Wrong. Roy is experiencing the Oedipus complex, a hallmark of the phallic stage, involving children ages 3-5.

9. D, Correct (p. 411)

   A. Wrong. One's personal traumas are placed in the personal unconscious.

   B. Wrong. The collective unconscious contains concepts passed through generations, not the ego.

   C. Wrong. Adler stressed inferiority/superiority, not Jung.

10. B, Correct (p. 407)

    A. Wrong. The pleasure principle is associated with the id, not the ego.

    C. Wrong. Reciprocal determinism is the interaction of beliefs, behavior, and environment.

    D. Wrong. Self-efficacy is a feeling of competence. The ego uses the reality principle.

11. D, Correct (p. 408)

    A. Wrong. He's attributing the cheating to others, not channeling them to acceptable forms.

    B. Wrong. He's attributing (projecting) the cheating to others, not explaining things away.

    C. Wrong. He's attributing (projecting) the cheating to someone else, not "forgetting" them.

12. C, Correct (p. 414)

    A. Wrong. Conditions of worth are expectations we believe others have of us, and they don't relate to peak experiences.

    B. Wrong. Internal locus of control is the belief that one has some control over what happens. It is not Maslow's concept, and it is not related to peak experiences.

    D. Wrong. Jung proposed the collective unconscious. It does not relate to peak experiences.

13. A, Correct (p. 413)

    B. Wrong. External locus of control involves a belief that luck or fate or external influences determine what happens.

    C. Wrong. Fixation is a psychodynamic (Freudian) concept, not a humanistic one.

    D. Wrong. Ted is not aware of the situation and changing his behavior to match it.

14. C, Correct (pp. 415-417)

    A, B. Wrong. These theories all emphasize inborn tendencies, not conditioning and interpretation.

    D. Wrong. The humanistic approach doesn't include conditioning.

15. B, Correct (p. 408)

    A. Wrong. An unresolved Electra complex is more likely to create relationship or sexual problems.

    C. Wrong. Lisa isn't attributing the problem to other people as occurs in the projection defense mechanism.

    D. Wrong. Lisa isn't forgetting an anxiety-producing thought or event.

16. C, Correct (p. 417)

    A. Wrong. Self-efficacy involves confidence in one's ability to do the job.

    B. Wrong. Self-monitoring involves changing behavior to fit a each situation.

    D. Wrong. Conditions of worth are the conditions tied to giving approval, a Rogerian concept.

17. A, Correct (p. 419)

    B. Wrong. Most theories assume consistency (e.g., if the self-concept is stable, so is behavior; conditioning produces consistency).

    C. Wrong. The debate questions behavioral consistency across situations, not across people.

    D. Wrong. The debate questions consistency across situations, not across people.

18. C, Correct (p. 416)

    A., B. Wrong. Nothing is said about how May feels about her own personal chance for success.

    D. Wrong. An external locus of control focuses on luck or external factors, not personal effort.

19. A, Correct (p. 417)

    B. Wrong. High self-efficacy would involve confidence in his abilities.

    C, D. Wrong. Lester's issue is self-efficacy, not his belief in what determines what happens.

20. B, Correct (p. 417)

    A. Wrong. Social-cognitive theories are criticized for not considering biological factors sufficiently.

    C. Wrong. Social-cognitive theories do include conditioning as an important determinant.

    D. Wrong. Freud's theory, not social-cognitive theories, is considered difficult to test scientifically.

21. D, Correct (p. 420)

    A, B. Wrong. Self-efficacy involves a person's feeling of competency.

    C. Wrong. A low self-monitor does not modify behavior to fit the situation. Consistency is seen.

CHAPTER **13**

SOCIAL PSYCHOLOGY

ESTABLISHING LEARNING GOALS

Use these learning goals as a preview of the chapter, a guide for active reading, and to evaluate your mastery of the material. Review the relevant goals as you begin and end your reading of each major section of the chapter.

I. Understand social cognition, interpreting the behavior of others.
   A. Discuss how physical attractiveness, stereotypes, and social schemas influence our impressions of others.
      1. Describe the impact of attractiveness and social schemas.
      2. Identify common types of stereotypes and explain factors that influence stereotyping.
      3. Describe self-fulfilling prophecy, and discuss how it can influence behavior.
      4. Define and discuss prejudice.
   B. Discuss how we attribute causality to the behavior of others, explaining our biases and errors.
      1. Define attribution, and describe the covariation model of attribution.
      2. Compare internal and external attributions, and describe the fundamental attribution effect, actor-observer effect, and the self-serving bias.
   C. Explain how attitudes are formed and changed.
      1. Describe the cognitive, affective, and behavioral components of attitudes.
      2. Explain how exposure, conditioning, and observational learning influence attitudes.
      3. Describe the elaboration likelihood model of persuasion.
      4. Define cognitive dissonance, and discuss the research on its effect on attitudes.
      5. Describe the self-perception theory of the relationship between behavior and attitude.

II. Understand how social influence affects behavior.
   A. Define and discuss social facilitation and interference.
   B. Describe the bystander effect and diffusion of responsibility.
   C. Describe how behavior changes in a group setting.
      1. Describe social loafing and deindividuation, and explain their possible causes.
      2. Describe Asch's research on conformity, and discuss the factors that increase conformity.
   D. Discuss some aspects of group decision making.
      1. Describe group polarization.

2. Describe groupthink.

E. Describe the Milgram experiment, and discuss what it implies about the power of authority.

F. Discuss how culture affects social influence.

III. Understand how relations with others are established.

A. Describe the factors that influence our perception of facial attractiveness.

B. Explain the factors that influence us to like or love others.

C. Define the components of romantic love, and explain the triangular theory of love.

MASTERING THE MATERIAL

PREVIEW & INTERPRETING THE BEHAVIOR OF OTHERS: SOCIAL COGNITION (PP. 429-444)

MASTERING THE VOCABULARY

Define or explain each of the following terms.

1. social psychology
2. social cognition
3. social schema
4. stereotypes
5. self-fulfilling prophecy effect
6. prejudice
7. discrimination
8. attributions
9. external attribution
10. internal attribution
11. fundamental attribution error
12. actor-observer effect
13. self-serving bias
14. attitude
15. elaboration likelihood model

16. source characteristics
17. cognitive dissonance
18. self-perception theory

MASTERING THE CONCEPTS

Fill in the blanks to create a summary of the section.

[1] ____________ psychology is the study of how people think about, influence and relate to other people. Three issues are discussed: How do people interpret the behavior of others? How do people behave in the presence of others? How do people establish relations with other people?

Social [2] ____________ is the study of how people use cognitive processes to understand other people and themselves. Impressions of other people are influenced by that person's physical appearance and the observer's [3] ____________ about the person. Expectations are based on [4] ____________ , knowledge structures about social experiences, and influence action.

[5] ____________ are schemas about the traits and behavior of people that belong to a group, especially groups based on race, [6] ____________ , or age. Stereotypes cause [7] ____________ prophecy effects in which expectations lead to behaviors which themselves cause the person to behave in ways matching the expectations. Prototype and exemplar theories have been proposed to explain stereotypes. Stereotypes may be adaptive heuristics, but they may lead to rigid interpretations, and increase the chance of [8] ____________ and discrimination. Prejudice is [9] ____________ with repeated, widespread social interactions with representative individuals from the group.

According to Kelly's [10] ____________ model, attributions, inferences about the cause of a behavior, are based on events occurring with a behavior, and the consistency, distinctiveness, and consensus of the relationship. [11] ____________ , or situational, attributions are likely if these factors are strong. If consistency is high, but the others are low, an [12] ____________ , trait-based, attribution is made. The [13] ____________ attribution error is a bias to make internal attributions about someone else's behavior. The actor-observer effect is the tendency to make [14] ____________ attributions about your own behavior. [15] ____________ bias is the tendency to make internal attributions about one's successes, but external ones about failures. Attribution biases allow quick decisions but possibly inaccurate decisions.

[16] ____________ , beliefs held about something, have three parts: a [17] ____________ part involving knowledge; an [18] ____________ part involving feelings; and a [19] ____________ part involving a predisposition to act. Attitudes develop through mere [20] ____________ , classical and instrumental conditioning, and [21] ____________ learning. The [22] ____________ likelihood model of attitude change states that change occurs through a central route where the content of a persuasive message is processed, or through a peripheral route where superficial cues are influential and the message is not processed directly. In peripheral processing [23] ____________ characteristics and heuristics are important influences.

Festinger's cognitive [24] ____________ theory states behavior inconsistent with attitude creates dissonance (tension) that the person seeks to reduce, usually by changing the [25] ____________ . People asked to lie changed their attitudes to fit the lie more if they were paid a little than if they were paid a lot. Bem's self-perception theory states people use their [26] ____________ to infer their [27] ____________ . The [28] ____________ technique shows that people who behave in small ways implying an attitude later engage in larger behaviors implying the attitude because self-perception is triggered. The low balling technique works similarly.

EVALUATING YOUR PROGRESS

Select the best response. If you make any errors, reread the relevant material before proceeding.

1. Darla's first impression of her blind date will be most strongly influenced by his
   a. name.
   b. apparent intelligence.
   c. physical appearance.
   d. first words.

2. When one's expectations about a person actually cause that person to behave in the expected way,
   a. a self-fulfilling prophecy effect has occurred.
   b. a social schema has been violated.
   c. a fundamental attribution error has been made.
   d. cognitive dissonance has developed.

3. The most common types of stereotypes are based on race, gender, and
   a. age.
   b. intelligence.
   c. hair color.
   d. occupation.

4. Consensus, distinctiveness, and consistency are central ideas in
   a. Festinger's theory of cognitive dissonance.
   b. Kelly's covariation model.
   c. Bem's self-perception theory.
   d. the elaboration likelihood model.

5. If Jess acts cranky only when she has been up late the previous night, crankiness has
   a. high distinctiveness.
   b. high consensus.
   c. low consensus.
   d. low consistency.

6. When Liz broke her leg this winter, you decided she probably fell because of all the icy sidewalks. Your decision is an example of
   a. an internal attribution.
   b. an external attribution.
   c. self-serving bias.
   d. cognitive dissonance.

7. People are more likely to make internal attributions about others more often than external attributions. This represents
   a. the self-fulfilling prophecy effect.
   b. the self-serving bias.
   c. self-perception theory.
   d. the fundamental attribution error.

8. When people explain their successes in terms of their personal characteristics, but explain their failures in terms of environmental events or situations, they are demonstrating
   a. the fundamental attribution error.
   b. the self-serving bias.
   c. self-perception theory.
   d. a self-fulfilling prophecy effect.

9. Which of the following is not a component of attitudes?
   a. cognitive component
   b. behavioral component
   c. affective component
   d. consensus component

10. An example of mere exposure as a means of attitude formation is
    a. liking a car because the music in the ads makes you feel happy.
    b. liking a brand of shoes because an athlete endorses them.
    c. liking a song after hearing it several times.
    d. liking a charity because it sent you a nice thank you letter.
11. The peripheral route of persuasion involves
    a. focusing attention on processing the content of the persuasive message itself.
    b. an evaluation of consensus, distinctiveness, and consistency.
    c. basing attitudes on celebrity, mere exposure, or other superficial cues in the message.
    d. creating a state of tension as a result of mismatched attitudes and behavior.
12. When attitudes and behaviors do not match, a tension develops that is then reduced by changing the attitude. This describes
    a. the elaboration likelihood theory.
    b. the cognitive dissonance theory.
    c. the self-perception theory.
    d. the covariation theory.
13. If you examine your past actions to determine your attitudes, your behavior is most consistent with
    a. cognitive dissonance theory.
    b. the self-fulfilling prophecy effect.
    c. the idea of social schemas.
    d. self-perception theory.

BEHAVING IN THE PRESENCE OF OTHERS: SOCIAL INFLUENCE (PP. 445-457)

MASTERING THE VOCABULARY

Define or explain each of the following terms.

1. social influence
2. social facilitation
3. social interference
4. altruism
5. bystander effect
6. diffusion of responsibility
7. social loafing
8. deindividuation
9. conformity

10. in-group
11. group polarization
12. groupthink
13. obedience

MASTERING THE CONCEPTS.

Fill in the blanks to create a summary of the section.

Social [1] ____________ involves how the presence of others affects behavior. Audiences may enhance performance, social [2] ____________ , or disrupt performance, social [3] ____________ .

In the [4] ____________ effect, the presence of others inhibits helping behavior, altruism, because of [5] ____________ of responsibility. Helping increases if the person has watched others be helpful. Diffusion of responsibility may explain [6] ____________ , working less hard when in a group, and might influence [7] ____________ , a depersonalization that can lead to destructive behavior.

People in groups often show [8] ____________ , behavior that shifts toward the group norm. Asch's research shows that people will give a wrong answer if everyone else does so, especially if the group contains 3-5 people for whom the person has respect or a sense of identification, such as in an [9] ____________ . Conformity may result from an attempt to get approval or avoid [10] ____________ , or because the group is seen as a source of information.

Group decisions differ from those of individuals. With time, a group decision grows more extreme, the group [11] ____________ effect. Close-knit groups make bad decisions when they value obtaining a consensus more than considering all the facts, a situation known as [12] ____________ .

As shown by Milgram's research, orders given by an authority often lead to [13] ____________ . Sixty-five percent of Milgram's subjects obeyed and gave what they thought were severe shocks to another person. Obedience is reduced when the prestige of the setting or the authority is low, and when the authority figure [14] ____________ the room. This study has been criticized as [15] ____________ .

Whether a person has an independent or interdependent sense of self is influenced by cultural factors. As a result, social phenomena like conformity may vary across cultures.

EVALUATING YOUR PROGRESS

Select the best response. If you miss any questions, reread the relevant material before proceeding.

1. Performance is sometimes worse with an audience than without an audience. This represents
   a. diffusion of responsibility.
   b. the group polarization effect.
   c. social interference.
   d. altruism.

2. Being unwilling to consider alternative views and overemphasizing obtaining a consensus of opinion is characteristic of
   a. groupthink.
   b. group polarization.
   c. social loafing.
   d. social facilitation.

3. The bystander effect is explained in terms of
   a. the suppression of dissent.
   b. greater obedience that is created by being a bystander in a group.
   c. the feeling that responsibility is shared by the other people present.
   d. the feeling that one shares certain characteristics with other members of a group.

4. Feeling anonymous, less self-conscious, and possibly depersonalized, and being willing to do things you normally wouldn't do are characteristic of
   a. social loafing.
   b. normative social influence.
   c. groupthink.
   d. deindividuation.

5. Which of the following does not increase the chance of conformity?
   a. increasing group size from 5 to 15
   b. having group members that have high status
   c. being a group that is an in-group
   d. perceiving group members as good sources of information

6. Group polarization involves the tendency
   a. to act like the other members of the group because they have important information.
   b. for a group decision to grow more extreme with increasing time.
   c. for a group to emphasize reaching a consensus rather than considering dissenting views.
   d. to separate into leaders and workers in groups working on a specific project.

7. In Milgram's experiment on obedience, 65% of the people
   a. refused to begin the experiment after hearing they would have to shock someone.
   b. began the experiment, but quit when they were faced with actually having to shock someone.
   c. participated in most of the experiment, but quit when the "learner" started screaming with pain.
   d. participated in the entire experiment, giving the highest level of shocks to the "learner."

ESTABLISHING RELATIONS WITH OTHERS (PP. 457-464)

MASTERING THE VOCABULARY

Define or explain each of the following terms.

1. reciprocity
2. passionate love
3. companionate love

MASTERING THE CONCEPTS

Fill in the blanks to create a summary of the section.

Physical appearance influences social relations. An evolutionary view of attractiveness predicts attractiveness should be related to [1] ____________ capacity (youth and health) and should be similar across cultures. Attractive faces tend to be [2] ____________ or prototypical faces. Although cross-cultural similarities in attractiveness exist, culture-specific attitudes are important also.

Primary determinants of relationships include [3] ____________ , the physical distance between the people's homes, [4] ____________ , the number of shared interests or characteristics, and [5] ____________ , a tendency to return feelings received. Physical nearness encourages relationships through mere exposure or a sense of connectedness developing from repeated contact. Similarity influences relationships by [6] ____________ a person's beliefs, because people dislike others that do not share their views, or because personal characteristics limit the range of choices.

Love can be [7] ____________ love, which is an intense desire, or [8] ____________ love, which is a less intense, but a more enduring feeling of trust and warmth. Sternberg's [9] ____________ theory of love classifies love based on three dimensions: passion or erotic attraction, [10] ____________ or the sharing of feelings, and [11] ____________ to remaining in the relationship. Passion may develop first, but often fades. Commitment and intimacy develop later, but are more likely to endure.

EVALUATING YOUR PROGRESS

Select the best response. If you miss any questions, reread the relevant material before proceeding.

1. The most accurate summary of research on facial attractiveness is:
   a. Universal, innate factors entirely determine what types of faces are most attractive.
   b. Cultural factors entirely determine what types of faces are most attractive.
   c. Both universal and cultural-specific factors determine what faces are most attractive.
   d. Attractiveness is entirely an individual matter; there is little consistency in choices.

2. Interpersonal attraction is primarily determined by
   a. proximity, similarity, and reciprocity.
   b. income, proximity and attractiveness.
   c. reciprocity, education, and attractiveness.
   d. income, education, and attractiveness.

3. Ralph Waldo Emerson wrote in Friendship, "To have a friend, you must be a friend." He seems to be referring to the determinant of love and friendship that social psychologists call
   a. similarity.
   b. proximity.
   c. reciprocity.
   d. conformity.

4. The type of love most likely to lead to self-disclosure and enduring feelings of trust and warmth is
   a. passionate love.
   b. companionate love.
   c. empty love.
   d. infatuated love.

5. Which is not a dimension in Sternberg's triangular theory of love?
   a. reciprocity
   b. passion
   c. intimacy
   d. commitment

MAKING FINAL PREPARATIONS

Complete these sections without consulting your book or notes. For a more accurate estimate of how well you know this material, wait at least a day or two after studying the chapter before working on the questions. Some of the material you "know" immediately after working with the chapter will be quickly forgotten. Exercises done too soon after studying will overestimate what you know well.

SHORT ESSAY QUESTIONS

Write a brief answer to each question.

1. Explain the adaptive value and disadvantages of stereotypes.

2. Compare Festinger's cognitive dissonance theory and Bem's self-perception theory.

3. Describe the bystander effect and give one primary explanation.

4. Explain why similarity might promote friendship.

5. Compare passionate and companionate love.

MATCHING

Select the correct definition or description for each item.

1. _______ reciprocity
2. _______ social interference
3. _______ elaboration likelihood model
4. _______ obedience
5. _______ social cognition
6. _______ Daryl Bem
7. _______ social facilitation
8. _______ Solomon Asch
9. _______ foot-in-the-door technique
10. _______ Stanley Milgram
11. _______ stereotypes
12. _______ self-fulfilling prophecy
13. _______ Leon Festinger
14. _______ social schemas
15. _______ attitude
16. _______ covariation model

a. compliance in response to an authority
b. get attitude shift by inducing attitude-consistent act
c. impaired performance in the presence of others
d. knowledge structures relating to social experiences
e. conducted obedience experiments
f. proposed theory of cognitive dissonance
g. conducted conformity experiments
h. how thoughts help people understand people
i. proposes central & peripheral route to attitude
j. beliefs about traits of a particular group
k. enhanced performance in the presence of others
l. tendency to return feeling shown toward oneself
m. positive or negative evaluation of something
n. expectation leads to behavior matching expectation
o. emphasizes consistency, distinctiveness, consensus
p. proposed self-perception theory of attribution

MULTIPLE CHOICE PRETEST 1

Select the one best response.

1. An evolutionary approach to attractiveness would suggest people are attracted to people
   a. who look like them (share the same gene pool).
   b. who are youthful and healthy looking.
   c. who have unusual features.
   d. who fit their cultural definition of beauty.

2. Based on research on first impressions, when Ed first sees a very attractive person he will assume the person is
   a. less intelligent than people with an average appearance.
   b. more self-centered than people with an average appearance.
   c. better adjusted than people with an average appearance.
   d. more likely to get into trouble than the average person.

3. Which of the following is false?
   a. Stereotypes are activated by recent exposure to stereotypic beliefs.
   b. The most common stereotypes involve age, gender, and race.
   c. Stereotypes produce an overemphasis on within-group differences.
   d. Repeated, widespread exposure to representative members of a group reduces stereotyping.

4. John acts nervous when he talks with his psychology professor. If many other students also act nervous in that situation, the covariation model would describe the behavior as
   a. low in consistency.
   b. low in distinctiveness.
   c. high in consensus.
   d. high in distinctiveness.

5. According to Kelly's covariation model, internal attributions are most likely when there is
   a. low consistency, high consensus, and high distinctiveness.
   b. low consistency, low consensus, and low distinctiveness.
   c. high consistency, high consensus, and high distinctiveness.
   d. high consistency, low consensus, and low distinctiveness.

6. Election commercials that attempt to persuade viewers by listing the candidate's views and accomplishments are using
   a. a peripheral route strategy.
   b. a central route strategy.
   c. the foot in the door strategy.
   d. the source characteristics strategy.

7. According to your text, negative evaluations of a group and its members defines
   a. discrimination.
   b. altruism.
   c. prejudice.
   d. source characteristics.

8. Cognitive dissonance occurs when
   a. a person's expectations produce changes in behavior that, in turn, confirms those expectations.
   b. a person makes internal attributions about good outcomes and external attributions about bad outcomes.
   c. a person's review of his/her past behavior is used to determine a current attitude.
   d. a person's behavior is not consistent with his/her attitude.

9. Abe had made 100% of his free throws when alone in the gym, but when the coaches showed up, he missed four in a row. This is an example of
   a. self-fulfilling prophecy.
   b. the bystander effect.
   c. the actor-observer effect.
   d. social interference.

10. When a student gets up and leaves during the middle of his lecture, Dr. Marsh is more likely to think, "That student is a rude fool" than "That student must be ill." This illustrates
    a. altruism.
    b. a self-fulfilling prophecy.
    c. the fundamental attribution error.
    d. cognitive dissonance.

11. When the quarterback threw a game-winning pass, he attributed his success to his great skill. When he threw a disastrous interception, he attributed his failure to a gust of wind. This pattern represents
    a. the fundamental attribution error.
    b. a self-fulfilling prophecy.
    c. elaboration likelihood.
    d. the self-serving bias.

12. Although at least 20 people saw Tyrone's serious fall, several minutes passed before anybody came over to help. This lack of action can best be explained in terms of
    a. the fundamental attribution effect.
    b. cognitive dissonance.
    c. diffusion of responsibility.
    d. reciprocal altruism.

13. Don is normally a hard worker, but when fifty people showed up to clean the ballpark, Don watched more than he worked. Don's behavior is most similar to
    a. the bystander effect.
    b. group polarization.
    c. lowballing.
    d. social loafing.

14. Bem's self-perception theory has been used to explain
    a. the foot-in-the-door technique.
    b. the fundamental attribution error.
    c. deindividuation.
    d. social loafing.

15. April knows she is 20 lbs too heavy to look good in low-rider jeans, but because everybody else is wearing them, so does she. April's behavior reflects
    a. obedience.
    b. group polarization.
    c. conformity.
    d. reciprocity.

16. In the aftermath of the World Trade Center attack, many people immediately stopped to help strangers who were injured. This behavior represents
    a. the bystander effect.
    b. altruism.
    c. deindividuation.
    d. groupthink.

17. Some critics have suggested that President Bush's staff were more concerned with getting a consensus on the issue of weapons of mass destruction in Iraq than listening to dissenting opinions. If true, this situation is an example of
    a. group polarization.
    b. low-balling.
    c. the fundamental attribution error.
    d. groupthink.

18. Research on obedience has shown that
    a. very few people obey orders to hurt someone unless the study is carried out in a highly prestigious location.
    b. most of the people who gave the highest shock in Milgram's study had figured out the hoax.
    c. obedience is most likely if the person giving the orders leaves the room afterward.
    d. Milgram's basic results can be replicated in many countries.

19. Which of the following sayings is best supported by research on friendships?
    a. Birds of a feather flock together.
    b. Absence makes the heart grow fonder.
    c. Familiarity breeds contempt.
    d. Opposites attract.

20. Mike and Carol share an incredibly strong need to be with each other and strong emotional arousal when together. Their relationship is an example of
    a. companionate love.
    b. empty love.
    c. passionate love.
    d. friendship.

MULTIPLE CHOICE PRETEST 2

Select the one best response.

1. Coach Bob has heard that Tim is not a very good baseball player. As a result, he gives Tim little time or attention in practice and little playing time in games. Sure enough, Tim was the worst player at the end of the season. This is best explained in terms of
    a. cognitive dissonance.
    b. self-serving bias.
    c. an actor-observer effect.
    d. a self-fulfilling prophecy effect.

2. Brad believes students of Asian heritage are excellent students and especially good at math and science. Brad's belief is an example of
   a. elaboration likelihood.
   b. the actor-observer effect.
   c. an external attribution.
   d. a stereotype.

3. Mira's recital performance was marred by several squeaks and honks. Before deciding why MIra's performance was poor, you considered whether she usually honks and squeaks in other situations. Your decision emphasized
   a. consistency.
   b. consensus.
   c. distinctiveness.
   d. expectation.

4. Kim complained to Flo, "You mostly make an internal attribution concerning *my* behavior, but you make external attributions about *your* behavior." If Kim's accusation is true, Flow's behavior illustrates
   a. the actor-observer effect.
   b. deindividuation.
   c. cognitive dissonance.
   d. a self-fulfilling prophecy.

5. If Anne makes the fundamental attribution error, she will explain her favorite politician's loss in the election by saying,
   a. "He just didn't have the campaign skills necessary to get his ideas across."
   b. "His opponent ran a dirty campaign that turned the voters away from the real issues."
   c. "He didn't have big money behind him, so he couldn't buy the advertising time he needed to win."
   d. "The voters were determined to get rid of all the incumbents, no matter how good they were."

6. The head of marketing often claimed, "Say it often enough, and people will start to believe it." This suggests she believes attitudes are influenced by
   a. mere exposure.
   b. classical conditioning.
   c. instrumental conditioning.
   d. deindividuation.

7. Sid is an Indianapolis Pacers basketball fan. He knows the team's win-loss record and the achievements of the individual players. He buys season tickets every year, and gets angry if anyone says they aren't the best. The behavioral component of Sid's attitude is
   a. knowing the team's win-loss record.
   b. knowing the achievements of the individual players.
   c. buying season tickets every year.
   d. getting angry at people who disagree with him.

8. In his re-election campaign President Bush ran a commercial in which images of the flag, firemen, the World Trade Center, and stirring music were prominently featured. This is an example of persuasion based on
   a. the peripheral route.
   b. the central route.
   c. cognitive dissonance.
   d. operant conditioning.

9. Kit, a volunteer, and Tom, a highly paid staff member, work on Candidate Smith's campaign. Although Candidate Smith recently admitted he has a criminal conviction, both Kit and Tom have continued to work for him. According to cognitive dissonance theory, how are Kit's and Tom's attitudes about Candidate Smith likely to have changed since the news about his criminal record?
   a. Both Kit's and Tom's attitudes became less favorable, but Kit's changed more.
   b. Both Kit's and Tom's attitudes became less favorable, but Tom's changed more.
   c. Both Kit's and Tom's attitudes became less favorable by an equal amount.
   d. Kit's attitude became less favorable, but Tom's attitude became more favorable.

10. Members of the Residence Hall Council initially felt that some minor changes were needed in the visitation policies. After a very lengthy, well-balanced, and thorough discussion, they produced a very extreme proposal restricting visitation to 1:00-7:00 pm. Their shift to a more extreme view illustrates
    a. groupthink.
    b. social facilitation.
    c. normative social influence.
    d. group polarization.

11. Charities emphasize getting any kind of donation at first, no matter how small. They know that having complied with a small request makes a person much more likely to comply with a large request later. This represents
    a. behavioral consensus.
    b. a self-fulfilling prophecy.
    c. normative social influence.
    d. the foot in the door technique.

12. Ben realized that every time he had an open elective, he took a psychology class. Based on his observation, Ben has decided he must like psychology. Ben's attitude is best explained by
    a. self-perception theory.
    b. cognitive dissonance theory.
    c. the fundamental attribution error model.
    d. the elaboration likelihood model.

13. Dozens of cars passed by before Jack got help when stranded on a busy road. Mike got help from the first person to pass by when he had car trouble on an almost deserted road. The difference in helping behavior they encountered is most consistent with
    a. the group polarization effect.
    b. the bystander effect.
    c. the elaboration likelihood theory.
    d. covariation theory.

14. In the large Mardi Gras crowd, Jill felt anonymous and depersonalized, and she did some things very uncharacteristic of her normal behavior. Jill seems to have experienced
    a. the group polarization effect.
    b. deindividuation.
    c. social facilitation.
    d. reciprocity.

15. "He told me to do it." "Everybody else did it too!" "Nobody else did anything either." These are comments likely to be heard when explaining behavior in situations like Milgram's experiment, riots, and the Kitty Genovese case. Each comment illustrates the importance of
    a. self-perception theory.
    b. diffusion of responsibility.
    c. internal attributions.
    d. reciprocity.

16. Which of the following is more typical in non-Western (e.g., Asian) cultures?
    a. the use of individualistic traits when describing oneself (e.g., I am an expert dancer.)
    b. perception of oneself as above average in intelligence
    c. an independent view of self
    d. an emphasis on shared characteristics

17. Research has found that people tended to rate as most attractive pictures of people
    a. who look similar to themselves.
    b. who have very distinctive features.
    c. created by averaging photos of many other people.
    d. who had asymmetrical faces.

18. Which is true?
    a. Newborns prefer faces rated as attractive by adults.
    b. Cross-cultural research supports the idea that attractiveness is determined entirely by cultural norms.
    c. Perceptions of attractiveness have remained the same over time.
    d. People tend to select as mates others who are about equal to them in attractiveness.

19. Georgia just met a woman who is like a twin sister. She likes the same things Georgia likes, she looks a little like Georgia, and she often starts to say the same thing as Georgia. Based on the research on interpersonal relationships, Georgia will probably
    a. feel really creepy about finding someone so similar to her and will avoid her in the future.
    b. very quickly become lasting friends with this person.
    c. become friends for a short while before becoming bored with someone so like her.
    d. become friends for a short while before the small differences cause her to lose interest.
20. If feelings of closeness, connectedness, and warmth characterize a relationship, Sternberg would say the relationship is high in
    a. commitment.
    b. reciprocity.
    c. passion.
    d. intimacy.

LANGUAGE DEVELOPMENT GUIDE

CORE TERMS

In the lectures on social psychology, your instructor may refer to ***pro-social*** behaviors, such as ***philanthropy***, or charity. These are behaviors that help others.

Your instructor may also use the terms ***legal***, ***ethical*** and ***moral***. These terms are not quite interchangeable. Something that is *illegal* breaks a specific law in a society; something that is *unethical* breaks the principles that guide conduct in a profession, such as those research psychologists must follow in designing their studies. Finally, something that is *immoral* violates public standards for good behavior.

IDIOMS

p. 429	itching for	wanting, restlessly waiting for
p. 429	spearheaded by	led by, directed by
p. 429	shortcomings	faults
p. 429	save one	except one
p. 432	judging a book by its cover	making assumptions about someone or something based upon its outward appearance
p. 433	seedy characters	people who seem to be likely to cause trouble or who are dressed poorly

p. 436	channel surfing	flipping from one television (TV) channel to another
p. 437	sour disposition	unpleasant personality
p. 438	bearing down on your bumper	coming closer and closer to the back of your car
p. 438	tailgated	followed very closely by another car
p. 439	switch gears	change topics or approaches to a topic
p. 440	landlord	owner of a rented property, such as a house or apartment
p. 440	pet deposit	money some landlords require pet owners to pay in order to keep their pets in the house with them
p. 440	classified ads	short advertisements in newspapers
p. 442	measly	tiny, inconsequential, nearly worthless
p. 445	underling	employee
p. 446	risen to the occasion	performed well when the situation called for it
p. 446	"choke"	to seize up, to fail to perform when the situation requires
p. 449	rigged	set up an event so that the outcome is certain
p. 452	watershed event	an event that serves as a critical point or dividing line
p. 452	devil's advocate	a person who deliberately takes a contrary position in an argument, especially to test the others' case
p. 453	toe the line	do what everyone else does; conform
p. 453	laced with	containing a small amount of an additive
p. 453	billed as	described or advertised as
p. 454	via intercom	by way of a room-to-room communication device
p. 454	in on	knowledgeable about some secret
p. 454	give a piece of your mind	express your opinion forcefully, usually with displeasure
p. 455	three-plus decades	more than 30 years
p. 457	paramount	most important
p. 460	a looming visual configuration	a large, or growing, visual image
p. 462	con job	a swindle; a deception
p. 462	ulterior motive	a hidden reason or motivation
p. 463	unrequited	unrewarded; unreturned
p. 463	bedrock	foundation, basis

PRONUNCIATION

deindividuation (dee-in-di-vi′-ju-ay′-shun) *p. 449* **reciprocity** (re-si-prah′-si-tee) *p. 462*

SOLUTIONS

PREVIEW & INTERPRETING THE BEHAVIOR OF OTHERS: SOCIAL COGNITION (PP. 429-444)

MASTERING THE CONCEPTS

1. Social (p. 431)
2. cognition (p. 431)
3. expectations (p. 431)
4. social schemas (p. 433)
5. Stereotypes (p. 433)
6. gender (p. 433)
7. self-fulfilling (p. 433)
8. prejudice (p. 435)
9. reduced (p. 435)
10. covariation (p.437)
11. External (p. 437)
12. internal (p. 437)
13. fundamental (p. 437)
14. external (p. 439)
15. Self-serving (p. 439)
16. Attitudes (p. 440)
17. cognitive (p. 440)
18. affective (p. 440)
19. behavioral (p. 440)
20. exposure (p. 440)
21. observational (p. 441)
22. elaboration (p. 441)
23. source (p. 442)
24. dissonance (p. 442)
25. attitude (p. 443)
26. behavior (p. 443)
27. attitudes (p. 443)
28. foot-in-the-door (p. 444)

EVALUATING YOUR PROGRESS

1. C, Correct (p. 432)

   A., B., D. Wrong. First impressions are most strongly influenced by physical appearance.

2. A, Correct (p. 433)

   B. Wrong. Expectations are upheld, not violated.

   C. Wrong. The fundamental attribution error is making internal attributions about other's behavior.

   D. Wrong. Cognitive dissonance is tension produced when attitudes and actions don't match.

3. A, Correct (p. 433)

   B., C., D. Wrong. Although stereotypes can include these, race, age, and gender are most common.

4. B, Correct (p. 433)

   A. Wrong. The central idea in cognitive dissonance is tension when behavior and attitude don't match.

   C. Wrong. The central idea in Bem's theory is examining your past behavior, not these dimensions.

   D. Wrong. The central ideas in this model are central and peripheral routes of persuasion.

5. A, Correct (p. 437)

   B., C. Wrong. There is no information about whether other people are cranky after staying up late.

   D. Wrong. There is no information to suggest the relationship between mood and late nights is limited.

6. B, Correct (p. 437)

   A. Wrong. You attributed her injury to an environmental, external cause, not an internal one like clumsiness.

   C. Wrong. This bias would suggest you'd make an internal attribution.

   D. Wrong. There is no tension due to a mismatch of attitude and behavior here.

7. D, Correct (p. 438)

   A. Wrong. Self-fulfilling prophesies don't involve different rates of internal and external attributions.

   B. Wrong. This bias involves making different attributions for your self than for others depending on the outcome.

   C. Wrong. This theory involves determining attitudes based on one's past behavior.

8. B, Correct (p. 439)
   A. Wrong. Attributions in this question are for people's own behavior, not someone else's.
   C. Wrong. Nobody is examining their own behavior to determine what their beliefs are.
   D. Wrong. Nobody's expectations are resulting in later behavior that matches their expectations.
9. D, Correct (p. 440)
   A., B., C. Wrong. These are all components of attitudes. Consensus is a dimension considered when making attributions.
10. C, Correct (p. 440)
   A. Wrong. This is classical conditioning in action.
   B. Wrong. This is a source characteristic in action.
   D. Wrong. This is instrumental conditioning in action.
11. C, Correct (p. 441)
   A. Wrong. This is the central route.
   B. Wrong. This occurs when making attributions, not in the peripheral route for persuasion.
   D. Wrong. This describes cognitive dissonance, not the peripheral route to persuasion.
12. B, Correct (p. 442)
   A. Wrong. Elaboration likelihood proposes central and peripheral routes to persuasion, not tension.
   C. Wrong. Self-perception theory states we use behavior to infer our attitudes. Tension isn't involved.
   D. Wrong. The covariation theory deals with how attributions are made, and tension is not involved.
13. D, Correct (p. 443)
   A. Wrong. This theory emphasizes reducing tension caused by mismatching attitudes and behavior, not examining past actions.
   B. Wrong. This effect involves the impact one's attitudes may have on another person's behavior.
   C. Wrong. Social schema are clusters of ideas about social experiences or people.

BEHAVING IN THE PRESENCE OF OTHERS: SOCIAL INFLUENCE (PP. 445-457)

MASTERING THE CONCEPTS.

1. influence (p. 445)
2. facilitation (p. 445)
3. interference (p. 446)
4. bystander (p. 447)
5. diffusion (p. 447)
6. social loafing (p. 448)
7. deindividuation (p. 449)
8. conformity (p. 449)
9. in-group (p. 450)
10. rejection (p. 450)
11. polarization (p. 451)
12. groupthink (p. 451)
13. obedience (p. 453)
14. leavcs (p. 455)
15. unethical (p. 455)

EVALUATING YOUR PROGRESS

1. C, Correct (p. 446)
   A. Wrong. This is a feeling of shared responsibility that affects behavior. It is not really a decline in performance.
   B. Wrong. The group polarization effect involves more extreme attitudes or decisions in groups.
   D. Wrong. Altruism is helping behavior.
2. A, Correct (p. 451)
   B. Wrong. Group polarization produces more extreme views, but it doesn't rely on inhibition of dissent or an emphasis on consensus.
   C. Wrong. Social loafing is not working as hard when in a group.
   D. Wrong. Social facilitation is improved performance with an audience.

3. C, Correct (p. 447)
   A. Wrong. This characterizes groupthink, not the bystander effect.
   B. Wrong. Obedience isn't relevant; the person is reluctant to help due to diffusion of responsibility.
   D. Wrong. This describes an in-group. In the bystander effect the key is diffusion of responsibility.
4. D, Correct (p. 449)
   A. Wrong. Social loafing is not doing your share of work when in a group. Anonymity and depersonalization are not typical.
   B. Wrong. Normative social influence involves conformity in order to fit in or be liked. Depersonalization, etc. is not involved.
   C. Wrong. Groupthink involves an emphasis on consensus and a failure to consider all information.
5. A, Correct (pp. 449-450)
   B., C., D. Wrong. These all are associated with increased conformity, but increasing group size above five is not.
6. B, Correct (p. 451)
   A. Wrong. This describes informational social influence.
   C. Wrong. This describes groupthink.
   D. Wrong. Group polarization involves the nature of group decisions, not division of labor.
7. D, Correct (p. 454)
   A., B., C. Wrong. Most people were distressed, but continued to the highest shock level.

ESTABLISHING RELATIONS WITH OTHERS (PP. 457-464)

MASTERING THE CONCEPTS

1. reproductive (p. 458)
2. average (p. 459)
3. proximity (p. 461)
4. similarity (p. 461)
5. reciprocity (p. 462)
6. validating (p. 462)
7. passionate (p. 463)
8. companionate (p. 463)
9. triangular (p. 463)
10. intimacy (p. 463)
11. commitment (p. 463)

EVALUATING YOUR PROGRESS

1. C, Correct (pp. 458-460)
   A. Wrong. Culture is influential.
   B. Wrong. Universal tendencies have been found.
   D. Wrong. General tendencies have been found.
2. A, Correct (pp. 461-462)
   B., C., D. Wrong. Income, education, and attractiveness are not primary determinants.
3. C, Correct (p. 462)
   A., B., D. Wrong. The quote suggests one person must act friendly for another to be friendly--reciprocity.
4. B, Correct (p. 463)
   A. Wrong. Passionate love is usually low in commitment and enduring trust and warmth.
   C. Wrong. Empty love has commitment, but little passion or intimacy.
   D. Wrong. Infatuated love is low in intimacy (self-disclosure).
5. A, Correct (p. 463)
   B., C., D. Wrong. The sides of the triangle are passion, intimacy, and commitment.

MAKING FINAL PREPARATIONS

SHORT ESSAY QUESTIONS

1. Stereotypes act as "rules of thumb" for how to organize the social world and how to act with new people. Stereotypes can be relatively accurate, although not always. The danger of stereotypes is that they emphasize differences between groups rather than differences within groups, and they may lead to prejudice and self-fulfilling prophesies. (pp. 433, 435-436)
2. Festinger's cognitive dissonance is a tension created by a mismatch of attitudes and behavior. The person then tries to reduce dissonance, mostly by adjusting the attitude to match the behavior. Bem's theory doesn't involve dissonance. Bem suggests that rather than trying to reconcile existing attitudes and behavior, people determine their attitude on the spot by examining their recent behavior. "If I did this, I must like that." (pp. 442-444)
3. The bystander effect is the reluctance to help when other people are present. The primary explanation is that responsibility for helping (or the consequences of not helping) are shared by all present, a diffusion of responsibility. Thus, the person feels less responsible for helping; someone else can help. (pp. 447-448)
4. Similarity might promote friendship because similar views validate our views, which is valued. We might associate with similar people to avoid associating with people who don't agree with us. Physical factors might limit the range of possible mates. Unattractive people might be limited to other unattractive people as companions, and economic or social similarity can restrict exposure to different people. (pp. 461-462)
5. Passionate love involves an intense erotic attraction to, and longing for, another person. It has intimacy but low commitment. Companionate love has less passion, but is high in intimacy and commitment. (pp. 463-464)

MATCHING

1. l (p. 462)
2. c (p. 446)
3. i (p. 441)
4. a (p. 453)
5. h (p. 431)
6. p (p. 443)
7. k (p. 445)
8. g (p. 449)
9. b (p. 444)
10. e (p. 453)
11. j (p. 433)
12. n (p. 433)
13. f (p. 442)
14. d (p. 433)
15. m (p. 440)
16. o (p. 437)

MULTIPLE CHOICE PRETEST 1

1. B, Correct (p. 458)
   A., C., D. Wrong. Evolutionary theory stresses reproductive and protective value.
2. C, Correct (p. 432)
   A., B., D. Wrong. Physical attractiveness is associated with positive first impressions.
3. C, Correct (pp. 433-436)
   A., B., D. Wrong. These are all true.

4. C, Correct (pp. 437-438)
   A. Wrong. Consistency is a measure of whether the behavior always occurs in that situation.
   B., D. Wrong. Distinctiveness relates to whether the behavior occurs in other situations – information we are not given here.
5. D, Correct (p. 437)
   A., B. Wrong. These patterns are not strongly associated with a particular type of attribution.
   C. Wrong. This pattern is associated with external attributions.
6. B, Correct (p. 441)
   A. Wrong. The peripheral route emphasizes emotions, attractiveness, and other non-factual aspects.
   C. Wrong. This strategy involves the idea that a small concession will lead to a larger one.
   D. Wrong. Source characteristics are associated with attractiveness, power or celebrity – peripheral items.
7. C, Correct (p. 435)
   A. Wrong. Discrimination is behavior that is directed against members of a group.
   B. Wrong. Altruism is acting in a way that shows unselfish concern for the welfare of others.
   D. Wrong. Source characteristics are features of the person presenting a persuasive message.
8. D, Correct (p. 442)
   A. Wrong. This describes the self-fulfilling prophecy effect.
   B. Wrong. This is the self-serving bias, if the attributions involve one's own situation.
   C. Wrong. This describes the self-perception theory, which is an alternative to cognitive dissonance theory.
9. D, Correct (p. 446)
   A. Wrong. A self-fulfilling prophecy involves the influence of expectations on behavior.
   B. Wrong. The bystander effect involves a reduced tendency to help if other people are present.
   C. Wrong. The actor-observer effect is a pattern of attributions, not an audience effect.
10. C, Correct (p. 438)
   A. Wrong. Altruism is helping behavior, not assigning blame for a failure.
   B. Wrong. Dr. Marsh is making an attribution, not letting expectations affect his behavior.
   D. Wrong. Dr. Marsh is making an attribution. There is no mismatch of belief and behavior.
11. D, Correct (p. 439)
   A. Wrong. He did not make an internal attribution about someone else's behavior.
   B. Wrong. He didn't change his behavior based on his expectations.
   C. Wrong. The elaboration likelihood model concerns attitude change, not attribution.
12. C, Correct (p. 447)
   A. Wrong. This effect involves the tendency to make internal attributions about other people's behavior.
   B. Wrong. Cognitive dissonance produces a change in attitude. It isn't an audience effect on helping.
   D. Wrong. Reciprocal altruism is helping in the expectation that in the future you'll be helped in turn. It doesn't explain a failure to get help if a lot of people are present.
13. D, Correct (p. 448)
   A. Wrong. The bystander effect is the reluctance to help if others are present.
   B. Wrong. Group polarization is the tendency to make more extreme decisions in a group.
   C. Wrong. Lowballing is a technique involving getting agreement to a low figure, then introducing a high one.
14. A, Correct (p. 444)
   B. Wrong. This error involves attributions. Self-perception theory involves attitudes.
   C. Wrong. Deindividuation is a loss of individualism in a group. Self-perception theory involves attitudes.
   D. Wrong. Social loafing is explained in terms of diffusion of responsibility. Bem's theory involves attitudes.
15. C, Correct (p. 449)
   A. Wrong. Obedience is following an order. April wasn't ordered to do anything.
   B. Wrong. Group polarization causes extreme decisions. April following the group is critical here.
   D. Wrong. Reciprocity involves returning the feelings of another individual in kind.
16. B, Correct (p. 446)
   A. Wrong. The bystander effect would involve a failure to help, not immediate help.
   C. Wrong. Deindividuation is a loss or personal identity, not helping behavior.
   D. Wrong. Groupthink involves group decisions. No decision is involved in this question.

17. D, Correct (pp. 451-452)
   A. Wrong. Moving to a more extreme view is not the key issue in this situation; a rush to consensus is.
   B. Wrong. Nobody is being offered a low price and then asked to pay a higher one, as in low-balling.
   C. Wrong. The fundamental attribution error involves internal attributions, not stressing consensus.
18. D, Correct (pp. 453-454)
   A. Wrong. Obedience is reduced but is still quite common when the setting is not prestigious.
   B. Wrong. The fact that they were very upset disproves the idea they knew about the hoax.
   C. Wrong. More obedience occurs if the authority figure leaves.
19. A, Correct (p. 461)
   B. Wrong. Friendships are facilitated by proximity and mere exposure.
   C. Wrong. Friendships are facilitated by proximity, mere exposure, and similarity.
   D. Wrong. Friendships are less likely when people are dissimilar.
20. C, Correct (p. 463)
   A., B., D. Wrong. These do not involve the intense arousal of passionate love.

MULTIPLE CHOICE PRETEST 2

1. D, Correct (p. 433)
   A. Wrong. Cognitive dissonance would occur if Bob's actions and attitudes didn't match.
   B. Wrong. Self-serving bias is making internal attributions for your success, external ones for failures.
   C. Wrong. The actor-observer effect is a pattern of attribution. The key in this question is Bob's expectations causing behavior which results in his expectations being confirmed.
2. D, Correct (p. 433)
   A. Wrong. The elaboration likelihood model contrasts central and peripheral routes to persuasion, not attitudes based on group membership.
   B. Wrong. The actor-observer effect is the tendency to make external attributions about our own behavior, but internal attributions about others' behavior.
   C. Wrong. Attributions are explanations of behavior. There is no behavior to be explained.
3. C, Correct (p. 437)
   A. Wrong. If you decide based on whether problems always occur in concerts, consistency is involved.
   B. Wrong. Checking what other people do involves consensus.
   D. Wrong. Expectation looks forward.
4. A, Correct (p. 439)
   B. Wrong. Deindividuation is a loss of personal identity in a group. It doesn't involve attribution style.
   C. Wrong. Cognitive dissonance relates to attitudes, not attribution style.
   D. Wrong. Self-fulfilling prophesies do not relate to different attributions for others versus one's own behavior.
5. A, Correct (p. 438)
   B., C., D. Wrong. These are all external attributions. Fundamental attribution error is a bias to make internal attributions about someone else.
6. A, Correct (p. 440)
   B. Wrong. The emphasis is on repetition, not an association of neutral and unconditioned stimuli.
   C. Wrong. The emphasis is on repetition. Responses (attitudes) are not being reinforced or punished.
   D. Wrong. Deindividuation occurs in a large group. The saying doesn't involve group influences.
7. C, Correct (p. 440)
   A., B. Wrong. These are cognitive components.
   D. Wrong. These are affective components.
8. A, Correct (p. 441)
   B. Wrong. He is not emphasizing direct facts. The ad emphasizes emotion.
   C. Wrong. There is no mismatch of behavior and attitude here. The key is his use of emotional input.
   D. Wrong. There is no reinforcement here. His use of emotional information is the critical factor.

9. B, Correct (pp. 442-443)

   A. Wrong. Tom can justify his work because he is paid, so no dissonance and no shift occur.

   C., D. Wrong. Kit has more dissonance than Tom. She is freely supporting Smith, so her attitude will remain more positive to better match her behavior.

10. D, Correct (p. 451)

    A. Wrong. The discussion was well balanced, so groupthink didn't occur.

    B. Wrong. An audience didn't improve performance. Positions became more extreme.

    C. Wrong. Conformity to be like the group is not an issue. The issue is the shift to an extreme view.

11. D, Correct (p. 444)

    A. Wrong. Consensus relates to whether others behave similarly.

    B. Wrong. Self-fulfilling prophecy involves the effect of one person's attitudes on another person's behavior, not the effect of compliance with small requests.

    C. Wrong. There is no indication that conforming to a group's standard is relevant in this question.

12. A, Correct (p. 443)

    B. Wrong. Ben is basing his attitude on his behavior, not changing it due to dissonance.

    C. Wrong. Ben is not making an internal attribution about someone's behavior.

    D. Wrong. Ben's attitude is based on an evaluation of his past behavior, not central or peripheral routes.

13. B, Correct (p. 458)

    A. Wrong. Group polarization is a move to extreme decisions. Altruism isn't involved.

    C. Wrong. Elaboration likelihood is a view of persuasion, not a model of altruism.

    D. Wrong. Covariation theory is a view of attribution and doesn't involve helping behavior.

14. B, Correct (p. 449)

    A. Wrong. Key here is not feeling like an individual, not a more extreme decision after discussion.

    C. Wrong. There was no improved performance due to an audience here.

    D. Wrong. Fred did not return the feelings shown toward him. The key here is loss of individuality.

15. B, Correct (p. 447)

    A. Wrong. Self-perception theory relates to attitude change, not the situations described.

    C. Wrong. These statements do not explain the cause of behavior in terms of personal traits.

    D. Wrong. The focus of the statements is on other people's participation in events, not on returning feelings shown by others toward oneself.

16. D, Correct (p. 456)

    A., B., C. Wrong. These are all characteristic of Western cultures.

17. C, Correct (p. 459)

    A., B., D. Wrong. Averaged, prototypical faces were preferred.

18. A, Correct (p. 458)

    B., C., D. Wrong. These are all true, but babies do tend to prefer attractive faces.

19. B, Correct (p. 461)

    A., C., D. Wrong. Similarity is a strong determinant of friendship.

20. D, Correct (p. 463)

    A. Wrong. Commitment is a decision to remain in the relationship.

    B. Wrong. Reciprocity isn't a dimension in Sternberg's theory. It is a tendency to like someone who likes you.

    C. Wrong. Passion involves intense erotic feelings.

CHAPTER **14**

PSYCHOLOGICAL DISORDERS

ESTABLISHING LEARNING GOALS

Use these learning goals as a preview of the chapter, a guide for active reading, and to evaluate your mastery of the material. Review the relevant goals as you begin and end your reading of each major section of the chapter.

I. Discuss the definition of abnormality.

   A. Evaluate the various criteria that have been used to define abnormality.

   B. Discuss the legal definition of insanity.

   C. Explain how the medical model classifies and categorizes abnormality.

   D. Discuss the effects of diagnostic labeling.

II. Discuss how psychological disorders are classified.

   A. Describe the DSM-IV-TR.

   B. Describe the common anxiety disorders.
      1. Compare the symptoms of generalized anxiety disorder, panic disorder, and specific phobias.
      2. Describe obsessive-compulsive disorder.
      3. Describe the influence of gender and culture on anxiety disorders.

   C. Describe the somatoform disorders.
      1. Differentiate hypochondriasis, somatization disorder and conversion disorder.
      2. Describe the influence of gender and culture on the somatoform disorders.

   D. Describe the common dissociative disorders.
      1. Compare dissociative amnesia and dissociative fugue.
      2. Describe dissociative identity disorder, and discuss why this disorder is controversial.

   E. Describe the common mood disorders.
      1. Describe the symptoms of a major depressive episode.
      2. Describe bipolar disorder.
      3. Discuss the risk factors for suicide and how suicide can be prevented.
      4. Describe the influence of gender and culture on mood disorders.

   F. Describe the characteristics of schizophrenia.
      1. Differentiate positive and negative symptoms and give examples of each.

   2. Describe the influence of gender and culture on schizophrenia.
  G. Describe the common personality disorders.
   1. Compare paranoid, dependent, and antisocial personality disorders.
   2. Explain why personality disorders are not listed as Axis I disorders.

III. Solve the practical problem of understanding the origin of psychological disorders.
  A. Explain how biological and genetic factors can contribute to psychological disorders.
   1. Describe the role of neurotransmitters in schizophrenia and mood disorders.
   2. Describe structural changes in the brain associated with psychological disorders.
   3. Describe the evidence for a genetic predisposition for schizophrenia and mood disorders.
  B. Explain how maladaptive thoughts can contribute to psychological disorders.
   1. Describe the types of attributions that are characteristic of psychological disorders.
   2. Explain the learned helplessness theory of depression.
  C. Explain how environmental factors can contribute to psychological disorders.

MASTERING THE MATERIAL

PREVIEW & CONCEPTUALIZING ABNORMALITY: WHAT IS ABNORMAL BEHAVIOR? (PP. 471-478)

MASTERING THE VOCABULARY

Define or explain each of the following terms.

1. statistical deviance
2. cultural deviance
3. emotional distress
4. dysfunction
5. insanity
6. medical model
7. diagnostic labeling effects

MASTERING THE CONCEPTS

Fill in the blanks to create a summary of the section.

Three issues are explored: How should abnormal behavior be defined? How can psychological disorders be classified? What are the underlying causes of psychological disorders?

Abnormality can be defined in terms of [1] ____________ deviance or infrequency, [2] ____________ deviance, emotional [3] ____________ , or [4] ____________ , a breakdown in normal functioning. Any one definition is insufficient to define abnormality, and some disorders involve exaggerations of normal behavior. Normal and abnormal behavior are considered to form a continuum, not clear-cut categories. [5] ____________ is a legal concept and is usually defined based on the person's ability to understand whether an action is right or wrong.

The [6] ____________ model views abnormality as a symptom of disease. Support for this includes the important role of neurotransmitters and the fact that disorders may be classified in terms of [7] ____________ . Criticisms focus on a lack of identifiable physical causes for some disorders, the idea that some problems are "problems in living," cultural differences in "abnormal" behavior, and the stigma of diagnostic [8] ____________ . Rosenhan's pseudopatient study shows that labels affect the interpretation of later behavior.

EVALUATING YOUR PROGRESS

Select the best response. If you make any errors, reread the relevant material before proceeding.

1. Behaviors that are very infrequent might be classified as abnormal using the criterion of
   a. statistical deviance.
   b. cultural deviance.
   c. dysfunction.
   d. emotional distress.

2. The criterion used to determine insanity is
   a. proof of a neurotransmitter imbalance.
   b. diagnosis of a mental disorder.
   c. statistical and cultural deviance of action, accompanied by emotional distress.
   d. an inability to understand the wrongfulness of the behavior due to a mental problem.

3. Some psychological disorders can be treated with drugs that affect neurotransmitters, and many psychological disorders may be reliably classified in terms of measurable symptoms. These facts support
   a. the legal definition of insanity.
   b. the medical model of abnormality.
   c. the need to consider the context of a behavior before labeling a person psychologically abnormal.
   d. the need for more than one type of deviance to declare a person psychologically abnormal.

4. Rosenhan's pseudopatient study is important because it showed
   a. psychologists are incompetent in most cases.
   b. patients in mental hospitals receive inhumane treatment.
   c. the medical model of psychological disorders is most appropriate.
   d. expectations and labels influence the interpretation of behavior.

CLASSIFYING PSYCHOLOGICAL DISORDERS: DMS-IV-TR (PP. 478-493)

MASTERING THE VOCABULARY

Define or explain each of the following terms.

1. DSM-IV-TR
2. anxiety disorders
3. generalized anxiety disorder
4. panic disorder
5. agoraphobia
6. obsessive-compulsive disorder
7. specific phobic disorder
8. somatoform disorders
9. hypochondriasis
10. somatization disorder
11. conversion disorder
12. dissociative disorders
13. dissociative fugue
14. dissociative amnesia
15. dissociative identity disorder
16. mood disorders

17. major depressive episode
18. bipolar disorder
19. manic state
20. schizophrenia
21. personality disorders
22. paranoid personality disorder
23. dependent personality disorder
24. antisocial personality disorder

MASTERING THE CONCEPTS.

Fill in the blanks to create a summary of the section.

DSM-IV-TR is a [1] ____________ system based on objective, measurable criteria without reference to therapy. Axis I, clinical syndromes, and Axis II, [2] ____________ disorders, classify abnormal behavior. Axis III notes [3] ____________ conditions, Axis IV notes [4] ____________ problems, and Axis V evaluates current daily functioning.

Persistent and intense anxiety that interferes with behavior characterizes the [5] ____________ disorders. In [6] ____________ anxiety disorder, the anxiety is free-floating and unrealistic and may cause physical symptoms related to the autonomic nervous system. In [7] ____________ disorder, anxiety is sudden, relatively brief, but intense. If an attack occurs in public, the person may develop [8] ____________ , a fear of going into public places. Obsessive-compulsive disorder involves obsessions, which are persistent [9] ____________ , and compulsions, a need to perform an action. A specific, irrational fear is found in specific [10] ____________ disorder. [11] ____________ are most likely to be diagnosed with anxiety disorders, and cultural differences are found, also.

[12] ____________ disorders focus on the body. In hypochondriasis, normal bodily reactions are interpreted as serious medical conditions. In somatization disorder, the focus is on [13] ____________ without a physical cause, rather than the possible disease. In [14] ____________ disorder, the person has a true symptom but no real physical disorder, such as paralysis when the nervous system is normal.

The [15] ____________ disorders involve a separation of conscious awareness from memories. Dissociative amnesia involves memory loss not due to head injury. Dissociative [16] ____________ involves a loss of memory for identity and a flight from the home. Dissociative [17] ____________ disorder involves more than one personality. This disorder is controversial, and not all psychologists accept it.

The mood disorders involve prolonged, disabling disruptions of emotional state, including depressive disorders and [18] ____________ disorders. A major depressive episode involves behavioral changes, low mood, and a pessimistic outlook. Milder, more chronic depression is [19] ____________ disorder. [20] ____________ depression is dysthymic disorder with a major depressive episode. Depression is more common in women, but occurs cross-culturally. In bipolar disorder, mood swings from depression to a [21] ____________ state of hyperactivity and abnormal thought. The risk factors for suicide include psychological disorders like depression, sudden stress, suicidal [22] ____________ , and prior attempts. Suicide among young adults can be reduced through gatekeeper training, [23] ____________ skills training, the availability of crisis centers, and increased media awareness.

[24] ____________ involves disordered thoughts, emotion, and behavior, but symptoms vary across cases. Symptoms are classified as [25] ____________ if they involve an excess or added behavior, and [26] ____________ if they involve a deficit. Schizophrenia often involves hallucinations, [27] ____________ without a sensory cause, and [28] ____________ , thoughts with inappropriate content. Speech may be disordered, thoughts may be disconnected, emotions may be flat, and bizarre postures may be held for long periods, [29] ____________ . Some gender and racial differences in onset and outcome occur with schizophrenia.

Axis II describes personality disorders, chronic patterns of behavior that lead to impaired [30] ____________ function. People with [31] ____________ personality disorder show a pervasive distrust of others, [32] ____________ personality disorder involves the need to be taken care of, and [33] ____________ personality disorder involves no respect for social customs and an absence of guilt. Personality disorders are more ingrained and inflexible than Axis I disorders, and some psychologists argue they are not true disorders, only extreme versions of personality traits.

EVALUATING YOUR PROGRESS

Select the best response. If you miss any questions, reread the relevant material before proceeding.

1. The DSM-IV-TR is
   a. a diagnostic system for psychological disorders.
   b. the three different major classifications of psychological disorders.
   c. the standard used to determine insanity in the United States.
   d. a series of guidelines used to determine the best therapy for a given problem.
2. Panic disorder and specific phobic disorder are two types of
   a. somatoform disorders.
   b. mood disorders.
   c. anxiety disorders.
   d. personality disorders.
3. The disorder in which a particular object or situation produces an intense, unrealistic fear is
   a. panic disorder.
   b. obsessive-compulsive disorder.
   c. manic state.
   d. specific phobic disorder.
4. Garth has to get up several times at night to check each door and window. His behavior is an example of
   a. a phobia.
   b. an obsession.
   c. a delusion.
   d. a compulsion.
5. Hypochondriasis and conversion disorder are
   a. somatoform disorders.
   b. personality disorders.
   c. dissociative disorders.
   d. anxiety disorders.
6. A loss of personal identity accompanied by escape or flight from the home environment represents
   a. agoraphobia.
   b. dissociative fugue.
   c. dissociative identity disorder.
   d. dysthymia.
7. Bipolar disorder is characterized by
   a. hallucinations and language disorders.
   b. alternation between depression and a manic state.
   c. dysthymia and a major depressive episode.
   d. two or more personalities.

8. All of the following are characteristic of schizophrenia except
   a. disordered thoughts.
   b. disordered language.
   c. inappropriate emotions.
   d. multiple personalities.
9. Fred hears voices in his head that tell him to injure himself. This is an example of
   a. a delusion.
   b. catatonia.
   c. an hallucination.
   d. conversion disorder.
10. Personality disorders are not on the same axis as the clinical syndromes of Axis I because they
    a. generally seem to be due to a specific brain dysfunction, unlike the clinical syndromes.
    b. are more ingrained and inflexible, and are resistant to treatment, unlike the clinical syndromes.
    c. come and go without treatment much more often than the clinical syndromes.
    d. involve statistically deviant behavior, but not maladaptive behavior.

UNDERSTANDING PSYCHOLOGICAL DISORDERS: BIOLOGICAL, COGNITIVE, OR ENVIRONMENTAL? (PP. 494-500)

MASTERING THE VOCABULARY

Define or explain each of the following terms.

1. bio-psycho-social perspective
2. learned helplessness

MASTERING THE CONCEPTS

Fill in the blanks to create a summary of the section.

The bio-psycho-social perspective recognizes the multiple causes of abnormality. Signs of abnormal brain chemistry or brain structures and evidence for a genetic component to disorders support a biological explanation of some psychological disorders. Schizophrenia may involve an excess of [1] ___________ or an interaction between dopamine and other neurotransmitters. Schizophrenia also is associated with low activity in the frontal lobes and enlarged [2] ___________ . For mood disorders, the monoamine neurotransmitters [3] ___________ , norepineprine and dopamine may be involved. The true role of these abnormalities is unclear, however.

There is a strong [4] ____________ predisposition for schizophrenia and mood disorders. Concordance rates for identical twins with schizophrenia are very high and also very high for [5] ____________ disorders. Children whose parents have these disorders are at greater risk, even if adopted into healthy homes. Genes are not the only important factor, however.

Thought patterns also may be a determinant of mood disorders. People prone to depression tend to make attributions that are [6] ____________ , stable, and global. If repeated failures occur, learned [7] ____________ can occur, leading to passive behavior and depression.

Evidence suggests some disorders may be learned or influenced by cultural factors. [8] ____________ might be classically conditioned, and abnormal behaviors, if reinforced, can be acquired through [9] ____________ conditioning. Observational learning also may contribute to the development of phobias.

EVALUATING YOUR PROGRESS

Select the best response. If you miss any questions, reread the relevant material before proceeding.

1. Although several neurotransmistters might be involved, dopamine appears to be especially important in
   a. personality disorders.
   b. schizophrenia.
   c. anxiety disorders.
   d. dissociative disorders.

2. If your identical twin is schizophrenic, the likelihood that you will develop schizophrenia is approximately
   a. 90%.
   b. 75%.
   c. 50%.
   d. 20%.

3. The data concerning genetic influences on mood disorders shows that
   a. mood disorders have no significant genetic component.
   b. mood disorders have a significant genetic component, but it is weaker than that for schizophrenia.
   c. mood disorders have a genetic component at least as strong as that for schizophrenia.
   d. mood disorders are entirely due to genetic factors.

4. Maladaptive attributions are more common when people are depressed. This is evidence that supports explanations based on
   a. cognitive factors.
   b. classical conditioning.
   c. modeling.
   d. operant conditioning.

5. Which disorder does animal research suggest may be learned?
   a. schizophrenia
   b. dissociative disorder
   c. panic disorder
   d. specific phobic disorder

6. Which neurotransmitter is affected by Prozac, an antidepressant, and may be involved in mood disorders?
   a. acteylcholine
   b. serotonin
   c. GABA
   d. lithium carbonate

MAKING FINAL PREPARATIONS

Complete these sections without consulting your book or notes. For a more accurate estimate of how well you know this material, wait at least a day or two after studying the chapter before working on the questions. Some of the material you "know" immediately after working with the chapter will be quickly forgotten. Exercises completed too soon after studying will overestimate what you know well.

SHORT ESSAY QUESTIONS

Write a brief answer to each question.

1. Identify the four criteria for abnormality and discuss why classifying abnormal behavior is difficult.

   ____

   ____

2. Discuss the purpose of Axes III, IV, and V of the DSM-IV-TR.

   ____

   ____

3. Explain how insanity differs from psychological abnormality.

____

____

4. Compare generalized anxiety disorder and specific phobic disorder.

____

____

5. Explain what positive and negative symptoms are, and give an example of each.

____

____

6. Explain how classical conditioning, instrumental conditioning and observational learning could influence the development of specific phobic disorder.

____

____

MATCHING

Select the correct definition or description for each item.

1. ________ dependent personality disorder
2. ________ catatonia
3. ________ double depression
4. ________ delusion of persecution
5. ________ anxiety disorders
6. ________ dysthymic disorder
7. ________ delusion of grandeur
8. ________ personality disorders
9. ________ dissociative disorder
10. ________ flat affect
11. ________ mood disorders
12. ________ somatoform disorders
13. ________ learned helplessness
14. ________ schizophrenia

a. belief that others are plotting against you
b. disorder with thought, emotion, and behavior defects
c. chronic behavior causing impaired social function
d. lack of emotion
e. disorders that focus on the body
f. involves excessive need to be cared for
g. chronic, moderate depression
h. tendency to hold strange postures for a long time
i. sense of helplessness after repeated failures
j. prolonged and disabling disruption of emotion
k. major depressive episode added to dysthymia
l. the thought you are someone famous
m. disorders with separation of awareness and memory
n. disorders with excessive, prolonged apprehension

MULTIPLE CHOICE PRETEST 1

Select the one best response.

1. If a behavior is classified as abnormal because it violates accepted rules of behavior, abnormality is being defined by
   a. cultural deviance.
   b. dysfunction.
   c. emotional distress.
   d. statistical deviance.
2. Criticisms of the medical model of psychological disorders include the idea that
   a. the medical model sees many disorders as problems with living.
   b. the medical model puts too much emphasis on cultural context.
   c. some mental disorders have no well-defined or consistent physical cause.
   d. behavioral symptoms allow reliable classification of many disorders.
3. Rosenhan's pseudopatient study is most important for demonstrating
   a. the impact of diagnostic labeling effects.
   b. the need to evaluate medical conditions, stressors, and general functioning when diagnosing disorders.
   c. the inconsistency of psychological diagnoses.
   d. that dissociative identity disorder is probably role-playing in many cases.
4. Axis III, IV, and V on the DSM-IV-TR focus on
   a. personality disorders, clinical syndromes, and developmental disorders.
   b. anxiety disorders, mood disorders, and schizophrenia.
   c. medical conditions, psychosocial problems, and general level of function.
   d. cause, recommended treatment, and prognosis (likely outcome).
5. Obsessive-compulsive disorder is an example of
   a. an anxiety disorder.
   b. a somatoform disorder.
   c. a dissociative disorder.
   d. a mood disorder.
6. Pam has been diagnosed with conversion disorder. She is likely to experience
   a. a loss of personal identity and memory.
   b. sudden onset of extreme anxiety.
   c. hallucinations, delusions, and disorganized thought.
   d. physical symptoms that have no detectable physical basis.
7. Which is a negative symptom of schizophrenia?
   a. flat affect
   b. catatonia
   c. delusions
   d. disorganized speech

8. Several times over the past month, Sam went to the hospital because he thought he was having a heart attack. His heart would race, he suddenly would be extremely anxious, and he could hardly breathe. If the diagnosis wasn't heart attack, it probably was
   a. generalized anxiety disorder.
   b. dysthymic disorder.
   c. bipolar disorder.
   d. panic disorder.

9. The disorder characterized by the existence of more than one personality, usually with little shared awareness, is known as
   a. dissociative identity disorder.
   b. schizophrenia.
   c. agoraphobia.
   d. bipolar disorder.

10. For weeks, Claire has mostly stayed in bed. Her mood is extremely negative, and she can't seem to force herself to do anything. Claire's problem is likely to be
    a. dependent personality disorder.
    b. major depressive episode.
    c. dissociative fugue.
    d. conversion disorder.

11. We know that schizophrenia is not entirely due to genetic factors because
    a. children raised apart from their schizophrenic parents have a greater rate of schizophrenia than their adoptive siblings.
    b. children raised apart from their schizophrenic parents have the same rate of schizophrenia as their adoptive siblings.
    c. the concordance rate for fraternal twins is very low.
    d. the concordance rate for identical twins is not 100%.

12. Which of the following will be least useful for improving suicide prevention among young people?
    a. Train teachers and coaches to recognize the warning signs for suicide.
    b. Improve availability of suicide hotline services.
    c. Increase media coverage of suicides when they occur.
    d. Teach coping and general life skills to young people.

13. The physiological factors associated with schizophrenia include
    a. brain swelling.
    b. higher than usual frontal lobe activity.
    c. larger than usual ventricles.
    d. neurofibrillary tangles in the cortex.

14. Micah is a serial killer who killed without guilt. Micah's behavior is characteristic of
    a. paranoid personality disorder.
    b. dependent personality disorder.
    c. antisocial personality disorder.
    d. multiple personality disorder.

15. Mood disorders seem to involve a problem with
    a. GABA.
    b. glutamate.
    c. monoamines.
    d. acetylcholine.

16. People prone to depression are likely to make attributions about failures that are
    a. global, stable, and internal.
    b. global, unstable, and internal.
    c. specific, unstable, and external.
    d. specific, stable, and external.

17. For years, Bonita has seen her mother's extremely fearful behavior at the sight of a dog. Now Bonita is showing the same reactions. This suggests Bonita's excessive fear was caused by
    a. operant conditioning.
    b. learned helplessness.
    c. modeling.
    d. observational learning.

MULTIPLE CHOICE PRETEST 2

Select the one best response.

1. Which of the following is an Axis II disorder in DMS-IV-TR?
    a. dependent personality disorder
    b. dissociative identity disorder
    c. schizophrenia
    d. somatoform disorder

2. Sal's ideas about germs and contamination make life very difficult. He eats little and is underweight. He won't go out in public, which cost him his job and friends. Sal's behavior would be considered abnormal based on
    a. statistical deviance.
    b. personal distress.
    c. cultural deviance.
    d. dysfunction.

3. Ted believes that drug therapy is the best approach for treating psychological problems because psychological problems are really illnesses caused by biochemical abnormalities. Ted believe in
   a. the results of the Rosenhan study.
   b. the medical model.
   c. the standard view of insanity.
   d. the DSM-IV-TR.

4. Yan, who has a history of depression, is likely to explain being laid off from work by saying,
   a. "It was just luck, I guess. I was one of the most recently hired, so I'm the first to go."
   b. "That foreman never liked me, no matter how hard I worked."
   c. "I'm just incompetent. I was rotten in school, and now I'm rotten in my job."
   d. "I wasn't very good at my job yet. I'll get more training, and this won't happen again."

5. You know your roommate has a history of anorexia nervosa. When you see her eat very little at dinner and then go to work out at the gym, you see this as a sign of another anorexic episode beginning. You don't think that when other people act the same way. Your behavior is consistent with
   a. a diagnostic labeling effect.
   b. Axis II of the DSM-IV-TR.
   c. dissociation.
   d. the medical model approach.

6. Last week, May was exceptionally excited and rushed around buying unneeded items and making wild plans – none of which were ever completed. This week May is extremely depressed and has talked about committing suicide. A psychologist is likely to diagnose
   a. double depression.
   b. dysthymia.
   c. schizophrenia.
   d. bipolar disorder.

7. A loss of memory for one's identity and personal history that is not caused by physical problems such as a stroke or head injury would likely be diagnosed as
   a. conversion disorder.
   b. dissociative identity disorder.
   c. dissociative fugue.
   d. dissociative amnesia.

8. Pat never seems relaxed, and she worries all the time about everything. As a result, he is finding it difficult to accomplish anything. Pat's diagnosis is likely to be
   a. obsessive-compulsive disorder.
   b. panic disorder.
   c. agoraphobia.
   d. generalized anxiety disorder.

9. Woody Allen's characters often interpret minor physical symptoms as major diseases. A headache means a brain tumor, and minor indigestion means stomach cancer. This behavior is characteristic of
   a. a somatoform disorder.
   b. a dissociative disorder.
   c. an anxiety disorder.
   d. a personality disorder.
10. Psychologists have noticed that agoraphobia is often associated with
   a. bad childhood experiences with spiders.
   b. having previously experienced a panic attack in public.
   c. early childhood sexual abuse.
   d. unusually "cold" parents.
11. Which of the following disorders does *not* appear more frequently in women than in men?
   a. schizophrenia
   b. depression
   c. conversion disorder
   d. generalized anxiety disorder
12. The primary difference in hypochondriasis and somatization disorder is that
   a. hypochondriasis focuses on the possible disease and somatization disorder focuses on the symptoms.
   b. the anxiety is general in hypochondriasis, but it is linked to a specific idea or thing in somatization disorder.
   c. there are actual physical problems in hypochondriasis but not in somatization disorder.
   d. hypochondriasis develops rapidly, but somatization disorder develops more slowly.
13. Mina's thoughts are extremely disordered and her emotions are either absent or inappropriate. She thinks she is Mother Theresa, and she was found wandering the streets in her nightgown. Mina's diagnosis is probably
   a. bipolar disorder.
   b. dissociative identity disorder.
   c. schizophrenia.
   d. generalized anxiety disorder.
14. Most drugs used to treat schizophrenia block the activity of
   a. dopamine.
   b. serotonin.
   c. acetylcholine.
   d. norepinephrine.
15. Sue is depressed. Her psychologist suggested that she has simply given up because of the many failures she has experienced. Apparently Sue's psychologist believes depression is the result of
   a. classical conditioning.
   b. modeling.
   c. learned helplessness.
   d. instrumental conditioning.

16. The hyperactive, euphoric periods of bipolar disorder are
    a. delusions.
    b. dissociations.
    c. fugue episodes.
    d. manic states.

17. The "schizo" in schizophrenia means "split." This split refers to
    a. consciousness and memory.
    b. personality or identity.
    c. attributions.
    d. the mind or thoughts.

18. Adam and Wilma both have schizophrenia. Their child, Thea, was raised in a healthy adoptive family without contact with Wilma and Adam. The likelihood that Thea will develop schizophrenia is
    a. equal to the general population's likelihood.
    b. equal to her adoptive siblings' likelihood.
    c. much higher than her adoptive siblings' likelihood.
    d. almost 100%.

LANGUAGE DEVELOPMENT GUIDE

CORE TERMS

In the lectures on this chapter, you are likely to hear terms like ***pathology***, ***impaired***, ***dysfunction***, ***lesion***, ***compromised*** and ***debilitating***. Not surprisingly, these are all words having to do with disease. A *lesion*, as you may remember from chapter 3, is a cut or injury; *pathology* refers to a disease that causes damage. A lesion of the brain is likely to cause *impairment* or *dysfunction* -- the injured part of the brain won't work properly anymore. Another way to say it is that the function of that part will be *compromised*. Such an injury would be *debilitating* -- it would destroy the ability of the brain to function properly.

Since there are many more conditions described in the DSM than are discussed in the book, don't be surprised if you hear about others in class. Your instructor is also likely to talk about some famous ***case studies***, or share ***anecdotes*** (brief stories) about patients they have heard about or treated. These can be both interesting and helpful when you study. Remember, elaborative thinking improves recall -- so thinking of interesting examples will help you recall the material you need to learn.

IDIOMS

p. 472	the general public	most people
p. 473	sole criterion for	the only way of judging something
p. 477	pseudopatient	someone who is pretending to be ill
p. 482	jingle	short song used in advertisements
p. 485	colorful types	people with unusual personalities
p. 485	Hollywood	California city where movies and TV programs are made
p. 485	the popular press	magazines or newspapers read by the general public
p. 485	amnesiac	someone suffering from amnesia
p. 487	the community at large	the whole community; most of the people involved
p. 488	grandiosity	a belief that you are much more powerful or important than you really are
p. 488	roller-coaster	a ride which sends you up and down hills very quickly
p. 490	gone awry	gone wrong; gone off course
p. 497	adoptees	those who have been adopted
p. 497	extraterrestrials	'people' from outer space; aliens
p. 498	plays a pivotal role	influences an important change

PRONUNCIATION

dysfunction (dis-funk′-shun) *p. 475*
anxiety (ang-zy′-i-tee) *p. 481*
agoraphobia (uh-gore-i-fo′-bee-a) *p. 481*
hypochondriasis (hy-po-kon-dry′-uh-sis) *p. 484*
fugue (fewg) *p. 486*
schizophrenia (skiz-o-fren′-ee-uh or skiz-o-freen′-ee-uh) *p. 490*

SOLUTIONS

PREVIEW & CONCEPTUALIZING ABNORMALITY: WHAT IS ABNORMAL BEHAVIOR? (PP. 471-478)

MASTERING THE CONCEPTS

1. statistical (p. 473)
2. cultural (p. 474)
3. distress (p. 474)
4. dysfunction (p. 475)
5. Insanity (p. 476)
6. medical model (p. 476)
7. symptoms (p. 476)
8. labeling (p. 477)

EVALUATING YOUR PROGRESS

1. A, Correct (p. 473)
   B. Wrong. Cultural deviance involves violations of cultural norms for acceptable behavior.
   C. Wrong. Dysfunction involves maladaptive behavior that might or might not violate rules.
   D. Wrong. Emotional distress involves personal feelings of emotional discomfort.
2. D, Correct (p. 476)
   A., B., C. Wrong. Insanity requires a lack of appreciation for the wrongfulness of the action.
3. B, Correct (p. 476)
   A., C., D. Wrong. Biological causes and "symptoms" relate to the medical model.
4. D, Correct (p. 477)
   A. Wrong. Diagnosis was based on reported symptoms. Absence of abnormality was later noted.
   B. Wrong. There is no indication of inhumane treatment.
   C. Wrong. This study says nothing about the validity of the medical model.

CLASSIFYING PSYCHOLOGICAL DISORDERS: DMS-IV-TR (PP. 478-493)

MASTERING THE CONCEPTS.

1. classification (p. 479)
2. personality (p. 480)
3. medical (p. 480)
4. psychosocial (p. 480)
5. anxiety (p. 481)
6. generalized (p. 481)
7. panic (p. 481)
8. agoraphobia (p. 481)
9. thoughts (p. 482)
10. phobic (p. 482)
11. Women (p. 483)
12. Somatoform (p. 484)
13. symptoms (p. 484)
14. conversion (p. 485)
15. dissociative (p. 485)
16. fugue (p. 486)
17. identity (p. 486)
18. bipolar (p. 488)
19. dysthymic (p. 488)
20. Double (p. 488)
21. manic (p. 488)
22. thinking (p. 488)
23. coping (p. 489)
24. Schizophrenia (p. 490)
25. positive (p. 491)
26. negative (p. 491)
27. perceptions (p. 491)
28. delusions (p. 491)
29. catatonia (p. 492)
30. social (p. 492)
31. paranoid (p. 492)
32. dependent (p. 492)
33. antisocial (p. 492)

EVALUATING YOUR PROGRESS

1. A, Correct (p. 479)
   B. Wrong. DSM-IV-TR is a classification or diagnostic system, and there are more than three major types of disorders.
   C. Wrong. The DSM-IV-TR is a diagnostic system. Insanity is a legal concept in which a disorder is only one of the criteria.
   D. Wrong. DSM-IV-TR says nothing about treatment. It only classifies disorders
2. C, Correct (p. 481)
   A. Wrong. Somatoform disorders include hypochondriasis, somatization disorder, and conversion disorder.
   B. Wrong. Mood disorders include depression and bipolar disorder, but not panic or specific phobic disorder.
   D. Wrong. Panic disorder and specific phobic disorder are Axis I clinical syndromes. Personality disorders are not clinical syndromes and are part of Axis 2 diagnoses.
3. D, Correct (p. 482)
   A. Wrong. Panic disorder involves sudden, nonspecific anxiety.
   B. Wrong. OCD includes intrusive thoughts and ritualistic behavior.
   C. Wrong. A manic state involves hyperactivity, not irrational fear of an object.
4. D, Correct (p. 482)
   A. Wrong. Phobias are intense, irrational fears.
   B. Wrong. Obsessions are persistent, uncontrollable thoughts. Getting up is a behavior.
   C. Wrong. Delusions are thoughts with inappropriate content.
5. A, Correct (p. 484)
   B. Wrong. Hypochondriasis and conversion disorder are Axis I clinical syndromes, not Axis II conditions like personality disorders.
   C. Wrong. Dissociative disorders involve consciousness and memory, not concern with the body.
   D. Wrong. Anxiety disorders do not focus on the body as do hypochondriasis and conversion disorder.
6. B, Correct (p. 486)
   A. Wrong. Agoraphobia is a fear of going out in public or leaving one's home.
   C. Wrong. Dissociative identity disorder is popularly called "multiple personalities."
   D. Wrong. Dysthymia is a chronic, low level depression.
7. B, Correct (p. 488)
   A. Wrong. Hallucinations and language disorders are characteristic of schizophrenia.
   C. Wrong. These are two types of mood states, but bipolar disorder doesn't include both of them.
   D. Wrong. Multiple personalities are characteristic of a dissociative disorder.
8. D, Correct (p. 491)
   A., B., C. Wrong. These are common in schizophrenia. Multiple personality occurs in a dissociative disorder.
9. C, Correct (p. 491)
   A. Wrong. Delusions are irrational thoughts.
   B. Wrong. Catatonia is the tendency to remain in a bizarre posture for hours.
   D. Wrong. Conversion disorder involves physical symptoms with no physical cause.
10. B, Correct (p. 492)
    A. Wrong. Personality disorders have not been linked to a specific brain dysfunction.
    C. Wrong. Personality disorders are more resistant to treatment than most clinical disorders.
    D. Wrong. Personality disorders produce maladaptive social behavior.

UNDERSTANDING PSYCHOLOGICAL DISORDERS: BIOLOGICAL, COGNITIVE, OR ENVIRONMENTAL? (PP. 494-500)

MASTERING THE CONCEPTS

1. dopamine (p. 495)
2. ventricles (p. 495)
3. serotonin (p. 495)

4. genetic (p. 496)
5. mood (p. 497)
6. internal (p. 498)
7. helplessness (p. 498)
8. Phobias (p. 499)
9. instrumental (p. 499)

EVALUATING YOUR PROGRESS

1. B, Correct (p. 495)
   A., C., D. Wrong. These disorders do not seem to be highly linked with dopamine. Schizophrenia is.
2. C, Correct (p. 496)
   A., B., D. Wrong. There is a 50% chance of the other twin developing schizophrenia.
3. C, Correct (p. 497)
   A., B., D. Wrong. Mood disorders have at least as strong a genetic component as schizophrenia.
4. A, Correct (p. 498)
   B., C., D. Wrong. These relate to learned behavior. Attributions are cognitive processes.
5. D, Correct (p. 499)
   A., B., C. Wrong. These disorders are unlikely to have a significant learned component.
6. B, Correct (p. 495)
   A., C., D. Wrong. Mood disorders involve the monoamine neurotransmitters: serotonin, norepinephrine, and dopamine.

MAKING FINAL PREPARATIONS

SHORT ESSAY QUESTIONS

1. The criteria are: statistical deviance (infrequent), cultural deviance (violates norms), emotional distress, and dysfunction (maladaptive). Problems arise because criteria can be violated, but the behavior might be considered normal, or a person who has a problem might not violate most criteria. Intense distress and maladaptive behavior is "normal" if linked to a death, but thought disorders that indicate mental problems might cause no serious problems, other than slight dysfunction. (pp. 473-475)
2. Axis III (medical conditions), Axis IV (psychosocial and environmental problems) and Axis V (level of function) provide a context in which symptoms are evaluated. This allows a very broad assessment and diagnosis and helps in treatment decisions. (pp. 479-480)
3. Insanity is a legal concept. Most definitions of insanity require the person not understand the wrongfulness of his or her actions as a result of a "mental disease." Thus, abnormality is a requirement, but the emphasis is on the lack of understanding of whether an action is right or wrong. (p. 476)
4. Both generalized anxiety disorder and specific phobic disorder are anxiety disorders and involve anxiety. In generalized anxiety disorder the anxiety is not tied to a specific object or situation; it is free-floating or a general state of anxiety. In specific phobic disorder the anxiety is focused on a specific object or event. (pp. 481-483)
5. Positive symptoms of schizophrenia are excessive or added behaviors, such as hallucinations (hearing voices) or delusions (thinking you're Napoleon). Negative symptoms are deficits in behavior, such as flat affect, a lack of emotional response. (pp. 491-492)
6. The specific fear found with phobias might be learned. If an object is paired with an US for fear, the object might become a CS for fear, setting the stage for a phobia. That is, if you fall off a high location, the height might become a CS for the US (sense of falling) for the UR (fear). If fear responses are reinforced by being given attention or other rewards, fear responses in that situation will become more common. Finally, watching someone exhibit fear responses to a situation can result in the observational learning of that behavior. Children who watch fear responses in the parents might learn to act the same way. (p. 499)

MATCHING

1. f (p. 492)
2. h (p. 491)
3. k (p. 488)
4. a (p. 491)
5. n (p. 481)
6. g (p. 488)
7. l (p. 491)
8. c (p. 492)
9. m (p. 485)
10. d (p. 492)
11. j (p. 487)
12. e (p. 484)
13. i (p. 498)
14. b (p. 490)

MULTIPLE CHOICE PRETEST 1

1. A, Correct (p. 474)

   B. Wrong. Dysfunction involves behavior that is not adaptive or prevents normal activities.

   C. Wrong. Emotional distress involves personal feelings of emotional discomfort.

   D. Wrong. Statistical deviance involves an infrequent behavior.

2. C, Correct (p. 476)

   A., B. Wrong. These are opposite to the actual criticisms.

   D. Wrong. This is a supporting fact, not a criticism.

3. A, Correct (p. 477)

   B. Wrong. Rosenhan's study revealed the impact of labeling effect, not the benefits of the DSM-IV-TR.

   C. Wrong. The pseudopatients were given relatively consistent diagnoses.

   D. Wrong. The pseudopatients were not faking a dissociative disorder.

4. C, Correct (p. 480)

   A. Wrong. These are on is Axis I and Axis II.

   B. Wrong. These are on Axis I.

   D. Wrong. DSM-IV-TR does not address causes, treatments, or prognosis.

5. A, Correct (p. 482)

   B. Wrong. The somatoform disorders discussed in the text include hypochondriasis, somatization disorder, and conversion disorder.

   C. Wrong. Dissociative disorders include dissociative amnesia, dissociative fugue, and dissociative identity disorder.

   D. Wrong. Mood disorders include major depressive episode, dysthymic disorder, and biopolar disorder.

6. D, Correct (p. 485)

   A. Wrong. This characterizes a dissociative disorder. Conversion disorder is a somatoform disorder.

   B. Wrong. This describes panic disorder, a type of anxiety disorder.

   C. Wrong. These are common in schizophrenia, not conversion disorder.

7. A, Correct (p. 491)

   B. Wrong. This is a disorganized symptom, not a negative symptom.

   C. Wrong. This is a positive symptom, not a negative symptom.

   D. Wrong. This is a disorganized symptom, not a negative symptom.

8. D, Correct (p. 481)

   A. Wrong. His anxiety is sudden and intense. Generalized anxiety disorder involves chronic anxiety.

   B. Wrong. Dysthymic disorder is chronic, relatively mild depression.

   C. Wrong. Bipolar disorder is the alternation of manic and depressed states, not anxiety.

9. A, Correct (p. 486)

   B. Wrong. Schizophrenia involves disordered thought, behavior, and emotion, not multiple selves.

   C. Wrong. Agoraphobia is a fear of going out in public places, not multiple personality.

   D. Wrong. Bipolar disorder is the alternation of manic and depressed states, not multiple personality.

10. B, Correct (p. 487)

    A. Wrong. Claire doesn't need others to take care of her all the time. She seems to be depressed.

    C. Wrong. Claire didn't lose her identity and flee the area.

    D. Wrong. Claire doesn't have great concern about bodily issues and changes.

11. D, Correct (p. 496)

    A. Wrong. This supports a genetic component but doesn't indicate how complete it is.

    B. Wrong. This is not true, but it would support a strong environmental component.

    C. Wrong. A low concordance rate for non-identical twins could be due to genes or environment.

12. C, Correct (p. 490)

    A., B., D. Wrong. These are all good proposals, but increased media coverage is likely to increase copycat suicides.

13. C, Correct (p. 495)

    A. Wrong. Brain shrinkage, not swelling, is associated with schizophrenia.

    B. Wrong. Frontal lobe activity is lower than normal.

    D. Wrong. Neurofibrillary tangles is characteristic of Alzheimer's disease, not schizophrenia.

14. C, Correct (p. 492)

    A. Wrong. Paranoid personality disorder involves a long-term distrust of other people.

    B. Wrong. Dependent personality is characterized by an excessive need to be cared for by others.

    D. Wrong. Multiple personality disorder involves having more than one personality, not distrust.

15. C, Correct (p. 495)

    A., B., D. Wrong. Mood disorders involve monoamines such as serotonin, dopamine, and norepinephrine.

16. A, Correct (p. 498)

    B., C., D. Wrong. Their attributions are global, stable, and internal.

17. C, Correct (p. 482)

    A. Wrong. There is no mention of being reinforced, so operant conditioning probably isn't a factor.

    B. Wrong. Bonita has not giving up trying. She is modeling things she has seen her mother do.

    D. Wrong. The key here is the observation of her mother's behavior, not the predictive value of dogs.

MULTIPLE CHOICE PRETEST 2

1. A, Correct (p. 479)

   B., C., D. Wrong. These are all Axis I clinical disorders, not Axis II personality disorders.

2. D, Correct (p. 475)

   A. Wrong. Statistical deviance deals with frequency of behavior. Sal's behavior is maladaptive.

   B. Wrong. There is no personal distress noted. Sal's behavior is maladaptive.

   C. Wrong. These behaviors don't seriously violate cultural norms. Of greater importance is the fact they are maladaptive.

3. B, Correct (p. 476)

   A. Wrong. The Rosenhan study examined expectancy or labeling effects.

   C. Wrong. Insanity is a legal concept that makes no assumptions about cause or treatment.

   D. Wrong. The DSM-IV-TR is a book describing diagnostic guidelines for mental disorders.

4. C, Correct (p. 498)

   A., B. Wrong. These are external attributions. Depression is linked to internal attributions.

   D. Wrong. This is an unstable attribution. Depression is linked to stable attributions.

5. A, Correct (p. 477)

   B. Wrong. Axis II involves personality disorders. Your behavior does not indicate a personality disorder.

   C. Wrong. Dissociation is abnormal consciousness, not reactions to a history of mental disorder.

   D. Wrong. Maladaptive attributions are dysfunctional attributions of one's own behavior.

6. D, Correct (p. 488)

   A. Wrong. May is alternating between a manic and a depressed state. There is no major depression coupled with dysthymia.

   B. Wrong. Dysthymia is a milder, more chronic form of depression. May is alternating between mania and depression.

   C. Wrong. May is alternating between a manic and a depressed state, which is probably bipolar disorder.

7. D, Correct (p. 486)

   A. Wrong. Conversion disorder does not involve amnesia.

   B. Wrong. Dissociative identity disorder involves multiple personalities.

   C. Wrong. There was no travel from home accompanying the amnesia.

8. D, Correct (p. 481)

   A. Wrong. His anxiety is non-specific. OCD has a more focused anxiety and compulsive behavior.

   B. Wrong. His anxiety is constant and non-specific. Anxiety has a sudden onset in panic disorder.

   C. Wrong. His anxiety is non-specific. Agoraphobia involves anxiety in a specific situation.

9. A, Correct (p. 484)

   B. Wrong. Dissociative disorders involve breaks in normal conscious awareness.

   C. Wrong. Anxiety disorders do not usually involve misinterpreting small symptoms as major disease.

   D. Wrong. Personality disorders involve chronic personality traits, not preoccupation with the body.

10. B, Correct (p. 505481

    A. Wrong. Agoraphobia is a fear of leaving home or being in public places. Arachnophobia involves spiders.

    C. Wrong. Childhood sexual abuse may be linked with dissociative identity disorder.

    D. Wrong. Parenting style is not relevant. Having had a panic attack in public is relevant.

11. A, Correct (p. 492)

    B., C., D. Wrong. These all are more common in females. Schizophrenia may be more common in males.

12. A, Correct (p. 484)

    B. Wrong. The anxiety is specific in both, but focuses on different things.

    C. Wrong. Physical symptoms or problems are present in both disorders.

    D. Wrong. These disorders do not differ greatly in rate of development.

13. C, Correct (p. 490)

    A. Wrong. Mina doesn't swing from depression to mania and back.

    B. Wrong. Mina doesn't have multiple personalities.

    D. Wrong. There is no free-floating anxiety, and delusions are not usually found in anxiety disorders.

14. A, Correct (p. 495)

    B. Wrong. Antidepressants, not drugs for schizophrenia, usually increase serotonin activity.

    C. Wrong. Acetylcholine is associated with Alzheimer's disease, not schizophrenia.

    D. Wrong. Some antidepressants, not schizophrenia drugs, influence norepinephrine activity.

15. C, Correct (p. 498)

    A. Wrong. Failures would not classically condition depression.

    B. Wrong. Sue is not observing and copying someone's behavior.

    D. Wrong. Depression is not being reinforced or punished.

16. D, Correct (p. 488)

    A. Wrong. Delusions are thoughts, not hyperactive periods.

    B. Wrong. Dissociations are a separation of normal consciousness and memory.

    C. Wrong. Fugue episodes are period of amnesia combined with travel.

17. D, Correct (p. 490)

    A. Wrong. Consciousness and memory problems are part of dissociative disorders, not schizophrenia.

    B. Wrong. Multiple personality is the common description of dissociative identity disorder.

    C. Wrong. There is no split of attributions in schizophrenia.

18. C, Correct (p. 496)

    A., B. Wrong. Schizophrenia involves a significant genetic component.

    D. Wrong. Even identical twins only have a 50% concordance rate.

CHAPTER **15**

THERAPY

ESTABLISHING LEARNING GOALS

Use these learning goals as a preview of the chapter, a guide for active reading, and to evaluate your mastery of the material. Review the relevant goals as you begin and end your reading of each major section of the chapter.

I. Discuss how the biomedical aspects of psychological disorders are treated.

   A. Explain how drug therapies are used to treat psychological disorders.
      1. Identify the uses and limitations of each major category of drugs.
      2. Explain how each major category of drugs work.

   B. Discuss and evaluate electroconvulsive shock therapy.

   C. Explain why psychosurgery is sometimes used to treat psychological disorders.

II. Discuss how the mental aspects of psychological disorder are treated.

   A. Evaluate psychoanalysis as a form of insight therapy.
      1. Discuss the basic philosophy of psychoanalysis.
      2. Discuss the role of free association, dream analysis, transference, and resistance.
      3. Describe how modern psychodynamic therapy differs from the psychoanalysis of Freud's era.

   B. Evaluate cognitive therapies.
      1. Describe rational-emotive therapy, and give examples of common types of irrational thought.
      2. Describe Beck's cognitive therapy, and compare it to rational-emotive therapy.

   C. Evaluate humanistic therapies.
      1. Describe client-centered therapy and the three essential core qualities a therapist should have.
      2. Describe Gestalt and existential therapies.

   D. Discuss group and family therapy.

III. Discuss how the environmental aspects of psychological disorders are treated.

   A. Explain how conditioning techniques can be used in therapy.
      1. Describe systematic desensitization.
      2. Describe aversion therapy.

   B. Explain how rewards and punishments can be used in therapy.
      1. Describe token economies.

2. Describe social skills training.

IV. Discuss how psychotherapy is evaluated and may be selected.

A. Discuss the major findings of clinical evaluation research.

B. Describe the factors that are common across psychotherapies.

MASTERING THE MATERIAL

PREVIEW & TREATING THE BODY: BIOMEDICAL THERAPIES (PP. 507-515)

MASTERING THE VOCABULARY

Define or explain each of the following terms.

1. psychotherapy
2. biomedical therapies
3. antipsychotic drugs
4. antidepressant drugs
5. antianxiety drugs
6. electroconvulsive therapy
7. psychosurgery

MASTERING THE CONCEPTS

Fill in the blanks to create a summary of the section.

[1] ____________ , treatment for mental, emotional or behavioral problems, can help both severe and more minor problems. This chapter considers how to treat mental problems by treating the body, mind, and environment, and how to evaluate and choose a therapy.

[2] ____________ therapies originated in ancient Greece. [3] ____________ therapy began in the 1950s with the discovery of chlorpromazine to treat [4] ____________ . [5] ____________ drugs used to treat the positive symptoms of schizophrenia reduce [6] ____________ activity. They don't affect negative

symptoms or work for all people, and they have side effects, including [7] ____________ dyskinesia, involuntary facial movements. The anti-psychotic drug Clozapine affects dopamine and serotonin and often works when chlorpromazine doesn't. Depression is treated with antidepressants. Tricyclics affect [8] ____________ , while SSRIs such as Prozac affect [9] ____________ . They are effective for over [10] ____________ of patients but require time to work, and they can have side effects. Bipolar disorder is treated with [11] ____________ carbonate. [12] ____________ drugs, such as benzodiazepine tranquilizers, affect [13] ____________ .

Electroconvulsive therapy is used to treat [14] ____________ that has not responded to other therapies. It is effective in 50-70% of cases. Controversies include not knowing why it works, reports of temporary [15] ____________ , the potential for brain damage, and the possibility of relapse. Brain surgery to alter behavior, [16] ____________ , is rarely performed today. In the 1930s, Moniz developed the prefrontal [17] ____________ procedure to calm patients. Major cognitive deficits occurred. Cingulotomy, an operation that removes a little [18] ____________ system tissue, occasionally is used today to reduce obsessive-compulsive disorder and depression.

EVALUATING YOUR PROGRESS

Select the best response. If you make any errors, reread the relevant material before proceeding.

1. Biomedical therapy was proposed as early as
   a. 400 B.C. by Hippocrates for treating depression.
   b. the 16th century by doctors for treating "evil spirits."
   c. the 19th century by doctors for treating the paranoia of syphilis.
   d. the 1930's by Moniz for treating violent disorders.

2. Biomedical therapies include drugs, psychosurgery, and
   a. systematic desensitization.
   b. electroconvulsive therapy.
   c. psychodynamic therapy.
   d. rational-emotive therapy.

3. Chlorpromazine (Thorazine), one of the original psychoactive drugs, is used primarily to treat
   a. depression.
   b. bipolar disorder.
   c. schizophrenia.
   d. anxiety disorders.

4. Most antipsychotic drugs slow or block the activity of
   a. serotonin.
   b. norepinephrine.
   c. dopamine.
   d. GABA.
5. Tricyclic drugs and serotonin-specific reuptake inhibitors (SSRIs) are examples of
   a. antipsychotic drugs.
   b. antianxiety drugs.
   c. antidepressant drugs.
   d. antimanic drugs.
6. The side effects associated with antianxiety drugs include
   a. tardive dyskinesia and blurry vision.
   b. drowsiness and psychological dependence.
   c. restlessness and diminished sexual desire.
   d. memory loss and possible brain damage.
7. The effectiveness of GABA is increased by
   a. antipsychotic drugs.
   b. anti-manic drugs.
   c. antianxiety drugs.
   d. antidepressant drugs.
8. When other therapies have been ineffective, cingulotomy is sometimes used to
   a. calm violent or agitated behavior.
   b. treat extreme panic disorder.
   c. treat the negative symptoms of schizophrenia.
   d. treat obsessive-compulsive disorder.
9. Electroconvulsive therapy is most commonly used to treat
   a. generalized anxiety disorder.
   b. schizophrenia.
   c. obsessive-compulsive disorder.
   d. depression.

TREATING THE MIND: INSIGHT THERAPIES (PP. 515-526)

MASTERING THE VOCABULARY

Define or explain each of the following terms.

1. insight therapies
2. psychoanalysis

3. free association
4. dream analysis
5. resistance
6. transference
7. cognitive therapies
8. rational-emotive therapy
9. humanistic therapy
10. client-centered therapy
11. group therapy
12. family therapy

MASTERING THE CONCEPTS.

Fill in the blanks to create a summary of the section.

[1] ____________ therapies are based on the idea that disorders involve maladaptive thoughts that can be reduced by self-knowledge. [2] ____________ , originated by Freud, emphasizes insight into conflicts repressed in the [3] ____________ mind. Dream analysis and [4] ____________ , saying what comes to mind, help determine those conflicts. Anxiety causes [5] ____________ , periods of poor cooperation. When conflicts near consciousness, [6] ____________ occurs as the client directs emotions felt about other people toward the therapist instead. The fact that classical psychoanalysis is very [7] ____________ and costly has led to brief forms in which the therapist is more active, focuses on selective problems, and emphasizes [8] ____________ , not sexual drives. This modern version is called [9] ____________ therapy.

Conscious beliefs are emphasized in [10] ____________ therapies. In Ellis' [11] ____________ therapy, the therapist challenges any irrational thoughts to guide the person to insight. In Beck's cognitive therapy, the therapist is not combative, and clients are encouraged to discover negative thinking themselves.

The goal of [12] ____________ therapy is to help clients understand their self-worth and value. In Rogers' [13] ____________ therapy the therapist must show [14] ____________ , genuineness, and unconditional positive regard to allow clients to analyze their own feelings freely. In Perl's [15] ____________ therapy the client's goodness is emphasized, but the therapist is more directive. Emphasis is on the [16] ____________ and expressing oneself as a "whole" person. Existential therapies encourage clients to take responsibility for their life decisions by providing a supportive environment.

Therapy is also done in a [17] ____________ setting. This cuts costs and provides insight and support from other people. [18] ____________ therapy involves the entire family, not just one person.

EVALUATING YOUR PROGRESS

Select the best response. If you miss any questions, reread the relevant material before proceeding.

1. The goal of psychoanalysis is to gain insight into disordered behavior by
   a. challenging the irrational beliefs held by the client.
   b. providing a supportive environment in which clients can explore their true self.
   c. bringing unconscious conflicts and memories into conscious awareness.
   d. having clients take notes about their feelings and behavior each day.
2. Expressing feelings and thoughts toward the therapist that really represent the patient's feelings about other people is an example of
   a. resistance.
   b. "musterbation."
   c. transference.
   d. incongruence.
3. How does psychodynamic therapy differ from classic psychoanalytic therapy?
   a. Psychodynamic therapy is faster.
   b. Psychodynamic therapy is a group therapy.
   c. Psychodynamic therapy is less confrontational.
   d. Psychodynamic therapy emphasizes personal choice.
4. "I must" beliefs lead to psychological problem, according to the theory behind
   a. Gestalt therapy.
   b. rational-emotive therapy.
   c. client-centered therapy.
   d. existential therapy.
5. The humanistic therapy that is more directive and more forceful than client-centered therapy and also stresses the "here an now" is
   a. family therapy.
   b. Gestalt therapy.
   c. rational emotive therapy.
   d. existential therapy.

6. Which is *not* an advantage of group therapy?
   a. It is cost effective.
   b. Other people can provide information about coping strategies.
   c. It shows other people have similar problems.
   d. It offers a quicker cure.
7. An emphasis on getting clients to recognize their irrational beliefs themselves, rather than confronting them with them, is characteristic of
   a. Ellis' rational-emotive therapy.
   b. Perls' Gestalt therapy.
   c. Rogers' client-centered therapy.
   d. Beck's cognitive therapy.
8. Carl Rogers, a client-centered therapist, suggested psychological problems develop because of
   a. incongruence.
   b. genuineness.
   c. unconditional positive regard.
   d. resistance.

TREATING THE ENVIRONMENT: BEHAVIORAL THERAPIES (PP. 524-529)

MASTERING THE VOCABULARY

Define or explain each of the following terms.

1. behavioral therapies
2. systematic desensitization
3. aversion therapy
4. token economy

MASTERING THE CONCEPTS

Fill in the blanks to create a summary of the section.

Behavioral therapy assumes psychological problems can be [1] ____________ , and the [2] ____________ should be treated, not thoughts or feelings. One type, [3] ____________ desensitization, replaces a negative response with a relaxation response. Relaxation is paired with successively higher stimuli in the client's [4] ____________ hierarchy. This is used to treat [5] ____________ . An unwanted response (e.g., drinking) can be eliminated by [6] ____________ therapy, in which a pleasant reaction to something harmful is replaced with something unpleasant. Problems include [7] ____________ if therapy is discontinued and ethical considerations. Rewards are used to modify behavior in token [8] ____________ . Tokens are later exchanged for goods or privileges. Reinforcement is combined with modeling in [9] ____________ training to improve the adjustment and social skills of people with serious disorders. [10] ____________ modifies behavior, but it can damage the client-therapist relationship, it teaches only what not to do, and it raises ethical concerns.

EVALUATING YOUR PROGRESS

Select the best response. If you miss any questions, reread the relevant material before proceeding.

1. The central idea in behavioral therapy is that psychological problems
   a. are the result of irrational thoughts.
   b. are due to neurotransmitter imbalances.
   c. may be learned and unlearned.
   d. are due to unconscious conflicts.

2. The therapy in which relaxation is paired with anxiety-producing stimuli of increasing intensity is
   a. aversion conditioning.
   b. token economy therapy.
   c. existential therapy.
   d. systematic desensitization therapy.

3. Conditioning an unpleasant response to replace a pleasant one describes
   a. systematic desensitization.
   b. aversion therapy.
   c. token economy.
   d. meta-analysis.

4. Using modeling and rewards to teach appropriate ways of interacting with other people in order to improve the quality of life of individuals with psychological disorders is called
   a. systematic desensitization.
   b. aversion therapy.
   c. social skills training.
   d. insight therapy.

5. Token economies
   a. are used to teach appropriate behaviors.
   b. are based on classical conditioning principles.
   c. use anxiety hierarchies to eliminate maladaptive behavior.
   d. are used to develop congruent self-concepts.

EVALUATING AND CHOOSING PSYCHOTHERAPY (PP. 530-534)

MASTERING THE VOCABULARY

Define or explain each of the following terms.

1. meta-analysis
2. spontaneous remission

MASTERING THE CONCEPTS

Fill in the blanks to create a summary of the section.

Valid evaluation of the effectiveness of therapy requires a [1] ____________ group and proper experimental procedures. The well-controlled Philadelphia study found that after four months, people receiving therapy were [2] ____________ improved than those on a waiting list, and that psychodynamic and behavioral therapies were [3] ____________ effective. After one year the three groups [4] ____________ , indicating the effect of therapy is to speed recovery. Researchers have used [5] ____________ to examine many studies and concluded that therapy is better than no therapy, and all therapies are about equal in effectiveness. Improvement without therapy, [6] ____________ remission, has raised questions about defining "treatment." The equal effectiveness of all therapies is also controversial and may reflect the effect of [7] ____________ variables. The similar results also might be due to therapies having certain shared features:[8] ____________ factors, learning factors, and action factors. Effective therapy is predicted by the amount of [9] ____________ between client and therapist, and the quality of the therapeutic alliance.

EVALUATING YOUR PROGRESS

Select the best response. If you miss any questions, reread the relevant material before proceeding.

1. According to the results of the Philadelphia study, psychotherapy
   a. has no effect.
   b. speeds up natural improvement.
   c. causes an improvement that is larger and longer lasting than getting no therapy.
   d. causes a significant number of people to get worse rather than better.

2. Based on recent meta-analysis of hundreds of studies, we can reasonably conclude
   a. psychotherapy doesn't work.
   b. therapy helps temporarily, but it has no lasting benefit.
   c. psychoanalysis is more effective than behavioral therapies.
   d. all types of therapy are effective, with no type better than the others.

3. Therapies are said to share the common feature of action factors. Action factors involve
   a. giving clients a better understanding as to the cause of their behavior.
   b. giving clients suggestions for how they can improve their behavior.
   c. developing a trusting relationship between client and therapist.
   d. giving clients the feeling that someone is concerned and wants to help them.

4. Which of the following is the best predictor of successful therapy?
   a. the amount of empathy the therapist exhibits
   b. the specific type of therapy
   c. the age and sex of the therapist
   d. the length of the therapy

MAKING FINAL PREPARATIONS

Complete these sections without consulting your book or notes. For a more accurate estimate of how well you know this material, wait at least a day or two after studying the chapter before working on the questions. Some of the material you "know" immediately after working with the chapter will be quickly forgotten. Exercises done too soon after studying will overestimate what you know well.

SHORT ESSAY QUESTIONS

Write a brief answer to each question.

1. Discuss the uses and limitations of ECT.

   ____

   ____

2. Compare Ellis' rational emotive therapy and Beck's cognitive therapy.

   ____

   ____

3. Compare the basic philosophy of insight therapies and behavioral therapies.

   ____

   ____

4. Summarize the conclusions about the effectiveness of various forms of psychotherapy.

   ____

   ____

MATCHING

Select the correct definition or description for each item.

1. _______ Jones & Wolpe
2. _______ anxiety hierarchy
3. _______ fluoxepine
4. _______ musterbation
5. _______ prefrontal lobotomy
6. _______ genuineness
7. _______ tricyclics
8. _______ Egas Moniz
9. _______ existential therapy
10. _______ resistance
11. _______ psychodynamic therapy
12. _______ Gestalt therapy
13. _______ Albert Ellis
14. _______ empathy
15. _______ benzodiazepines
16. _______ meta-analysis

a. anti-anxiety tranquilizers affecting GABA
b. Ellis' description of an irrational way of thinking
c. open, honest, without phoniness
d. stresses expressing feelings as a whole person
e. ordered list of fear-inducing stimuli
f. understanding; seeing client's point of view
g. stresses accepting responsibility for decisions
h. technique to compare data from many studies
i. developed prefrontal lobotomy
j. modern, shorter form of psychoanalysis
k. anti-depressants that affects norepinephrine
l. developed systematic desensitization
m. unconscious attempt to hinder therapy
n. psychosurgery to calm patient
o. developed rational-emotive therapy
p. Prozac; anti-depressant affecting serotonin

MULTIPLE CHOICE PRETEST 1

Select the one best response.

1. When did modern drug therapy begin?
   a. 1930s
   b. 1940s
   c. 1950s
   d. 1960s

2. The benzodiazepines are examples of
   a. antipsychotic drugs.
   b. antianxiety drugs.
   c. antidepressant drugs.
   d. antimanic drugs.

3. Dopamine antagonist antipsychotic medications are affective primarily for reducing
   a. the positive symptoms of schizophrenia.
   b. the negative symptoms of schizophrenia.
   c. both positive and negative symptoms of schizophrenia.
   d. the tardive dyskinesia that can occur with schizophrenia.

4. May suddenly began to forget her appointments, to misplace her dream diary, and to be unwilling to talk during her therapy sessions. A psychoanalytic therapist would interpret her behavior as
   a. transference.
   b. incongruence.
   c. resistance.
   d. musterbation.

5. Side effect associated with serotonin specific reuptake inhibitors (SSRIs) include
   a. tardive dyskinesia.
   b. drowsiness and impaired motor coordination.
   c. additions or dependence.
   d. agitation, weight gain, and reduced sexual desire.

6. Saul is taking lithium carbonate for a psychological disorder. The disorder is most likely
   a. schizophrenia.
   b. obsessive-compulsive disorder.
   c. depression (a major depressive episode).
   d. bipolar disorder.

7. Which of the following is not a concern psychologists have about electroconvulsive therapy (ECT)?
   a. ECT reduces depression in very few people.
   b. ECT causes loss of memory for events surrounding the treatment.
   c. ECT's method of action is unknown.
   d. The long-term effects of repeated ECT treatments is not known.

8. Ali is recovering from a cingulotomy. The outcome that might be expected is a reduction of
   a. obsessive-compulsive behavior.
   b. hallucinations and delusions.
   c. the manic periods in bipolar disorder.
   d. the ability to plan and coordinate actions.

9. In hopes of discovering clues to the contents of the unconscious mind, Ed's therapist had him relax and say anything that came to mind. This describes
   a. transference.
   b. free association.
   c. systematic desensitization.
   d. the empty chair technique.

10. The idea that disorders develop because of irrational or overly negative beliefs is central to.
    a. humanistic therapy.
    b. Gestalt therapy.
    c. cognitive therapy.
    d. psychodynamic therapy.

11. Dee's therapist strives to provide genuineness, unconditional positive regard, and empathy. Dee's therapist probably practices
    a. client-centered therapy.
    b. cognitive therapy.
    c. psychoanalytic therapy.
    d. behavioral therapy.

12. Tim's therapist isn't "warm and fuzzy." In fact, she is quite aggressive in confronting Tim when he makes an irrational statement like, "I'm a total failure, and there's nothing I can do about it." Tim's therapist is using
    a. Freud's psychoanalytic therapy.
    b. Beck's cognitive therapy.
    c. Perl's Gestalt therapy.
    d. Ellis' rational-emotive therapy.

13. Joe tends to shout and stare. Because Joe soon will leave the hospital, his therapist is using rewards, modeling and role-playing to teach him to interact more appropriately. In other words, he is applying
    a. systematic desensitization.
    b. social skills training.
    c. aversion therapy.
    d. client-centered therapy.

14. Systematic desensitization is most likely to be used by a therapist who believes phobias
    a. are the result of irrational thoughts.
    b. reflect unconscious conflicts or traumas.
    c. phobias are learned fear responses.
    d. reflect an overactive perceptual system.

15. Some pedophiles have been given therapy that includes pairing child pornography with shock in an attempt to condition an unpleasant response to sexual thought about children. This is an example of
    a. Gestalt therapy.
    b. systematic desensitization.
    c. aversion therapy.
    d. a token economy.

16. The Philadelphia study of the effectiveness of therapy found
    a. people who got therapy of any type were better after four months than people put on waiting lists.
    b. people who got therapy of any type were better off after one year than people put on waiting lists.
    c. people who got behavioral therapy improved more than people who got psychodynamic therapy.
    d. people who got psychodynamic therapy improved more than people who got behavioral therapy.

17. Spontaneous remission of psychological problems occurs about 30% of the time. This means the disorder
    a. responded very rapidly to therapy.
    b. failed to respond to therapy.
    c. increased in severity.
    d. improved without treatment.

18. Smith's early meta-analytic study found the average therapy client
    a. was better off than 80% of the people who did not get therapy.
    b. was better off than 30% of the people who did not get therapy.
    c. was not better off than the people who did not get therapy.
    d. was worse off than the people who did not get therapy.

19. All therapies allow greater personal insight or understanding about the disorder. This common factor is
    a. a support factor.
    b. a learning factor.
    c. an action factor.
    d. empathy.

20. Emma, age 14, is depressed. Her therapist believes not only Emma should receive therapy, but also her parents and siblings. Emma's therapist is probably
    a. an existential therapist.
    b. a behavioral therapist.
    c. a Gestalt therapist.
    d. a family therapist.

MULTIPLE CHOICE PRETEST 2

Select the one best response.

1. Soren had always been on good terms with his therapist, but recently he became hostile, started accusing her of wanting to run his life, and said she was never satisfied. He even referred to her as "mother" once. Soren's therapist saw this as a sign the cause of Soren's problems was nearing consciousness. In psychoanalytic theory, Soren's behavior represents
    a. transference.
    b. free association.
    c. resistance.
    d. incongruence.

2. For patients with schizophrenia, what will a psychiatrist most likely prescribe to reduce the hallucinations and delusions?
    a. cingulotomy
    b. electroconvulsive therapy
    c. an antipsychotic drug
    d. systematic desensitization.

3. Tardive dyskinesia, a neuromuscular disorder, is a side effect associated with
   a. prefrontal lobotomy.
   b. cingulotomy.
   c. electroconvulsive therapy.
   d. long term chlorpromazine use.

4. Flora is taking a drug that slows the reuptake of serotonin. This drug is most likely
   a. a tranquilizing drug like Xanax.
   b. an antianxiety drug like Valium.
   c. an antipsychotic drug like Thorazine.
   d. an anti-depressant drug like Prozac.

5. Snooping in the medicine cabinet of a friend, you see a bottle of Xanax, a benzodiazepine drug. You should suspect your friend is being treated for
   a. generalized anxiety disorder.
   b. schizophrenia.
   c. depression.
   d. bipolar disorder.

6. As a result of treatment in 1946 for a violent psychological disorder, Craig is calm, but he has cognitive deficits, including the inability to plan and coordinate actions. The treatment probably was
   a. drug treatment using an SSRI (e.g., Prozac or Zoloft).
   b. a prefrontal lobotomy.
   c. drug treatment using a benzodiazepine (Xanax).
   d. electroconvulsive therapy (ECT).

7. Electroconvulsive therapy works by
   a. blocking reuptake of serotonin.
   b. decreasing utilization of dopamine.
   c. modulating norepinephrine activity.
   d. some yet-to-be-determined action.

8. Electroconvulsive therapy (ECT) is most likely to be prescribed when a person
   a. fails to respond to antidepressant drugs.
   b. develops tardive dyskinesia and must give up drug therapy.
   c. develops very violent behavior as part of schizophrenia.
   d. develops very severe obsessive-compulsive disorder.

9. How does modern psychodynamic therapy differ from classical psychoanalysis?
   a. Psychodynamic therapy is usually done as group therapy.
   b. Psychodynamic therapy is usually briefer.
   c. Psychodynamic therapy emphasizes working on the entire personality rather than limited issues.
   d. Psychodynamic therapy emphasizes aggression and sexual drives.

10. Kim's therapist is very non-judgmental and merely reflects back what Kim says. Kim's therapist is
    a. a behavioral therapist.
    b. a client-centered therapist.
    c. a rational-emotive therapist.
    d. a psychoanalytic therapist.

11. Dr. Yi believes that psychological problems are the result of anxieties caused by the personal choices people must make during their lifetimes, and that a goal of therapy is to accept responsibility for those decisions. This approach represents
    a. psychoanalysis.
    b. Beck's cognitive therapy.
    c. behavioral therapy.
    d. existential therapy.

12. Ron's therapist wants Ron to discover his irrational beliefs. She asked him to keep track of his thoughts and feelings throughout the day, and each night to write rational responses to those thoughts. This perspective and "homework" is common in
    a. Freud's psychoanalysis.
    b. Roger's client-centered therapy.
    c. Beck's cognitive therapy.
    d. Perl's Gestalt therapy.

13. The goal of humanistic therapy is to
    a. get the client thinking more logically and rationally.
    b. bring unconscious conflicts into consciousness where they can be resolved.
    c. help the client gain insight into his or her self-worth and value as a person.
    d. condition adaptive behaviors to replace maladaptive ones.

14. Dan's therapist is never critical and is always accepting and respectful of him. His therapist is showing
    a. empathy.
    b. unconditional positive regard.
    c. genuineness.
    d. congruence.

15. Sabeen is trying to maintain a state of deep muscle relaxation as she works through her anxiety hierarchy. This represents
    a. existential therapy.
    b. systematic desensitization therapy.
    c. psychoanalytic therapy.
    d. aversion therapy.

16. What is most likely to occur if aversion therapy is ended too soon?
    a. The aversive response will extinguish.
    b. Incongruence will develop.
    c. The client-therapist relationship will be damaged.
    d. A new psychological problem will develop.

17. At Riverside Psychiatric Hospital, patients are given a ticket each time they engage in certain desirable behaviors (e.g., dressing appropriately, taking medications). The tickets are exchanged later for snacks or various special activities. This describes
    a. systematic desensitization.
    b. social skills training.
    c. a token economy.
    d. rational-emotive therapy.

18. Ida is in psychodynamic therapy, Jo is in behavioral therapy, and Vi is not in therapy. We should expect
    a. Ida will improve greatly, Jo will improve modestly, and Vi will not improve.
    b. Jo will improve greatly, Ida will improve modestly, and Vi will not improve.
    c. Jo and Ida will show equal improvement, and Vi will not improve.
    d. Jo and Ida will show equal improvement, and Vi may improve, but not as quickly.

19. Rodrigo asked your advice about how to find a good therapist. What advice would be most accurate?
    a. "Find one that uses a cognitive approach. That's the best approach to therapy."
    b. "Pick any therapist. Every therapist is just as effective as the others."
    c. "Find one with whom you feel comfortable and who understands you."
    d. "Find one that uses a behavioral approach. That works best for most problems."

LANGUAGE DEVELOPMENT GUIDE

CORE TERMS

In the lectures on this chapter, you will be learning about drugs that affect the mind, so you can expect to hear the term ***psychoactive drugs***. You already learned a bit about one kind of these in the chapter on consciousness; ***psychotropic drugs*** like marijuana and LSD alter consciousness. But in this chapter you will be learning about ***psychopharmaceuticals*** --drugs that are ***therapeutic*** (helpful in treating illnesses). When referring to non-biological treatments, your instructor may use the terms ***counseling***, ***therapy*** and ***psychotherapy*** fairly interchangeably.

One more thing: you may wonder why counselors need to have ***empathy*** rather than ***sympathy*** for their clients. The answer to this can be found in the word parts: if one has *sympathy*, then one feels along with the other person. A counselor needs to be a bit more objective; in *empathy*, the emphasis is on understanding the feelings rather than participating in them.

IDIOMS

p. 511	"even keel"	avoiding extremes; not rocking from one side to the other, stable (a keel is the bottom of a boat)
p. 512	a downside	a negative perspective; reason something is not so good
p. 513	of last resort	the least preferred option
p. 514	cognitive deficits	problems in thinking well
p. 516	maneuver around a number of roadblocks	find a way around many difficulties
p. 517	contemporaries	those who live at the same time
p. 517	streamline	to smooth the edges of something, to make it move more easily through air, water, etc.
p. 520	a more subtle tack	a less direct or forceful way
p. 524	odds of	chances, likelihood, probability of

PRONUNCIATION

tranquilizer (tran′-kwill-eye-zer) *p. 512*
prefrontal (pree-front′-al) *p. 514*
lobotomy (low-bot′-o-mee) *p. 514*
eclectic (ek-lek′-tik) *p. 533*

SOLUTIONS

PREVIEW & TREATING THE BODY: BIOMEDICAL THERAPIES (PP. 507-515)

MASTERING THE CONCEPTS

1. Psychotherapy (p. 507)
2. Biomedical (p. 509)
3. Drug (p. 510)
4. schizophrenia (p. 510)
5. Anti-psychotic (p. 510)
6. dopamine (p. 510)
7. tardive (p. 510)
8. norepinephrine (p. 511)
9. serotonin (p. 511)
10. 50% (p. 511)
11. lithium (p. 511)
12. Antianxiety (p. 512)
13. GABA (p. 512)
14. depression (p. 513)
15. memory loss (p. 513)
16. psychosurgery (p.514)
17. lobotomy (p. 514)
18. limbic (p. 514)

EVALUATING YOUR PROGRESS

1. A, Correct (p. 509)

   B., C., D. Wrong. These were much later.
2. B, Correct (p. 512)

   A. Wrong. Systematic desensitization is a kind of behavioral therapy that emphasizes learning.

   C. Wrong. Psychodynamic therapy is the modern version of psychoanalysis, an insight therapy.

   D. Wrong. Rational-emotive therapy is a cognitive therapy, a type of insight therapy.
3. C, Correct (p. 525106)

   A. Wrong. Chlorpromazine is an antipsychotic, not an antidepressant.

   B. Wrong. Lithium carbonate is mostly used to treat bipolar disorder. Thorazine is an antipsychotic.

   D. Wrong. Thorazine is an anti-psychotic, not an anti-anxiety drug.
4. C, Correct (p. 510)

   A. Wrong. Clozapine affects serotonin, but most antipsychotics don't. Prozac affects serotonin.

   B. Wrong. Tricyclic antidepressants, not antipsychotics, affect norepinephrine.

   D. Wrong. Antianxiety drugs, not antipsychotics, affect GABA.
5. C, Correct (p. 511)

   A., B., D. Wrong. Tricyclics and SSRIs are antidepressants.
6. B, Correct (p. 511)

   A. Wrong. These are side effects of antipsychotic drugs.

   C. Wrong. These are side effects of antidepressant drugs.

   D. Wrong. These are side effects of ECT.
7. C, Correct (p. 512)

   A. Wrong. Antipsychotics are dopamine antagonists.

   B. Wrong. The action of lithium carbonate is unclear.

   D. Wrong. Antidepressants generally affect norepinephrine or serotonin.
8. D, Correct (p. 514)

   A. Wrong. Pre-frontal lobotomy once was used for this purpose, but cingulotomy isn't.

   B. Wrong. Psychosurgery is not used to treat panic disorder.

   C. Wrong. Psychosurgery is not used to treat schizophrenia.
9. D, Correct (p. 512)

   A. Wrong. Anti-anxiety drugs and insight therapy is used to treat generalized anxiety disorder.

   B. Wrong. Anti-psychotic drugs are used to treat schizophrenia.

   C. Wrong. Anti-anxiety drugs or (rarely) cingulotomies are used to treat obsessive compulsive disorder.

TREATING THE MIND: INSIGHT THERAPIES (PP. 515-526)

MASTERING THE CONCEPTS.

1. Insight (p. 515)
2. Psychoanalysis (p. 515)
3. unconscious (p. 515)
4. free association (p. 516)
5. resistance (p. 516)
6. transference (p. 517)
7. lengthy (p. 517)
8. social skills (p. 517)
9. psychodynamic (p. 517)
10. cognitive (p. 517)
11. rational-emotive (p. 518)
12. humanistic (p. 520)
13. client-centered (p. 521)
14. empathy (p. 521)
15. Gestalt (p. 523)
16. here & now (p. 523)
17. group (p. 541)
18. Family (p. 541)

EVALUATING YOUR PROGRESS

1. C, Correct (p. 515)

   A. Wrong. This describes Ellis' rational-emotive therapy.

   B. Wrong. This describes Rogers' client-centered therapy.

   D. Wrong. This describes Beck's cognitive therapy.
2. C, Correct (p. 517)

   A. Wrong. Resistance involves uncooperative behaviors, not transferring feelings toward the therapist.

   B. Wrong. Musterbation involves a series of irrational thoughts, not transferring feelings toward the therapist.

   D. Wrong. Incongruence is the mismatch of self-concept and reality.
3. A, Correct (p. 517)

   B. Wrong. Both are individual therapies.

   C. Wrong. Psychodynamic therapists are more directive than psychoanalytic therapists.

   D. Wrong. Personal choice is not emphasized in psychodynamic or psychoanalytic therapy.
4. B, Correct (p. 519)

   A., C., D. Wrong. Ellis, of rational-emotive therapy, outlined the problem of "musterbation."
5. B, Correct (p. 523)

   A. Wrong. Family therapy isn't necessarily a humanistic therapy.

   C. Wrong. Rational-emotive therapy is a type of cognitive therapy.

   D. Wrong. Existential therapy is not usually described as forceful and directive.
6. D, Correct (p. 524)

   A., B., C. Wrong. These are all advantages of group therapy.
7. D, Correct (p. 520)

   A. Wrong. Ellis confronts clients with their illogical thoughts.

   B. Wrong. Gestalt therapy doesn't emphasize illogical thoughts. It's a humanistic therapy.

   C. Wrong. Client-centered humanistic therapy doesn't emphasis the role of irrational thoughts.
8. A, Correct (p. 521)

   B. Wrong. Genuineness is a desirable, therapeutic condition.

   C. Wrong. Unconditional positive regard is a desirable situation.

   D. Wrong. Resistance is a psychoanalytic concept, not a client-centered (humanistic) one.

TREATING THE ENVIRONMENT: BEHAVIORAL THERAPIES (PP. 524-529)

MASTERING THE CONCEPTS

1. learned (p. 525)
2. behavior (p. 525)
3. systematic (p. 525)
4. anxiety (p. 526)
5. phobias (p. 526)
6. aversion (p. 526)
7. extinction (p. 527)
8. economies (p. 528)
9. social skills (p. 529)
10. Punishment (p. 529)

EVALUATING YOUR PROGRESS

1. C, Correct (p. 525)
   A., B., D. Wrong. Behavioral therapy focuses on learning appropriate behaviors, not thoughts, neurotransmitters, or the unconscious.
2. D, Correct (p. 525)
   A. Wrong. Aversion therapy replaces a pleasant response with an unpleasant one.
   B. Wrong. Token economies use rewards to increase desired behaviors.
   C. Wrong. Existential therapy encourages people to take responsibility for their decisions.
3. B, Correct (p. 526)
   A. Wrong. This replaces an unpleasant response with a pleasant one.
   C. Wrong. Token economies don't replace pleasant responses, they reward appropriate behavior.
   D. Wrong. Meta-analysis is a research tool, not a therapy.
4. C, Correct (p. 529)
   A. Wrong. Systematic desensitization reduces anxiety. It doesn't each appropriate social behavior.
   B. Wrong. Aversion therapy doesn't use modeling or rewards, and it doesn't teach communication.
   D. Wrong. Insight therapy strives for insight into the problem. It doesn't teach social behavior.
5. A, Correct (p. 528)
   B. Wrong. Token economies are based on operant conditioning.
   C. Wrong. This describes systematic desensitization.
   D. Wrong. This describes client-centered therapy.

EVALUATING AND CHOOSING PSYCHOTHERAPY (PP. 530-534)

MASTERING THE CONCEPTS

1. control (p. 530)
2. more (p. 531)
3. equally (p. 531)
4. were equal (p. 531)
5. meta-analysis (p. 531)
6. spontaneous (p. 532)
7. client (p. 532)
8. support (p. 533)
9. empathy (p. 533)

EVALUATING YOUR PROGRESS

1. B, Correct (p. 531)
   A., C., D. Wrong. Control groups caught up with therapy groups, so therapy primarily speeds up a natural improvement.
2. D, Correct (p. 531)
   A. Wrong. Psychotherapy does work.
   B. Wrong. Meta-analysis shows there is a lasting benefit of therapy.
   C. Wrong. Meta-analysis finds no particular therapy is consistently better than another.
3. B, Correct (p. 534)
   A. Wrong. This is part of the learning factor.
   C., D. Wrong. These are part of the support factor.
4. A, Correct (p. 533)
   B., C., D. Wrong. Empathy is one of the best predictors of an effective therapist.

MAKING FINAL PREPARATIONS

SHORT ESSAY QUESTIONS

1. ECT is used to treat depression that has not responded to other therapies. It is highly effective, but its use has been limited by several concerns. Although reports of serious memory deficits have not been found in controlled research, ECT causes memory loss for events close to the treatment. Because ECT involves several treatments, there is worry that brain damage might occur. Also, why it works is unknown, causing caution. (pp. 512-513)
2. Both therapies view abnormality to be due to irrational thoughts. In Ellis' therapy the client is aggressively confronted concerning irrational thoughts. Beck's therapy is not as confrontational. Clients are encouraged to discover their own irrational thoughts. (pp. 518-520)
3. Insight therapies are based on the idea that by gaining insight into a problem, a person can resolve the problem and become psychologically healthy. The thoughts or conflicts are treated. Behavioral therapies treat behaviors, not thoughts. Any underlying problem is almost irrelevant; if a behavior is unwanted or inappropriate, change the behavior. This assumes that abnormal behavior can be learned, and unlearned. (pp. 515, 525)
4. Repeated evaluations of therapy suggest that any major type of therapy is better than no therapy, but that no one type of therapy is significantly better than the others. Untreated people do improve, and may catch up to treated people eventually, but therapy speeds the improvement. (pp. 530-534)

MATCHING

1. l (p. 525)
2. e (p. 525)
3. p (p. 511)
4. b (p. 517)
5. n (p. 514)
6. c (p. 522)
7. k (p. 511)
8. i (p. 514)
9. g (p. 523)
10. m (p. 516)
11. j (p. 517)
12. d (p. 523)
13. o (p. 518)
14. f (p. 522)
15. a (p. 512)
16. h (p. 531)

MULTIPLE CHOICE PRETEST 1

1. C, Correct (p. 510)

   A., B., D. Wrong. Drug therapy was first recognized as an alternative in the 1950s.
2. B, Correct (p. 512)

   A., C., D. Wrong. Benzodiazepines are antianxiety drugs.
3. A, Correct (p. 510)

   B., C. Wrong. Dopamine antagonists primarily affect the positive symptoms.

   D. Wrong. Dopamine antagonists cause tardive dyskinesia, they don't reduce it.

4. C, Correct (p. 516)
   A. Wrong. In transference, behavior reflects how the client feels about someone else.
   B. Wrong. Incongruence is a concept in humanistic therapy and involves the self-concept.
   D. Wrong. Musterbation, holding irrational "I must" ideas, is a cognitive therapy concept.
5. D, Correct (p. 511)
   A. Wrong. This is a side effect of antipsychotic drugs.
   B., C. Wrong. These are side effects of antianxiety drugs.
6. D, Correct (p. 511)
   A. Wrong. Schizophrenia doesn't necessarily involve mania, the primary target of lithium carbonate.
   B. Wrong. Obsessive-compulsive disorder doesn't involve mania, the primary target of lithium.
   C. Wrong. The major target of lithium is manic behavior, not depression.
7. A, Correct (p. 512)
   B., C., D. Wrong. These are all points of concern, but ECT is very effective.
8. A, Correct (p. 514)
   B., C. Wrong. Cingulotomy is used to treat obsessive-compulsive disorder.
   D. Wrong. These are side effects of prefrontal lobotomy, not cingulotomy.
9. B, Correct (p. 516)
   A. Wrong. This situation involves transferring toward the therapist feelings felt about another person.
   C. Wrong. Systematic desensitization involves relaxation when faced with anxiety-producing stimuli.
   D. Wrong. This technique involves clients projecting their feelings at an empty chair and talking back.
10. C, Correct (p. 517)
    A. Wrong. Humanistic therapy is based on getting the client to develop congruence.
    B. Wrong. Gestalt therapy is based on getting the client to function as a "whole" person.
    D. Wrong. Psychodynamic therapy is based on resolving unconscious conflicts.
11. A, Correct (p. 521)
    B., C., D. Wrong. Genuineness, empathy, and unconditional positive regard are the hallmarks of humanistic client-centered therapy.
12. D, Correct (p. 518)
    A. Wrong. Psychoanalytic therapy doesn't challenge irrational beliefs in a confrontational manner.
    B. Wrong. Beck's therapy is less confrontational than this.
    C. Wrong. Gestalt therapy doesn't focus on irrational thoughts.
13. B, Correct (p. 529)
    A. Wrong. Systematic desensitization eliminates anxiety responses; it doesn't teach social skills.
    C. Wrong. Aversion therapy replaces pleasant responses with unpleasant ones.
    D. Wrong. Client-centered therapy focuses on thoughts, not behaviors.
14. C, Correct (p. 525)
    A. Wrong. Systematic desensitization is a behavioral therapy. This view is cognitive.
    B. Wrong. Systematic desensitization is a behavioral therapy. This view is psychoanalytic.
    D. Wrong. Systematic desensitization is a behavioral therapy. This view does not emphasize learning.
15. C, Correct (p. 526)
    A. Wrong. Gestalt therapy is a humanistic therapy. It doesn't condition unpleasant responses.
    B. Wrong. Systematic desensitization conditions a pleasant, not an unpleasant response.
    D. Wrong. Token economies reward desired behavior. They don't condition an unpleasant response.
16. A, Correct (p. 531)
    B. Wrong. Therapy groups didn't differ from the waiting list people after one year.
    C., D. Wrong. Type of therapy did not matter.
17. D, Correct (p. 532)
    A., B., C. Wrong. Spontaneous remission is an improvement without treatment.
18. A, Correct (p. 531)
    B., C., D. Wrong. The average therapy patient is better off than 80% of those getting no therapy.

19. B, Correct (p. 534)
A. Wrong. Support factors involve someone who wants to help them get better, not how.
C. Wrong. Action factors give solutions to problems, not just understanding of the problem.
D. Wrong. Empathy is the understanding of the client's point of view, part of the support factor.

20. D, Correct (p. 524)
A. Wrong. Existential therapy focuses on the individual accepting responsibility for life choices.
B. Wrong. Behavior therapy focuses on changing the target behavior, not treating the family.
C. Wrong. Gestalt therapy focuses on the individual, not the family.

MULTIPLE CHOICE PRETEST 2

1. A, B. Wrong. Free association is a technique in which the person says whatever comes to mind, not when feelings are directed toward the therapist that actually relate to another person.
C. Wrong. Resistance does not involve directing feelings toward the therapist that actually relate to another person.
D. Wrong. Incongruence is a concept in humanistic therapies, not psychoanalytic therapy.

2. C, Correct (p. 510)
A. Wrong. Cingulotomies are rare and used mostly for obsessive-compulsive disorder.
B. Wrong. ECT is used almost exclusively for depression, not schizophrenia.
D. Wrong. Systematic desensitization is used for specific phobic disorder, not schizophrenia.

3. D, Correct (p. 510)
A. Wrong. Prefrontal lobotomy doesn't produce tardive dyskinesia. Some antipsychotic drugs do.
B. Wrong. Cingulotomy doesn't producc tardive dyskinesia. Some antipsychotic drugs do.
C. Wrong. ECT doesn't produce tardive dyskinesia. Some antipsychotic drugs do.

4. D, Correct (p. 511)
A. Wrong. Tranquilizers affect GABA, not serotonin.
B. Wrong. Antianxiety drugs affect GABA, not serotonin.
C. Wrong. Antipsychotics usually affect primarily dopamine, not serotonin.

5. A, Correct (p. 512)
B., C., D. Wrong. Benzodiazepines are antianxiety drugs.

6. B, Correct (p. 514)
A., C. Wrong. These drugs weren't available until some time later, and do not have these side effects.
D. Wrong. ECT isn't used to calm people; it's used for depression.

7. D, Correct (p. 513)
A., B., C. Wrong. The way ECT works is unknown at this time.

8. A, Correct (p. 513)
B. Wrong. ECT is a treatment for depression. Tardive dyskinesia occurs with antipsychotic drugs.
C. Wrong. ECT is used to treat depression, not to reduce violence in schizophrenia.
D. Wrong. ECT is used to treat depression, not obsessive compulsive disorder.

9. B, Correct (p. 517)
A. Wrong. Psychodynamic therapy still involves one client at a time.
C. Wrong. Psychodynamic therapy is more likely to focus on more limited issues.
D. Wrong. Psychodynamic therapy is more likely to focus on social skills than on sex or aggression.

10. B, Correct (p. 521)
A. Wrong. Behavioral therapists modify behavior. The client's thoughts are not the focus.
C. Wrong. A rational-emotive therapist is judgmental and much more assertive.
D. Wrong. Psychoanalysts are more directive and actively interpret the client's comments.

11. D, Correct (p. 523)
A. Wrong. Psychoanalysis focuses on unconscious conflicts, not anxieties created by life decisions.
B. Wrong. Beck's cognitive therapy stresses the importance of irrational beliefs in creating problems.
C. Wrong. Behavioral therapy stresses learned behavior, not anxiety about decisions.

12. C, Correct (p. 520)

    A. Wrong. Homework of this sort is not typical of psychoanalysis.

    B. Wrong. Client-centered therapy does not emphasize irrational thoughts.

    D. Wrong. Gestalt therapy does not focus on irrational thoughts.

13. C, Correct (p. 520)

    A. Wrong. This is the goal of cognitive therapy.

    B. Wrong. This is the goal of psychodynamic therapy.

    D. Wrong. This is the goal of behavioral therapy.

14. B, Correct (p. 522)

    A. Wrong. Empathy is seeing things from a client's perspective.

    C. Wrong. Genuineness is openness, honesty, and an absence of phoniness.

    D. Wrong. Congruence occurs when the self-concept and reality match.

15. B, Correct (p. 525)

    A. Wrong. Existential therapy stresses taking responsibility for one's decisions. It doesn't use relaxation.

    C. Wrong. Psychoanalysis doesn't teach relaxation responses.

    D. Wrong. Aversion therapy uses an unpleasant response, not relaxation, a pleasant one.

16. A, Correct (p. 526)

    B. Wrong. Incongruence involves the self-concept. Aversion therapy doesn't deal with self-concept.

    C. Wrong. Damage to the client-therapist relations is a problem when punishment is used, not when aversion therapy is brief.

    D. Wrong. The old problem might reappear, but a new one would not be expected to develop.

17. C, Correct (p. 528)

    A. Wrong. Systematic desensitization conditions relaxation. It doesn't reward appropriate behavior.

    B. Wrong. Social skills training focuses on teaching social skills to be used outside the institution. Although reinforcement is sometimes involved, it is not the primary activity.

    D. Wrong. Rational-emotive therapy tries to modify irrational thoughts. It doesn't use tokens as reinforcers.

18. D, Correct (p. 531)

    A., B., C. Wrong. Studies consistently find equal improvements across therapies and a greater effect for therapy than for no therapy.

19. C, Correct (p. 533)

    A., B., D. Wrong. Empathy and trust are primary determinants of successful therapy.

CHAPTER **16**

STRESS AND HEALTH

ESTABLISHING LEARNING GOALS

Use these learning goals as a preview of the chapter, a guide for active reading, and to evaluate your mastery of the material. Review the relevant goals as you begin and end your reading of each major section of the chapter.

I. Discuss the definition of stress and describe how stress is experienced

   A. Describe the stress response.
      1. Define stress, and explain how it is an adaptive reaction.
      2. Discuss Selye's General Adaptation Syndrome view of the physiological components of stress.
      3. Describe the psychological aspects of stress and gender differences.

   B. Explain the function of cognitive appraisal as part of the stress response.

   C. Discuss external sources of stress.
      1. Describe the Holmes and Rahé Social Readjustment Rating Scale and explain what it predicts.
      2. Define daily hassles, and compare their effects to those of life events.
      3. Identify other external stressors likely to be studied by environmental psychologists.

   D. Discuss internal sources of stress.
      1. Specify the relationship between perceived control and stress.
      2. Specify the relationship between explanatory styles and stress.
      3. Identify the personality characteristics related to stress and their possible health outcomes.

II. Identify and discuss the physical and psychological effects of prolonged stress.

   A. Describe the physical consequences of prolonged stress.
      1. Discuss the link between stress and the immune system.
      2. Discuss the link between stress and cardiovascular problems.

   B. Describe the psychological consequences of prolonged stress.
      1. Describe the symptoms of posttraumatic stress disorder.
      2. Describe the symptoms of burnout and the conditions likely to produce burnout.

III. Discuss how to cope with stress.

   A. Explain how relaxation techniques can be used to reduce stress.

   B. Explain how stress can be managed through cognitive reappraisal of the stressful situation.

IV. Discuss how to live a healthy lifestyle.

A. Discuss the physical and psychological benefits of aerobic exercise.

B. Discuss the consequences of tobacco use, and explain why quitting smoking is so difficult.

C. Discuss the value of proper nutrition.

D. Describe the different types of prevention programs and explain how they're used to target AIDS.

MASTERING THE MATERIAL

PREVIEW & EXPERIENCING STRESS (PP. 541-552)

MASTERING THE VOCABULARY

Define or explain each of the following terms.

1. health psychology
2. stress
3. stressors
4. general adaptation syndrome
5. cognitive appraisal
6. environmental psychology
7. perceived control
8. Type A
9. Type B

MASTERING THE CONCEPTS

Fill in the blanks to create a summary of the section.

[1] ____________ psychology, part of behavioral medicine, studies the role of biological, psychological, environmental, and cultural factors in promoting physical health. Four issues are considered: What are the causes and effects of stress? What are the effects of prolonged stress? How can people reduce or cope with stress? What factors promote physical and psychological health?

Stress is the physical and psychological [2] ____________ to demanding situations. Stress can be adaptive because it [3] ____________ the body to respond, but it can have negative effects. Selye proposed the general [4] ____________ syndrome to describe general physiological reactions to all stressors. In the [5] ____________ phase, the sympathetic nervous system is activated, causing general arousal. In the [6] ____________ phase, arousal is still high, but the body maintains resources and function. Susceptibility to other stressors is high and health problems may begin to develop. In the [7] ____________ phase, the body starts to give up, maladaptive behavior occurs, and serious damage is possible. Criticism of Selye's proposal involves evidence that the response to stress is variable and depends on a cognitive [8] ____________ of the situation and coping resources. Stress involves emotional and behavioral components. Dealing successfully with stress can lead to improved self-image and immune system strength. Gender differences occur, with [9] ____________ being less likely to show a fight or flight response.

The Holmes and Rahé social Readjustment Rating Scale uses significant [10] ____________ to predict health problems. Life events involve either positive or negative [11] ____________ . Although criticized for some limitations, the scale is still widely used. Little irritations, [12] ____________ , also correlate with health problems. [13] ____________ psychology studies environmental influences on health and behavior. For example, noise and crowding are stressors that produce health problems.

Internal determinants of stress include perceived [14] ____________ , [15] ____________ style, and personality characteristics, including the [16] ____________ personalities. If attributions about negative events are [17] ____________ , stable, and global, stress is more likely. Optimism and perceived control reduce stress, and cardiovascular problems are more likely with a hostile Type A personality.

EVALUATING YOUR PROGRESS

Select the best response. If you make any errors, reread the relevant material before proceeding.

1. The author of your text defines stress as
   a. a stimulus that places a demand on the person.
   b. a feeling of being overwhelmed.
   c. the physical and psychological reaction that people have to demanding situations.
   d. demanding situations that threaten the well-being of the person.

2. Alarm, resistance, and exhaustion are
   a. the three "basic" stressors.
   b. the dimensions of the Holmes & Rahé scale.
   c. the stages of Selye's general adaptation syndrome.
   d. the dimensions of the Hassles scale.

3. Which of the following is false concerning Selye's general adaptation syndrome?
   a. It proposes that different stressors produce the same stress reactions.
   b. It proposes that stressors cause physiological arousal.
   c. It proposes that extended stress causes health problems to develop during the alarm stage.
   d. It proposes that the body cannot experience high stress for long periods without suffering damage.

4. The Holmes & Rahé Social Readjustment Rating Scale is based on the idea that
   a. events involving change produce stress.
   b. stress occurs only for events that have negative consequences.
   c. stress is dependent on people's perception of the situation.
   d. perceived control is critical to the impact of stress.

5. Emphasis on people's perceptions of a situation and their ability to deal with that situation is characteristic of
   a. Selye's general adaptation syndrome view of stress.
   b. the cognitive appraisal view of stress.
   c. Holmes and Rahé's life events view of stress.
   d. the tertiary prevention view of stress.

6. Which is most associated with the development of stress-related problems?
   a. lack of perceived control over a situation
   b. external, situational, and temporary attributions about negative events
   c. Type B personality
   d. optimistic personal style

7. Type A personality is characterized by
   a. cool, calm, and collected behavior.
   b. an optimistic, but dependent, style.
   c. hard-driven, ambitious, and impatient behavior.
   d. external, stable, and situational attributions.

8. Some researchers suggest that the critical aspect of Type A behavior that relates to heart disease is
   a. working long hours.
   b. the need to be in control.
   c. the feeling that everything must be done quickly.
   d. the tendency to be hostile or angry.

REACTING TO PROLONGED STRESS (PP. 552-557)

MASTERING THE VOCABULARY

Define or explain each of the following terms.

1. lymphocytes
2. posttraumatic stress disorder
3. burnout

MASTERING THE CONCEPTS.

Fill in the blanks to create a summary of the section.

Stress increases susceptibility to illness because it suppresses the [1] ____________ . People with high stress were more likely to catch the common cold in one experiment, and other studies found lower levels of [2] ____________ , a type of white blood cell, and more rapid growth of tumors. Stress increases the risk for cardiovascular disease, possibly because stress increases [3] ____________ and cholesterol.

Stress influences psychological health, but is not sufficient to cause major problems for most people. One serious condition due to traumatic events is [4] ____________ stress disorder. Symptoms include [5] ____________ , avoidance of stimuli linked to the trauma, and chronic [6] ____________ symptoms, such as sleep problems and irritability. [7] ____________ is a state of physical, emotional, and mental exhaustion caused by long-term involvement in emotionally demanding situations. Sufferers are usually highly motivated, but become disillusioned and perhaps feel as if life is meaningless.

EVALUATING YOUR PROGRESS

Select the best response. If you miss any questions, reread the relevant material before proceeding.

1. People under high stress are more likely to get sick because stress inhibits
   a. the cardiovascular system.
   b. the endocrine system.
   c. the sympathetic nervous system.
   d. the immune system.

2. One reason stress might increase the risk for developing heart disease is that stress
   a. increases cholesterol.
   b. increases the number of lymphocytes in the blood.
   c. reduces autonomic nervous system activity.
   d. reduces blood pressure.

3. Posttraumatic stress disorder is characterized by
   a. loss of memory for the traumatic event.
   b. avoidance of stimuli associated with the traumatic event.
   c. a tendency to become dependent on family and friends.
   d. chronic low arousal symptoms.

4. Burnout is most likely to occur in people who
   a. are idealistic.
   b. have a Type B personality.
   c. are not very committed to their job.
   d. have had little experience on the job.

REDUCING AND COPING WITH STRESS (PP. 557-563)

MASTERING THE VOCABULARY

Define or explain each of the following terms.

1. coping
2. biofeedback
3. social support

MASTERING THE CONCEPTS

Fill in the blanks to create a summary of the section.

Ways to cope with stress include [1] ____________ techniques, forming [2] ____________ systems, and reappraising the situation. In [3] ____________ muscle relaxation, specific muscle groups are relaxed, one after the other until all the body is relaxed. Autogenic relaxation focuses on directing [4] ____________ to a muscle group to warm and relax it. Meditation sometimes is also used. Providing information about relaxation through [5] ____________ is helpful, but the sense of [6] ____________ it produces might be critical. Misleading feedback produces equal pain relief.

Social support reduces health and mental problems, perhaps because healthy [7] ____________ are encouraged, or because there is opportunity to talk about problems, which reduces stress. Pets also provide positive support. Social support can have negative effects, reducing [8] ____________ and perceived control. Some people increase stress by [9] ____________ situations too negatively. Events can be made less stressful by taking attention off of the disturbing aspects, reappraising the outcome, or by planning for future situations.

EVALUATING YOUR PROGRESS

Select the best response. If you miss any questions, reread the relevant material before proceeding.

1. Progressive relaxation involves
   a. mental repetition of a word and the focusing of attention inward.
   b. relaxing one muscle group after another until the entire body is relaxed.
   c. using monitoring equipment to provide information about the state of the body.
   d. concentrating on directing blood flow to particular muscle groups to relax them.

2. Research on the effects of misleading biofeedback suggests that
   a. improvement in physical symptoms (headache) is due to greater relaxation with biofeedback.
   b. biofeedback is another form of meditation, which is known to reduce tension.
   c. biofeedback gives a sense of control that reduces stress and stress-related disorders.
   d. biofeedback provides a sort of social support that reduces the impact of stress.

3. Compared to people with little social support, people with well-established social support systems show
   a. improved physical health and psychological health.
   b. the same physical health, but better psychological health.
   c. lower death rates from cancer, but higher death rates from cardiovascular problems.
   d. the same levels of physical and psychological health.

4. Based on research by Karen Allen and colleagues, your best chance of avoiding a high stress reaction during a difficult problem solving task is to
   a. be alone while working.
   b. have your dog with you.
   c. have your close friend with you.
   d. have either your dog or your friend in the room with you (equal effects).

5. Rethinking a situation and focusing on more positive or realistic perspectives is characteristic of the stress management technique of
   a. social support.
   b. cognitive reappraisal.
   c. autogenic relaxation.
   d. tertiary prevention.

LIVING A HEALTHY LIFESTYLE (PP. 564-568)

MASTERING THE VOCABULARY

Define or explain each of the following terms.

1. aerobic exercise
2. primary prevention
3. secondary prevention
4. tertiary prevention
5. AIDS

MASTERING THE CONCEPTS.

Fill in the blanks to create a summary of the section.

Healthy lifestyles can reduce the impact of stress. [1] ____________ exercise improves mental and physical health and increases resistance to stress, although a placebo effect might be involved. Smoking contributes to many deaths and increases birth [2] ____________ , and it is [3] ____________ . Withdrawal is a DSM-IV diagnosis and often includes insomnia, irritability, difficulty concentrating, and weight gain or increased appetite. Most Americans have a poor diet that is too high in [4] ____________ , calories, cholesterol, sugar, protein, and salt. Fat and cholesterol are linked to [5] ____________ problems.

AIDS is caused by a [6] ____________ and transmitted through contact with bodily fluids, most often by blood or semen. Health psychologists use three types of prevention programs to combat unhealthy lifestyles and disease. Primary prevention centers on [7] ____________ about ways to avoid problems. Secondary prevention involves early identification of risk factors or looking for early signs of disease. Tertiary prevention handles an illness or habit once it is present.

EVALUATING YOUR PROGRESS

Select the best response. If you miss any questions, reread the relevant material before proceeding.

1. The relationship between aerobic exercise and psychological health is
   a. imaginary; no controlled studies have found any benefit other than improved physical health.
   b. questionable; positive results are supported only by correlational data.
   c. questionable; research shows that people report feeling psychologically healthy, but psychological tests show no change in psychological status, especially concerning depression.
   d. significant; people who exercise have reduced depression and react less to stressful situations.
2. Cigarette smoking
   a. has increased in frequency over the past two decades, in spite of anti-smoking campaigns.
   b. introduces a central nervous system depressant to the brain.
   c. does not produce an addiction, although it is a habit that is difficult to break.
   d. during pregnancy is associated with an increased risk of birth defects.
3. When health psychologists focus on educating the public about the danger of unprotected sex, they are using
   a. primary prevention.
   b. secondary prevention.
   c. tertiary prevention.
   d. terminal prevention.
4. The primary problem associated with AIDS is
   a. cholesterol-related heart disease.
   b. emphysema.
   c. damage to the immune system.
   d. stroke.

MAKING FINAL PREPARATIONS

Complete these sections without consulting your book or notes. For a more accurate estimate of how well you know this material, wait at least a day or two after studying the chapter before working on the questions. Some of the material you "know" immediately after working with the chapter will be quickly forgotten. Immediate tests will overestimate what you know well.

SHORT ESSAY QUESTIONS

Write a brief answer to each question.

1. Discuss the role of cognitive appraisal in stress and stress management.

____

____

2. Explain why stress management should be a part of the treatment given people who are HIV-positive.

____

____

3. Discuss the role of perceived control in stress.

____

____

4. Explain why social support seems to be an effective way to reduce the impact of stress.

____

____

MATCHING

Select the correct definition or description for each item.

1. _______ tertiary prevention
2. _______ stress
3. _______ Holmes & Rahe
4. _______ explanatory style
5. _______ primary prevention
6. _______ health psychology
7. _______ Selye
8. _______ burnout
9. _______ stressor
10. _______ posttraumatic stress disorder
11. _______ lymphocytes
12. _______ Type A personality

a. serious trauma-induced psychological disorder
b. program to deal with problem once it develops
c. attribution patterns that impact stress
d. physical, emotional, & mental exhaustion
e. study of biological, emotional, environmental, and cultural effects on health
f. demanding or threatening situation
g. program to educate in order to prevent a problem
h. hard-driving behavior linked to heart diseasc
i. white blood cells in the immune system
j. devised "life event" scale
k. proposed general adaptation syndrome
l. physical & emotional reaction to demanding event

MULTIPLE CHOICE PRETEST 1

Select the one best response.

1. The stage in Selye's general adaptation syndrome that corresponds to the fight-or-flight response is
   a. the activation stage.
   b. the resistance stage.
   c. the exhaustion stage.
   d. the alarm stage.

2. Which freshman should experience the most stress as he begins his first semester at State College?
   a. Ron, who expects State College to be very competitive and very difficult.
   b. Clay, who expects State College to be moderately competitive and moderately difficult.
   c. Ely, who expects State College to be no more difficult than high school.
   d. All of them should experience the same stress because they are in the same college situation.
3. The relationship between daily hassles and the chance of developing stress-related health problems is
   a. nonexistent because daily hassles do not produce significant stress.
   b. strong, but negative, because people with many daily hassles have fewer health problems.
   c. significant, but not as strong as for major life events.
   d. at least as strong as the relationship between major life events and stress-related illness.
4. Max is 45. He will be most likely to develop a stress-related illness if his attributions about negative events are usually
   a. reflexive Type A.
   b. reflexive Type B.
   c. internal, global, and stable.
   d. external, situational, and specific.
5. In one experiment, the people who were most likely to get sick after being exposed to the common cold virus were those who
   a. were Type B personalities.
   b. had high stress lives.
   c. had low stress lives.
   d. felt in control.
6. Carla blows little hassles out of proportion and creates stress unnecessarily. Being caught in traffic means she will never be able to fix dinner or do her homework, when it just will delay things a few minutes. Carla could avoid much of the stress she now experiences if she would try
   a. developing social support.
   b. meditation.
   c. exercise.
   d. cognitive reappraisal.
7. Ellie keeps seeing images of the World Trade Center collapse, and sometimes seems to feel the dust filling her lungs. She refuses to go back to New York City and is having trouble sleeping. Ellie's behavior is consistent with
   a. Type A personality disorder.
   b. burnout.
   c. generalized anxiety disorder.
   d. posttraumatic stress disorder.

8. The University has built one massive high-rise dorm for all students. Research on environmental psychology predicts there will be
   a. improved physical health in the residents.
   b. improved psychological health in the residents.
   c. increased tolerance to daily hassles by the residents.
   d. increased aggressive behavior by the residents.

9. Keisha quit her high stress job. In six months she will probably find
   a. her lymphocytes will be reduced.
   b. her cholesterol level will be reduced.
   c. her blood pressure will be higher.
   d. her heart rate will be higher.

10. Emilio has devoted his life to teaching in urban schools. After a particularly stressful period in which several of his programs were eliminated, Emilio began to act exhausted mentally and physically, and he began skipping all the extra activities he had sponsored in the past. Emilio is showing the symptoms of
    a. posttraumatic stress disorder.
    b. burnout.
    c. Type A personality.
    d. a dissociative disorder.

11. To help Tyce learn to relax the muscles of his forehead, his psychologist has hooked him up to a machine that presents a tone when muscle tension drops. Tyce is using
    a. the progressive muscle relaxation technique.
    b. the autogenic relaxation technique.
    c. meditation.
    d. biofeedback.

12. One reason social support reduces stress-related health problems is that it may tend to
    a. encourage healthy behaviors.
    b. take control of the situation and the person in need.
    c. allow the person to avoid talking about or facing the situation.
    d. increase autonomic nervous system activity.

13. Nicotine withdrawal
    a. is included in the DSM-IV-TR.
    b. often leads to deceased appetite.
    c. often leads to extreme sleepiness.
    d. is so unpleasant that people rarely smoke again.

14. Counseling an HIV-positive individual about how to avoid transmitting the virus to other people is
    a. ancillary prevention.
    b. primary prevention.
    c. secondary prevention.
    d. tertiary prevention.

15. Chuck is tensing and then relaxing each of the muscle groups in his body, moving from his head down. What stress-reduction technique is Chuck using?
    a. biofeedback
    b. progressive muscle relaxation
    c. autogenic relaxation
    d. the general adaptation syndrome

16. Depressed college students were asked to either engage in aerobic exercise, use relaxation techniques, or do nothing to treat their depression. After 10 weeks researchers found
    a. the relaxation group's mood improved more improved than that of the other two groups.
    b. the exercise group's mood improved more than that of the other two groups.
    c. all three groups' moods improved equally.
    d. the relaxation and exercise groups' moods didn't improve, but the control group's mood worsened.

MULTIPLE CHOICE PRETEST 2

Select the one best response.

1. Between working two jobs, facing three major exams this week, and finding out he is being evicted, Sam is feeling overwhelmed. Your text's definition of stress would identify the stress to be
    a. working two jobs.
    b. facing two exams.
    c. being evicted.
    d. feeling overwhelmed.

2. For the past year Helena's life has been one disaster after another. She has felt a lack of control and hopeless, and she has developed some serious stress-related illnesses. In which stage of the general adaptation syndromes is Helena?
    a. exhaustion stage
    b. resistance stage
    c. alarm stage
    d. burnout

3. If stress hormone levels are recorded for everyone taking the SAT, an achievement test used for college admissions, the hormone levels should be correlated most strongly with
    a. the student's sex.
    b. the student's IQ.
    c. the student's age.
    d. the student's income.

4. The Holmes & Rahé Social Readjustment Rating Scale score is used to predict
    a. Type A or B personality.
    b. locus of control.
    c. explanatory style.
    d. risk of developing health problems.

5. Russ is most likely to develop stress-related problems if he
   a. feels competent and able to succeed in his very difficult new job.
   b. shares a crowded apartment with four other people.
   c. has a Type B personality.
   d. has an optimistic outlook.

6. Nan's life is very stressful now that she is a single parent, and she has noticed that she catches every illness that her little girl gets. If Nan had a complete physical, she would probably be found to have
   a. lower blood pressure than usual.
   b. lower lymphocyte levels than usual.
   c. lower hormone levels than usual.
   d. lower blood cholesterol than usual.

7. When their trip home was interrupted by car trouble, Sam got very upset even though they had no reason to hurry and the repairs were covered by a warranty. Trudy said, "This isn't so bad. We can relax by the pool and the car will be better than before." Trudy experienced less stress because
   a. she had good social support.
   b. she has an internal, global, and stable attributional style.
   c. she used autogenic relaxation.
   d. she used cognitive reappraisal.

8. Tallal is a straight-A student who insists all assignments be done perfectly and devotes all his attention to being the best student in every class. Tallal quickly becomes impatient with anyone who doesn't perform to his standards. Tallal's behavior is characteristic of
   a. a negative explanatory style personality.
   b. a controlling personality.
   c. a Type A personality.
   d. a Type B personality.

9. Melvin narrowly escaped death when a tornado destroyed his home. Two years later, Melvin still has flashbacks of the storm and has withdrawn from family and friends. Hc even moved to a milder climate to avoid the intense anxiety any storm produced. Melvin's behavior is most consistent with
   a. burnout.
   b. post-traumatic stress disorder.
   c. daily hassles.
   d. generalized anxiety disorder.

10. Mary tries to direct increased blood flow to each muscle group, one by one. Mary is using
    a. biofeedback.
    b. autogenic relaxation.
    c. meditation.
    d. progressive relaxation.

11. Without Paul's knowledge, his son changed the settings on his biofeedback equipment so that it will sound a tone when muscle tension increases, rather than decreases. We should expect Paul's headaches to
    a. immediately increase in frequency.
    b. continue to decrease in frequency.
    c. temporarily decrease, then increase in frequency.
    d. stay the same frequency.

12. After the tornado destroyed most of the town and killed over 100 people, counselors came in to help the survivors and rescue workers cope. Some counselors just let the people talk about their experiences. Based on Pennebaker's research, this procedure was probably
    a. helpful; talking about troubles leads to better coping and less stress.
    b. harmful; trauma victims always need intense psychotherapy.
    c. harmful; talking just reopens the wounds so that they are slower to heal.
    d. neutral; talking doesn't hurt, but it doesn't help, either.

13. Men interested in reducing the impact of stress by exercising should remember that research shows
    a. aerobic exercise works better than strength training.
    b. strength training works better than aerobic exercise.
    c. aerobic exercise and strength training work equally well.
    d. neither aerobic exercise nor strength training reduces stress or its impact.

14. In hopes of reducing the incidence of heart disease and stroke, a company offered free cholesterol tests each year. This is an example of
    a. primary prevention.
    b. secondary prevention.
    c. tertiary prevention.
    d. quadratic prevention.

LANGUAGE DEVELOPMENT GUIDE

CORE TERMS

In discussing stress and health, your instructor is likely to use the term ***optimal***. That means best or highest level; *optimal health* is the best level of health of which your body is capable. But stress and injuries may add up and have a ***cumulative*** (added together) effect. One stressor after another may ***compromise*** (damage) your health. If the damage cannot be cured, you might end up with a ***chronic*** condition (one that lasts for a long time). As the text suggests, good diet, exercise and so on can help you avoid this unpleasant scenario -- your instructor may call these good habits ***preventative maintenance***.

IDIOMS

p. 541	claim exclusive rights	say that we are the only ones who deserve something
p. 543	jack-knifed tractor trailer	a large truck which has gone out of control and is blocking the road
p. 543	life-threatening jams	situation that might kill you
p. 545	a black belt in the martial arts	the highest level of training in a specialized form of fighting (such as karate)
p. 546	exhaustive list	complete list; a list of all
p. 549	in the eye of the beholder	depends upon who is looking at it or experiencing it
p. 549	manned space program	project to send people into space
p. 554	compromising the function of	causing something to not work properly
p. 554	wear and tear	rough usage; damage through use
p. 555	vet	short for veteran, that is, a soldier in a past war
p. 556	syndrome	a set of symptoms of an illness
p. 557	skirts	goes very near
p. 557	a regimen of	a fixed set of
p. 561	buffer	that which protects from outside influences

PRONUNCIATION

lymphocyte (lim′-fo-site) *p. 553*
aerobic (a-row′-bik) *p. 564*
tertiary (ter′-shee-air-ee) *567*

SOLUTIONS

PREVIEW & EXPERIENCING STRESS (PP. 541-552)

MASTERING THE CONCEPTS

1. Health (p. 541)
2. reaction (p. 543)
3. activates (p. 543)
4. adaptation (p. 543)
5. alarm (p. 543)
6. resistance (p. 544)
7. exhaustion (p. 544)
8. appraisal (p. 545)
9. females (p. 544)
10. life events (p. 546)
11. change (p. 547)
12. daily hassles (p. 548)
13. Environmental (p. 548)
14. control (p. 546)
15. explanatory (p. 547)
16. Type A and B (p. 548)
17. internal (p. 548)

EVALUATING YOUR PROGRESS

1. C, Correct (p. 543)
   A., B., D. Wrong. These may be alternative definitions, but not your author's.
2. C, Correct (p. 543)
   A. Wrong. No such group exists. The stages of the general adaptation syndrome are listed here.
   B Wrong. This scale gives values to various life events, not the described reactions or stages.
   D. Wrong. These are the reactions to stress, not part of the Hassles scale.
3. C, Correct (pp. 543-544) A., B., D. Wrong. These are all true, but health problems occur *after* the alarm stage.
4. A, Correct (p. 546)
   B. Wrong. Some of their "life events" are positive events (vacation, marriage).
   C., D. Wrong. Their scale does not consider the person's perceptions at all.
5. B, Correct (p. 545)
   A., C. Wrong. These do not emphasize perceptions. They emphasize the stressor itself.
   D. Wrong. This is not an actual approach to stress.
6. A, Correct (p. 549)
   B., C., D. Wrong. These are associated with reduced stress.
7. C, Correct (p. 550)
   A., B., D. Wrong. Type A people are ambitious, easily annoyed, impatient, and hard driving.
8. D, Correct (p. 551)
   A., B., C. Wrong. Hostility is the factor receiving the focus of attention currently.

REACTING TO PROLONGED STRESS (PP. 552-557)

MASTERING THE CONCEPTS.

1. immune system (p. 553)
2. lymphocytes (p. 553)
3. blood pressure (p. 554)
4. posttraumatic (p. 555)
5. flashbacks (p. 555)
6. arousal (p. 556)
7. Burnout (p. 556)

EVALUATING YOUR PROGRESS

1. D, Correct (pp. 552-553)
   A., B., C. Wrong. These systems are more active during stress, but the immune system is not.
2. A, Correct (p. 554)
   B., C., D. Wrong. Stress has the opposite effect listed.
3. B, Correct (p. 555)
   A., C., D. Wrong. These are the opposite of the true symptoms.

4. A, Correct (p. 555)
   B. Wrong. Personality type is not strongly predictive.
   C. Wrong. Burnout occurs in highly committed people.
   D. Wrong. Burnout requires a long-term experience.

REDUCING AND COPING WITH STRESS (PP. 557-563)

MASTERING THE CONCEPTS

1. relaxation (p. 557)
2. social support (p. 557)
3. progressive (p. 558)
4. blood flow (p. 558)
5. biofeedback (p. 558)
6. control (p. 559)
7. lifestyles (p. 560)
8. self-reliance (p. 560)
9. interpreting (p. 563)

EVALUATING YOUR PROGRESS

1. B, Correct (p. 558)
   A. Wrong. This describes meditation.
   C. Wrong. This describes biofeedback.
   D. Wrong. This describes autogenic relaxation.
2. C, Correct (pp. 558-559)
   A., B., D. Wrong. Symptoms improved even with misleading biofeedback, leading researchers to propose the key is perceived control, not actual relaxation.
3. A, Correct (p. 559)
   B., C., D. Wrong. These are not true. Social support generally aids both physical and psychological health.
4. B, Correct (p. 561)
   A. Wrong. Being alone led to intermediate levels of stress.
   C., D. Wrong. A human companion was associated with the highest levels of stress.
5. B, Correct (p. 562)
   A. Wrong. Social support is help received from others, not reinterpreting a situation.
   C. Wrong. Autogenic relaxation is a way to relax muscles, not a reevaluation of a situation.
   D. Wrong. Tertiary prevention is treating the effects of stress, not reducing the source of stress.

LIVING A HEALTHY LIFESTYLE (PP. 564-568)

MASTERING THE CONCEPTS.

1. Aerobic (p. 564)
2. defects (p. 565)
3. addictive (p. 565)
4. fat (p. 566)
5. cardiovascular (p. 566)
6. virus (p. 567)
7. education (p. 567)

EVALUATING YOUR PROGRESS

1. D, Correct (p. 564)
   A., B., C. Wrong. Controlled studies support a positive relationship.
2. D, Correct (p. 565)
   A. Wrong. Smoking has decreased over the past few decades.
   B. Wrong. Nicotine stimulates the central nervous system.
   C. Wrong. Nicotine is considered addictive by most researchers.

3. A, Correct (p. 567)
   B. Wrong. Secondary prevention identifies risk factors or screens for early signs of a problem.
   C. Wrong. Tertiary prevention seeks to handle an illness or habit once it has been acquired.
   D. Wrong. This is not a health psychology prevention program.

4. C, Correct (p. 567)
   A. Wrong. Cholesterol is associated with poor diet and little exercise, not AIDS.
   B. Wrong. Emphysema is associated with smoking, not AIDS.
   D. Wrong. Stroke is associated with poor cardiovascular fitness, not AIDS.

MAKING FINAL PREPARATIONS

SHORT ESSAY QUESTIONS

1. One's cognitive appraisal of a situation is critical in determining whether stress results. If the situation is not perceived to be demanding, or people perceive they have the resources to deal with the situation, stress is eliminated or reduced. By reappraising a potentially stressful situation (e.g., seeing a death as a release from pain), stress is reduced. Personality factors that lead to negative appraisals increase stress. (pp. 545-546, 562-563)
2. An HIV-positive diagnosis brings with it situations involving stress---employment concerns, social stigma, and the prospects of a terminal disease. HIV itself suppresses the immune system, so stress management will reduce the additional impact that stress has on the immune system and will help to maintain other aspects of physical health. An HIV diagnosis has psychological effects which stress management can address. (pp. 553-554, 567)
3. Perception of control reduces stress. Animals able to terminate a shock by making a response showed fewer stress-related physical problems (ulcers) than animals experiencing the same amount of shock but given no control. Control relates to the evaluation of one's ability to cope with a stressor, and this is critical in determining whether stress results. (p. 549)
4. People with social support systems show fewer physical and psychological stress effects. This might occur because the social support system encourages the individual to maintain a healthy lifestyle and to follow medical prescriptions. Social support provides a chance to talk about problems, which has been shown to reduce stress. Social support may boost the evaluation of coping resources, which can reduce stress effects. (pp. 559-562)

MATCHING

1. b (p. 567)
2. l (p. 543)
3. j (p. 546)
4. c (p. 550)
5. g (p. 567)
6. e (p. 541)
7. k (p. 544)
8. d (p. 556)
9. f (p. 543)
10. a (p. 555)
11. i (p. 553)
12. h (p. 550)

MULTIPLE CHOICE PRETEST 1

1. D, Correct (p. 543)
   A. Wrong. This is not one of Selye's GAS stages.
   B., C. Wrong. Fight-or-flight is rapid physiological activation, which occurs during the alarm stage.
2. A, Correct (p. 545)
   B., C. Wrong. Clay and Ely perceive State as less of a threat than Ron does.
   D. Wrong. Their perceptions differ, which is very important to the stress experienced.
3. D, Correct (p. 548)
   A., C. Wrong. Daily hassles are at least as predictive of stress-related illnesses as life events.
   B. Wrong. The relationship is a positive correlation.
4. C, Correct (p. 550)
   A., B. Wrong. Reflexive Type A and Type B are not styles of attributions.
   D. Wrong. This is the opposite pattern associated with stress-related illness.
5. B, Correct (p. 553)
   A. Wrong. Type A, not Type B, personality is more associated with stress-related illness.
   C. Wrong. Low stress is not associated with illness.
   D. Wrong. The perception of control reduces stress.
6. D, Correct (p. 563)
   A. Wrong. Social support assists coping, but doesn't necessarily eliminate the source of stress.
   B. Wrong. Meditation won't stop the catastrophizing or eliminate the stress; it reduces its impact.
   C. Wrong. Exercise moderates the effects of stress, but doesn't stop it at the source.
7. D, Correct (p. 555)
   A. Wrong. Type A personality disorder involves impatient, hard-driving competitiveness.
   B. Wrong. Burnout involves feeling emotionally drained and losing a sense of accomplishment.
   C. Wrong. Generalized anxiety disorder is a chronic state of anxiety unrelated to any specific event.
8. D, Correct (p. 548)
   A., B., C. Wrong. High-rise housing is more crowded, which is associated with greater stress and greater aggression.
9. B, Correct (p. 554)
   A., C., D. Wrong. The opposite would be expected.
10. B, Correct (p. 556)
    A. Wrong. There is no trauma, flashback, avoidance, or arousal in Emilio's case.
    C. Wrong. He isn't competitive and driven.
    D. Wrong. There is no loss of memory or abnormal consciousness.
11. D, Correct (p. 558)
    A. Wrong. This involves relaxing one muscle group after another, without feedback.
    B. Wrong. This involves directing blood flow to a muscle group, not using feedback about tension.
    C. Wrong. This involves concentrating on a word or image and clearing the mind.
12. A, Correct (p. 560)
    B. Wrong. A lack of personal control increases stress.
    C. Wrong. Talking about negative events improves coping.
    D. Wrong. Increased nervous system activity is associated with increased stress.
13. A, Correct (p. 565)
    B. Wrong. Withdrawal often causes increased appetite and weight gain.
    C. Wrong. Nicotine withdrawal often leads to insomnia and restlessness.
    D. Wrong. Relapse is very, very common.
14. D, Correct (p. 567)
    A. Wrong. This is not a type of prevention.
    B. Wrong. Primary prevention involves education to prevent a problem.
    C. Wrong. Secondary prevention involves identifying risk factors or early signs of the disease.
15. B, Correct (p. 558)
    A. Wrong. There is no external feedback concerning the state of his muscles.
    C. Wrong. Chuck is not directing blood to his muscles, as characteristic of autogenic relaxation.
    D. Wrong. The general adaptation syndrome describes the stages of physiological changes with stress.
16. B, Correct (p. 564)
    A., C., D. Wrong. Exercise was associated with the greatest improvement.

MULTIPLE CHOICE PRETEST 2

1. D, Correct (p. 543)
   A., B., C. Wrong. These are stressors (situations), not stress (reaction to stressors).
2. A, Correct (p. 544)
   B. Wrong. This the second stage, before major problems develop.
   C., D. Wrong. These are not Selye's stages.
3. B, Correct (p. 546)
   A., C., D. Wrong. Studies show high IQ is associated with lower stress levels prior to exams, probably because the test is not perceived as very threatening.
4. D, Correct (p. 547)
   A., B., C. Wrong. This scale predicts stress-related health problem, not any personality characteristics.
5. B, Correct (p. 548)
   A. Wrong. Feelings of competency reduce or eliminate stress, but crowding increases stress.
   C. Wrong. Type B personality is not associated with stress-related problems.
   D. Wrong. An optimistic style is associated with lower stress, but crowding increases stress.
6. B, Correct (p. 553)
   A., C., D. Wrong. Stress increases these, but decreases lymphocytes.
7. D, Correct (p. 562)
   A. Wrong. She is receiving no help from other people.
   B. Wrong. She isn't making attributions about causes.
   C. Wrong. Autogenic relaxation involves directing blood to muscles to relax them.
8. C, Correct (p. 550)
   A., B., D. Wrong. Competitive, impatient, ambitious, and hard-driving describes Type A personality.
9. B, Correct (p. 555)
   A. Wrong. Burnout is associated with long term stress, not a sudden traumatic event.
   C. Wrong. These are typical daily events that are stressors. Trauma is not involved.
   D. Wrong. This involves chronic anxiety not related to any specific situation.
10. B, Correct (p. 558)
    A. Wrong. Mary wasn't getting feedback from a machine that monitored her bodily responses.
    C. Wrong. Meditation doesn't typically involve directing blood flow to parts of the body.
    D. Wrong. Progressive relaxation involves relaxing muscles, not increasing blood flow.
11. B, Correct (p. 559)
    A., C., D. Wrong. When misleading biofeedback is given, symptoms continue to improve, perhaps due to perceived control.
12. A, Correct (p. 560)
    B., C., D. Wrong. These are not true. Talking about negative experiences has been shown to help.
13. A, Correct (p. 564)
    B., C., D. Wrong. Aerobic exercise works best.
14. B, Correct (p. 567)
    A. Wrong. Primary prevention involves education, not screening for risk factors or early problems.
    C. Wrong. Tertiary prevention involves managing and containing an illness once it has developed.
    D Wrong. Quadratic prevention is not a level of prevention.